Not Quite a Memoir

Not Quite a Memoir

Of Films, Books, the World

Judy Stone

SILMAN-JAMES PRESS   LOS ANGELES

First Edition

10   9   8   7   6   5   4   3   2   1

Library of Congress Cataloging-in-Publication Data

Stone, Judy, 1924-
Not quite a memoir : of films, books, the world / by Judy Stone. -- 1st ed.
p. cm.
ISBN 1-879505-91-6 (alk. paper)
1. Stone, Judy, 1924- 2. Film critics--United States--Biography.   I. Title.
PN1998.3.S758A3 2006
791.43092--dc22
[B]
2006012168

ISBN: 1-879505-91-6

Cover design and photography by Wade Lageose for Lageose Design
Cover photo of Judy Stone by Celia Gilbert

Silman-James Press

3624 Shannon Road
Los Angeles, CA 90027

To Barbara Baer, a wonderful friend, exemplary editor, and intrepid sleuth tracking down the master of pomegranate lore from Turkmenistan to Israel.

Contents

viii

x

ABBAS KIAROSTAMI AND JUDY STONE. PHOTO BY MOHAMMAD NIKBIN.

The title *Not Quite a Memoir* might seem curious, but how else to explain my lucky life interviewing creative people who range from Zacharias Kunuk, the pioneer Inuit filmmaker, to Czeslaw Milosz, the great Polish poet/essayist; from Abbas Kiarostami, the innovative Iranian director, to the writer/provocateur Jean Genet; from Orhan Pamuk, the tantalizing Turkish storyteller, to Jia Zhangke, the "underground" Chinese filmmaker. From Israeli Amos Gitai to Palestinian Elia Suleiman, whose films are devilish irritants to their own "tribes." From playwright Rolf Hochhuth's *The Deputy*, criticizing Pope Pius XII for silence about the wartime murder of European Jews, to John Duigan, whose film *Romero* honors the Salvadorean Archbishop who was murdered for raising his voice against injustice.

Many of these stories appeared first in the *San Francisco Chronicle* where I worked for thirty years, a wonderful job that enabled me to meet international filmmakers and writers who broadened my understanding of their worlds and mine.

It all started in Philadelphia at Jay Cooke Junior High School and Olney High, where I wrote film reviews praising Shirley Temple and scriptwriter Clifford Odets. And, believe it or not! in ninth grade, I already had the chutzpah to write "*Dead End* compensates for all the other trivia Hollywood has produced." I also started doing interviews: Theodore Dreiser, Paul Robeson, Walter Huston, William Saroyan, Langston Hughes, Ruth (*My Sister Eileen*) McKenney, Eve Curie, Erika Mann, Sholem Asch,

Haakon Chevalier. The list indicates my growing social curiosity. If they showed up in Philly, I'd find a way to get to them!

Some of the people interviewed in this book are close to my heart because they dealt in personal terms with the history of our times: such as cantankerous Meyer Levin, haunted by the ghost of Anne Frank; Milosz, who observed the worst of times and vowed never to forget; Amos Oz, an Israeli "peacenik"; William Abrahams and Peter Stansky, who looked into the life of George Orwell, a prophet of political double-talk; Olga Carlisle, engaged in a distressing dispute with Solzhenitsyn; Azar Nafisi, author of *Reading Lolita in Tehran*, who brought a breath of fresh air to stifled Iranian women.

All those conversations enriched my life, but this can't be any kind of a memoir without mentioning my brother Izzy, aka I.F. Stone. Unfortunately, I never interviewed Izzy, but I wish I had. I recall luncheons only too vaguely with a Hungarian writer and a Chinese landscape architect who were as amazed as I was about his knowledge of the literature and histories of their countries. I remember a long walk in London when Izzy talked about his assignment to review a book on mysticism, and I longed for my tape recorder, but thought, "Oh well, I'll read the review." It's not for nothing that he was a unique investigative journalist, digging into the Congressional Record for stories other reporters missed. But after he delved into the great mystics of the ages, he was so disgusted with mysticism that he never wrote the review. Later, he was more forthcoming with *The Trial of Socrates*, which had its origin in his desire to study the roots of free speech.

But like my idiosyncratic brother, who had a great and corny sense of humor, I have included my idiosyncratic collection of personalities:

Jeremy Irons and his wife Sinead Cusack at an irresistibly funny press conference, confounded (he was, she wasn't) by a question on how Anglo-Irish history affected their marriage.

Joe Levine, portly producer of *The Night Porter*, a movie I hated because of its salacious sex scenes between a former Nazi officer and his Jewish prisoner after the war was over.

Alfred Hitchcock, inscrutable when an electronic pixie jinxed a mammoth televised press conference in New York, Los Angeles, Dallas, and Chicago. It was just too much fun to omit.

Leonard Wolf, author of *The Annotated Dracula* and *The Annotated Frankenstein*.

And Luna, the fabulous black model who wanted to be Snow White, but had her only moment of fame as God's mistress in Otto Preminger's lackluster comedy *Skidoo* and whom I thought of as an American tragedy.

So here it is, a lifetime of memories but not quite a memoir.

Acknowledgements

To Celia Gilbert, my first-born niece (and I was only nine!), artist, poet, and a very tough critic, the first person to read most of my interviews and provide a very enthusiastic boost to my morale.

To two fellow book writers who exchanged worries with me about titles, deadlines, the high price of photos, and everything including events beyond their control: Myra MacPherson, author of *All Governments Lie: The Life and Times of Rebel Journalist I.F. Stone*, and my nephew, Peter H. Stone, trying to absorb ongoing revelations into his book about Lobbyist Incarnate Jack Abramoff. (These are unsolicited, but loving, plugs.)

To my friend Alan Freeland, ardent defender of intellectual property rights and a born-again film buff.

To my cousins, novelist Peter Delacorte (who knows more about movies than I'll ever know) and his sister Erika for delectible goodies under my mailbox, computer first-aid and for indispensable help with photos by her late husband, David Gong.

To Sharon Silva, who often interrupted her own editing to provide critical help when I had questions about grammar, spelling, what have you.

To former *San Francisco Chronicle* staff writer Frank Viviano, who suggested my article from the Cairo Film Festival that eventually enabled me to report on one Iraqi's exile and subsequent returns, his hopes and misgivings.

To indefatiguable *San Francisco Chronicle* librarians Kathleen Rhodes and Johnny Miller, who never made me feel I was nagging them when—to compensate for my bad habits—they provided dates I needed for articles in this book.

To Leslie Katz, my editor at *The Oakland Tribune* and the late tabloid *Examiner*, who helped me get time (after my retirement) with some filmmakers in order to give press agents newspaper gratification when they couldn't be satisfied with future book publication. And they're here!

To Phil Bronstein, executive vice-president and editor of the Hearst-owned *San Francisco Chronicle* for his help with this book.

To professor Jamsheed Akrami for introducing Iranian cinema through his documentaries *Friendly Persuasion* and *Iranian Political Films in the '70s*—they helped us to understand "how such humane images could have emerged in such a tense and problem-filled society."

To Nikzad Khansari, not only for interpreting Farsi-speaking Iranian filmmakers, but for her critical knowledge of films worldwide.

To Milos Stehlik, owner of Facets, Inc. and Don Krim, owner of Kino, who have helped to preserve and circulate many films that might otherwise have been forgotten.

And for loving support throughout the years, from old friends Doris Samitz and Christie Rigg, as well as my former *Chronicle* colleague Genevieve Stuttaford, who helped me get *Publishers Weekly* assignments.

1

A Hot War Here/
A Cold War There

Czeslaw Milosz

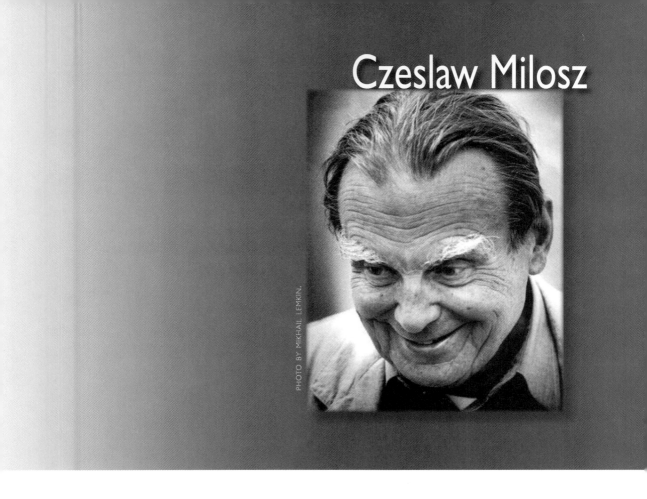

PHOTO BY MIKHAIL LEMKIN.

"Ill at ease in the Tyranny/ Ill at ease in the Republic."

Berkeley, California

Czeslaw Milosz was on the phone. He wanted to postpone our talk for an hour so that he could attend a memorial service for Nadezhda Mandelstam at the Russian Orthodox Church in Berkeley. It was an entirely fitting delay. "Those who are alive," Milosz had said when he accepted the 1980 Nobel Prize for Literature in Stockholm, "receive a mandate from those who are silent forever." It is a mandate implicit in all his work, whether as witness for those who died in the Holocaust or on behalf of those, like Osip and Nadezhda Mandelstam, whose voices were silenced by totalitarian rule.

Nevertheless, in the study of his hillside home in Berkeley, not far from the University of California where he is a professor of Slavic language and literature, Milosz, who is seventy years old, admits that he is wary about becoming a Polish freedom

4

symbol. As he speaks, he looks severe in his blue denim jacket over a dark blue shirt that seems oddly formal on him. The rebellious eyebrows protrude as fiercely as horns on a Viking's helmet over vivid blue eyes in a craggily handsome face.

He begins our conversation by apologizing for the "mess" in his study. It is simply the scholar's overflow of books, obscure tomes touching on his current translation of the Bible into Polish, *Analytical Hebrew and Chaldee Lexicon*, *The Septuagint with Apocrypha* in Greek and English, the *Jerome Biblical Commentary*, Kierkegaard's *Stages on Life's Way*, *Young's Analytical Concordance to the Bible*. On the wall, a small color picture of Pope John Paul II looking at his translation of the Book of Psalms. There is a lovely old photograph of his wife, Janka; a simple, inconspicuous painting of the head of Christ; a medal, sculpted by a friend, of Thaddeus Kosciusko, the Polish general who fought in the American Revolution.

Milosz acknowledges his skepticism about the inevitable simplifications of a newspaper interview, a natural qualm for a man appalled by "one-dimensional images of human fate," for a poet troubled by the "inadequacy of language when confronted with the fantastic, the horrible and grotesque of this century."

But as he answers a question about the official publication of his poetry in Poland, he brightens, spicing his remarks with a sudden grin. He tells of his insistence that a Catholic publishing house in Krakow which had taken an option on his work years ago, be given the right to issue the first volume. People in Warsaw signed up many days in advance for a first edition of 20,000. It sold out in one day. Since then 200,000 copies of his collected poems have been published by three state presses. "For poetry , that's not bad!" he remarked.

Milosz foresees a "more touchy problem" when Polish censors are faced with his prose works, notably *The Captive Mind* (1953) and *Native Realm: A Search for Self-Definition* (1968). Both were written after Milosz had broken with the government. He had served with the Polish Embassy in Washington for four and a half years until he could no longer stomach the discrepancies between his non-Marxist beliefs and official dogma. Rather than take the easy way out by seeking asylum in the West, he courageously—and not without a gnawing fear—returned to Warsaw. He left Poland soon after, under dramatic circumstances too complex, he feels, to be discussed in an interview.

When he left Poland for France after his resignation in 1951, he was desperate. It was during that period in France that he wrote *The Issa Valley*. Milosz considers this book his link between poetry and prose; he wrote it when he was unable to compose poetry. "I felt a poet could write only in his own language. Technically, I can write in French or English, but I made a decision and stuck to my Polish. I have never regretted it. I always write in Polish except when I am cornered and have to do an article in English. The only poem I have ever written first in English was when I got angry with an English-speaking friend."

His English poem, "To Raja Rao," eloquently expresses his distress at being trapped between two worlds: "Ill at ease in the tyranny/Ill at ease in the Republic./In the one I longed for freedom/In the other for the end of corruption."

Milosz made a conscious decision in France to work in isolation. "I had a moment of fame after I received the first Prix Littéraire Européen for my novel *The Seizure of Power* (1953). All I would have had to do was step on the gas and publish constantly. I opted against that move. Besides, there was a conflict between myself and French intellectuals who—with a few exceptions like Albert Camus—were looking for new revelations about ideal communism somewhere, and I didn't share their illusions."

But things have changed, and privacy is now not always possible. "Because of the victory won by Polish workers, suddenly my poetry appearing in print became a symbol of the relaxation of censorship. This is very awkward for somebody who is rather solitary by nature. So I have to cope with a new situation. My guess is that when one is aware of the impact of playing a role, one may be able to save himself. Otherwise, there is a great danger of becoming a pompous ass."

It is not the first time Milosz has rejected being pigeonholed. He detested being used as a Cold War tool when his book *The Captive Mind*, a complex study of the "mental acrobatics" that led Polish intellectuals down the path to Stalinist dogma, was published in 1953. He wriggles out from under magisterial robes by calling himself a poet, "a mandolin player." He writes ironic lines about "Wrong Honorable Professor Milosz/ Who wrote poems in some unheard-of tongue." He mockingly writes his "obituary" in his poem "The Accuser": "Oh, yes, not all of me shall die/There will remain an item in the fourteenth volume of an encyclopedia/Next to a hundred Millers and Mickey Mouse."

In fact, Milosz is glad that the Nobel Prize was given to him, more, he feels, for his poetry than for his prose, and he discounts any political significance to the award. He pointed out that the Swedish Academy decided on his award in May 1980. The Academy could not have known that Solidarity's strikes in Gdansk in August would affect the course of Polish politics.

"My 'return' to Poland as a writer," Milosz said, "coincides with the disappearance of double-talk. Let us not exaggerate; of course, censorship in Poland exists, but the basic system of double-talk is no more."

Milosz recalls the censorship he faced years ago: "When I was still published in Poland, what I was afraid of most was a slow erosion of truth. Usually it comes by small compromises—one sentence here, one sentence there. A word. Anything that might anger the Russians was deleted or changed. Once you agree, you introduce an internal censorship and censor yourself. Now I would insist on the integrity of my text."

There was actually some thaw toward Milosz even before the Nobel announcement in October. (A year earlier the Catholic University of Lublin planned to present him with an honorary doctorate. The ceremony was eventually held June 11, 1981, a week after Milosz returned to a tumultuous reception on his first visit since he left the country thirty years earlier.) And long before Milosz's existence was again noted officially in the press, or on radio and television, his work was circulated through Samizdat. Independent publishers issued his poetry as well as *The Captive Mind*.

After he received the Nobel prize in December 1980, Milosz was overwhelmed by the flood of congratulatory messages from Poland. Among them was a request for a poem from the committee that was building a monument in memory of workers killed in Gdansk in 1970.

"I could not write a poem on request," he said, but the committee picked up something he had written in 1950, a short poem never translated into English. It begins with the lines "You who harmed a simple man/Don't feel secure/Because a poet remembers./You can kill him/but another will appear."

He had suggested a fragment from Psalm 29 in his translation: "The Lord will give strength to his people, the Lord will give to his people the blessing of peace."

Milosz has been a reader of the Bible since his youth, although he rebelled against Jesuitical interpretations at the Catholic schools he attended before earning a law degree. Early on, along with "foggy socialist principles," he developed a "loathing for religion as a national institution." Even as an avant-garde poet in the 1930s, he was influenced by the Bible. The poets who inspired him—William Blake, Walt Whitman, and the French poet, his relative Oscar Milosz, who introduced him to the beauty of the Old Testament—shaped their verse in a biblical way.

Czeslaw Milosz's decision to translate the Bible developed as he saw the inadequacies of recent Polish translations: "I found a beautiful version of the Psalms from the fifteenth century, compared it with a modern translation, and said, 'My goodness! Is it the SAME book?' Not at all. I thought maybe I could compete with that anonymous translator."

The task of translating the Bible, he suggests, has helped to restore his equilibrium after the intrusion of the Nobel prize. "You should consider," he says with laughter, "that this may be a somewhat crazy enterprise to sit in Berkeley and translate the Bible into Polish, but it proves that one is completely immersed in the language."

It is not only a problem of language. In his Nobel address, Milosz said that "for a poet of the other [Eastern] Europe, the events embraced by the name of the Holocaust are a reality, so close in time that he cannot hope to liberate himself from their remembrance unless, perhaps, by translating the Psalms of David." And, as he wrote at the end of his 1943 poem "A Christian Looks at the Ghetto":

What will I tell him, I, a Jew of the New Testament,

Waiting two thousand years for

the second coming of Jesus?

My broken body will deliver me

to his sight

And he will count me among the

helpers of death:

the uncircumcised.

I ask if his wartime experiences in Poland had influenced his decision to translate the Bible.

"To some extent, my memories elude my consciousness," Milosz replies. "I suspect it's been operating on a much deeper level of horror, so translating the Bible is a quite logical way of coping with some subconscious things . . . like dreams."

In his Nobel address, Milosz referred to the number of published books that have denied that the Holocaust ever took place, suggesting that it was invented by Jewish propagandists. "If such an insanity is possible," he asked, "is a complete loss of memory as a permanent state of mind improbable? And would it not present a danger more grave than genetic engineering and/or poisoning of the natural environment?"

Such a loss of memory is probable, he reasons. Referring to the television miniseries *Holocaust*, he asks with a sense of horror: "Do people have to see reality changed into melodrama to come a little closer to visualizing how it really was?"

Milosz has played a role in stimulating different levels of consciousness in Poland— for instance, through his 1958 translation into Polish of the writing of Simone Weil. The book is required reading, a Polish bishop told him, in the seminaries of his diocese. Milosz sees it as a "weapon" in the theological fight between Marxism and Polish Catholicism, which has many diverse strands.

"I have been influenced by Weil in a profound way," Milosz says. "Primarily because of her very deep concern with evil. That was her main preoccupation: suffering, pain, the evil of the world. This goes back to my preoccupations when I was a schoolboy. I was interested in heresies which were concerned with evil and with suffering, and Simone Weil is a slightly heretical writer."

Milosz's preoccupation with Weil and Dostoyevsky is linked to his meditations on the figure of Job, who dared to question God but whose faith withstood the test of all calamities.

"Job is at the center of Weil's attention, and I quote at length from her in my introduction to the Book of Job. We are again close to the Book of Job with Dostoyevsky. It plays a crucial part in the structure of *The Brothers Karamazov*. I have never taught other Russian writers. Only Dostoyevsky. I laughingly tell my students that Dostoyevsky, who hated Poles and Catholics, is taught by a man who is very far from Dostoyevsky's Russian Orthodox views. But I'm fascinated by those deeply felt contradictions in Dostoyevsky and his sensitivity to the question of evil. So you see, we are always turning around the same problem."

I ask if he sees the world in terms of good and evil.

"Unfortunately, I guess I do," Milosz replies. "I have a very clear, very strong feeling of opposed forces of good or evil. It's something which you acquire only through experience and it's very elemental. That's precisely the gist of what Nadezhda Mandelstam says in her memoir. This is characteristic of her and of Solzhenitsyn and all who went through misfortune, affliction. In those extreme situations, good and evil acquire elemental force. Western civilization is losing that clear distinction: Everything can be explained away; everything is relative. In dramatic circumstances, you feel clearly the good forces and the demonic forces in action."

And is Milosz now a practicing Catholic?

"Yes," he responds. "But I have always stressed that I do not see a great chasm today between believers and nonbelievers because all these things are in a very strange state. We are going through a very profound change of mentality and imagination. We are all affected by those changes, by the impact of science, of biology, natural sciences. I am searching for an answer as to what will result from an internal erosion of religious beliefs."

Milosz has referred to those "who sense that we went on the wrong track sometime in the eighteenth century and we have been continuing ever since on the wrong track."

Blake, he says, led a lifelong battle against the three he considered Satanic figures: Bacon, Locke, and Newton, all adherents of mechanistic philosophies. "To Blake, they were the epitome of modern science. Blake wanted to defend imagination and the unity of man who was being divided into reason and emotionality. Perhaps the day will come when science will become more open to poetry. But we are conditioned in such a way that we are in a world of separation, of division, of fragmentation. It's difficult to put it together. You know Humpty Dumpty on the wall? Humpty Dumpty had a great fall. How to put those pieces together again?"

July 1981
The New York Times

Olga Carlisle

"I longed to be free of the heavy spell which Russia and her past had cast upon my life."

San Francisco

> " . . . and the simple course of the simple brave man is not to partici-
> pate in the lie and not to support lying actions. Even if they come
> into the world and reign in the world, let it not be through me."
>
> —Aleksandr Solzhenitsyn, Nobel Prize address, 1970

> "Solzhenitsyn, whom I had served with joy, and in having done so,
> lost my family's homeland, was now obliterating my Russian origins.
> [To him] I was another dry Western mercenary . . . I longed to be free
> of the heavy spell which Russia and her past had cast upon my life."
>
> —Olga Andreyev Carlisle: *Solzhenitsyn and the Secret Circle* (1978)

Olga Carlisle's deepest desire is to paint: vivid still lifes or graceful landscapes in the manner of Matisse or Bonnard. But fate casts her as a controversial footnote in the history of a literary giant.

Even now, she should simply be celebrating the publication of her new book, *Island in Time*, about her girlhood under the Nazi occupation of France. Instead, she is awaiting, with weary curiosity, American publication of Solzhenitsyn's *The Oak and the Calf*. That memoir in earlier Russian and French editions dismissed her—anonymously—as a "dry Western mercenary" and impelled her to write an answer: *Solzhenitsyn and the Secret Circle*.* It was a meticulous, moving account of seven years dominated by the task he once thrust upon her: that she represent him in obtaining Western publication of *The First Circle* and, later, *The Gulag Archipelago*. Then he switched signals and their unwritten agreement ended.

The intensity of her feelings about her family's homeland and Solzhenitsyn's present messianic role in Western exile seems incongruous in the airy, elegant San Francisco apartment she shares with her husband, Henry Carlisle, novelist and former editor at Knopf. From the peak of Russian Hill, she can look out over the Bay, which is mirrorlike in the sunshine and seems to reflect hundreds of white sails. The spacious beige-toned living room is dominated by her large, spiky, black-on-white drawing of the ancient walled French hillside town of Murs where they once lived.

She was born in Paris but her first language was Russian, spoken in a home bubbling with fervent discussions about literature and humanitarian socialism. The passion was passed on to this small, spirited woman now walking around barefoot, toenails painted bright red. As she recalls the past, her gray eyes sometimes cloud with family memories, then flash with anger over injustice—ancient, contemporary.

Tradition. She doesn't take it lightly. Her father's father was the avant-garde Symbolist writer Leonid Andreyev. She shows a wide, loving smile when she refers to his "extraordinarily romantic-looking face." There's pride when she recounts how he and Maxim Gorky fought the anti-Semites of their day, as well as cool criticism of Andreyev's less-realistic work. She's working on a new translation of his play *He Who Gets Slapped*, with its contemporary relevance about a man who leaves the "establishment" to become a clown.

Her mother's life was dominated by the fateful figure of her adoptive father, Victor Chernov, a leader of the Socialist Revolutionary Party, chairman of the Constituent Assembly, the only parliamentary body ever assembled in Russia through democratic process. It convened in January 1918, and after one dramatic session was disbanded by the Bolsheviks. While Chernov went into hiding, his wife was sent to prison for nearly three years. Her twin teenage daughters, Olga and Natalia, were in and out of jail until Gorky interceded on their behalf.

Olga Chernov Andreyev, gave "a very nice portrait of Gorky in her memoir, *Cold Spring in Russia*," Olga Carlisle said. "This was the best period of Gorky's life. He had not yet joined Lenin. He was rather appalled by what the Bolsheviks were doing and tried to counteract it. He helped lots of Russian writers in that period. When he asked Lenin to let Chernov's family emigrate, Lenin refused, but Gorky told him, 'You wouldn't want it said in Europe that Lenin is keeping Chernov's children in prison.' Lenin thought about it and said, 'All right, let them go.'

"They were extremely fortunate; I want to stress that. Of my mother and grand-mother's milieu, almost no one survived. Their kind of non-Marxist Socialists were the majority in Russia before the Bolsheviks' October takeover. Lenin hated those social-ists and only a few dozen of them survived out of hundreds of thousands of people."

Despite those memories, in France the family was optimistic "that somehow Russia would be transformed," Olga Carlisle said. "The great purges were very hard for my parents to comprehend and everyone was very worried, but then the war came and somehow wishful thinking made a lot of people everywhere believe that Russia would simply not go back to the terror after that experience. Had Stalin died at that time, it would all have been different."

The outbreak of war in 1939 caught the Andreyev family vacationing on Oleron, an island off the western coast of France that became part of Hitler's Atlantic Wall fortifications. Olga was nine when they were trapped there. The next six years, which she writes about in *Island in Time*,** were marked by fear of the German occupation troops and by the strange, dramatic transformation of a woman who found refuge in their home—arriving as an anti-Fascist and then becoming a Nazi collaborator. She had been referred to them by the Modiglianis—members of the artist's family—whom her grandmother, a leftist journalist, had known before the Russian revolution.

Not until the publication of Pasternak's *Dr. Zhivago* did Olga Carlisle first see her parents' country. By that time, she already had a mixed introduction to the United States. At eighteen, she spent one year at Bard College in New York. Appalled by the McCarthyite atmosphere, she hastened back to France, where she met and married Carlisle, an American Navy veteran studying at the Sorbonne.

She was busy raising their son and studying painting under Robert Motherwell in 1960 when the editors of the *Paris Review* asked her to interview Pasternak. "Here was the opportunity to do something that served a measure of social use," she said. "At that time, it was important for Americans to learn more about Russia." Because of the Mc-Carthy era, Russian studies in the universities had dwindled, she explained.

Her family relationship to Andreyev eased her way to meetings with Pasternak, Ehrenburg, Yevtushenko, and Sholokov, as she collected material later published by Random House as *Voices in the Snow* and *Poets on Street Corners*. Solzhenitsyn had met her parents and admired her father's memoir on the elder Andreyev. In 1967,

Solzhenitsyn asked her to represent him in the West with *The First Circle*, his initial attack on the Soviet ruling class. To protect Solzhenitsyn, publication had to be worked out with maximum secrecy and without written authorization. Publishers Harper & Row mapped out a careful strategy for the book's release.

Later, at a signal from Solzhenitsyn, Carlisle was to release the first part of the *The Gulag Archipelago*, his devastating expose of the Soviet forced labor-camp system. But, unknown to her—at first—Solzhenitsyn had begun working with other representatives in Switzerland and France. A Russian-language edition of *Gulag I* appeared in Paris in December 1973, and a German edition in January 1974. In February, Solzhenitsyn was summarily expelled from the Soviet Union. He later charged that Carlisle was responsible for delaying American publication of *Gulag I* until four months after his expulsion. Solzhenitsyn called the postponement a "catastrophe" for himself and the whole dissident movement. Olga Carlisle and her husband had both worked on the project; both denied Solzhenitzyn's charges. They declared that *Gulag I* had been ready for publication in 1970 and that Solzhenitsyn himself ordered the delay.

This would be ancient history if it were not for the forthcoming American publication of *The Oak and the Calf*. Harper & Row discussed changes in a "controversial footnote" involving Carlisle's role but declined to reveal the text.

In the European edition, Solzhenitsyn chronicles his life as a public writer and "describes his moment of exaltation when he begins to count as a force in Russian politics," Carlisle said. "It is very detailed about the Russian literary scene. It is a very Soviet book with a lot of innuendoes and accusations that could be devastating to the people accused." She stressed that her observations were based on the first European editions of *The Oak and the Calf*.

Carlisle's overall view of Solzhenitzyn remains "extremely positive: What he has achieved is extraordinary in alerting the world to what has been going on in the Soviet Union.

"But the principal thing that upsets me is that Solzhenitsyn confers upon himself the right to say who loves Russia and who is a Russia-hater. In his terms, a hater is whoever feels that something was lacking in Russia before the revolution. The kind of socialism my grandmother's family was involved with is anathema to the Russian right wing and Solzhenitsyn. The fact that they were not Marxists is forgotten; they are seen as the people who brought into Russia the foreign ideas that caused all the touble. Solzenitsyn believes that Russia was a happy authoritarian kingdom . . . until those troublemakers who had Western educations and befriended Jews caused the revolution. In indirect ways, Solzhenitsyn says this in his book *Lenin in Zurich*.***

"I think the Russian revolution was brought about by the fact that the czars were inept and incapable of reform when it was needed," she declared.

Originally, Carlisle didn't have a clue about Solzhenitzyn's hostility to Western democratic ideas nor his nationalistic and mystical Russian Orthodox beliefs. After his interview on BBC-TV and his controversial speech at Harvard University attacking the lack of spiritual fiber in the West, she became increasingly angry with the man whom few people dared to challenge.

Carlisle—who is not Jewish—said that one of her great quarrels with Solzhenitzyn is his pressure on people not to leave the Soviet Union. "He is reading declarations about the fact that those Jews who leave are really not Russian at all, that they have no identification with or responsibility to Russia. Of course, he was thrown out so he is fine. But those people who are in impossible circumstances and decided to leave voluntarily, he feels they are no longer entitled to a place in the Russian community.

"What is so bad about Solzhenitsyn is that he makes ideas respectable that have not been respectable from the nineteenth century on. You might be anti-Semitic, but except among yourselves you wouldn't discuss it.

"But Solzhenitsyn—because he was heroic and wrote the *Gulag*—is presumed to have a right to say what he pleases . . . The anti-Semitic White Russians were dying out. Now Solzhenitsyn comes and it is like pouring fertilizer on those people. Their ideas and their publications, their sense of self, and their opposition to the Jews who emigrate have been tremendously reinforced by Solzhenitsyn. I think that is shocking."

April 13, 1978

Los Angeles Times

*Published in Russia in 2004
**Published in France in 2005 as part of a World War II commemoration.
***Recently, Solzhenitsyn elaborated on his theories about the historical relationship between Russians and Jews in a "grandiose, controversial, two-part volume" Carlisle noted.

Pascal Aubier

"Godard would ask me to do the most incredible things."

San Francisco

As a boy in Paris, Pascal Aubier listened to the Russian fairy tales told by his surrealist artist father, as well as true stories about the Soviet people's fierce resistance to the Nazis at Stalingrad. Later, as an impressionable teenager, he learned some idiosyncratic lessons in filmmaking from his father-figure, Jean-Luc Godard.

Aubier's affection for the people, not the politics, of Russia and his love for the New Wave French cinema of the sixties merge in his ebullient comedy-romance, *Son of Gascogne*. He talked about all of that when *Son of Gascogne* was screened at the 1995 San Francisco Film Festival.

In the movie, as if it's not enough for Harvey, a fatherless Parisian guide, to be responsible for a rambunctious bunch of singers from ex-Soviet Georgia, there's a key question he has to face: "Is he or is he not the son of Gascogne?"

The answer is "yes," according to Marco, a burly con-artist chauffeur (Jean-Claude Dreyfus) who took one look at the winsome Harvey (Gregoire Colin of *Olivier, Olivier*) and decided to pass him off as the son of a fictional sixties director Gascogne, a legendary Lothario who died while making his last film.

While Harvey and the charming Dinara, the singers' interpreter (Dinara Droukarova), are discovering each other, Marco, who claims to be a former child star, is introducing Harvey to all of Gascogne's old actors and other associates from the '60s.

So there are sixties cameos galore, whether the viewer can recognize these old stars or not: Stephane Audran, Marie France-Pisier, Claude Chabrol, Bernadette Lafont, Bulle Ogier, Richard Leacock, and many more. Only two of the sixties luminaries turned Auber down: Anna Karina, Godard's first wife and frequent star, didn't want to play herself, and Jean-Pierre (*400 Blows*) Leaud didn't like being one of many, declaring, "I *was* the New Wave."

The notion of the fatherless French tour guide came from Aubier's co-writer, Patrick Modiano, who was obsessed by the fact that he never knew much about his father. And Aubier got the idea of having Georgian singers in the film when he attended a festival on a Black Sea boat that offered musical entertainment.

Which brings us to Gascogne's other famous character, the irrepressible Georgian director Otar Iosseliani, who introduced Aubier to Russia at the Moscow airport in 1967 with the unforgettable query, in French: "Do you enjoy drinking?" And off the two went at 10A.M. for a vodka or two or more.

"We started speaking and became close friends at first sight," Aubier said, relishing the recollection and clicking his fingers expressively. "Otar was speaking beautiful French, although he had never been to France at that time, but as a prince from a former aristocratic Georgian family, he had been taught the language. He was absolutely an unofficial person. We spent two weeks together running around Moscow, and one day he showed me his film, *Dead Leaves*, and it was beautiful."

In the film, Iosseliani showed the corruption that overtakes a shy but principled young man who tries to correct the mismanagement of a Tbilisi distillery where the quality of the wine is being tampered with to meet the demands to overfill the production plan.

"It was the Brezhnev era," Aubier said, "and I could have lost my many illusions about Russia, but I met great people, and that made the difference. They had had hard times but they knew how to find their way and they had these warm, human relationships. The depth of their relationships was fantastic and that is still there. Russia taught me a lot. I was with people who cried because they were so happy to be together, but we French were not supposed to cry. Even though the Russians are miserable today, they're great human beings, and that's one of the things I wanted to show in my movie. Nothing to do with politics."

Iosseliani was only one of the exceptional characters Aubier met in his life. His father, Jean Aubier, an artist and publisher who had been in the French Resistance, died when Pascal was thirteen, but he had introduced the boy to his avant-garde friends. Aubier fondly recalls "endless luncheons with Picasso, who was very funny, very sharp," and riding on a bicycle with Tristan Tzara, the artist and poet who helped found the Dada-ist movement, which called for the "abolition of all logic."

Logic was not necessarily intrinsic to what Aubier learned about filmmaking when he was studying anthropology at the Sorbonne. A classmate, Barbet (*Reversal of Fortune*) Schroeder, asked for his assistance on a film he was producing after school hours. *Six in Paris* was a compilation of brief views of the city as seen by six directors, including Godard, Chabrol, and Rohmer. Godard asked Aubier to continue working for him in *Pierrot le Fou* and *Masculin, Feminin*.

"I was very shy," Aubier recalled with a laugh, "and Godard would ask me to do the most incredible things. Whatever he does, you feel very embarrassed to be around him."

Despite many embarrassing experiences, Aubier was convinced that film was "like magic." And, it was Godard who taught him the most important lesson. "Godard would tell people, 'You want to make a movie? Do it. It's not difficult. You can be a good or bad filmmaker, but you'll be a filmmaker.'"

Advice that Aubier took to heart.

May 23, 1998
The San Francisco Examiner

E.L. Doctorow

PHOTO BY: PAUL BACON.

People caught up in history.

San Francisco

E.L. Doctorow is part of what *Time* or *Life* and some Big Media Man called the "silent generation." A cold war here. A hot war there. Korea. They went. Who asked questions? Joe McCarthy had lists up his sleeves. Reds under the pumpkin patches. On June 19, 1953, Ethel and Julius Rosenberg were executed at Sing Sing prison for conspiracy to commit espionage. Millions protested, especially in other countries. Survivors of history were heard from: a sister of Bartolomeo Vanzetti, a daughter of Colonel Alfred Dreyfus.

Ed Doctorow was sweeping up the bathroom in a theater in Westport, Conneciticut. He thought he might learn to become an actor while waiting to be drafted. He wasn't interested in the Rosenberg case.

In a sense, he still isn't, even though his brilliant novel, *The Book of Daniel*, will undoubtedly raise questions all over again about the Rosenbergs. And whatever did happen to their two little boys? Doctorow doesn't know. He doesn't have any theories as to whether the Rosenbergs were guilty or innocent. He doesn't want his book discussed in terms of the Rosenbergs.

He says it a little helplessly, knowing it will be—and a little apologetically, for lecturing on about how he doesn't want his book analyzed. He stopped overnight in San

18

Francisco on his way home to Connecticut. He is a tall, sturdy, kind-looking man, balding, with longish brown hair and a neat brown beard. He has a burly warmth, sensitivity and humor, a certain amount of shyness.

The Book of Daniel takes off from the point when Daniel Isaacson and his little sister, Susan, attempt to come to grips with their lives and those of their parents, executed for conspiring to steal atomic secrets. From that vantage, Doctorow has tried to make the novel "big news" again, "as it was in the nineteenth century." But he has abandoned traditional techniques and captured the fragmented rhythm of life today, presenting a striking kaleidoscope of people caught up in history.

"Novels should be about large social things, not the problems of homosexual teenagers," Doctorow said. "This is a novel that covers twenty-five years of American history. It takes everything on. It doesn't duck anything. It's nothing if not ambitious. Does it say something a sociologist or the Gallup Poll couldn't have told you? I hope people will read there the spiritual history of the Cold War.

"The idea that fascinated me was discovering and investigating what happens to a family when all the antagonistic force of society turns upon it, how does it feel, what does it mean, what does it lead to, what are the consequences? My book is about the lives of children, the way children live and perceive, it's about Jewish sensibility, the peculiar relationship between humanist politics, between socialist politics and Jewishness. I think there is a relationship in the great romantic sense of the belief that it is possible to perfect the world. It comes right out of the Jewish prophets. My book is about the nature of the left, what the life of the left is, what its peculiar bitterness is and its humanity and its function in American politics, which I think is largely sacrificial."

Doctorow grew up in a Jewish middle-class family in the Bronx with *New York Post* liberal-left sympathies. He went through undergraduate school at Kenyon College, Ohio, took his master's degree at Columbia, and served two years in the army in Europe without any particular political commitments. While a reader at Columbia Pictures, he wrote his first novel, the well-received *Welcome to Hard Times*, about the destruction of a Western town by a bad man, and *Big as Life*, which dealt with the chaos in New York when two giant human figures appear in the harbor.

"What is common to all three novels," Doctorow ventured, "is an involuntary oscillation beween hope and despair." After nine years as an editor in two New York publishing houses, he became a writer-in-residence for a year at the University of California at Irvine.

A few years ago, Doctorow began to worry about political trials in general and then remembered what he had "perhaps repressed" during the fifties. He saw that the conspiracy charge leveled against the Rosenbergs was relevant today. "The use of conspiracy to secure an indictment is a very convenient legality to use against someone you cannot prove did anything illegal. Going after the Catholic radicals, the Berrigans and so on. The use of this kind of law in political trials is to punish people whose politics are disagreeable to the establishment."

The atmosphere is in many ways worse today, Doctorow believes, as wiretapping and surveillance are condoned and the tolerance level rises for "really totalitarian" government techniques.

"The heart of the politics in the book comes to explicit expression at only one point," Doctorow said. "That's when Daniel is trying to figure out why he's not applying for a fellowship under the National Defense Education Act. He begins to speculate on how he stands in relationship to the government that has killed his parents. He knows they keep a dossier on him and he knows they are not worried about him. He talks about *Paths of Glory*, in which the soldiers are killed in effect by their own officers, and he finds in that the metaphor about how all citizens stand in relationship to their country. He says, 'Every citizen is an enemy of his own country.' Daniel stands at a point of absolute distrust of any kind of state, whether it be called capitalism or communism, any nationhood that exists to use its own citizens for its protection. I explain why Daniel was so fascinated by Bukharin's trial in the Soviet Union. It was a mirror image of what happened to someone on the other side. Bukharin confessed and he got killed: Daniel's parents didn't confess and they got killed. It doesn't matter if you confess or don't confess, you're going to be destroyed if it's convenient—which ties in to the nature of trial and what trial is in any society and what it's used for."

Doctorow is now writing a book for children on the history of revolution. "The only kind of revolution I could believe in is different from any that has ever occurred," he said. "It's totally non-violent. The only kind of thing which will work and redeem us all. The historical message is you can't hammer your way to it because when you get there, you still have the hammer in hand and you can never let go and you become your own enemy. You become the bad guys. That's what happened to us in Vietnam.

"There's a point in the book where it says that the Isaacsons were convicted of conspiracy to steal the atom bomb or the hydrogen bomb or the cobalt bomb, or napalm. That's a crucial passage because in the spirit of the kind of sensibility of young people today, by becoming the rigid guardian of truth and justice you somehow pervert your own nature. Protecting the free world with one bomb after the other, you suddenly discover you're what the world has to worry about. But I'm talking politics again and I don't want to talk politics. The book is about human beings. I want people to read it and cry at the right places and try to lead better lives."

June 20, 1971
San Francisco Chronicle

Thomas Keneally

"*Jews were even a more unknown people than the Aborigines.*"

Sydney, Australia

Afew days short of becoming a Catholic priest, Thomas Keneally decided he'd rather write books than save souls. Now, all because of a broken briefcase, he is the author of a prize-winning novel about an unlikely but real savior, Oskar Schindler, a Sudeten German and "back-slid" Catholic industrialist who actually did preserve the lives of more than 1,300 Jews during World War II.

That wartime rescue is not a story one had anticipated hearing in this gorgeously remote location: a book-cluttered house perched on a cliff above the red sands of Bilgola Beach, overlooking the South Pacific Ocean. A genocidal tale closer to home and more remote in memory would have been the British obliteration of the Aboriginal tribes in Tasmania. In fact, Keneally, author of *The Chant of Jimmy Blacksmith*, is currently at work on a nonfiction book, *The Outback*, about the Aborigines and white settlers of Central and Northern Australia.

This impish-looking scholar is bubbling with information on the differences between the tribal Aborigines who still believe profoundly in their prehistoric "Dream Time" and the more rootless Aboriginal city-dwellers. Keneally regrets that he didn't have that knowledge when writing about the missionary-raised Aborigine, Jimmy Blacksmith. "I was making easier, middle-class, humanist judgments then," Keneally said. He believes now he had not really understood the Aboriginal relationship to ritual, to their mystical connection with the earth.

If tribal Aborigines were strangers to him, Jews were an even more unknown people. In Keneally's mind, they were the exotic men and women in novels by Saul Bellow, Bernard Malamud, and Isaac Bashevis Singer.

"I had rarely met anyone Jewish before I started writing *Schindler's List*," Keneally said.

He grew up in a rigidly Irish Catholic atmosphere, not unlike that of Belfast. In Australia, it was cause for excommunication if Catholic children weren't sent to parochial schools. A special aura was attached to the priesthood, but after six years in a seminary, Keneally said, "I was mentally exhausted by the strain of being a seminarian. I was very doubtful about that old-style, rather anti-human, Catholicism."

Later he wrote a book about the crisis in Catholicism, *Three Cheers for the Paraclete* (Holy Spirit), a book that "did well" in the United States. "Now I don't think I'm a Catholic," Keneally said, "except in the tribal sense." His wife, Judy, an ex-nun, is smilingly obstinate in her refusal to talk about her defection.

When writing about Orthodox Jews in *Schindler's List*, Keneally commented, "I found it enormously helpful to have a tribal background myself. There are great similarities in mentality between the Jews and the Irish. I think the Jews are tougher. This tradition of failing fatally against overwhelming odds—it's in both races and it's very strong. The Jews do more about it: they subscribe to fighter planes and the Irish just get drunk. But, there is a genuine set of symbols which both parties share."

But Keneally said he wouldn't have made that connection if it hadn't been for Paul Page, a loquacious Los Angeles luggage dealer who sold him a new briefcase in October 1980 and asked what he did for a living. Page got his answer and uttered the phrase writers dread: "I've got a book you ought to write."

The way Keneally tells it—with a fondly mimicking Central European accent—Page, a Polish Jew, said, "I was saved by a Sudeten German, a wild man, an industrialist, a bon vivant. He got my wife out of Auschwitz. I think he's a God, but he was a scoundrel, a black-marketeer, a drunk, and a womanizer."

Page—"this little nugget of a bloke"—was not about to lose his prospective historian. He put his son in charge of the store, hustled Keneally off to his bank, and conned an obliging clerk into copying a box of documents for Keneally to study. Keneally was hooked.

"The rudimentary story was astounding," Keneally said. "Schindler was about thirty-one when he moved to Krakow, Poland, on the heels of the invading army in 1939. He was an agent of Admiral Canaris' intelligence unit, the Abwehr—which made him exempt from army service. He started an enamel works in a suburb of Krakow and began cooperating with Jewish leaders very early. He was young, fairly well-off, extremely handsome, a Hitlerite dream. The factory became a refuge for Jewish workers, and eventually he founded a 'concentration camp' in his own backyard—but nothing evil happened there. This a preposterous claim, and it is absolute truth. The SS were not permitted in its perimeter, except for the most senior officials. He couldn't prevent them from coming in occasionally. The place was 'paradise,' compared to what was happening elsewhere in Europe. I've heard survivors in Australia, Austria, Brazil, and Israel use that word 'paradise' over and over."

In *Schindler's List*, which won the prestigious Booker prize, Keneally created a stunning, meticulous work of real suspense to show how one determined man outwitted a murderous system. What possessed Schindler to save Jewish lives in a Europe that closed its eyes is still a mystery. Schindler himself may not have understood his driving obsession. Even after being arrested twice by the SS, he convinced German authorities to release Jewish people for a new factory camp he was planning in Czechoslovakia. When the men were first sent to Gross-Rosen, another huge slave-labor camp, and the women to Auschwitz, Schindler bribed and finagled their transfer to his Czech haven.

On the eve of liberation, in *Schindler's List*, an extraordinary drama was played out in his factory under the eyes of the SS. When the Schindlerjuden—as Schindler's Jews called themselves—said farewell, they presented him with a gold ring, fashioned by a jeweler from his own false teeth. It was incribed in Hebrew: "He who saves one soul, it is as if he saved the entire world."

November 21, 1982
San Francisco Chronicle

Lajos Koltai

PHOTO BY JUDY STONE.

"What happened in the past can happen today..."

Mill Valley, California

In 1975, Lajos Koltai, the noted cinematographer, was like all the other Hungarians who ignored the publication of *Fateless*, Imre Kertész's semi-autobiographical account of a Jewish boy's survival in three concentration camps. Ten years later, a major Hungarian literary critic proclaimed it a "great, great" book and urged people to read it.

Then in 2002, Kertész won the Nobel Prize for literature. Readers began to pay attention to the stark and understated account of the Holocaust that never becomes melodramatic, and some directors tried to figure out how to create a film out of material that seemed to defy cinematic possibilities. In 2000, a friend had sent the novel to Koltai, who was shooting a film in Morocco, and the cinematographer was stunned by its simplicity and power.

24

Koltai recalled his first reaction when *Fateless* was shown at the 2005 Mill Valley Film Festival. "It was so special," he said in heavily accented English. "I had never read anything like that in Hungary. As I read the sentences, I immediately saw how things were. I could see the concentration camps in my mind. I'm always reading visually. I'm thought of as a cinematographer. That's why I was given the book. Nobody asked me to direct, but it was the first time I had something in my hand that I thought was really for me to direct."

Nominated for a 2001 Academy Oscar for his cinematography on Giuseppi Tornatore's *Malena*, Koltai had collaborated as a director of photography on fifteen Istvan Szabo productions, including *Being Julia*, starring Annette Bening, and the 2006 *Relatives*, a Hungarian political comedy. He also shot many American films. "Everything was planned for me to direct my first movie and I had the money but I gave it back, hoping to direct *Fateless*."

Kertész had refused giving *Fateless* film rights to many aspirants, but had arranged with mutual friends to meet Koltai. "I tried to explain how much I loved the book," Koltai said, recalling the way Kertész had blushed at his praise. He handed Koltai a script and asked if it was good enough for a film. It wasn't.

When the two met again, Kerész had a key question for Koltai: "What do you think about a linear narrative? A straight story?" The novelist knew that approach was usually not attractive for filmmakers because they prefer more flexibility.

"I told him," Koltai replied, "this is what I like. I don't want to use the same elements as every other Holocaust film that starts outside and goes inside. We can go inside the boy and see outside. Finally we are interested in a human being who's been there. It's much more important than seeing something about how the Germans are coming or how someone hides from one place to another. That's not important. The most important thing is to spend this terrible time in the camps."

Koltai asked if Kertész was that boy. "Imre said, 'It's not me. This boy is created by the words, by the sentences that become literature. When you're writing down something, it's the creation of the literature. Of course I was in the camps, but I was just one of the boys.'"

To make his personal background clear, Koltai said he wanted the writer to know that he is not Jewish. Recalling Kertész's positive response, Koltai quoted him as saying: "'That's a good thing. If you are Jewish, you can't go away from it because then you would go in a sentimental way. The book is very objective, very dry. You are a person who can keep a distance because you are not Jewish. You are not inside.'"

Nevertheless, as Koltai directed the horrendous day-to-day ordeals facing the Jewish prisoners, he felt "inside," identifying with them. As for the main character, the once-carefree adolescent's boy body becomes bent and his eyes haunted in the mesmerizing performance of Marcell Nagy. Selected from among 4,000 youngsters, he is the son of Protestant parents, both sports figures. "At first I thought Marcell was too beautiful," Koltai said, "but then I decided I didn't care about beauty anymore. I showed his picture to Imre, who thought it was a great face, and my friend, the director Istvan Szabo, said, 'It's unbelievable.' The boy who was twelve when we started had no knowledge about the Holocaust, but he went through so much in the film, he's a grown-up person now. He has wisdom. There's something in him forever."

With agreement on how to handle the difficult story, Kertész decided to write his own script, relying on the director to elicit the emotions that words couldn't express. In one new scene, an American Jewish soldier who has helped liberate the camp tries to warn the boy not to return to Hungary. Although this scene is not in the novel, Kertész said it was based on a real occurrence.

Koltai talked to people in the cast every day, discussing the history and why the film was being made and what the emotion of the moment should be. "I didn't want to get a letter from anybody saying, 'It wasn't like this.' This film is a little like a history, a book, and you have to be very careful. Imre said, 'It's very much as it happened. Very.'"

People fought to get in the film. Everybody seemed to have had relations in the camps. "It was like a memory of family to be there. The extras would come to me in the evening, after a day of lying in the mud and cold, and say, 'Thank you, Lajos.' It was fantastic."

When the film opened in Hungary, "The audiences loved it and they hated it. Some people went against it a little bit because the film opened a subject that nobody wanted to talk about: the way Hungarian officials supported the Germans and got people into the trains that went to the concentration camps. And before the film, they never talked about what happened when the survivors returned home."

Although Koltai doesn't want to make any more films about the Holocaust, he believes that all the arts in Europe are affected by the wars that dominated the twentieth century. "What happened to your family is always in the background, even in painting. I think I just have to make films about human relations because what happened in the past can happen today—anywhere and anytime."

Feburary 24, 2006
The Oakland Tribune

Joseph E. Levine

"I'm here to sell my fish."

Beverly Hills

J oe Levine, the mighty mite who became a movie mogul overnight by parlaying *Hercules*, a spaghetti spectacular, into a multi-million-dollar grosser, is happy to be back in business again with a new "people's picture."

A "people's picture," he explained expansively, "is one that no matter what high-class critics on *The New York Times* and *The New Yorker* say, you can't keep the people away from."

He was expounding on his theory before a covey of critics, friends, and flacks assembled for an intimate little screening of *The Night Porter,* the movie that saved him from retirement. Or "How an ex-Nazi officer and his former concentration camp victim found sado-masochistic bliss on a bed of ground glass twenty years after that beastly little war."

"I am here," said Levine, who doesn't call himself a hustler for nothing, "to sell my fish." He look very natty in a black suit, blue shirt with white collar, and maroon

26

tie as he ordered a Perrier instead of his usual Black & White before lunch at the Beverly Hills Hotel. The producer, hunched over his 300-year-old Chinese bamboo-engraved silver-tipped ebony cane, his left wrist resplendent in a Piaget onyx and tiger's eye checkerboard watch, shrewdly surveyed the unfamiliar faces through his gray-tinted glasses.

He had been begging for retirement from Avco-Embassy productions for two years, Levine said amiably, and when he got it he couldn't stand it.

What was he going to do—go fishing? Count his Monets, Vuillards, Toulouse-Lautrecs, and Renoirs? Was this, after all, a life for a man who had worked since age fourteen? Who went from manufacturing statues of Daddy Grace, the Negro evangelist, to discovering the paydirt in sound-alike double bills such as *Captain Fury* and *Captain Caution* at his Boston theaters? Who revolutionized the art-film business by touting *Two Women* like a Hollywood spectacle and promoting the first Oscar for a foreign actress for its star, Sophia Loren? Who did so much for Italian movies that he received the order of Merit of the Republic of Italy in the grade of Cavaliere Ufficiale and, what's more, got a mezuzah blessed by Pope Paul VI for the doorway of his New York Sutton Place apartment?

Did Horatio Alger stop to go fishing?

After six days in retirement, Joe Levine did what came naturally. He took an ad in *Variety* and announced to the world: "At liberty. Have tux. Will travel."

Once more, it was an Italian movie, *The Night Porter*, directed by Liliana Cavani, that put the bounce back into the old maestro.

No sooner did he get to Paris than he was shown Miss Cavani's new film.

"I noticed one thing," said Levine. "We went to lunch and everybody talked about it. In France, *Paris-Match* hated it, *Figaro* loved it. It was doing a land-office business in Italy. In England, the ones who didn't like it all used the same word, 'sado-masochistic.'"

"I didn't know what it meant," said Levine, the family man playing know-nothing. "I just turned thirty-nine.

"United Artists owned the picture for France," Levine said. "It earned over $1 million in Paris alone. But now I own half the world rights."

"What," asked one fact-seeker, "has it done so far in New York, Joe?"

"We opened at the 414-seat Baronet," Levine answered, checking with the New York team at the end of the table. "We did $50,000 the first week, which is capacity; $49,000, the second, $39,000 the third week. The previous house record was $41,000, racked up by *Serpico*. It beat out *A Touch of Class*.

"We did get some bad reviews," Levine conceded cheerfully. He not say that Vincent Canby called it "a piece of junk" in *The New York Times*. Instead, Levine turned up truffles for his ad, and quoted Canby on "romantic pornography" and "a kinky turn-on."

"This is a people's picture," Levine reiterated. "Some pictures are hurt by reviews and some not. I hate to minimize the power of the press.

"The picture reminds me of *8¹/₂*. I produced that with Fellini. I asked him 'Federico, what does it all mean?' Fellini said, 'I don't know. It's a cocktail picture. People just talked about it.'"

The producer ranged widely over the field of all the Levine pictures that people have talked about, from *Lion in Winter* to *The Graduate*, while murmurs of appreciation hummed steadily through the room.

Considering all those accomplishments, said one reporter, struggling to be polite, "Wasn't there something better you could have done with your retirement than buy *The Night Porter*?"

Levine, a little plaintively: "The only thing I know how to do is buy or make pictures."

Portly senior columnist, in the manner of Merriman Smith adjourning a presidential press conference: "Thank you, Mr. Levine."

But Levine wasn't finished with dessert or the skeptical reporter. "You haven't asked me the $64 question," Levine said in a quiet aside. "Do you like this picture, Joe?"

"Do you like this picture, Joe?"

"No," Levine responded. "Now you should ask, 'Why did you buy it then, Joe?'"

"It had two great performances," he said, answering his own question. "And I saw the making of a great director in this woman.

"I also bought it because it's my kind of picture to sell. Nobody can sell a picture like I can.

"As for me," said Levine, good guy to the end, "I personally would not go to see it after reading my own ads."

November 30, 1974
San Francisco Chronicle

Gillies Mackinnon

PHOTO BY JUDY STONE.

"T'is sweet and fitting to die for one's country."

Toronto

"T'is sweet and fitting to die for one's country," wrote the Roman poet Horace, but that sentiment is nailed as "an old lie" in *Regeneration*, a riveting British film set in a mental hospital designed to cure the psychological wounds of World War I veterans and send them back into battle.

The film, based on Pat Barker's prize-winning wartime trilogy, is a fictionalized account of the real relationships among Dr. William Rivers, the head neurologist (Jonathan Pryce), poet Siegfried Sassoon, a decorated war hero turned passionate anti-war polemicist (James Wilby), and poet Wilfred Owen (Stuart Bunce), who switched from romantic verse to blistering evocations of battlefield horrors.

Sassoon, a decorated battalion commander who had just made a public declaration against the continuation of the war and thrown his Military Cross medal for bravery into the River Mersey, continued his protest with a written declaration: "I believe that this war, upon which I entered as a war of defence and liberation, has now become a war of aggression and conquest. . . . I am not protesting against the conduct of the war, but against the political errors and insincerities for which the fighting men are being sacrificed."

Sassoon wanted to be court-martialed for the publicity it would bring, but a friend, writer Robert Graves, convinced him instead to go along with a medical board convened to assess Sassoon's mental state. As a result, Sassoon was sent to Craiglockart War Hospital in Scotland. The film contains a running dialogue between Sassoon and Dr. Rivers about how they should respond to the war. As the doctor begins to win his trust, the poet describes his visions of dying soldiers as "the nightmares that go on after waking."

Oddly enough, director Gillies Mackinnon, who has always been haunted by the murderous devastation of the first Great War, said he didn't think of his production as an "anti-war" vehicle. "The people who see this don't need to be converted," he commented at the 1997 Toronto Film Festival. "I assume they already feel the First World War was a horrible, horrible event and should be unrepeatable, but of course it isn't unrepeatable. After all that carnage in Yugoslavia. It seems that human beings haven't learned a lesson."

Pryce, interviewed by telephone, thought it was particularly appropriate that *Regeneration* was opening in the United States almost simultaneously with *Saving Private Ryan*, which deals with the Second World War. "I thought the first twenty minutes of *Ryan* seriously demystifies war. You can feel the trauma and agony the soldiers endured and the lack of comprehension on their faces when they see the deaths around them. After that, it turns into a kind of wartime heroism shown in many American films."

But neither man, both aged fifty, took a strictly pacifist position. They agreed with Sassoon, who said he did not believe that no war was ever justified. Sassoon was known as "Mad Jack" because he took so many dangerous risks, but two years on the batttle-field convinced him that the war was "being deliberately prolonged by those who have the power to end it."

Mackinnon noted that Sassoon's eloquent anti-war statement is the backbone of the story. The director of *Playboys* and *Small Faces* couldn't quite account for his early identification with World War I veterans. His grandfather, a veteran, would never talk about it.

"That whole generation was paralyzed in some way. Wounded inside," Mackinnon observed. "This was a different kind of war. You can understand the appalling reasons for World War II. This wasn't like the Holocaust. There wasn't even a crazy philoso- phy like Hitler's. This was like you didn't understand why millions of men had to walk into machine guns. Everybody went there to be destroyed. I had a sense of guilt that I should have been there—or maybe," he added obliquely, "I was there."

In Glasgow, his hometown, he used to meet WWI veterans who had survived bloody battles fought in France's Somme valley. One veteran told him, "I was brought up a Catholic and all my life I believed in God. Then I went to the Somme and I couldn't believe in God anymore."

That remark made a lasting impression on Mackinnon. "He was a simple man and the one thing he had was a belief in God."

Mackinnon, who was educated at the Glasgow School of Art, added softly, "I believe in art, I suppose."

His art training stood him in good stead when it came to incorporating poetry—Sassoon's and Owen's—in the film. "We introduced poems that were not in the book, but we needed them for our story. (For instance: Owen's "red lips are not so red as the stained stones kissed by the English dead.")

"As soon as you use poetry in a film it becomes something different because poems are not supposed to have visual images, it changes them."

Dr. Rivers, who empathizes with his patients and learns from them, had his own misgivings about repairing them to fight again, but he also felt that Sassoon's proclamation would accomplish nothing. "It was wonderful to play a man who is learning about his profession," Pryce said, "while I'm going through the same process learning to be Rivers. If you put it into another context, the Gulf War soldiers were complaining about the same sort of neuroses as the men in *Regeneration*. I think the film is very important because it shows how to vocalize one's objections to war."

August 1998

The San Francisco Examiner

Menno Meyjes

PHOTO BY JUDY STONE.

"Let's not forget that Mussolini and Hitler were elected."

Toronto

The Nazi architect Albert Speer said, "If you want to understand Hitler, you have to understand he was an artist first."

That quote inspired Menno Meyjes to proceed with writing and directing his first feature film, *Max*, a bound-to-provoke controversy about the relationship between Max, a genial Jewish art dealer, and a bitter would-be artist who went on to create one of the greatest catastrophes the world has ever known.

A graduate of the San Francisco Art Institute and Oscar nominee for his *Color Purple* script, Meyjes, a native of Holland, doesn't mind playing "devil's advocate" because he sees his film as a cautionary tale for today. "If we say this guy is a monster, then what we do by definition is place him outside of human reckoning. I was very mindful of the enormity of this man's crimes, to the dead looking over my shoulder as it were, but at the same time I thought that if we x-ray this little window into his character, we can actually glean something from his views on art."

Speaking at the 2002 Toronto International Film Festival, Meyjes, a towering figure at 6'4" with a low-key manner, said he was sorry if his work disturbs viewers, but it is meant to be disturbing. "Hitler wasn't born a monster. What we are showing is a man making a conscious decision to become a monster. I think in ourselves we have that struggle on a daily basis. The roots of anti-Semitism and the roots of Nazism and Fascism are the same. It's fear, anger, envy, frustration—emotions that are not strange to any of us and they'll always be with us. Let's not forget that Mussolini and Hitler both ran on totalitarian platforms and people elected them."

If Hitler is placed outside of human reckoning, Meyjes warned, "It all becomes mysterous. Then we won't recognize it if it invades our lives. Take the guys playing the anti-immigration card in Europe today, they know what they're doing and we have to be mindful of it. I think it's a good thing to energize this debate."

Although Meyjes, forty-eight, was too young to have had direct experience of World War II, he grew up with family memories of the Nazi occupation of Holland. His father was arrested at seventeen in a round-up on the street and held in a German prisoner-of-war camp for two years until the war ended in 1945. His paternal grandparents died in what became known as the Hunger Winter of 1945. Anxious to forget about Europe, Menno's father took off for Indonesia and work in an import-export firm. He also engaged in a proxy marriage to the girl he knew before the war and she later joined him in Indonesia. When they returned to Holland, he became a manager for the Philips electronics firm.

Menno recalls growing up in a "very cosmopolitan, very liberal" home. Both parents were interested in modern art and African art. They would take the boy to museums and talk about their belief that modern art was political and its value was political. "When I was brought up, I was steeped in that."

So it became natural for him to conceive of Max, based on several real people, as a person "who believes something nobody believes anymore which is that art can change the world." With the loss of his right arm in World War I, Max had to give up his own desire to paint, but he kept his sense of humor and poured his enthusiasm into embracing the avant-garde of the art world, men who expressed the wartime horrors they had experienced: George Grosz, Hans Richter, Max Ernst. They were artists incomprehensible to Hitler, the former army corporal, who preferred to paint kitschy portraits of dogs and flat battlefield landscapes. He doesn't really understand Max's advice for him to dig for deeper emotions to explore in his art. Egged on by an army propaganda officer who recognizes his skill as a demagogic orator, Hitler finds it easier to express his anger at Germany's wartime loss and his own artistic frustration in anti-Semitic diatribes and comes to believe that "art plus politics equals power."

Once Meyjes got the idea for the film, he wondered if he had the nerve to make it. At the frightening final shot of Hitler shouting an anti-Semitic speech right out of *Mein Kampf*, Meyjes, slightly taken aback, thought, "I hope to God we're doing the right thing!" Most financiers didn't want anything to do with the production. At first, neither did Andras Hamori, who had produced Istvan Szabo's *Sunshine*, about three generations of a Hungarian Jewish family. Hamori, whose parents managed to evade capture and stay hidden in Hungary during the war, recalled that "the very word Hitler was taboo in my home."

Ultimately, Hamori agreed to meet Meyjes and explain that "politically and emotionally, I couldn't imagine making this movie. Then Menno showed up, this tall, crazy Dutchman with a huge album—an entire storyboard almost like a comic book of the movie—and I thought, 'Oh no!' But he started showing me these wonderful, starkly drawn, moody scenes and we began talking about ideas and philosophies and the hours just evaporated. By the time I got up to go, I was convinced the movie had to be made." Hamori signed on as producer, but it remained difficult to get the $10 million financing for the film even after John Cusack enthusiastically signed on to play Max. Eventually Francois Ivernel and Jerome Seydou of Pathe, the French-English distributors, agreed to take on the project.

When Noah Taylor (who played the teenaged David Helfgott in *Shine*) was hired to portray Hitler, he delved into the history of that time, but what he found especially useful was a photo of Hitler taken when he was eight years old. Taylor has said, "There was this intensely angry, incredibly serious little boy with his arms crossed, and that to me was the core of him."

But an eight-year-old boy was not the core of Hitler to those who began to protest the film before they even saw it. Referring to recent portrayals of Hitler on film, Abraham Foxman, national director of the Anti-Defamation League, told *The New York Times*, "There are documentaries about Hitler the man, Hitler the lover, Hitler the young person. I find that trivializing and offensive." However, after seeing *Max*, Foxman issued a press release apologizing for his premature judgement.

More important to Meyjes than such premature opinions was that his Jewish wife, Natalie Kohn, was "hugely supportive" and contributed her expertise to the film. Formerly principal dancer and soloist with the San Francisco Ballet, Kohn later studied painting and sculpture at the San Francisco Art Institute. She did the choreography for the ballet exercise performed by Max's wife. She also painted all the art collages—in the style of Hannah Hoch, the feminist Dadaist—shown in the studio of Max's mistress. Menno and his wife now live near London with their three daughters.

His fifteen years in the Bay Area affected him "hugely," he said. He soaked up the independent work of his teacher, George Kuchar, as well as that of Larry Jordan and Joseph Cornell, but he took his first filmmaking step when he wrote *Lionheart* (1978), a script for Francis Ford Coppola about a children's crusade. Coppola never made the film but sold it "for a big profit," although none of the proceeds went to Meyjes. "It was my introduction to the movie business," he said with a laugh.

Following his success with Steven Spielberg's *The Color Purple*, he went on to write scripts for *Indiana Jones and the Last Crusade* and *Empire of the Sun*. He credits a lot of what he has learned in directing from observing Spielberg on all three sets. "Steve is amazingly writer-friendly," Meyjes said. "The most important thing I learned was that he has a very strong grasp on what the essence of a scene is, and that's what he's selling and that's what he's going for."

But looking at many of today's blockbusters, Meyjes thinks of them as "a business proposal on celluloid. How much money can they make? I never thought I was going to make any money working on movies. It's amazing to me that I can eke out a living." In fact, Cusack, Hamori, and Meyjes donated what would have been their salaries to the budget in order to get the film made.

"So," Meyjes concluded, "I did put my money where my mouth is. We all did."

January 22, 2003
The San Francisco Examiner

2

One Land/Many Voices

Amos Gitai

"The biggest crisis that Jews face with Israel is that it is not a Utopia. That's why it is difficult for them to take criticism . . . they are left with a broken dream."

Montreal

An architect before he became a filmmaker, Amos Gitai was born in 1950 in Haifa, where some Arabs stayed on after the Palestinian exodus in 1948 when the state of Israel was proclaimed.

"This event gave Haifa a modern quality," Gitai explained at the 1999 Montreal World Film Festival, which presented *Yom Yom* (*Day After Day*), his fictional feature about a Jewish-Arab family in Haifa.

The stocky, ebullient director didn't get hooked on film until he came to the University of California, Berkeley, to do graduate work in architecture. He was sidetracked for life when he saw the works of Jean-Luc Godard, Rainer Werner Fassbinder, Brazil's Glauber Rocha, and other innovators at the Pacific Film Archive.

His subsequent unorthodox films embroiled him in so much controversy in Israel that Gitai and his family spent the next ten years in France where his productions— ranging from the Philippines to Bankok and Germany—won an international reputation. When he returned to his hometown, it became the location for *Yom Yom*.

"A unique situation developed in Haifa," he explained, "thanks to the fact that the Arab population stayed. Palestinians are heads of hospitals, they are lawyers and chiefs of education departments. This is what the city symbolizes. Although it is far from perfect, it is a micro-model for the possibility of people to exist."

Yom Yom is the second part of his trilogy based in three Israel cities. *Devarim* [*Commentaries*, 1995] explored the generational differences in Tel Aviv by three sons of fictional Israeli state founders. The third feature, *Kadosh* [*Sacred*], shot in Jerusalem, was accepted at the Cannes Film Festival, the only Israeli film in nearly twenty-five years to be selected for the competition. Modern Jerusalem, Gitai said, "a city constructed for eternity has the problem of living the daily life. In contrast, Haifa has found some form of daily life."

In *Yom Yom*, Moshe, a forty-year-old hypochondriac, the son of a Jewish mother and Arab father, can't get his act together. While Moshe (also called Mussa) works in the family bakery, he cheats on his Jewish wife with Grisha, who is also intimate with his best friend, Jule. Moshe's parents' love for each other is poignant, in heightened contrast to Moshe's frenzied couplings.

Gitai pointed out that in the 1940s and '50s, some Jewish women married Arabs as a sort of "declarative act," expressing their egalitarian beliefs. His own maternal grandparents arrived in Haifa from Russia in 1905, although his Orthodox maternal great-grandmother considered her daughter as dead for emigrating, an action she considered against the Messiah. But when her own death neared, she traveled to Palestine to be buried. "This somehow made my mother an atheist," Gitai commented. A self-professed "liberated woman," his mother studied psychoanalysis in Vienna and returned to Palestine in 1933, aligning herself with the leftist Hashomer Hatzair kibbutz movement.

Gitai's father, born in Poland, studied architecture at the famed Bauhaus in Germany under Mies van der Rohe until he was arrested by the Nazis in 1933. After a painful incarceration, he escaped and eventually made it to Palestine, where he met his future wife.

In 1973, Gitai, then twenty-three, served in an airborne unit in the Yom Kippur War until his helicopter was shot down by the Syrians. He was the only one to survive uninjured, and it took him six months to come to terms with his survival and to process the anti-heroic images in his mind for an anti-war film without any Hollywood clichés. He returned to that scene with his film *Kippur* in 1995. He then prepared a fictional version of that time, a "pacifist approach to show the way the war changed my generation's concept of this country. We realized the military is no solution."

He explained that the Israelis had not been ready for Syria's surprise attack on Yom Kippur, a day that is traditionally very quiet in Israel. It broke the silence both physically and metaphorically, Gitai recalled. "It also broke in a way the somewhat naïve trust that the Israelis used to have in their leaders. Unlike the easy and victorious success of the Six Day war in 1967, the heavy losses and chaos in the three-week Yom Kippur battles seemed to traumatize the whole nation. People of my generation asked themselves: 'why?' Big anti-government demonstrations started. Some soldiers came from the battlefields. Some went to the homes of Moshe Dayan and Golda Meir and asked them to resign. I didn't speak about my own experience until recently. People who knew my work as a critical filmmaker were astonished to discover that I was a soldier in the Yom Kippur war and was almost killed."

Learning about his war experience was what finally seemed to convince the military officials to cooperate in supplying tanks and helicopters for the $4-$5 million *Kippur*. In a final meeting with the head of the air force, who originally seemed to distrust the project. Gitai was asked why they should cooperate. "I told them I knew they had supplied equipment for *Rambo*, but this is a story of our troubled land and I think it struck something in him. When he realized it was a real story and my own story, it was difficult for him to refuse."

To say that Gitai is an embattled filmmaker is an understatement. Two projects commissioned by Israeli television were censored and/or banned: *Political Myths* (1977) had three sequences, including one "against that kind of vulgar religiosity that sees Judaism as something physical, something with territorial borders" and another reflecting on the mass suicides at Masada in 73 A.D. *House* (1980) documented the life of a home, originally owned by a Palestinian, rented to Algerian Jews and sold to an Israeli professor while renovation is carried out by Palestinians refugees, Israeli soldiers, and Israeli settlers. *Field Diary* (1982), shot before and during the 1982 invasion of Lebanon, was met with considerable hostility due to its explicit anti-militarism. "I wanted to examine how violence against the Palestinians is 'legitimized.'"

And *Esther* (1985), his first fictional film, is faithful to the Biblical account of how the oppressed Jews become, in revenge, murderous oppressors of their enemies. It was shown only once in Israel, after a Cannes Festival screening. Shot in an Arab section of Jerusalem, Mordecai, the Jew, is played by the Arab actor, Mohammed Bakri. Juliano Mer, son of an Arab father and Jewish mother, portrays the evil Haman. At the end, the actors talk about their personal histories and so link the old myth to modern history.

With those films, Gitai remarked, "They thought every film I did was threatening to the tender soul of the nation."

July 22, 1999

The San Francisco Examiner

Amos Oz

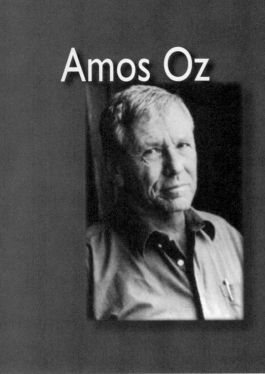

"It's time for us to stop acting stupid."

Arad, Israel

One of Israel's finest novelists and a prominent "dove," Amos Oz in person seemed more concerned when we met with speaking out to the Israelis than talking about the forthcoming American publication of his fifth novel, *The Black Box*. His epistolary narrative traces the wreckage of an Israeli marriage and attempts to study fanaticism in unexpected places.

"I wanted to decipher the emotional, psychological, and should I say psychotic mechanisms of fanaticism, discovering that fanaticism does not lie where people expect it. It can be everywhere. I've seen left-wingers, pacifists, liberals—people who waved tolerance and patience—catch fanaticism and they will shoot anyone who is not open-minded, and they will kill anyone who is not pluralistic enough."

In his book-lined study, a special shelf is reserved for Oz's own work, translated from Hebrew into nineteen languages, including Japanese. For the last few years, the fifty-year-old novelist and his family have lived in this small new city in the Yehuda Desert, overlooking the Judean hills.

During our talk, he didn't want to waste time discussing the way the American or Western media deal with Israel. "There's obviously a standing expectation that Israel be the most Christian nation, if not the only Christian nation, on earth," he said with just a hint of irony in his lightly accented English. "It's probably a tough realization for some American Jews, this expectation that Israel set a world record in morality. It's unrealistic. Perhaps unjust."

His tone is harsh but always eloquent when he talks to the Israelis. "I say it's time for us to stop acting stupid. It is a historical fact and anyone who isn't blind can see it—that this is the homeland of two people. The consequences are that under certain circumstances and certain technical arrangements, the land must be divided among its two people. It's as simple as that. There are parts of the land which are heavily populated by Arabs. They should become part of an Arab homeland and those parts heavily populated by Jews should be part of the Jewish homeland. As for deserts and empty spaces, they should be carefully negotiated."

For stating this position, Oz said, "I have had the honor of being called traitor by some of my own people and have provoked frustration from some radical left-wingers who assume that I am a reactionary chauvinist because I am not in love with the PLO, and because I keep repeating that this particular national movement is the most stupid and cruel in modern history, but we ought to do business with it. We don't have the luxury of selecting our enemy. This is the enemy and you make peace with the enemy. You can't make peace with nice neighbors."

His 1983 nonfiction book, *In the Land of Israel,* provides a vivid picture of the volatile cross-currents there. "Israel speaks in about four million different voices about the present situation," Oz said. "And everyone is infuriated with everyone else. The diversity here, the individual sense of involvement, is unique in the world. Everyone is a potential prime minister if not a self-appointed prophet or an aspiring Messiah. Everyone knows better, including yours truly."

When the Israeli army adopted a policy of beating Palestinian protesters in the occupied West Bank and Gaza Strip, Oz felt that "Israeli stupidity had reached a point that was more than I could cope with. The Israeli government seems to assume that what happens there are 'disturbances,' that riots are problems of law and order. They fail to realize that what we have there right now—and what we have had for decades—is a tragic clash between two national movements. It's not a police problem."

The stone-throwings and beatings are terrible, he said with a sigh, "but they are symptoms. You don't heal symptoms. It's the conflict that must be treated and dealt with and healed. To me as an Israeli dove, the immediate question is not civil rights for the Palestinian Arabs. It's the question of their right to self-determination. Once they have it, it's up to them, not to me, to worry about their civil rights. They never had civil rights before the Israeli occupation and I'd be extremely surprised if they have civil rights after they form their own state, but this is none of my business. The only right I want to grant them—and quickly—is the right to self-determination."

44

Oz took his own right to self-determination at the age of sixteen when he rebelled against his father, a right-wing militant Zionist, literary scholar, and librarian who left Russia for Jerusalem in the early 1930s.

"It was a house full of footnotes, so to speak, floating in the air," Oz said. He decided to go to Kibbutz Hulda and become a "simple, uncomplicated tractor driver. No intellect. No brainwork. No books. So like many revolts, mine was also almost a full circle. Here I am in a roomful of books."

He had not rebelled against Zionism, he explained, but against his father's interpretation. "I still am a deeply commited Zionist. There are as many ways of being a Zionist as of being a Jew, and obviously every Jew is a bad Jew to some other Jew. So to many Zionists, I am obviously a bad Zionist, if not a disgrace to Zionism, but I have always believed that those Jews, including myself, who want to conduct a national life as Jews—not just a religious life or a cultural life—are not only entitled to do so, but even wise to want to do so. This is my Zionism. A to Z in a nutshell. The long course takes a trilogy."

While he has not been a chauvinist or an expansionist for Israel, Oz confesses, "I'm a terrible expansionist for the language. I wish the whole world would read our literature." However, translating Hebrew into English "isn't difficult, it's impossible," he said. "Hebrew is very far away from any European language. It has a different system of tenses and consequently a different concept of time, possibly a different idea of reality."

He provided a simple example. "There is no Hebrew word for 'to have,' no way of saying in Hebrew, 'I have a wife' or 'I have a tape recorder with me.' Which probably reflects a very ancient nomadic concept of property. 'It's with you today, it's with someone else tomorrow.' Here today and gone tomorrow. Which I like. To this day when I have to say in English, 'I have a wife and three kids,' I feel uneasy because in my heart of hearts, I don't feel possessive about them."

Hebrew is also more compact than English. His novella *Crusade* began with a three-word Hebrew sentence but required ten words in English: "It all began with outbreaks of discontent in the villages."

To say that he "works with" his English translators is a "nice way" of describing the process: "We are like worst enemies." And when he reads an English translation, no matter how good, "It hurts like hell."

For readers of *The Black Box*, Oz has a warning: Nearly all his letter-writing characters are lying. "It's up to the reader to decipher a bunch of lies. There's no big brother of a narrator guiding you through the jungle. You have to find your own path. The idea is that truth is elusive, complex, and sometimes extremely hard to decipher in human affairs."

May 1988
San Francisco Chronicle

Hany Abu-Assad

"I wanted to understand how life changes when you have an appointment with death."

San Francisco

The Palestinian director Hany Abu-Assad can't resist challenges, but he still has nightmares and second thoughts about the way he chose to dramatize the lives of two would-be suicide bombers.

He doesn't regret his determination to show the human side of the two men in his critically acclaimed film *Paradise Now*. In hindsight, however, Abu-Assad thinks it was "kind of insane" to insist on absolute realism by filming in beleaguered Nablus on the West Bank. The seventy-member crew had to avoid almost daily tank and missile attacks by the Israeli army searching for terrorists, gun-wielding threats from rival Palestinian factions, and the kidnapping of the film's local location manager.

"If I had the chance to go back and not to do it there [in Nablus], I'd rather not to have made the movie, but to be able to sleep again," he said when in the Bay Area to promote the film. It was an unexpected admission from this man who speaks with quiet, understated authority. "My body is still in pain from the tension." He was worried most about the life of the international crew. Finally, circumstances forced them to complete shooting in Nazareth, Abu-Assad's hometown.

At forty-four, Abu-Assad still remembers the humiliation he felt as a child when he went to a checkpoint with his father for a visit outside Nazareth and saw Israelis passing through, but the Palestinians had to wait. "When you are a Palestinian, you are immediately a threat. When you go to Tel Aviv, you try not to speak Hebrew with an accent. You hide in the bus because you're afraid if they knew I was an Arab."

He had left Nazareth at nineteen, to study airplane engineering in Amsterdam in order to prove to himself and others that he could do something difficult. Suddenly in Amsterdam, the fear he felt in Israel was gone. There were no checkpoints and no ethnic discrimination. "I felt very free. I didn't have to hide that I was Palestinian."

After several years as an airplane engineer in Amsterdam, where he still has a home, Abu-Assad began working on Dutch television programs about foreign immigrants. In 1992, he wrote and directed his first short film, *Paper House*. It depicted the adventures of a thirteen-year-old Palestinian who tries to build his own house after his family's original home was destroyed. He showed what was to become his trademark light touch on serious subjects when he made the documentary *Nazareth 2000* for Dutch TV. The turmoil in the city between quarreling Christian and Muslim inhabitants is viewed humorously through the eyes of two gas-station attendants.

Abu-Assad said that his ability to see comedy in tragic moments stems from the way he protected himself from being mocked for not being good in high school sports. "It was scary to feel the girls laughing at you, so I made myself a clown to hide my weakness. With humor, I could make it bearable."

Rana's Wedding in 2002 brought him international praise for its comic depiction of a hazardous day in the life of an independent young Jerusalem woman trying to get married to the man she loves against the wishes of her father before his 4 o'clock deadline. In the film, Abu Assad said, "I was challenging everything: the occupation, the society, the politics, and her fears. These things attracted American audiences because Americans like the idea of one person fighting against the rest."

Earlier, in 1999, he had begun co-writing a thriller involving a suicide bomber. "But, why a thriller?" Abu-Assad began asking himself. "I wanted to know more about this man. I wanted to understand how life changed when you have an appointment with death. What is the point of killing yourself at the same moment that you are a killer? Because in general either you kill people and you stay alive or you kill yourself."

That last moment of decision for a would-be martyr became very important for him. "I wanted to know more about it. When the first Intifada didn't bring solutions, people became more frustrated and started to go to the streets. Palestinians from Gaza went with knives to Tel Aviv and killed people. It was a kind of suicide action. I wondered what kind of desperation did these people feel when they came to the moment that their lives were not worth it because if they can't be equal in life, they try to be equal in death. It's a very important concept to look at."

His questions found support in two suicide stories in the Bible: Samson, who preferred to die with his Philistine enemies, and Masada, where the Jews chose mass suicide rather than surrender to the Romans. "From the Bible I understood that you don't accept inferiority, even if it costs your life or the life of others. You prefer to destroy everything rather than accept the idea that you are less."

Researching the subject, Abu-Assad spoke to many people who knew suicide bombers, but the most important information came from a lawyer who represented people who failed in their mission. He first heard about an educated young woman whose boyfriend had been killed by the Israelis. "She felt she had to defend her society and that women should be equal in defending the society. It's very human, but it's a wrong conclusion for a very wrong situation. Her family in Bethlehem is happy she's in jail and not dead, but they couldn't imagine that this girl would try to do it because she was someone who helped everybody and didn't use violence to defend her rights."

The suicide bombers had surprisingly different backgrounds, he noted, but mostly they came from refugee camps in the West Bank. "They wanted to be human beings, to have fun and chase women, and their biggest dream was to go out and be free, but in reality they lived their entire life under occupation. Some of them hated their fathers for not being able to fulfill a father's role to protect the family."

Some Palestinians thought Abu-Assad was denigrating the suicide bombers by showing their doubts and confusion. "They didn't like it because they wanted to see them as super heroes. They want to shout about their pain and this film is not shouting. It is just making reality a tragic story. It upset them that one suicide bomber was afraid and another's father was a collaborator. He had to be clean, not the son of a collaborator who was killed by the resistance. Perhaps a father collaborates in order for his sons to have work or to be less hurt by the occupation. Collaboration is a crime, but I understand why people do it. At least it's a crime I wanted to talk about."

As for a peaceful resolution in that troubled land, Abu-Assad believes, "It doesn't matter if there will be a bi-national country or a two-state solution, but it has to be based on the principle that both parties have equal rights. That the Jews have the right to be there and the Palestinians have a right to be there, but they have to accept each other. We have to solve the fear of the other because without each other we cannot live."

November 7, 2005
The Oakland Tribune

Dan Wolman

"The story of Israel's foreign workers is very important."

San Francisco

Dan Wolman, an Israeli film director with childhood roots in Ethiopia and years of TV work there, explores the problems of Israel's immigrants through a dramatic story about a Jewish housewife and her Ethiopian maid in *Foreign Sister* which won first prize at the 2000 Jerusalem International Film Festival.

Wolman's empathy for the plight of the Ethiopian immigrants can be traced to his father's background and an almost-forgotten page of World War II history. After receiving his medical education in Mussolini's Italy, Wolman's father emigrated to Palestine, where he joined the British army. He served under the daring leadership of Major General Orde Charles Wingate, who led a guerrilla force into Italian-occupied Ethiopia and helped to restore Haile Selassie to his throne in 1941. Dr. Wolman became the emperor's personal physician and eventually brought his wife and one-year-old son Dan to join him. The family returned to Israel in 1946.

After finishing high school in Jerusalem, Dan studied cinema at the Film Institute of New York City College and New York University. He became best known abroad in 1975 for *My Michael*, based on the novel by Amos Oz, and received the Jerusalem festival's Lifetime Achievement Award in 1999.

When the emigration of Ethiopian Jews to Israel began with "Operation Moses" and "Operation Flying Carpet" in the mid-eighties, Wolman, who had learned Aramaic, began training the new arrivals in communication.

"I had the feeling there was a lot of patronizing in the way the media treated them," Wolman said. "On the one hand, they were romanticized and on the other hand, there was a lot of patronizing them as the carriers of disease and as people 'who didn't know how to use toilet paper.'"

He thought the immigrants should tell their own stories and inaugurated a still-ongoing television program in Aramaic called *Through Our Own Eyes*. Meanwhile, Wolman and his Ethiopian partner began frequent travels to Ethiopia to set up a television program there and train directors, writers, and editors to carry on with their own work.

He met Askala Markos when she acted in several TV programs Wolman produced. Speaking in Hebrew and occasionally in English, Markos, who has lived in Israel for twelve years, took up her own story. Born in Addis Ababa, she is the daughter of an Eretrian journalist and an Ethiopian Jewish mother. When she was sixteen, against her parents' wishes, she married an Ethiopian Jew who wanted to emigrate to Israel, and she converted to Judaism there.

But expecting to be taken to a modern town, she said, "I cried for a year" when they were temporarily housed in a caravan in a small absorption center in Kiryat Gan, near Beersheba.

After her divorce, from 1992 to 1998 she supported her three children, a boy and two girls, by doing housekeeping and any work she could find. But then her parents' illnesses disrupted her life. She became very depressed when she was told that she couldn't leave her children and visit her dying mother in Ethiopia. Six months later, her father became ill and she again asked permission to visit him. She was told she could go if the children's father took care of them. But after visiting her mother's grave in Ethiopia, she was unable to meet her father in Eritrea because war had broken out between the two regions.

Trapped in Ethiopia for a month and a half, she finally returned to Israel, too distressed and too weak to go to court and regain custody of her children. Meanwhile, her ex-husband, who had been tortured in Ethiopia for his attempts to emigrate, exists on an Israeli pension given to people who are called "prisoner of Zion" (like those Jewish activists who were arrested and tortured in the Soviet Union). Wolman has made a documentary, *Prisoner of Zion*, about three Ethiopians who suffered a similar fate.

Markos, an Israeli citizen, now lives in Jerusalem, works as a hostess in the dining room of a nearby kibbutz, and manages to see her children about once a week.

Although she is Jewish, Markos portrays Negist, an Ethiopian Christian in *Foreign Sister*, Wolman said, so that he could reveal the fear within the Ethiopian Christian community and its exploitation.

Without any sentimentality, the film shows Naomi (Tamar Yerushalmi), a good-hearted, overworked Jewish housewife, becoming close to Negist, her new part-time maid, an illegal Christian. In the course of meeting Negist's friends and trying to help a seriously wounded man in a wild car ride from Tel Aviv to a Jerusalem hospital, Naomi begins to learn some things about herself and her own community.

As for the reaction to the production, an Israeli Palestinian told Wolman, "The film is really about us." And an Iranian director wanted to know if there were other people like Wolman in Israel.

The fearful life of illegal Ethiopian Christians began to come to Wolman's attention when he observed an incident at the airport. Many Israeli Ethiopians were flying back to visit their old hometowns while handcuffed illegal immigrants who were Christian Ethiopians were being deported.

Another episode that was re-created for the film involved Wolman's Ethiopian music arranger, who failed to show up for a recording session because he had been in a car accident in Tel Aviv. He asked to be taken to an Arab hospital in Jerusalem.

"I visited him and asked why he had gone to Jerusalem. He told me he was a Christian and afraid he'd be asked for his papers in the local Israeli hospital and be arrested for being illegal." (Since that time, in 1991, the Israeli hospitals treat everyone, no questions asked.)

The story of Israel's foreign workers—Romanians, Bulgarians, Turks, Thais, Poles, and Africans—is a very important one, Wolman said. "There is a lot of unemployment among Israelis who think certain jobs are beneath their dignity, but there is a bad feeling about foreign workers who were brought in because they thought Palestinians could not be trusted. Now a lot of prostitutes are coming in from the Eastern Bloc countries and the trafficking is a really horrible story."

But what Wolman always bears in mind is his favorite line from Deuteronomy: "Love the sojourner for you were sojourners in Egypt."

February 28, 2003
Forward

Michal Aviad

"If we don't think things will improve what reason is there to live?"

San Francisco

Whether it's a film about aging California women, Israeli adolescent girls itching for love, or the rights of Palestinians, there's always an edge to the work of Michal Aviad, Israel's leading woman director.

By the age of fourteen, she was reading Tolstoy, Dostoyevsky, Thomas Mann, later studying philosophy and literature for a master's degree, but a bit of a barefoot hippie, too. In the late seventies, she was already protesting Israel's occupation of the West Bank and Gaza. "Then one day, out of the blue," Aviad recalls, "I thought maybe if I could make a documentary, I could change the world."

Six documentaries later, she still hasn't stopped trying, but along the way, there's a family history—Hungarian, Irish Catholic, Italian, socialists, skeptics—to share.

It's there in *For My Children*, shown at the 2003 San Francisco Film Festival. The impressionistic film—with historic newsreel clips and home movies—shifts back and forth in time, telling the stories of the grandparents: the Jewish anti-Zionist Briton who married the New York Irish Catholic convert to Judaism, the Hungarian socialist who married and divorced an Italian Jew, once a young admirer of Mussolini. Back in Israel after ten student years in the U.S., Aviad and her husband, Shimson, a psychotherapist, worry about the future of their children in a strife-torn land.

San Francisco was an appropriate showcase for *For My Children*, Aviad, the vibrant mother of two, said in an interview after the festival screening. She and Shimson met when they were both studying literature and politics. He wanted to get a doctorate degree in psychology and she wanted to study filmmaking. "In 1981, we thought peace with Egypt was on the verge of happening and we decided to come here because we heard that San Francisco is progressive and revolutionary and we would fit in."

She was studying film at San Francisco State while making a living as a waitress at David's Delicatessen when Israel invaded Lebanon with massive force in June 1982. Michal and Shimson linked arms with anti-war Palestinians, Lebanese, and Jewish peaceniks to picket the Israeli consulate in protest. The next day, Aviad's picture was on page one of the *San Francisco Chronicle* and her boss, David, a Holocaust survivor, was very upset that his waitress was demonstrating against Israel. He didn't fire her but gave her a work station notorious for small tips.

After earning her master's degree in 1984, Aviad started to work on her first film, *Acting Our Age*, trying to deal with what it means for a woman to grow old. It went to the Sundance and Telluride festivals, opened the first *Point of View* program on public television in 1987. In retrospect, she said, "It was a very pedestrian film. The next year I gave birth to my son and it looked as if the political situation in Israel was changing. Palestinians were revolting against the occupation and it appeared as if a Palestine-Israel two-state solution might be possible. So we started thinking about going back."

When they returned to Israel, she worked on her next film, *The Women Next Door*, in which she talks to Arab and Jewish women about their relationship to the occupied territories.

The documentary also expressed Aviad's political opinions. "I proposed that in all situations women are the ultimate victims in that they bring children to the world and then send them out to be killed. But on a different, more complicated, level, the film indicated that women collaborate with this. They are not just innocent in this violence." When the film came out in 1992, no one in Israel wanted to broadcast it, but *Point of View* did. It won the Berlin Festival's peace prize and was shown at the liberal

Jerusalem Film Festival. It is still being screened in many countries—even, Aviad said with a surprised laugh, Albania. Why not?

Women Next Door was shown at a 1993 Swedish conference designed to encourage a dialogue between Israelis and Palestinians. Aviad couldn't go because she was pregnant with her daughter. She later learned from a conference report that Professor Edward Said said, "Israelis not only occupied Palestinian land, but Israelis are also writing Palestinian history."

"It would be strange if Said said that since he did his dissertation on Joseph Conrad and Conrad was writing other people's history," Aviad commented. "I feel that Palestinian history is part of my history as well. If I don't see and look closely at everything Palestinian, then I wouldn't be able to understand my own history."

Although *Women Next Door* was never shown on Israeli TV, all of her other documentaries were. *Ever Shot Anyone?* (1995) was her attempt to analyze Israeli male culture and what militarism has done to Israeli society. She met with a group of reserve soldiers stationed at the Syrian border and stayed there for most of their thirty-two days of duty. She wanted to ask them personal questions about love, marriage, and their children, but they wanted a monument to their platoon demonstrating how far they could shoot, their military exercises and training.

"The film shows that the soldiers were very critical of me, saying, 'If I were your husband and you left your children at home, I would divorce you.' They said they wouldn't let me go ahead unless they filmed me and showed how ridiculous I was with my questions. Their film was very funny and they were surprised that I incorporated their footage into mine. So the documentary is not only about male culture, but the power of the camera too. In a sense I was a threat to their unity as a group of men. They would do anything for each other, but wouldn't take one step forward about how they destroy other people's lives or consider how the women and children they left behind suffer while they're having fun."

She was unable to screen the documentary in the West Bank or Ramallah. "A Palestinian cultural administrator wrote politely to me that 'We're not interested in this kind of issue. We only show films about the life of artists.' It's very hard to make most Palestinians interested in Israeli culture," Aviad noted.

In fact, most Israelis were not very interested in another part of their own culture until they saw Aviad's *Jenny & Jenny* (1997) about adolescent cousins who are part of a new generation of Jews from North African countries. They live in a town near Tel Aviv where the Arab Jews were sixty percent of the population and declined to forty percent after Russians settled there, but they're all part of a working-class culture. "It's political in the sense that it tries to deal with the heavy stereotyping Israelis have about the young generation of Mizrachi, as the Arab Jews are known. You basically get a window into their world which was invisible to Israelis before this film came out. I wanted

54

the audience to identify with these appealing girls. They don't have ambitions to save the world. They're trying to figure out their relationship to religion. They're burning with curiosity about sex. All they want is to get a job, get married, and have children. I wanted the audience to struggle with their own stereotypes. If you love the Jennies, you can't look down on them. It's considered my most popular film, and it had an overwhelming response, winning the Best Film award from the Israeli Film Institute."

For the next three years, she worked on *Ramleh*, the name of an old town between Jerusalem and the sea. It was inhabited by Palestinians until July 11, 1948, when the Israel Army drove them out as part of the War of Independence. In the 1990s, a huge number of Russian Jews came to live there. Now the town of 60,000 people is a microcosm of Israel with Indian Jews, Bulgarian Jews, Iraqi Jews, Kurds, Bedouins, Moroccans, and Palestinians from destroyed villages near Ramleh.

When Aviad went there in 1998, she observed the phenomenon of that population becoming newly religious. "These communities have nothing to do with each other and they don't get along with each other, but they have a lot in common. You can't tell them what to be an Israeli is all about. This is different from the Zionist idea that we all become the new Israelis. The word Sabra doesn't apply. Each one of them is Israeli and each one is different from the others. They belong to the party of SHAS, which is the second or third biggest party of Israel, and they combine in some way a new interpretation of Judaism and nationalism—and I consider that a kind of fundamentalism. So they really live a new way of life. There is no question that part of that phenomenon is their reaction against the racism they have suffered from Ashkenazi Jews."

At the time we talked, Aviad was busy raising money for her new film, *Hope*. "I'm trying to look for the moments of hope in the last ten years of relationships between Palestinians and Israelis. I'm tracking down those people—workers, refugees, soldiers, intellectuals—who were hopeful at a particular moment and I beg them to find extracts of hope. It's a Don Quixote type of journey . . . "

But does she have any hope for peace?

"Yes," Aviad responded, "but it doesn't make any sense. It's not rational. I think it's insane, but yeah, I hope there will be peace. If we don't believe that some things will improve, what reason is there to live? So I hope there will be peace. Otherwise I wouldn't stay in Israel."

May 2005
The Oakland Tribune

Meyer Levin

PHOTO BY: M. LEVIN.

"The Orthodox implementation of Judaism in Israel is cult worship."

Beit Yanai, Israel

I t's just the luck of Meyer Levin that there was a minor plumbing flood in his one-room seaside studio here, north of Tel Aviv, the night guests arrived.

A handyman had dumped some earth on the property and buried all the water pipes in the process. After struggling in the dark to find the shut-off valves, Levin appeared, drenched to the skin, with the cheerful scowl of a man who has overcome his natural enemies.

It was a kind of portent that there are still battles to be fought even in Israel, where Levin has spent the happiest six years of his life since leaving New York and the bitter fights over the dramatization of *The Diary of Anne Frank* and *Compulsion*, his best-selling novel based on the Leopold-Loeb case.

In the warmth and friendliness of Israel, Levin has managed to achieve a truce, if not peace, through his work, putting his own final word on the Broadway scene in his new novel *The Fanatic*, published by Simon & Schuster.

"I have never seen Meyer so happy as in these last few years," Levin's wife, Tereska Torres, the novelist, said as we drove to the studio from Kfar Shmaryahu, a suburb of Tel Aviv where they are building a home.

Always in the past, Levin's stubborn honesty and his insistence upon his identity as a Jew and his own worth as a writer have brought him into repeated conflict with editors and publishers.

The peacefulness of the last few years may be shattered again with the appearance of *The Fanatic*, which Levin had originally called *Obsession*.

Discussing the book prior to its publication, Levin said, "It's the story of a Jewish obsession for justice, a fight for justice carried out by an individual. It's about whether a survivor of the concentration camps finds it worthwhile living in New York.

"You might also say it's a roman à clef about certain people in theatrical circles in New York, and it bears a slight resemblance to the *Anne Frank* and *Compulsion* cases. The book also deals with the suppression of Jewish identity in Russia and as that bears on more of the same in the United States."

Levin also saw an obscure analogy with the President's assassination. "The book can even be tied to the Kennedy assassination. In a way, something similar happens in my book where a rabid Jewish Marxist carries on a Marxist action, not acting on party orders or the party line, but because of a history of indoctrination on the Jewish question."

The author, who calls himself "an old Zionist hand," wrote about his own search for identity in his powerful autobiography, *In Search*, but with Levin's luck, it has still not been translated into Hebrew.

In *The Fanatic*, he pointed out, an anti-Zionist Jewish Communist—acting without party connections—does great harm. "It's the same way in which Oswald was rejected by left-wing groups. In this case, there's a literary murder instead of a physical murder."

Speaking of the element in the new book that can be compared with *Compulsion*, Levin pointed out that "*Time* magazine now calls Oswald a compulsive murderer. The murderer is acting out in a specific way because of his philosophy rather than a personal family constellation. Just as Leopold and Loeb took their philosophy from Nietzsche, Oswald took his from Marx. The murderer feels justified because he is carrying out a philosophy he feels to be his truth.

"I'm telling about a guy, an American Communist who picks a target because of his convictions. The concentration camp survivor, a woman, is one of the victims."

Levin, still bitter about "the Broadway cabal operating against me," said that there had been one delay on the publication of his new book. It resulted from the threat of a lawsuit by Otto Frank's lawyer after pre-publication announcements indicated the book contained a parallel to the Anne Frank drama lawsuit. Publication was postponed for a couple of months while a firm of lawyers re-checked the novel.

"While this book is not about the Anne Frank case," Levin said, "people can be reminded that such things can happen and do happen. They might want to go back and see what actually happened in the Frank case.

"I'm not interested," he stressed, "in evoking any discussion of the Frank case. This is the one thing you must print in your story. Like any other writer, I have used some material out of that experience which has been fictionalized for the truth value it contains. I extracted the truth matter. I want it read and judged as a novel and not for any similarities to any actual case."

In 1954, Levin sued Otto Frank and Broadway producers Kermit Bloomgarden and Cheryl Crawford on grounds of fraud and plagiarism. He charged that in 1950, before the diary was even published, he had suggested its dramatization to Otto Frank. At the point when it was about to be produced, Cheryl Crawford changed her mind about using Levin's version.

Levin contended in court that Communist influence had been brought to bear on this decision. He claimed that Albert and Frances Hackett, who did the final stage adaptation, were selected precisely because they were not Jewish.

"The main difference between the two versions," he said, "was that they left out the Jewish character and concentrated on the schmaltz."

When the plagiarism charge went to the jury, it handed Levin an award of one-quarter of the royalties, based on Levin's contention that the Hacketts had included in their work some of the scenes created by Levin that were not actually in the diary.

During this same period, *Compulsion* was published and Levin became involved in a fight with the Broadway producers who, he claimed, had sensationalized the text of his dramatization.

"It was my play, but dirtied up," Levin said. "The critics later said the same thing, but they didn't say that was my complaint also. Since then, my version has been given in other cities of the United States and England with a favorable response."

Meanwhile, Levin charged, his Broadway antagonists "smeared me by saying that I always sued everybody. They poisoned people against me and it still goes on."

Levin had suggested a compromise to settle the Anne Frank case: permission to allow Jewish groups to put on his version of the play. He sent the defendants an appeal signed by Albert Camus, 400 rabbis and ten Hadassah groups who were interested in Levin's version, but he was turned down.

"*Anne Frank*, the prize-winning play," he commented with some bitterness, "today stands on the books convicted of plagiarism, but some of my opponents were so powerful that no one in the press commented on this.

"After the untouchability of the play wore off," he said, "more critics began saying that the dramatization was phony because it left out the Jewish identification or the fact that Anne had any thought of Zionism. In her diary, she writes about going to Zionist meetings, and her whole book asks the question: 'Why is this being done to us as Jews?'

"Instead the play was filled with bathos," he said, "and commercialized to an extreme." But some people said to him, "What are you complaining about? It's good for the Jews, isn't it?"

"By that time," Levin said, "I was completely smeared. The play had been de-Judaized. They said, 'It's more universal if it's less Jewish,' but they were wrong. As far as literature is concerned, the more specific it is, the more universal it is."

Completely exhausted by the two fights, Levin, his wife, and their three children decided to go to Israel. Levin had first visited there in 1925. He had returned there after every defeat in his life. After years of experiencing the extraordinary turbulence of his own "Jewish obsession," he finally faced the reality of living in the state of Israel.

He is now writing an Israeli novel and is engaged in a project with the Association of Americans and Canadians in Israel to have translated into Hebrew books dealing with American Jewish life, a subject on which most Israelis entertain many misconceptions.

Although he had often thought of becoming a citizen of Israel, he said, "Under some of the present conditions, I have very sharp reservations. Some of them have to do with the religious dictatorship aspects here and the undemocratic positions of the Orthodox religious groups."

Levin's wife, Tereska Torres, author of *Women's Barracks*, and *By Cecile*, said that these problems had impelled her to begin work on *The Converts*, a book she had thought about for many years: the story of her own parents, Marek Scwarc, the famous sculptor, and his wife, who had secretly converted to Catholicism, although they both came from devout Polish Orthodox families.

Their conversion stemmed from aesthetic and ethical beliefs, but they never ceased regarding themselves as Jews and considered their Christianity an extension of their Judaism. When their conversion was finally discovered in France, it caused a scandal among intellectuals, which brought them terrible suffering. The same type of religious intolerance that young Tereska felt then, she senses today in Israel.

"If I were a good deal younger," the fifty-eight-year-old Levin said, "I might think it my duty to enter into Israeli citizenship to combat these restrictions. In my case, I don't think it is necessary. I have taken part as much as I could in establishing a Reform synagogue. I even carried a case to the Supreme Court of Israel to compel equal treatment in the use of public buildings with the Orthodox religious group."

The couple also joined the League for Freedom from Religious Coercion and an Arab-Jewish friendship group.

"The Orthodox implementation of Judaism in Israel," Levin said, "is cult worship. You never hear of rabbis here talking of any ethical issues. But to me, religion and ethics are synonymous."

Levin's sharp criticism was not unexpected. His conception of the writer's crusading role was never so clearly expressed as in *In Search*:

"Whether he writes fiction or reportage, each serious writer considers himself a little bit of the conscience of the world, and his place most closely approximates that of the Biblical prophet: he is the one who may speak out, rebuke kings and rulers and populace, recall them to what is just."

And Levin has spent his life trying to do just that.

February 16, 1964
San Francisco Chronicle

Dover Kosashvili

"*There is no life without tradition.*"

Toronto

Love, marriage, matchmaking. Sex and loneliness. Tradition vs. today. Philosophically speaking, Dover Kosashvili is of a mixed mind on these subjects. After all, he was catapulted at age five and one-half from the tightly knit Jewish community of Soviet Georgia into the frenetic, secular society of Israel. His way of juggling these problems in his first feature, *Late Marriage*, has brought unprecedented acclaim from east to west, with *The New York Times* calling it a "grotesquely funny . . . powerful, and very bitter comedy."

In real life, it wasn't so funny when Kosashvili's Orthodox family tried at least twenty times to make a traditional match for their twenty-five-year-old son until they finally gave up. Now thirty-six, he's still not married, but that's not the fate he teases the audience with for his hero, Zaza, thirty-one, who has a secret, incredibly sensual love affair with Judith, a thirty-four-year-old Moroccan immigrant and the divorced mother of a little daughter. Kosashvili insists that the film is not strictly autobiographical, but merely informed by certain life experiences and his imagination.

During Dover's own parents' matchmaking frenzy, "I had a few girlfriends, but I didn't intend to marry any of them," he explained in heavily accented English at the 2001 Toronto International Film Festival. "I'm *crazy* about women," he insisted, shifting easily from a mournful to a merry look. "I *love* women. Without women, I wouldn't be here."

In fact, without the most essential woman in his life—his mother, Lili Kosashvili—he might not have been able to make his $850,000 movie. There were no professional actresses in Israel who could speak both Georgian and Hebrew, so he finally prevailed upon his mother to take on that role. It was difficult for her in more ways than one. While she is storming into Judith's apartment to demand that she give up Zaza, the film touches on the trouble in her own arranged marriage back in Georgia.

At that wedding, her husband was twenty-eight, a late age for a bridegroom in Georgia. He had been in love with another woman and continued the affair for a while after the marriage. As far as the community was concerned, he had settled down to carry on the Orthodox Jewish tradition of marriage and family in Georgia. Dover, the first of their four offspring, said that his mother was very moved by the film. However, his father, played by Moni Moshonov, a Bulgarian immigrant who took five months to learn to speak Georgian, made no comment after the family screening. The film has been a box-office hit in Israel, although it's inevitably stirred some mixed feelings among the country's 115,000 Georgians.

So how does Dover feel about tradition? After a long silence and a sigh, he answered like the philosophy student he once was. "There is an advantage and disadvantage in this. What is tradition? Some things you call tradition, but modern also is a tradition. There is no life without tradition. Any culture is tradition. Any point of view is tradition. In Georgia, the tradition is less individual. It's a more social culture in the connection within the family and between the families. Western culture is much more individual. In Georgia, maybe one gave up some priorities for others, and in the West, it is considered stupid to give up your priorities: what you desire if the family doesn't agree. In the Georgian culture, they get married by matchmaking; in the West, they get married for love and then they don't get married at all. I see a lot of young people who don't believe in marriage. I see how the process is starting in Israel. It's behind Europe, but it's getting stronger here. There is the phenomenon of living alone. I don't know why because we'll be vanishing one day."

In the film, Zaza, still a philosophy student at thirty-one, cannot come to a final decision about which woman is best for him. "He's attracted to more than one woman. There could be a problem with his parents or a problem with the woman he's in love with. It's not a matter of love anymore. It's a matter of womanhood. Love is too complicated for him. I wanted to bring him to that point."

Before Zaza gets to that point, he and Judith engage in one of the most genuinely erotic love scenes on film. "It's not about sex," Kosashvili said. "On the surface, you see sex, but it's not dealing with sex. For me, what the scene is about is that you can be in love and doing sex, but you still can be very lonely. Yes, I've had that feeling."

It was a difficult scene to shoot, but thanks to the professionalism of Ronit Elkabetz, who plays Judith, she made it easier for everyone, particularly Lior Ashkenazi, who portrays Zaza. The scene was rehearsed during five months of pre-production with both performers clothed. "We wanted to make a sex scene that was natural," Lior has said, "similar to what takes place night after night in thousands of homes throughout the world. But when Ronit and I came to the actual shooting, I was very nervous. To Ronit's credit I can say that she acted naturally and helped me to overcome my awkwardness and shyness. But it was still very difficult to deal with. It was filmed over fourteen hours and it unravels over fifteen pages in the script."

What enabled Elkabetz to deal with the scene was her feeling that "Judith's was a naked soul in a naked body, not solely a naked body. My soul was so exposed, so bare, that there were long moments when I forgot that I was standing in the center of the set, in front of a camera and twenty crew members, each staring at me in frozen silence. Even the director couldn't watch the scene for long—his eyes kept escaping to the monitor."

Kosashvili will still be dealing with love—and a bunch of diamond-smuggling Georgians—in his next ironic comedy, which may or may not touch on how the Russian and Georgian Jews get along in Israel. "It will take time," says Kosashvili, who believes that human beings are still in diapers. "Time fixes everything—if you don't get killed first."

June 2002

The San Francisco Examiner

Ali Nasser

PHOTO BY VERED PE'ER.

"I found it impossible to understand the fanatics – Arabs and Jews."

Montreal

When Arab farmers collected their harvest in a village in the Galilee, the children would gather there at night, talking without fear and looking up in wonder at the Milky Way.

For Ali Nasser, those stars became a symbol of the path that used to bring prosperity and food to his people, and might one day light their way again to a harmonious life. However, as the peace process has stalled, this gentle and quiet man is feeling "very pessimistic," he said in halting English at the 1997 Montreal World Film Festival, where his production *The Milky Way* was screened.

In the film, set in the 1960s under Israeli military rule, the future looks bleak indeed for Mabruq, an orphan who plays the part of the village fool. He is secretly in love with Jamileh, who became mute after seeing her mother killed.

When the Israeli authorities discover that valuable work permits have been forged, the village Mukhtar incriminates a politically troublesome teacher, who is beaten and jailed. A new chain of circumstances is set in motion when Mabruq's courageous friend Mahmud challenges the Mukhtar and looks for the real culprit.

The humor and communal tensions so vividly explored in the film have resulted in two singular honors for Nasser. It is one of the first Arab productions to be financed by the Fund for the Promotion of Israeli Quality Films. Arabs have criticized Nasser for accepting Israeli support, but that situation changed recently. The second recognition accorded *The Milky Way* was being accepted into competition at one of the most prestigious festivals in the Arab world, held in Paris.

It has been a long journey since the time Nasser herded his family's goats and escaped to watch wonders unfold on the one TV set in his village of 10,000 people.

He didn't have money for movie tickets, but he would climb up on the window sill to peer at the miracles displayed on Lebanese TV. Only five or six years old, he thought the TV antennae would find him way out in the fields and show him on the screen. When he went to secondary school far from his home, he began to see Italian productions and to identify with those heroic cowboys in American movies.

On fire to emulate the brave characters he saw on screen, and keenly feeling the discrimination Arabs suffered, he joined the Israeli Communist Party at nineteen because he believed it was against discrimination and for the establishment of two independent states.

Until he visited Haifa while in secondary school, all he knew about Israeli Jews was that they had confiscated Arab land. When he began to meet Jews, he realized that "there were good Jewish people fighting against racism and discrimination." The people he found impossible to understand were the fanatics—Arabs and Jews. "They were in another world from me," he said, using Hebrew to explain himself more precisely.

He found another world, indeed, when the Israeli Communist Party helped him get a scholarship to study directing at the prestigious Moscow film school, known as VGIK. He was impressed by the great Russian directors and actors, but quickly grew to distrust the similarity of the themes forced upon them.

He observed the difficulties experienced by a unique director like Andrei Tarkovsky, who had made *The Childhood of Ivan*, *Stalker*, and *Solaris*. "They didn't give money to him, but to those who belonged to the regime, like Sergei Bondarchuk. He was a great actor but a bad director. I didn't like him." On the other hand, the Georgian and Armenian films seemed freer and more capable of touching audiences.

"I changed so much in those years," Nasser said. "I saw that the Communist Party was not dialectical. They used communism like a very tough religion. Everything was for people sitting up high, but the simple people worked like horses for them and got nothing. I wanted from communism that people be equal, to love each other and human rights, not to be fanatical. It was fanatical in Russia and in the Israeli CP the same thing.

"There are good people in the Israeli CP and they want to fight for Jews and Arabs to live together without war, but the leaders are fanatical. They don't want you to think, to have your own ideas, to discuss, to say no."

He realized how those contradictions affected him when he ran into trouble in Moscow with his graduation film, *Eternity*. "They weren't happy with me because I look for eternity through simple people. Marxism doesn't believe in the spiritual eternity of human beings. My mother's spirit is eternity for me, because I loved her and had a life with her. Her ideas and mind are within me, and it will pass through me to other people. . . . In *The Milky Way*, I was inspired to portray weak people. They can't do anything to change their lives, but I like them in spite of the fact that I want them to make more of themselves and the bad situation in which they are living."

Nasser, who still lives in his native village and goes to Tel Aviv two or three times a week, says with genuinely sweet simplicity, "I love the earth, I love my land, and I love my movie. The movie is like the earth for me."

July 20, 1998
The San Francisco Examiner

Elia Suleiman

PHOTO BY JUDY STONE.

"If it rains on the West Bank, it falls on Israel too."

Toronto

Oddly enough, it was cinema—which Elia Suleiman first learned about from books—that liberated him from narrow ideas of nationalism, religion, and tribalism.

As a Palestinian from a secular Christian family in Nazareth, Suleiman provokes controversy and confusion among both Jewish Israelis and Arabs with his poetic, absurdist approach to Israeli reality. When he won the special jury prize and the critics' award at the 2002 Cannes Film Festival for his *Divine Intervention: A Chronicle of Love and Pain*, it was a cause for celebration among Arabs, who felt that they were recognized somewhere in the world.

At the 2002 Toronto International Film Festival, Suleiman, forty-two, explained how he came to believe in a bi-national democratic secular state. With low-key humorous charm in real life, on film, he's as deadpan as Buster Keaton.

In *Divine*, the idiosyncratic writer-director features himself as the alter-ego E.S. waiting in his car near an Israeli army checkpoint while trying to navigate between the shoals of death and desire, torn with worry about his dying father and the impossible barriers facing a new romance. Meanwhile, a wild balloon with Arafat's face drifts high above the scene, Arab neighbors bad-mouth each other, fiery explosions wreak havoc in a quiet suburb, and a serio-comic fantasy fight erupts between acrobatic Israeli soldiers and a free-floating Arab woman warrior with a sheaf of spectacular lethal arrows. It is, to say the least, a movie that defies easy description.

When Suleiman was growing up, the only time he saw Israelis was when the family went shopping in the cities and his mother, a teacher, would warn him to speak quietly. "If they knew you were an Arab, they kind of looked down on you," he said. As a boy with a "compulsion" to reflect on himself and learn how to better himself, he found that he wanted to express his feelings through film to counteract the stereotypes of Arabs he saw in "politically correct" Israeli movies. With the help of his brother, a teacher at Haifa University, the self-taught youngster began to check out library books on cinema. They opened new worlds to him—of Godard, Antonioni, Bresson, and Ozu. Soon he was saving money earned at odd jobs to travel to New York and see their films.

Much later Suleiman was living in Montmartre when he began "playing around" with an idea for a script in the thriller genre when he learned that his father was dying of cancer and he returned to Nazareth. He was shooting his completely new script when the Intifada broke out, and he went back to France to work on post-production. He's staying in Paris for the time being, but despite the death and destruction he saw on the West Bank, he still doesn't think it's too late for a bi-national state to emerge.

"It's possible that people get a little bit over the pain and the hurt. It's possible that they slowly start to forget like a lot of histories show," he said. "If it was impossible, I wouldn't make the film. We all have dreams and opinions. We don't have to be pragmatic. We leave the pragmatism to the politicians who are always manipulating us.

"Working in the cinema," he said, "taught me and continues to teach me that the only thing that could liberate us and make us better people is to be able as much as possible to carry on values that free us from all constraints and bad notions that control our minds. Cinema is a poetic site, a flow by itself. You don't determine its limitations. You cannot tell the edges of an image. Its associations to you and me are different. It depends on our memories, associations, intellect, desire, pleasure. Once you let yourself go in that direction and take the risk of not putting yourself in an ideological position, you discover that nationalism is not good, and you discover that religion and tribalism are awful because they do not free you. You don't take pleasure from them. It just gives you antagonism and a kind of angry energy."

Suleiman came to international attention when his ironic episodic feature *Chronicle of a Disappearance* won the Best First Feature prize at the Venice festival in 1996. Since then, he said, "There are Arabs who look at me with ambiguity because I don't deal with cliché and propaganda cinema and feel suspicious about who I am and what I stand for because I'm not raising flags. At the moment I am a sort of point of pride for Palestinians because, in the midst of all the horrible things happening, I was receiving a prize at Cannes. They didn't see the film but felt that at least the Palestinians are being recognized somewhere in the world."

He doesn't take any obvious political stands in his wry films, but Suleiman is as emphatically against a Palestinian state as he is against a Zionist Israeli state. "This place is too claustrophobic for two states. It's too small. Why divide people who look so much alike and have the same culture? If it rains on the West Bank, it falls on Israeli land too and the reverse is true. Why not give up this tribal ideological bullshit? Israel has to cease to exist as a state for the Jewish people. Anyway it cannot continue. There are a million Palestinians living there. How can Israelis control the demographic situation? The other way around is to open up and stop being racist and stop denying people rights and oppressing the Palestinians in Israel psychologically, economically, and putting them in ghettoes. It's a horrific thing for someone who calls himself a Jew to do. It's completely the antithesis of what Jewishness is about. These people arrived there, got to carry arms, and began to feel the strength of it, and I think it's horrible that a Jew is shooting. It's against all their values. And I think that something's wrong there when a country is ruled by a war criminal—Sharon."

Although invited to bring *Divine* to the Jerusalem Film Festival, he refused because he had wanted to premiere it in Ramallah, but the Israeli army destroyed its theater and the Dolby sound system, as well as the House of Culture in Jerusalem. He wanted the Israelis to pay for the damage and to offer an official apology "for consistently trying to eliminate the culture of the Palestinians," Suleiman said. "Their idea was to erase memory, and they're never going to manage that anyhow."

October 9, 2002
The San Francisco Examiner

3
Eastern Lights

Joan Chen

"I was indoctrinated to crave for something bigger than myself."

San Francisco

In 1978 when Joan Chen was seventeen, the darling star of *Little Flower*, she rocketed to fame and became a role model in China, but she never dreamed that one day she'd have to pay a $50,000 fine in order to act in another Chinese film.

That big penalty was for having directed an unauthorized production, *Xiu Xiu: The Sent Down Girl*, set in Tibet during the Cultural Revolution. The subject was not one calculated to gain official approval. It portrayed a young student's loss of innocence and idealism when she goes to a remote area to learn horse-herding and later desperately uses sex in the hope that one of the men she meets in casual encounters will help her to get back home.

Chen had become a famous Hollywood actress for her performances as the enigmatic mill owner in David Lynch's TV series *Twin Peaks*, as the Empress in Bernardo Bertolucci's *The Last Emperor* and a Vietnamese mother in Oliver Stone's *Heaven and Earth* (1993), but she was increasingly dissatisfied with the lack of challenging roles and films without substance. Stardom hasn't spoiled her. Refreshingly unpretentious and candid, she still retains some of the quality of innocence that made her a role model in China.

The way innocence can be destroyed is what attracted her to *Celestial Bath*, the short story that eventually became the basis for *Xiu Xiu*, as a film she would like to direct. The author, Geling Yan [see interview on page 104], had met Chen briefly in China when the actress was eighteen and astonished the writer by professing her love for Kafka's work. When both women eventually relocated in the San Francisco Bay Area, they would see all the art-house movies and share their enthusiasm for the novels of Gabriel Garcia Marquez, Manuel Puig, Vladimir Nabokov, Marguerite Duras, Mario Vargas Llosa, and Julio Cortazar.

When I caught up with Chen in 2003 at her San Francisco home, she had just re-turned from China, where she played two mothers *and* a grandmother in *Jasmine* and was enjoying *being* the mother of her two little daughters.

For a few years after she made *Xiu Xiu* in 1998, she kept hoping the fine would be forgotten, as well as the order to ban her from work in China. At the time, a Film Bureau official had denounced *Xiu Xiu* as a film that "traces the dark side of life, does not conform with history, and has a negative effect on the socialist system and the reputation of the nation."

"I could go back to China to visit my parents, but I couldn't work," Chen said. "Some Chinese reporters told me that they got a formal document never to talk to me or report anything about me. Every reporter, every news agency, every TV station and film studio got formal documents to not be related to me on any level. I thought, 'Wow, I didn't imagine it would be that way.'"

Finally, after she dutifully bowed to the required self-criticism and paid the fine, she got a formal document stating that she had recognized her "sin" and the press reported that she could work again. That marked an interesting development in her career. "When you're in your mid-thirties, there are not a lot of good parts in China. But now that I'm forty-two, all of a sudden I have a new life, a new lease on my acting career because now I can play the *mother* of a twenty-year-old." (Two years later, she got rave reviews for her role as a widowed mother with a secret in the American film *Saving Face*.)

She rediscovered the joy of acting when she was challenged to play three different roles in *Jasmine*, which was adapted from a novella written by Su Tong, the author of *Raise the Red Lantern*. "It's a very odd story to come from China because it's about a mother-daughter relationship. I think it's a very personal film for Hou Zhou, the director. I think he has this great disappointment in human relationships. It's a man's point of view on the definition of women. He feels great sympathy toward females and he often said, 'I feel so sorry for women.'"

The film is set in Shanghai from 1937 to the mid-1980s when so many changes hap-pened. Chen's co-star is Zhang Ziyi (of *Crouching Tiger, Hidden Dragon* fame). Chen said, "*Jasmine* tries not to be political because the changes were unimaginable, so it was dealt with in a subtle way and I like that."

The last time Chen acted in China was as a seductive wife in Stanley Kwan's 1994 *Red Rose White Rose*. Now, having directed *Xiu Xiu*, *Autumn in New York*, and planning to direct again, she brought a different perspective to *Jasmine*. "I loved to watch the set, to observe. Now I know what to look for, what to see, and also to have a mind game of my own on how I would have done it and how the director is doing it. Also, acting is just so easy compared to directing because your responsibility is limited to creating one character. It was almost a good vacation. Ever since I had my children, they have been the focus in our lives. Being back in China, I felt that I was focusing on myself again."

After marrying Dr. Peter Hui, a cardiologist whom she had met on a blind date, Chen left Los Angeles and moved to San Francisco, where she was living a quiet, relatively easier life. "I was working here and there, but it was almost like professionally, I was in hibernation." The challenge of *Xiu Xiu* "just woke me up."

When Geling Yan first told her the story, based on her friend's true experience, it struck a responsive chord in Chen, who urged her to write it. Although Chen was too young to have taken part in the Cultural Revolution, she felt the reverberations. Her parents, both physicians, were sent to the countryside, and her beloved grandfather, a famous professor of medicine and medical text writer who had studied at Oxford, committed suicide when he was accused of being a spy.

After Geling Yan wrote the tale as a novella, Chen told her, "'We'll make this movie,' and she didn't believe me."

Chen began re-working it into a script one winter while she was a juror at the Berlin Festival, where she was unhappy with the films she saw. "I felt some kind of emptiness, end-of-the-century emptiness and desperation. I was disgusted. I saw the work of a lot of young filmmakers and you expect something so fresh, something so inspired, even though flawed, and it wasn't there. You want to be inspired by their youthful imagination, by everything that is young, that is good about being young and new. Usually when you make a movie, it's because you really, really must say something. They said nothing. I thought, 'I feel I have something to say. I feel the urgency to make this film, and I think I'll do better.'"

She told a Chinese reporter that she had been "indoctrinated to crave for something bigger than my self-interest and that thirst is part of what is driving me. I see beauty in sacrifice and suffering, communism gave me that . . . For me, I don't care what I earn on a job. I'm more idealistic."

Yan, who had been a soldier-performer in Tibet, took the script to the Beijing Film Bureau where she was told they didn't like subjects about the Cultural Revolution or young intellectuals going to the countryside. And they wanted sexual and "pessimistic" scenes cut.

"They wanted this change and that change and that would have made the movie unworthy," Chen said. "Not my movie anymore—so why make it?"

Chen did have some misgivings before she got to the remote location in the high Tibetan plateaus in Sichuan province. "I thought, 'What am I doing here? I know nothing.' I was convinced I knew nothing about filmmaking and I was convinced this was a total mistake. But once I was there, we'd just go through every day and you don't have this wild imagination about what you don't know and what mistake you're making."

She was determined to proceed, even without a permit, but she had no idea of how difficult it would be in an area so remote that there was only one telephone line that hand-cranked to Beijing at certain hours and no fax machines. "The living conditions were incredibly awful in a two-story hostel. They supposedly gave me the best room. The toilet was totally broken. A lot of us just used the grassland. I remember squatting there, wearing my earphone, listening to Dvorak, and holding a candle to light my way. We couldn't wash. There was a quilt on the bed that was not washed or aired for the entire stay. We were just supposed to hang it out when the sun was out." At one point, she laughed, remembering how she said, "Hey, you know, this is quite poetic."

Still, being in the remote area with no producers at her back was great. "I could concentrate most of my energy and thoughts on the artistic side of directing. Directing in a formal studio situation, there is a lot of wheeling and dealing you have to do every day. We felt a lot of anxiety about being caught and thrown out. Other than that, it was just concentrating on making the story and that was very, very good."

Although she regrets having lied to Film Bureau officials about what she was doing, they never actually realized that the movie—which won a lot of Golden Horse awards in Taiwan—was the one she made without a permit.

When she learned that she couldn't make another film in China, "I was hurt, but at the same time I was kind of nonchalant about it. I did it, and I had to take the responsibility."

At the same time, she's relieved that she won't have to get Film Bureau permission when she directs her next film, *Fu Sang* (based on Yan's novel *The Lost Daughter of Happiness*), about a Chinese woman sold into prostitution in San Francisco and her love affair with a white man.

Has motherhood changed her feelings about working? "Obviously it's slowed me down a little bit and it's supposed to. If I don't work for a long time, I do miss it. But they need me and there's no one else, no movie in the world, and nobody else that needs me as much as they do. The movie is more or less for myself. Honestly, most filmmakers make movies for themselves. It's a very selfish desire. It is something that you must do, you must do for yourself because if you don't do it, you don't feel right. But now I have to do something for them, and they're totally worth it."

2003

Unpublished

Ann Hu

"I still think the Chinese culture had the most devout, profound, and rich wisdom of the world."

Toronto

From Mao Tse-tung to Indiana Jones and profitable commodity-trading, it's been a long march for Ann Hu to emerge as director of *Shadow Magic*, an entrancing tale about the introduction of motion pictures in China circa 1902.

When Liu, a curious young photographer, meets a visiting British citizen (Jared Harris) with a newfangled camera, he sees images move for the first time and wants to become a part of this exciting phenomenon. However, his interest brings him into conflict with two traditional gentlemen: his photo shop boss, who is afraid of Western influences, and the country's most famous opera star, who only wants a portrait taken of his beautiful daughter. This first official co-production between China and Taiwan includes four clips of Chinese films shot before 1905.

As Hu recalled the frustrating steps to her production at the 2000 Toronto International Film Festival, she burst into hearty laughs about her inability to accept any kind of control, but she couldn't hide tears remembering some bitter times during the Cultural Revolution.

As the daughter of high-ranking Communists in the Ministry of Propaganda, she had met the leaders of the country and enjoyed a "golden childhood" until Mao who had seemed "so human and so protective," inaugurated the Cultural Revolution in 1966. When she was eleven, her father, Ping Hu, was sent to the Mongolian border and her mother to farm labor in the south. Banishment turned out to be ten years of unfettered freedom for thousands of Chinese youngsters like Ann and her younger brother. Although the schools were closed, Ann found English-language books in the library that had never been translated into Chinese. With only a smattering of primary-school English lessons, she began the painstaking job of translating some works, including Mark Twain's "The One-Million Pound Bank Note."

When her parents came home in 1976, she said, "They couldn't recognize us. We were like totally little monsters. We didn't share the same values. We had our first confrontation when I came home late after seeing my boyfriend. My father slapped my face and said, 'If you keep going like this you will become a bad element in the society.' They wanted to control me and they couldn't."

Even at the Foreign Languages Institute, she couldn't stand the regulations. "Everyone there was trying to be part of a team. I didn't think that was for me. I was too outspoken and too personality-driven. I was always an outcast. After two years, I grabbed the first chance to go to America in 1979."

Settling in the San Francisco Bay Area, she took adult classes in Berkeley, then entered Contra Costa College and Golden Gate University, working her way through school as a waitress, chauffeur, house-cleaner, and instructor in Chinese. She renewed her acquaintance with Charles Xu, her future husband, when he was a graduate scholar in history at University of California, Berkeley. After he became a chemical trader for a German company in New York, Hu earned a bachelor's degree in business at New York University and eventually became a "top profit-producer as well." Soon she and her husband started their own investment company, but restless, as always, she began to think, "I didn't come to America just for this."

In 1987, they met director Chen (*Yellow Earth*) Kaige, who became a frequent visitor to their home. He was "like a window for me," Hu said. "I hadn't had access to film, but he talked about all the great aspects of filmmaking. He wanted my husband to be the producer of his *Life on a String*, and listening to him, I thought this is something I can do too. I just knew I had that talent. He took us to see *Indiana Jones and the Last Crusade* and my husband and I were laughing like kids. Kaige was so upset. He said, 'You people have poor tastes.' That was the time I began to realize there are entertain-

ment films and art films. I started to watch films so I could judge them and their different qualities. I looked at other people's work with a critical eye and every single masterpiece I watched, I could pick out some problem and thought I could do better."

She was amazed by *Lawrence of Arabia*. "It made me realize you could tell a story
about history, about a person and many other things in such a powerful way. It gave me
a kind of inspiration, but even then I thought I could do better."

Her initial self-confidence hit a few bumps on the way, she acknowledged with another hearty laugh. She was eager to try a theme that would combine something about
her past with her feelings about Chinese culture. "I still think Chinese culture has the
most devout, profound, and rich wisdom in this world. Anyone can challenge me on
that and I will win the debate!"

In 1994, she made a short 16mm experimental film, *Dream and Memory*, loosely
inspired by a famous Chinese painter who had been sent to the countryside to
paint propaganda portraits and fell in love with a local girl. Twenty years later in
New York, in a fictional twist, the artist, who was by then blind, began to love an
African girl, not knowing she was black. Expanded to an eighty-minute feature, the
film had a one-week release in New York, but contrary to Hu's great expectations,
it didn't win any Academy Awards.

She realized that she needed a "rock-solid" script, a lot of planning, an experienced technical crew, and a distributor if she was going to succeed as a director. She bought a documentary-like Chinese script about early movies and had it
translated into English, but nobody was interested. She studied books on how to
write a screenplay and worked with many American writers for three and a half
years. When she finally had a script she liked, it was sent to American producers,
and everyone rejected it. Eventually, she decided to go into production with her
savings of $500,000, including a "very reluctant" contribution from her husband.
Finally, Sandra Schulberg, founding director of the Independent Feature Project
and co-founder of First Run Features, overcame her initial reluctance and signed
on as co-producer.

When Hu went to the Beijing Film Studio for financial help, "They said, 'Get out
of here. You need ten times more money,' but basically I talked them into it. Two or
three weeks into production, I knew it was not possible to do what I wanted to." She
then managed with a bit of flattery to get production help from Zhang Xia, the powerful woman who is head of the co-production office in Beijing. Assistance that Hu will
never forget came from the crew that chipped in by bringing props from their own
homes. An assistant to director Ang Lee who knew Taiwanese investors convinced
them to visit the Beijing set, and they agreed to cooperate in financing the film which
eventually cost $5 million. Soon, they were getting financial help also from Road Mov-
ies Vierte Produktionen, the German company started by director Wim Wenders, as

well as from a Japanese private investor. Even so, they had barely enough cash to finish the shoot.

Back in New York, Post-Production Playground contributed its services as three sets of editors worked on it for the next three months, but the director's cut was not considered good enough to survive. "When many people say it's wrong, you have to pay attention," Hu conceded. They hired two more editors, who worked for two weeks to show her another cut. When Hu saw it, she said, "I felt big pain. You feel like you're raped or had brain surgery. But I realized that cut showed me another way to complete the film. It was a learning process. I feel it was a blessing to incorporate help in a correct way and make it become yours."

Her breakthrough came at the Sundance Film Festival when Sony Pictures signed on as distributor. At the Shanghai Film Festival, Hu beat Ang Lee's *Crouching Tiger* by winning the two top prizes, the government award, and the Golden Rooster, equivalent of an Academy Award. *Shadow Magic* took the best screenplay award at the Taiwan Festival.

Now she's working on the script for her next film. "Based on something real," she said. "It will be a shocking Chinese love story with sex and violence." With all her trials and tribulations in the past, she says there's "definitely been a change in my perspective. *Shadow Magic* made me aware of my own limitations and now I want to go beyond them."

April 13, 2001
The San Francisco Examiner

Im Kwon Taek

PHOTO BY JUDY STONE.

"I believe that the Korean culture must be revived."

Toronto

Although Im Kwon Taek has made ninety-seven films and is considered the Akira Kurosawa of South Korea, he is only now receiving his first American distribution with *Chunhyang*, a nominee for Best Foreign Film Oscar.

This gorgeous, inventive production was adapted from an eighteenth-century Korean classic folk song about a stately courtesan's daughter who stays loyal to her young scholarly lover in his absence, defying a governor's brutal attempt to make her his mistress.

The beloved tale, originally rendered by "pansori" singers, has inspired 120 novels and fourteen movies, Im, sixty-five, explained with a glint of humor in his eyes. Speaking through an interpreter at the 2000 Toronto International Film Festival, he said he took a calculated risk by creating a production that is both traditional and experimental.

80

It is the first film in which a pansori singer periodically interrupts the dramatic action with his vocal narrative. The risk paid off: *Chunhyang* became the first Korean film ever invited to the prestigious Cannes Film Festival and was acclaimed as a "masterpiece" at the Telluride, Toronto, and New York festivals. Earlier recognition had come when the San Francisco International Festival presented Im with the Kurosawa Award for lifetime achievement in 1998.

The international response to *Chunhyang* helped him in Korea, where censors were concerned about a nude scene with the sixteen-year-old girl (Lee Hyo Jung) who plays the title character (her age in the original song). Im had a difficult enough time getting the inexperienced girl to undress and create the emotion of someone falling in love for the first time. Then, a prosecutor thought that might involve a violation of Korea's juvenile protection law under which a minor cannot be exploited. And the press blew up the matter, Im said. He believes that the international reaction saved the film "from being forgotten in disgrace."

The earlier thirteen films concentrated on the classic love story. Some included "bits and pieces" of pansori, but they didn't really tell the audience how important pansori is, Im said. He hadn't realized it himself until he heard a four-hour pansori version. "I had never thought it could be so emotional and touching. For persons to really understand the movie, they have to understand that pansori is one of the most authentic expressions of Korean art and culture. It is hard to sing and hard to listen to, so its popularity is now going down." He had actually begun to explore the meaning and contemporary legacy of pansori with *Sopyonje* (1993), his first important international success.

Im has been feeling an increasing need to preserve what is special about Korean culture in an age of globalization when American films dominate Korean and world screens.

"What happens to the culture of a people who have kept themselves, for the most part, historically self-contained?" he asked during an interview with the *Harvard Asia Pacific Review*. "I believe that Korean culture must be revived and brought into the international context . . . I can't say that this influx of American films hasn't hurt us at all. I don't think that the overabundance of Hollywood movies with prominent sex or violence themes contributes to social consciousness in a beneficial way."

American films had influenced Im's early commercial productions at the beginning of a career that started in a most unusual fashion. Born in a town that was a Japanese colony, Im became a "juvenile vagabond" just before the Korean war ended. He was hired by some merchants who bought American shoes and re-made them into Korean-style footwear. At that time, a film called *Chunhyang Jun* became a commercial success. The merchants thought they could make a lot of money producing films and hired Im as an errand boy.

It was a very difficult time for Im. His father was a left-wing intellectual who suffered a great deal in his rebellion against the southern right-wing government. Although he survived the Korean war, he died shortly afterward and Im's mother became the family's support. Im's admiration for her strength and that of all Korean women during the years of warfare and poverty was particularly apparent in the 1986 films *Ticket*, a prostitution melodrama, and *Surrogate Woman*, a medieval period piece. A similar admiration for women's sturdiness is also apparent in the character of Chunghyang and her mother. They all illustrate director Peter Sellars' observation that in Im's films, "Women re-emerge, first of all as the embodiment of the suffering of the country, and then in the explosive and shocking renewal and reclaiming of identity. That positioning of women is a tremendously radical act in a highly patriarchal society."

2000

The Oakland Tribune

Gus Lee

"I learned that Chinese fathers do NOT have to have the power of life and death…"

Colorado Springs

Looking back on his life, Gus Lee, at forty-nine, says: "I'm very lucky in my background because the muses could have given me a much more pedestrian environment."

Growing up as a Chinese-American in the poor, predominantly black, San Francisco neighborhood called the Panhandle, Lee yearned to be black. Later, he attended West Point, became an attorney, investigated corrupt U.S. Army recruiting officers, and transformed himself into the author of the acclaimed autobiographical novels *China Boy* and *Honor and Duty*. A third novel, *Tiger's Tail*, is a political thriller set in postwar Korea.

In each of these novels, the protagonist wages a relentless search for moral truth, for a way to live that reconciles Chinese roots and American ways. Lee's unswerving need to honor his personal past is manifested in the story of how, after a hiatus of thirty years, he was reunited in 1991 with his childhood friend, Toussaint, an African American descendant of Caribbean pirates, who taught young Gus how to defend himself. The boys had lost track of each other when they entered different high schools, but Toussaint was vividly rendered as a major character in *China Boy*, the fictionalized tale of Lee's childhood.

His need to resume contact with Toussaint was a compulsion for Lee, who had, over the years, checked records of the U.S. Army, the Motor Vehicle Bureau, the FBI, and Social Security without success. Toussaint, it seemed, had vanished.

Lee and his wife, Diane, took up the tale of their search in 1993 at their five-bedroom stucco-and-frame home in Colorado Springs. Three years ago, they and their two pre-adolescent children moved from the posh San Francisco Bay Area suburb of Burlingame so that Lee could be a full-time writer without the need to augment their income with his legal work. At the time of this interview they were preparing to move into a smaller house that would be more manageable. The packing boxes were out of sight and the dining room was an oasis of calm. A portrait of Lee's beautiful mother hangs on the wall, along with framed displays of his first two book covers and an antique calligraphy scroll inscribed "longevity and prosperity."

Diane, a psychiatric nurse and editor "numero uno" on all Lee's books, talked about her determination to help her husband keep up the search for Toussaint. When one of her nurse's aide students, an African American, mentioned having seen Gus Lee discussing *China Boy* on television, Diane told her about the book's black characters, including nine-year-old Toussaint. The aide replied that she knew a Dr. Toussaint "Street," who had moved from the Bay Area to Fresno, where he was in charge of family practice at the Kaiser Hospital.

"All my old prejudices came out," recalled Diane, who called herself a WASP from Kansas City. "I thought there is no way that a little black boy from a slum could be a doctor!" One phone call to the stunned physician erased her stereotypes. A wildly excited Mrs. Lee sped home to her husband, whose computer searches had been off by one letter: Toussaint's surname was Streat, not Street. The susequent reunion between Dr. Streat and Lee reaffirmed their old friendship.

"Toussaint was the Good Samaritan," Lee said fervently, recalling his boyhood in the Panhandle. "I appreciated anyone who wasn't trying to kill me." Today, almost six feet tall, Lee still has the strong, broad shoulders he developed by studying boxing and lifting weights. "I'm not a natural warrior, just as I'm not a natural boxer. I'm not a fighter," he noted with the ease of a man finally at peace with himself.

While the body-building was a means of survival, Lee preferred books, devouring the works of Twain, Dickens, and Jane Austen. However, he was pressured by his father, Tsung-Chi (aka T.C.) Lee, a former major in the Kuomintang army.

It was a major disappointment to T.C. that Gus flunked out of West Point after three years because he couldn't pass the engineering/math requirements. Gus went on to get B.A. and L.L.B. degrees from the University of California, Davis, before serving in the army as a criminal defense lawyer and command judge advocate.

That achievement was small consolation to T.C. The elder Lee had arrived in San Francisco in 1939 to work at the Bank of Canton as an assistant to T.A. Soong (Chiang Kai-shek's brother-in-law), a former classmate at Shanghai's prestigious pro-Western St. John's University. Those connections—and the sale of Mrs. Lee's jewelry (she came from a powerful family of Suzhou scholars)—finally helped her and their three young daughters to make an arduous journey in 1944 across wartorn China to India and the U.S.

In San Francisco, Mrs. Lee gave birth to their long-hoped-for son, Augustus. When Gus was five, Mrs. Lee died of breast cancer. Two years later, T.C. married a Pennsylvania Dutch woman whose severe discipline was to haunt Gus for years. His stepmother, Edith, has reappeared as a formidable, ghostly presence in all Lee's books.

Lee hadn't ever considered writing until his then-seven-year-old daughter asked him about her Chinese grandmother. Lee realized he had no vivid memory of her, so he interviewed his three sisters, keeping a record of their diverse recollections. He thought that the family journal might be a basis for an article, but Diane declared, "It's a book!"

Lee pointed out that both of his parents were rebels, considering the times in which they lived. When his father joined the Kuomintang army, it was an "unthinkable" act for a wealthy young man. His mother—who had received a rare formal education for a girl—converted to Christianity and refused to consent to an arranged marriage. She had her eye on T.C., the adventurous boy next door in Shanghai.

Lee believes there was even a bit of a rebel in his stepmother, Edith. She had left her close-knit Pennsylvania Dutch community and married a young Oregon law student who was killed by Chinese Communist soldiers while serving with the 2nd U.S. Infantry near the Imjin river in Korea. Ironically, twenty years later, Gus Lee himself served with the 2nd U.S. Infantry near the Imjin river during his first tour of duty in Korea in 1977.

His novel *Tiger's Tail* was inspired by his second Korean assignment. Lee was among ten Army attorneys in the Connelly Commission, set up by the U.S. Senate's Armed Forces Committee, to investigate illegal recruiting practices. Korean nationals—many of whom had served in the South Korean army—were paying up to $10,000 to bribe their way into the peacetime all-volunteer American army as a means of becoming citizens. A "couple of hundred" recruiters were pocketing payoffs for enlisting them.

The investigation in 1979-80 began like an adventure story, Lee recalled. Eventually, hundreds of recruiters and senior commanders were relieved of their duties, massive reforms were instituted, and suspect enlistees were separated from the service.

Although *Tiger's Tail* is fiction, the army atmosphere in Korea is real, Lee emphasized. Reflecting on the Korean experience, Lee said he had met officers who believed the North Koreans were planning to cross the border again. "Some of our guys thought, 'Why not hit them first? Why should we wait to take the first blow?'"

But Lee said, "The U.S. military is premised NOT to deliver the first blow. We'll take a savage first blow often unaware and unfortunately unprepared, but attacking another country in your own self-defense is what Hitler claimed to be doing when he invaded Poland.

"That kind of first-strike talk exists," Lee said. "I didn't have to invent it." He is forthright in admitting that invention doesn't come as easily to him as describing his own experiences. "*China Boy* wrote itself in three months. It was like going down whitewater rapids. The other books took much more navigation and thought," he said. In 1992, he took four months of unpaid leave from his executive job with the California State Bar Association to write *Honor and Duty*.

Writing the books based on his life was more than a career change for Lee. Talking to his sisters about the family opened a window into his past and occasioned often painful insights. "I discovered my mother, not only who she was but also what she wished for me and how far away I had traveled from her hopes. The last thing she wanted me to be was an agnostic and I was. The last thing she wanted me to be was a stern father and I was with my son. I had begun preparing him for a hard life. I was yelling at him and acting as if I were putting him through boot camp."

When Diane challenged him to get some professional counseling, the therapist pressed Lee to explain the source of his severity toward his son. To his dismay and astonishment, Lee recalled, he replied, "It's not me he has to worry about, it's Edith"— and burst into tears. "She had died fifteen years earlier," he said, "but her strict parenting pattern and my father's was deep in me.

"My journeys as a boy and man have been chronicled in three books, but my most difficult journey was as a father," Lee continued. "I thought that once I understood my emotions I would change." But his stern behavior persisted. Rather than give up, Lee joined, albeit reluctantly, a small male covenant group at the First Presbyterian Church in Burlingame. Five men would meet every morning and pray for each other. Though he admitted that at first he thought it was "asinine," he eventually became a believer in Christianity. The entire experience, Lee admitted, "went against all my intellectual will and training."

In Colorado Springs, he attends the First Christian Church. "It's still hard for me to talk about this," he said. "But Christianity gave me a sense of genuine humility and hope for my children. I no longer have the things I feared most in myself, attitudes that I saw in my father and stepmother. Without my faith, I couldn't have done it. In my original culture, Chinese fathers literally have the power of life and death. What I found through faith is that children learn respect if you respect them."

March 18, 1996
Publishers Weekly

Edward Yang

PHOTO BY JUDY STONE.

"*Everyone wonders if they could have a second chance.*"

San Francisco

Twenty years ago, Edward Yang, then thirty-three, a computer scientist in Seattle, had a sleepless night. Suddenly, he felt himself growing old in a seven-year job he could not longer relish. It took three more years for him to break loose into a film career.

Now, Yang's seventh feature, *Yi Yi*, examining the trials and tribulations in a Taiwanese family from birth to death, has been named Best Foreign Film of the year by the New York Critics Association and Best Film overall by the National Society of Film Critics.

However, in San Francisco to promote his film, Yang, fifty-three, was more excited talking about his first child, three-month-old Sean. Beaming with joy, he exclaimed, "You never know how happy you are until you have a child!"

He was eager to return home to his wife, Peng Kaili, a cellist and pianist who arranged the film's music and production design—and, demonstrating, to cradle that baby in his arms.

Meanwhile, the lead actor who is charming *Yi Yi* audiences was eight-year-old Jonathan Chang, who plays Yang Yang, an imp with a stolid air. He once dumbfounded the director when he asked, "If nothing means nothing, why do we have to worry about calling it 'nothing?'"

Yang considered that a "very philosophical question to ask" at such an early age. "Because," Yang elaborated, "zero is a zero, so why call it zero because zero means something and zero is supposed to be nothing?"

Ponder that one!

Jonathan came to the attention of Yang's casting director, who had originally spotted a cute kid walking home from school and asked him if he would like to audition for a TV commercial.

Too young for the role, Jonathan, the son of a high-tech engineer, felt rejected because he didn't get the job, so when the second opportunity arose, he asked if he could join Yang's acting workshop.

"It was kind of an ego thing," Yang said.

The workshop was designed to make youngsters think of acting as play. "I noticed that a lot of Jonathan's body language was like that of old people, the way he rubbed his hands, for instance. He thought that was something everyone should do."

He seemed to be copying the movement of the grandparents with whom his family lives.

The title *Yi Yi* literally means "One One" (or *individually* in Chinese), but to make it sound jazzier, Yang calls it "A One and a Two." Yang filmed almost everything in long shots and very few close-ups so that the viewer never seems to intrude in the characters' lives.

"The film was developed over many years from things I think about a lot," Yang said. "If we look for a way to reassess our own lives, we ask, 'What haven't we done?' Everyone wonders if they could have a second chance."

NJ, who portrays Jonathan Yang's father, the partner in a computer company sinking into bankruptcy, is particularly troubled abut his own life when he goes to Japan for work and renews his relationship with an old sweetheart.

He seems very indecisive, but Yang said, "There are a lot of Chinese men like him. Even some of the macho-looking guys can sometimes be very weak. Lots of men are not tested. When they are put into a real situation, they would probably chicken out. Men may be called the head of the household but women run a lot of things."

In the film, Jonathan doesn't have much to say but his reactions are eloquent when he's the butt of teasing girls when his father is away in Japan, when his grandmother suffers a stroke, when his unhappy mother goes off on a religious retreat, and his adolescent sister suffers the pangs of first love.

His big moment comes when he reads a very moving letter to his grandmother at her funeral.

What about that letter? Edward Yang is silent until he sighs and gives a long, drawn-out, "Ahhh.

"It's a letter I would write to my grandmom," Yang said, "although I never knew my grandparents."

However, he enjoys telling the story with bursts of laughter and an occasional stutter. "My mom's family, who were from the north of China, were first-generation Christian. Her father worked for a warlord and because he was educated, he ran some offices for him. When that warlord was defeated by another warlord, he was thrown into jail. An American missionary who was helping prisoners convinced the warlord to release him. My father's family who came from a southern village were Buddhists, but he converted after he met my mother at the Shanghai bank where they both worked."

They were married during the Japanese invasion of China, and Edward was born in Shanghai in 1947. Two years later, when the Communist Party was consolidating its control, the bank moved to Taipei.

"I was eight-and-a-half when we moved to Taiwan. My parents talked to me about the war years. It was something they never forgot."

Taiwan under Chiang Kai-shek wasn't much better, with people under suspicion for alleged political opinions and personal vendettas.

"My parents lived through some of the most miserable years of recent Chinese history. That's why after they retired they wanted to get out and move to Seattle where my brother was working.

"The first time I realized this world could be ugly, I was nine. My dad was confined for a week in what they called guest houses for 'conversations.' They weren't called interrogations. Everyone was suspected—not only because of Chiang, but a lot had to do with people trying to get rid of you. At school nobody talked about anything like that. When I got older, I realized that all my friends' fathers went through these same things. I put a lot of those experiences in my film *A Brighter Summer Day* (1989)."

While studying electrical engineering in Taiwan, he didn't consider filmmaking as a career, although he went to many movies, especially American ones, and he still recalls being baffled by the works of Robert Bresson and Fellini's *8½*.

When he got a scholarship to do graduate work at the University of Florida, Yang's first stop in the new world was Seattle. "My first impression was that the air was so clean. It's very difficult to explain my sensation. 'How can it be this fresh?' I felt joy and weightlessness."

Why, then, did he return to Taiwan if he was so happy in the States?

"It was a low point in Taiwan's history," he acknowledged. The country had been expelled by the United Nations and President Carter had recognized Red China. "But I think my generation—we were rebellious at the time—was quite confident we could make some kind of contribution."

If any proof were needed, *Yi Yi* is it.

January 2001
The Oakland Tribune

Hirokazu Kore-Eda

He marches to a different taiko.

San Francisco

Death and loss, as well as the taboo subjects of minorities—Koreans and people with AIDS—are portrayed with rare sensitivity by Hirokazu Kore-eda, who gently marches to a different taiko in Japan.

With *Maborosi*, his first feature, poetically filmed in light and shadow, Kore-eda was credited with the birth of Japan's art-house genre in 1995. The unpretentious director, speaking quietly through an interpreter, discussed the origin of the film when he presented it at the San Francisco Festival in 1996.

Maborisi was fully developed after he made a documentary about a woman whose husband took his own life. "I wanted to do something more with her feelings of loss and her urge to find some kind of explanation for why her husband committed suicide." In the feature film, her search for an answer continues even as she tries to create a new life for herself and her small son in a second marriage.

90

To show the changes in the way the heroine feels, Kore-eda didn't want to picture her in the Hollywood style "of taking a head shot and showing the character laughing when happy or crying when sad. I wanted to depict the people as they lived there in the same way that time flows or the air permeates the scene in a natural way. What becomes most important in doing this is what kind of light comes into the scene or what kind of darkness drifts in. In the important places where the heroine exists—at a window, on a veranda, in a tunnel—I have shown a shift in the border between light and shadow. I have made that her space. In Western thought, there is life and when life ends, there is death. But in this film, what I have tried to depict as life and death or light and shadow does not have a sharp distinction, but is intermingled. I have treated light and shadow, the symbols of life and death, not as contrasting each other but as shadow within light and light within shadow to symbolize the way she lives on."

In demonstrating how people live in real scenes, he also wanted to use real sounds, rather than film music. "I wanted the audience to hear the kinds of sounds that enter in from the outside."

Apologizing for his lengthy explanation, Kore-eda said he had been surprised that audiences at festivals understood his approach. At the Chicago International Film Festival, one viewer spoke about how in Christianity life and death are concepts that are antagonistic to each other, and that death starts after life ends. "When I heard her comment, I realized that I don't think of life and death in that way. But this was a conclusion I reached only after hearing her question."

(He was to continue his exploration into memory, life, and death with *After Life* (1998), in which the dead relive their fondest memories before moving on to the hereafter.)

Initially, it was very difficult for Kore-eda to get financing for the $1.3 million *Maborosi*. Nobody wanted to invest in such a depressing subject until TV Man Union, a television company to which he belongs, decided to risk financing the first film in its history. At a time when the most popular production in Japan was *Die Hard 3*, Kore-eda was pleasantly surprised by the number of young people who came to see *Maborosi*, although they usually prefer American movies and rarely think about life and death.

At the start of *Maborosi*, there is a scene where the grandmother wanders off to try to get back to her hometown. "My father was something like that," Kore-eda recalled. "In a way, his life had ended once, as a prisoner of war in Siberia. Nothing mattered to him after that. He would drift off at times; his presence was like that of the husband in the film who commits suicide. In reading the original story that the film is based on, I was able to overlay my own experience with my father, whose presence was rather weak. He would be living in a normal way, but then one day disappear for three or four weeks and then wander back home."

His father's intermittent absence took a toll on the youngster, who was often left alone when both parents worked. His mother had to help support the family with her job in a scrap recycling place. Reading was the lonely boy's solace, which may account for his initial ambition to be a novelist.

Although Kore-eda was born in 1962 in Tokyo and raised in Tokyo, his father was born in Taiwan, then a colony of Japan. During the Second World War, he served in Manchuria with the Japanese army until the end of the conflict, when the Russians captured him. Sent to a labor camp in Sibera for two years, he underwent a Communist re-education program. As a result, Kore-eda said, "He had hatred toward Russia, but he also had hatred toward Japan, its imperialism and its emperor system."

When Kore-eda saw the films of Hou Hsiao-Hsien, like *The Time to Live and the Time to Die* (1985), the images perfectly fit his father's stories about Taiwan. "I felt very happy about this," Kore-eda said.

Asked about Japan's reluctance to talk about Japanese imperialism in Korea and reluctance to apologize for its wartime murderous actions in China, the director noted that those issues still remain and nothing has been resolved. "While making television documentaries, I have dealt with minorities, such as the Koreans living in Japan. I think hardly any people of the younger generation feel any guilt or responsibility for the past. As for me, I believe we need to think more deeply about these issues. Although they are not related to *Maborosi*, I hope to continue to deal with such subjects in the future."

In one of his TV documentaries, Kore-eda showed the experience of a Korean-born man who was brought to Japan when he was four years old. He used a Japanese name and lived in the postwar years as a Japanese. "As we can't distinguish between Japanese and Koreans by looking at them," Kore-eda said, "many resident Koreans hide their real identity. My subject could not be registered as a Japanese and couldn't get a Japanese passport. Even his wife and children didn't know he was Korean. As a result of all these conditions, he decided to go to Korea, but he was caught with a forged passport and criticized by the media for living a lie." Although the unfortunate man does not appear in the documentary, Kore-eda interviewed Japanese people close to him and raised the issue of why he felt he could not live as a Korean and had to live a lie.

When Kore-eda made a documentary about a gay man who contracted AIDS from sexual contact, he followed him for the last two years of his life. "I was allowed to have the valuable experience of thinking deeply about what it means for a person to be born and to die. It had a major effect on me." Although there is some sympathy among Japanese for those who get AIDS from blood transfusions, "They are very cold toward gays who contract the disease through sexual contact."

When the program was aired, there were calls to the TV station asking why it had shown the documentary and saying that it served the man right to get AIDS.

After each controversial program, Kore-eda was asked if he was Korean or if he had AIDS. His response was that he can only see through the eyes of a Japanese, but despite his sympathies, minority people see him as a perpetrator of injustice. "I can never forget that I am one of the majority. I always want to think about what my responsibility is and what I can do as a member of the majority. Even if I am not one of the involved parties, it is still my problem and that is how I express it in my work."

1996

San Francisco Chronicle

Postscript: In 2005, Kore-eda won international acclaim with *Nobody Knows*, his most accessible film. Continuing to reflect his sense of responsibility, Kore-eda portrayed the harrowing story of four abandoned Japanese youngsters struggling, despite the death of one sibling, to maintain their zest for living. It was based on a newspaper story about a similar case, Kore-eda told reporters at the 2004 Cannes Film Festival, and he emphasized that the film implicitly indicts "the loosening of neighborly and community ties . . . with no will or impulse to intervene."

Joris Ivens

"Don't make it rosy!"

San Francisco

When Premier Chou En-lai encouraged his old Dutch friend, Joris Ivens, to make a film about the daily lives of the Chinese people, he offered only one sentence of advice: "Don't make it rosy!"

What Ivens and his ebullient French wife, Marceline Loridan, finally did in their twelve-hour documentary was simple and unprecedented in Chinese film history: by conveying the individual personalities and spirit of many Chinese men, women, and children, they showed something of the real life that lies within that incomprehensible, amorphous mass of 800,000,000 people.

"We wanted to make a film about people, not statistics," the filmmakers said when they were in the San Francisco Bay Area to promote *How Yukong Moved the Mountains*. They repeatedly refused to generalize about their experiences in China. The country was too complex, the civilization too old, the political changes too dynamic and contradictory for them to indulge in easy oversimplifications.

"The film isn't even about China," they say. The faces of this great seventy-nine-year-old filmmaker and his tiny, redheaded wife glow with warmth and laughter as they quote a Chinese saying: "If you come for fifteen days, it's easy to write a book of 700 pages; if you stay three months, it becomes difficult. You can write only 400 pages. If you stay longer, you don't write a book."

A year and a half of work went into producing 120 hours of film. For Ivens, it was a logical extension of his past: shooting the Spanish Civil War, Japan's invasion of China, war in Vietnam, the revolution in Cuba, the reconstruction of eastern Europe, and changes in Chile.

Although a passion against injustice drove him to "nerve points" all over the world, most of his work was disciplined. An International Film Guide tribute noted in 1968, that his films demonstrated "modesty, discretion, artistry, and intelligent observation" whether it was the lyrical expression of the Dutch campaign against the sea, a dazzling photographic exercise on *Rain*, or the brutal realism and the misery of Belgian miners.

But this new work was also something completely different, he emphasized, a total collaboration with the perky woman he had fallen in love with when he saw her in *Chronicles of a Summer*, a French cinema-verité film in which she told of her years in Auschwitz and terrible personal problems after the war. What she wanted to learn in China was "if another way than our way is possible."

"She deepened the sensitivity toward human effects," Ivens said proudly, obviously eager for her to share equally in credit for the film.

For a while, they felt crushed by the enormity of the challenge that faced them after Chou En-lai chided them for not bringing their cameras to China in 1971. He urged them to return and make a documentary that would help the outside world understand what was happening in China without hiding the weaknesses. Ivens who had made a film in China in 1958 and taught filmmaking there for several months in the 1960s was assured of total freedom to film with the exception of military installations.

Freedom to travel made an interesting contrast to 1938 when Ivens had been there to make a documentary that would show the outside world what the Japanese invasion was doing to China: the Chiang Kai-shek government restricted his movements, had him under surveillance, and censored his film.

This time, there was total silence in China for months after *Yukong* had its successful opening in Paris in 1976. Chinese correspondents in Paris filed stories about the film's acclaimed premiere, but although countries all over Europe ordered prints, no such request came from China. When they returned to Peking early in 1977, journalists and filmmakers told them that the influence of Mao's widow had prevented publication of the reviews "because the film showed the reality of China and they just wanted to show beautiful things."

But by then, Mao's widow no longer had power. After the film was shown at the International Club in Peking, the Chinese film industry decided it was a good documentary for home consumption and, soon afterward, opened *How Yukong Moved Mountains* in thirty cities with Chinese subtitles for the European commentary.

Much to the astonishment of the filmmakers who thought the Chinese might be bored by a documentary showing their daily lives, they were fascinated. No previous film ever showed them so naturally at work, speaking in their own voices without a superimposed and didactic commentary about their activities. When the filmmakers expressed the thought that this might start a whole new trend in Chinese productions, some of the workers said, "Maybe," but they looked skeptical.

April 15, 1978
San Francisco Chronicle

Donald Richie

"I approve of Kurosawa, but Ozu's work is closer to my heart."

San Francisco

Donald Richie, a "Renaissance Man" from Lima, Ohio, is best known in the United States for his superlative study, *The Films of Akira Kurosawa*, but his heart belongs to the family-oriented work of Yasujiro Ozu.

An experimental filmmaker himself, novelist, pianist, composer, and critic, Richie expressed his personal preference when he was in San Francisco to offer a sometimes tart appraisal of Kurosawa in a lecture under the sponsorship of the Japan Society and the Surf Theater.

Richie, a resident of Japan for almost forty years, introduced Japanese film to New York when he was curator at the Museum of Modern Art from 1968-74, and has written a number of books on Japanese life, from etiquette to the art of Japanese tattooing and gardening. His *The Inland Sea* is a superb work that balances travel, a quest for personal identity, and a commentary on Japanese life.

It took one summer for him to write his Kurosawa book—which is considered a masterpiece of readable scholarship—but it was ten years "up the cliff" to finish his study of Ozu's life and work, including *Tokyo Story*, *Late Autumn*, and *Early Summer*.

"I like the Ozu book better. It's much closer to my heart," Richie said in an interview. "I *approve* of Kurosawa—which sounds very stuffy—but I *love* Ozu's work. I get all choked up and I cry . I threw away page after page on Ozu because it was turning into a mushy mash note.

"The humanity in Ozu is what you love but what really puts it in your head forever is his extraordinarily stringent technique. Less means more all the way. It's an almost Mondrian grid with real human emotions, all curves and idiosyncrasies working so well against this very rigid esthetic. If Ozu's wonderful people had been done in the style of the Andy Hardy films, you couldn't care less. That makes Ozu one of the greatest of all twentieth-century artists."

This is not to say that Richie approves of everything Ozu did. He thinks both Ozu and Kurosawa have "tin ears." According to Richie, the musical scores in Ozu's films are "four-square vapid, sweet to an uncommon degree, and sound like a dreadful combination of old-fashioned salon music and hymns played on a harmonium. It's gravy poured on the images."

As for Kurosawa, he's notorious for "sitting on" his composers, noted Richie, a comparatively self-taught composer who wrote original scores for a number of his plays that have been produced in Japan. As a young clerk-typist working under the U.S. occupation forces in Japan, he introduced such contemporary composers as Aaron Copland and Roger Sessions to Japanese musicians.

"When Kurosawa was young," Richie said with a note of caution, "I *think* this true—someone gave him an album of the 100 best classics. He knows these chestnuts extraordinarily well, but he doesn't know anything else. He almost ruined *Rashomon* by using Ravel's 'Bolero.'"

Kurosawa only met his match once, Richie recalled. "He called in Toru Takemitsu and showed him a rough cut of *Dodes'ka-den* with temporary music—the final score had yet to be written." Richie hummed some familiar tunes. "Takemitsu said, 'I don't think I'm the proper composer for this. I know who is, but you may have difficulty getting him—Georges Bizet, and he's dead.' Then he turned and walked out."

"That never had happened before to Kurosawa," Richie said. "The director ran after Takemitsu, saying it was only a *suggestion*. It was the first time a composer was given full range to do what he wanted. Takemitsu's score—which is very tender, very simple—is the best thing about *Dods'ka-den*. There's a fair amount of Mahler in *Ran*, but Takemitsu turned in a gorgeous score that rings tears out of stones."

With *Red Beard* in 1965, Kurosawa came to the end of a major cycle. "After that, we're in some other country," Richie emphasized. His favorite Kurosawa work is *The Seven Samurai*. He was so disappointed in *Dodes'ka-den* and *Dersu Uzala* that he couldn't wrote about them for the revised edition of his Kurosawa book. Those assessments were written by Joan Mellen.

"The original script for *Dersu Uzala* was wonderful. For reasons I still do not understand, he didn't use that script, and used one much more simplistic. I keep comparing it to this unfilmed original."

He also has reservations about *Kagemusha*, but he knew what happened there also. "It was originally supposed to have been a comedy in the style of *Yojimbo* and *Sanjuro*. It was written for the comedian who stars in the *Blind Swordsmen* films, but he behaved badly, bringing his own cameraman to the set, and was removed from the production on the first day of shooting.

"So old Nakadai was called in. He's not a comic and the script was not changed, so there's a tremendous focus problem going on all the time. Other people thinks this gives it interest because it's so ambiguous."

Kurosawa's most underrated film, according to Richie, is *The Lower Depths*, based on Maxim Gorky's work. "He rehearsed everybody for one month. It resulted in one of the miracles of ensemble acting. Toshiro Mifune did his finest work in that film."

The Mifune-Kurosawa collaboration came to an end with *Red Beard*, Richie said, because of a two-month hiatus in production that resulted when Kurosawa, ever the perfectionist, insisted on waiting for real snow for some crucial scenes.

Because he had such a bushy beard for that part, Mifune couldn't get other roles. "Mifune is a simple man," Richie said wryly. "He likes horses, cars, and fast women—and they all cost money."

Mifune's dismay at being out of work was silently conveyed to Kurosawa, who likes having his cast and crew around him like a family. "If you don't want to be woken up early to go fishing with Kurosawa or stay up late at night talking about ideas for his next film, Kurosawa finds it very suspicious," Richie recalled. "The atmosphere became so cool that they weren't speaking. The ice was not broken when I tried to get them together in Europe for a TV documentary. There were many awkward silences, while Kurosawa blandly talked about the cold and snow in the Soviet Union where he had been filming *Dersu Uzala*."

Later, when Richie tried to get Kurosawa to hire Mifune for *Ran*, Kurosawa turned on him in anger. "I would never hire *anyone* who appeared in *Shogun*," Kurosawa said. "That was very unfair," commented Richie, "since the only reason Mifune appeared in *Shogun* was because Kurosawa wouldn't use him in his films."

Now that it's so difficult to get financing for his films, Kurosawa has mellowed to the point where he goes to film festivals and gives interviews.

"Nevertheless, his prior attitude has been properly high-handed for such a high and mighty director as Kurosawa. In Japan, he has completely alienated the press. There's a cabal that is quite unfair to him, but he didn't get that reputation as 'the emperor' for no reason. He can't stand people who don't do their jobs properly, but he does it only to people who don't really matter. He will never push his major actors."

Richie said he finds himself more and more in agreement with Kurosawa. Once when he had the temerity to ask what a film means, Kurosawa turned on him with exasperation and said, "Look, if I had known what it means, I needn't have made a film about it."

May 22, 1985
San Francisco Chronicle

Jia Zhangke

"I believe that in Chinese society today there are moments when what's going on is a show."

Paris

J ia Zhangke, the elfin "underground" Chinese writer-director with a formidable international film-festival reputation, flatly declares that he's not as gentle as he looks. "I'm quite wild at heart," he insisted when we met in Paris in June 2003.

That all goes back to a childhood experience that later influenced his three films, banned in China, about the impact of Western influence and new consumer values on small town life.

Born in 1970 in the northern village of Fenyang when the Cultural Revolution disrupted his family's life, he was left as a little boy in the care of a "woman who sold tea and lived in a courtyard that was home to more than ten families. Because of my early life," he said through an interpreter, "I stayed in a different home every night, and that influenced my character. I paid more attention to other people's lives. I cannot be quiet. I cannot be still. I'm wild at heart. I want to move." And movement away from provincial restrictions is the dream of the listless young people in his films *Platform*, *Pickpocket*, and *Unknown Pleasures*, all shot in Fenyang, Shanxi Province, where even sexual attraction sinks into the doldrums and all roads lead nowhere.

The three important points in his trilogy involve friendship, life in a small town, and the portrait of young people today. "I had only one simple idea: to tell what my own life was like. You rarely see life in a small town today, especially the pace of life. It is not like life in the big city, and there are very few people who want to show this kind of experience."

Now he lives in Beijing with his wife, a teacher, but at the time Jia and I met she was studying photography in Paris.

Jia ran into trouble in 1997 with his first "underground" film, *Pickpocket*. It was banned in China for a "very simple reason: a pickpocket cannot be the hero of a [Communist] film." As a result of the ban, when he tried to apply for formal government approval in 2000 for *Platform*, it was denied, as was *Unknown Pleasures* in 2002. Even after he won recognition at many international festivals, the ban remained in effect. (It was lifted only after our interview in January 2004 for *The World* in which provincial people go to Beijing hoping for work and a look at another life in a theme park with famous international landmarks like the Eiffel Tower, the Taj Mahal, and the Pyramids.)

Jia had begun to get into mischief when his father, the son of a doctor, was sent to the countryside and his mother was involved as a soldier in the little civil wars at that time. Like other kids his age, he would try to find saleable rubbish in order make some money. When his father returned in 1977, he never talked about his experience, but he taught Jia to be a good citizen and to obey the law. Instead, Jia began rebelling, listening to music from Taiwan and Hong Kong on "The Radio of the Enemy." The music represented a free life to him, he said, as he recalled a song about wanting a cup of good wine mixed with coffee. Another song, popular with youngsters, asked, "If your mother and your wife dropped at the same time in the water, who will you save first?" It must have been a rhetorical question because he didn't know any of the answers. He just knew that the songs represented something different from their circumscribed existence.

As a teenager, Jia found his own way out while traveling with a performing dance troupe. Later singing and dancing became an integral part of his films. At the same time, he was observing how "all the people hated this culture. I thought at that time, we live in a disaster, but people were not aware of it until they were affected by their poverty." Even the children recognized the inequality that existed in their small town with Communist bureaucrats helping themselves to food and cigarettes out of the reach of ordinary citizens.

He wanted to tell many stories about the injustice he noted and was trying to figure out how to express them. At first, he wrote a lot of poetry and painted, but at twenty he was still uncertain about what path to follow. He saw revolutionary heros in official films and another kind of hero in American movies like *Rambo* with Sylvester Stallone. "I was touched by them, but those heroic characters were very far away from me." The first time he saw a reflection of his own life and experience was in *The Yellow Earth*, directed by Chen Kaige with cinematography by Zhang Yimou, and he realized that cinema could offer the answer for his visions.

When Jia asked a writer in his town how he could become a director, he was told about the experience of Zhang, who had spent ten dismal years as a farm hand and textile worker during the Cultural Revolution. When Zhang applied to the newly reorganized Beijing Film Academy, he was rejected twice for the cinematography division because he was way over the age limit of twenty-two. Eventually, Zhang became the oldest student—and the most famous—in the first Academy class that became known as the "Fifth Generation."

Jia, at twenty-three, also made it into the Academy on his third try, but entered the literary department to learn film theory because the examinations for director and cinematography were too difficult to pass. In the literary department, students were tested for their basic knowledge of cinema: for instance "What is the New Wave in France?" Although he had studied books on cinema, he had never seen anything by Jean-Luc Godard. Nevertheless, he wrote about the rebel hoodlum and cop-killer in the French director's revolutionary film *A Bout de Souffle* (*Breathless*). Six months later, he saw the film and thought it was more powerful than anything he had imagined.

In finding his own oblique way to present the bleak, complex reality of young provincial lives, Jia expressed a calm disappointment that the people who worked on his productions and saw them later on videocassettes didn't understand them. "They thought those were not films. They couldn't understand them. It was normal; it was natural because they had a different experience in watching films."

When Valerie Jaffee, a visiting film scholar, asked Jia why performance plays such a large part in all his films, he replied, "I think that in Chinese society today there are a lot of moments where what's going on could be called a *show*. It's something I find strange. The economy's doing very well, and everywhere you look you have these 'shows,' sort of like economic bubbles, filling up every sector of our lives. I find I can't get away from that topic."

He couldn't anticipate what the reaction would be when *The World* with its humor and gentle satire will be shown "above ground" in China. He thinks that the fake international landscapes in the World Park "can satisfy people's longing for the world. They reflect very strong curiosity and the interest they have in becoming a part of the international culture. I saw all the tourists at the World Park and how overjoyed they were to be there. At the same time this is very strange. To me, it makes for a very sorrowful scene."

June 2003
Unpublished

Geling Yan

PHOTO BY JUDY STONE.

An ambiguous reaction to sexual slavery.

San Francisco

When Geling Yan began trying to discover the life behind the portrait of a famous gold-rush-era prostitute, she had no idea that she would wind up rediscovering herself.

That particular prostitute remained a fascinating mystery, but she assumes the irresistible shape of Fusang in Yan's novel *The Lost Daughter of Happiness*. Not only is she irresistible to Chris, the white boy who falls in love with her when he is twelve, but she is irresistible to the author, who constantly inserts her twentieth-century self into the narration to question Fusang's ambiguous reaction to her sexual slavery.

Although she has had six novels published in China, *Lost Daughter* is her first to be translated into English.

Xiu Xiu: The Sent-Down Girl, a short story originally called *Celestial Bath* in her collection *White Snake*, was made into a critically acclaimed film directed by Joan Chen, who is also preparing the production of *Lost Daughter*.

Yan, forty-two, an Alameda resident, first saw her *Lost Daughter* on display at the Chinese Historical Society, but no other information was available. "But I'm as curious as a cat," she says in only slightly accented English. A slim bundle of nervous energy, she looks quite pleased at her self-description. Soon she got a list of 160 books referring to Chinese prostitution from Larry Engelmann, a San Jose professor who wrote *Daughter of China* with his wife, Meihong Xu.

Yan's husband, Lawrence A. Walker, a former foreign-service officer who had been stationed in China and Taiwan before they met in Washington, D.C., winnowed the list down to determine which books would be relevant, and she began reading.

There was a "wild innocence" to that era, Yan learned, with no formal police or judicial structure in place. People were coming to California from all over the world. Because of the huge disparity between men and women, no formal concept of prostitution existed.

"The women were pets, lovable, respectable creatures desired by men. More than 2000 boys between eight and fourteen had regular visits to the Chinese prostitutes, paying them maybe twenty cents of their candy or lunch money. The boys from inland America had never seen anything like them. These women were so delicate in their totally different costumes and tiny feet. To me that was a great story!"

What wasn't so great was what she learned about white society then, which often viewed Chinese the way it viewed blacks.

"They almost had what Hitler considered as a 'scientific analysis' of race, talking about bound feet, opium smoking, and a decadent lifestyle. I was shocked, totally infuriated that my race was considered so low. What I did was to examine how this prejudice developed. I was very angry at my own people, too. The Jewish people always remembered so clearly the confusion and hatred between them and other races.

"But when my book was published in Chinese in 1995, nobody had any idea that the Chinese had almost as bad treatment as the Jewish. One of the most famous critics in China said he was shaking when he read about the pain the Chinese suffered. The Chinese are very proud of their own culture. It never occurred to them that other races would treat them like a lower race, that they were lynched and killed. One Taiwan critic said the book didn't make him feel comfortable. But you know, the truth doesn't make you comfortable."

Some readers found it strange that Fusang could forgive someone who harmed her. Yan never made it clear whether Fusang continued to love Chris after he participated in her gang rape or if her marriage to Da Yong, her owner, was an act of revenge.

Some women critics wrote that Fusang is Yan's idea of "inner freedom."

"She's a woman who looks vulnerable, who is caged," Yan says. "She can take suffering and accept whatever fate brings her. By accepting it and not fighting it, she becomes invincible. Actually she is so free that she enjoyed sexual pleasure even when she was exploited and enslaved. She feels a physical pleasure in her suffering. If you relax about pain, it's really not so horrible."

Yan said she started playing with that idea years ago when she saw Chinese peasant women carrying babies on their back and on their chests. "They had to do all things on the bottom of the social scale. I wondered how come a person living like an animal, like livestock, is able to enjoy life. Then I started to think that ninety percent of Chinese women are like that. They never thought of fighting it and, by accepting it, they are able to enjoy it a little."

She says when she read the women critics, "They made me re-discover myself. Was that what I envied in Fusang? That I envy someone who is that natural? Because I'm a bunch of bullshit?!" She giggles. "I'm just a bunch of ideas. Instead of living life, I'm so busy analyzing it."

She calls herself a "born loner." Growing up in China when all schools closed during the Cultural Revolution seemed a "heaven-sent" time for the little girl who accompanied her parents to Horse Saddle Mountain City, where her father, a novelist, was condemned to work in a steel mill.

Surprisingly, they had been able to save their valuable library of Chinese and Western classics, collected by Han's U.S.-educated paternal grandfather, who had translated Thomas Hardy's work into Chinese.

The precocious child devoured books as diverse as Lord Byron's *Don Juan* and Romain Rolland's *Jean-Christophe*. Her mother, an actress, worried that the books were too advanced for her. To broaden her interests, Geling joined a performing troupe of the People's Liberation Army as a dancer from ages twelve to nineteen.

"It was fun to be a little soldier and so respected. Other kids followed me and called me 'Liberation Army Aunt.'" But it was a hard life, with dance practice, military training, political lessons, and tours as far away as Tibet, the region she later used for *Xiu Xiu*. Worst of all, other teenagers didn't trust her. Although they cried when she told them bedtime stories like *Les Miserables*, they thought her vocabulary "bourgois and disgusting." To gain respect, she would get up at 4:30 AM to do her dance exercises, then take care of the pigs. "I tried like crazy to show them I could work like a peasant."

In 1979, when the Chinese had a border conflict with Vietnam, Yan applied for a job as war correspondent with the People's Liberation Army newspaper, observing field hospitals. "Mainly what I wrote was anti-war. Seeing young people wounded and dying, I was disillusioned with 'heroism'; and all the propaganda. It was the first time I felt that way."

Beginning to have confidence in her work, she wrote her first script for the Beijing Film Studio in 1979. It was based on *A Song Without Words*, a story about an army musician during the 1950s' Korean conflict, written by her father, who had once been a war correspondent.

While in Beijing, she looked up an older childhood friend who unwittingly became the inspiration for Xiu Xiu. "She told me that when she had to do farm work during the Cultural Revolution, she slept with all the influential men who might have helped her get a residential permit to return to the city, but none of them did. She had been a strong believer in Communism, but after ten years in the countryside, she became very cynical."

Yan was shocked by her friend's experience. "I didn't think that life could be so desperate. I realized I was ignorant and naïve. I began to think about the fact that parts of our nature are hidden in normal life, but an extreme situation can trigger the darkest part of our being." When she started to write novels, she put her characters in extreme situations in order to examine their whole psychology.

After the failure of Yan's youthful marriage and brief trip to the United States, sponsored by the U.S. Information Service, she was studying in Beijing when the protests at Tiananmen Square exploded. Frightened by the gunfire and killings on June 3-4, 1989, she thought, "I cannot tolerate this country anymore."

She left China at the end of 1989 to study English at New York State University's campus in Buffalo. A year later, she was taking a graduate writing course in Chicago to gain an American perspective on fiction when she began to be questioned by the FBI, an interrogation she fictionalizes in her novel *The No Exit Café*. The book has already been published in China and Taiwan.

She was engaged to Walker when she was called into the Chicago office of the FBI after he, in accordance with government regulatons, notified State Department officials that he was engaged to a Chinese woman. She was interrogated for four months, until the Gulf War broke out. After the war ended, they called her in again.

"Larry couldn't understand why the FBI was so interested in me. When they asked me to take a polygraph test, he said, 'I'm quitting this government. That's the way they treat criminals.' He quit on the day I was supposed to take the test. Then someone came from the Security Office of the State Department. He couldn't understand why the FBI was on my case. He was angry. He said, 'This is our domestic problem.'"

After a three-hour interview, "He told me, 'Your fiancé is going to Rome and you're going to get married.' But then Larry had his security clearance suspended. I think the State Department played good cop, and the FBI bad cop with me. I wasn't very surprised because in China you're treated the same way—only they call it 'self-criticism.'"

July 20, 2001
The San Francisco Examiner

Yuan-tsung Chen

The hunger in Jiangsu haunts her.

Berkeley

Yuan-tsung Chen is a tiny, vivacious, and irreverent woman with an incongruously booming laugh, but her voice drops to a whisper when she talks about her year of excruciating hunger during China's Great Leap Forward in 1959-60.

The once-pampered Shanghai girl had left her year-old son and her husband in Peking to go to a remote northern province to prove that she wanted to share the suffering of the peasants. She thought that the books she took along would be her salvation, but after a few days of back-breaking work in the blistering sun and bare-minimum meals (a thin pancake of rough cornmeal—if she was lucky), she dreamed only about food.

Not even her scorn for the excesses of the Cultural Revolution can diminish the lesson of that terrible period. "What are human rights?" she asks quietly. "The first human right is to eat." She tells about that numbing experience in her autobiographical novel *The Dragon's Village*, which Harrison Salisbury called "The Chinese equivalent of Sholokhov's *And Quiet Flows the Don*." The heroine of *The Dragon's Village* is Guang Ling-ling, an apolitical middle-class Shanghai teenager, delighted to get a job away from home as a librarian at the Central Film Bureau in Peking. A year later, she eagerly shares in the new Communist government's initial step toward land reform in 1951.

The first time Yuan-tsung Chen herself "went to the countryside," she was only nineteen. She was staggered by the harshness of the peasants' lives in Gansu province in northwest China and the poverty she shared with them. She was one of a group of seventy, but only four or five were Communists.

"We went not because we understood Marxism, but to help the poor. Land reform was a dream of many centuries, especially among the intellectuals," she said, as we talk in the modest frame house she shares with her husband, Jack Chen, an artist and author of *Inside the Cultural Revolution* and *A Year in Upper Felicity*. He is a British citizen, born in Trinidad, son of a French Creole mother and Eugene Chen, a British solicitor and crusading journalist who became Dr. Sun Yat-sen's foreign minister in the Wuhan Revolutionary Government in 1927. They have lived in the United States since 1972, first in Albany, N.Y., where Mr. Chen was a consultant on Chinese studies for the New York State Department of Education.

Yuan-tsung Chen's original exposure to rural life lasted about five months. Later, she would "go to the countryside" near Peking for a month or so almost every year until she volunteered to join in the Great Leap Forward during a time of terrible food shortages brought on by what she called the government's mistaken policy of taking small plots of land away from the peasants and offering no incentives to work.

Although food was scarce then, the Chens were among the privileged. The Chinese Foreign Press Office, which employed her husband, took care of its valuable overseas workers. Additional food was brought to their home by her sister-in-law and her American husband, Jay Leyda, the American film historian.

But Yuan-tsun felt guilty about the country's hardships. "I ate very little for lunch. I tried not to eat eggs. Here an egg is nothing. There it was a luxury. To ease my conscience, I volunteered to go to the country again, this time for a year, and they sent me to Jiangsu province. It was very hard to leave our baby. Later, I cursed myself when I was in that mess. But since I survived it, I would not like to have missed that experience. It was unique. Without it, I couldn't have written that chapter, 'Spring Hunger,' in my book."

As a girl, when she had read about people starving and later gorging themselves to the point of death, she couldn't believe it. Then something similar happened to her the day before she returned to Peking from Jiangsu province.

110

"Several villages invited us for a meal. It was not good food, but I ate, ate, ate. I nearly died of overeating. After I came back to our own courtyard, I couldn't stand. I couldn't sit. It was awful, but when I heard there was porridge in our canteen, I went to get some. I couldn't eat it. I just *wanted* it."

The hunger of that year haunts her. "I never forget those people. I felt guilty and I'm still feeling guilty because I'm so lucky. One of the reasons I drive myself so hard to write, to convey something to Western readers, is because it eases my conscience that I'm not just sitting here and enjoying myself."

She doesn't stay somber for long. Her irrepressible sense of humor erupts in laughter as she tells her story, interspersing it frequently with the phrase, "I am frank with you" or "Now here is my weak point—I always have a very sharp tongue."

The first time she recalls using that tongue was to lash out at her family's older servants when they beat a younger one, a slave who used to steal their belongings. Her mother had bought the girl "for maybe nine silver dollars" because the child's father threatened to sell her to a brothel. Yuan-tsung's family was not wealthy, but comfortably well-off in the French quarter of Shanghai. Her father, sometimes a banker and sometimes an engineer, had studied at Columbia University for six years, and her mother had been educated at a missionary school. Yuan-tsung was taught that her pretty face was less important than a well-developed mind.

Even as a child, her sharp eye didn't miss much when she observed the spoiled, elegant, selfish Shanghai women. "I think we were rather decadent in Shanghai," she laughed. "It was a very strange world." Too frail to attend school regularly, she immersed herself in European books translated into Chinese: Dostoyevsky, Chekhov, Turgenev, Dickens, and Zola. She was nicknamed "the little old lady." By the time she was twelve, she had decided to have her own career as a writer because she never saw a happy woman in her family's circle.

The war years were spent mostly in Chungking, the nation's capital, but she never recalled hearing anything about the Communist-led Eighth Route Army. After she returned to Shanghai, with the Communists advancing on the city, her schoolmates advised her to leave, but she already thought that Hong Kong was too small for her ambitions.

She had heard that a "writer could only grow in his own country, on his own soil. At that time, I didn't know how tough the Communists could be," she said. "Like a typical young person, I thought I could deal with them."

Just before the Communist takeover, one friend gave her a pamphlet, Mao's *New Democracy*, and advised her to "accumulate some political capital." She never did. "They gave up on me," she said pertly, looking about half of her forty-seven years. "They always criticized me, but you can see they didn't do a very good job. I was never interested in politics. Never or now."

She loved her job as a translator of English-language books and articles on film because it kept her in touch with the outside world. Later during the Cultural Revolution, she had access to the personal libraries of her husband's friends in the Foreign Press Office, and she said with some pride that she read the angry young men of England and the work of the Beat Generation in the United States.

The chapter in her book about Chinese writers—whose real names are used—is based on her notes from actual discussions. "Many of them died in the Cultural Revolution, and the others are precious now [because they are reinstated] to the new government. Nothing I wrote would hurt them. They always talked a lot about how to write a good book and a good play, but I realized I couldn't write that way. It was like collective work."

Ai Qing, one of the best contemporary poets, did influence her. "He read my short stories and said, 'You have a rich imagination. The stories are good, but I don't think we can publish them. In China, if you choose to write, you have to prepare to go all alone sometimes.' A friend of his, a French translator, was having tea with us and he told me, 'Even when you are alone, you should go on.'"

In China, she pointed out, all the stories had to have formulas: "There had to be a party secretary, a Communist. The Communist must be good. You must speak certain things. If I describe the moonlight as beautiful, a Communist must not think that way. He must think of something more important. Moonlight is petty bourgeois."

Although at times she tried to fit her stories to the formula, she didn't succeed by Party standards. "I wrote about a girl who worked in a factory. She tried to improve her work, but she was not thinking only for the Party, for the revolution. She was disappointed in love. She wanted to show she was not the kind of old-fashioned girl who would stop her work just because she was disappointed in love. But they didn't like it because you should *only* think of work for the revolution, for a great ideal."

Her hopeful novel *Sisters*, about the economic struggle of a family before 1949, was written along the accepted lines of "exposing the old society," but it had no Communists in it. Despite this, the novel was going to be published during the liberal "100 flowers of thought" period, but they bloomed too briefly and the book never came out.

During the Cultural Revolution, when her husband was attacked, reading became even more important to them. One day, she borrowed a book about Tom Paine. When the Chens learned how the American revolutionary was imprisoned by the Jacobins and narrowly escaped the guillotine, they couldn't help laughing. "I was comforted," she said, "that other people were stupid like us."

That thought didn't help the day the Red Guard cadre from the Foreign Press office invaded her home and tore down a print of Botticelli's *Birth of Venus*, which they called "decadent," and her husband's early paintings. They confiscated precious art books, their sofa and electric stove, as well as some jewelry that had mainly sentimental value. The cadres warned that they could return at any time.

As soon as the "scoundrels" left, she burned the manuscripts of her two novels and a collection of short stories she had hastily hidden.

"Life is more important than manuscripts," she said. "I didn't cry, but I felt as if I was burning myself. I thought, 'I will remember everything and some day, I will settle accounts with them.'"

May 4, 1980

The New York Times Book Review

4

Transitions

LeRoi Jones

PHOTO BY LEROY MACLUCAS.

"People have said that I'm hateful and bitter."

"My God, where are we? What is this place? What is the reason . . . .
and in this most prosperous of all utopias . . . for the existence
everywhere in it, of filth, ignorance, cowardice?"

—LeRoi Jones

Asilomar, California

It was not a comfortable prospect to face an interview with LeRoi Jones, while still feeling the shock, the power, the hatred, the yearning, and the terrible perception of his two plays, *Dutchman* and *The Slave*.

Everywhere, at the 1964 Negro Writers' Conference in Asilomar, people were talking about Jones, about how he shook everybody up. So that finally, when we met, it was the softness of his voice that was startling, his composure, and the very slightest tinge of anxiety under the curiosity when he asked, "You didn't think I was hateful, did you?"

We had been talking about *The Slave* and *The Toilet* (to be published on his thirtieth birthday along with *Dutchman*). *The Toilet*, about a seduction in the subway shocked white critics and won the annual Obie Award for the best American play done off-Broadway. *The Slave* is set in a white professor's home under siege of a black revolutionary army. Walker Vessel, its leader and a poet, confronts his former wife, a white woman who is the mother of his two children, and her husband, the professor and Vessel's former friend. The encounter is black, terrifying, hopeless, and poignant.

"People have said about me that I'm hateful and bitter," Jones said. "Sure I'm bitter about a lot of things. I'm trying to work with complications of feelings, love and hate at the same time . . . What I'm after is clarity. If it sounds like anger, maybe that's good in a sense."

But this business of being a Negro writer, he said, "That's finally the worst of it, because you have to be faithful as an artist, but you have to carry the weight around of knowing that anything you say is going to be misunderstood simply because you're a Negro. They have to be racial dramas because they're about Negroes."

"Then people want to take your plays and make them strictly social. Melville was a social worker in the same sense I strive to be. But no one would call *Pierre* a novel of racial hatred or *Omoo*. Jesus, nobody calls Mark Twain's *Pudd'nhead Wilson* a novel of racial protest, but the comment it makes on what they call race relations is pretty strong. It's a wild book. I've never seen anything so strong. Nobody would say that's social protest, but it's more so than *The Toilet*."

Jones seemed to be thinking back to Twain admiringly, and said, "The aphorism from Twain is from Pudd'nhead's calendar: 'It was great to discover America, but it would have been better to have missed it . . . ' which is pretty good," Jones grinned, "for Columbus."

Jones didn't discover he was meant to be a writer until his Army experience: the Army shocked him into it. As a kid in Newark, New Jersey, the son of a postal supervisor and a social worker, he had fooled around with writing comic strips and science-fiction, won a lot of scholarships, and went for a year to Rutgers University.

The effort of trying to prove himself in an essentially mediocre situation and the experience of always being an outsider in any school social activities made him transfer to Howard University. At first he was going to major in religion because he thought what he was feeling was religious. "It was the only reference I had." But he switched to chemistry with medicine in mind, then went on to philosophy and English.

"The Howard thing let me understand the Negro sickness. They teach you how to pretend to be white. But the Air Force made me understand the white sickness. It shocked me into realizing what was happening to me and others. By oppressing Negroes, the whites have become oppressive, twisted in that sense of doing bad things to people and justifying them finally, convincing themselves they are right, as people have always convinced themselves."

In 1939, by then married and the father of two, he wrote his first play, *Revolt of the Moonflowers*, but the manuscript was lost. "It was a bad play anyway," he said with a shrug. Mostly he wrote poetry, published *Preface to a Twenty Volume Suicide Note*, *Blues People: Negro Music in White America* and *The Dead Lecturer*.

"I have to write poetry," he said. "Without it, I'd last about maybe a day if I didn't, I'd go crazy. Any artist has a lot of energy that won't respond to anything else. The reason I'm not a violent man—that's what I'm trying to say in *Dutchman*—is that art is the most beautiful resolution of energies that in another context might be violent to myself or anyone else. Artists are out of their minds. They're crazy. When I was in high school, I used to drink a lot of wine, throw bottles around, walk down the street dressed in women's clothes, just because I couldn't find anything to do to satisfy myself. Neither sex, nor whiskey, nor drugs would do it. People need something to do. If you really have something to do, you use up all that energy and violence in making sure you do it right."

In 1960, he started work on a book of fiction, *The System of Dante's Hell*, as well as two other plays, *The Baptism* and *Experimental Death: Unit No.1*. In six "inspired" hours one night, he wrote *The Toilet*, the story of some Northern Negro and white boys, about "how they love and hate and desire and suffer in the limited world they know: the only place where they can be themselves.

"I like it best," Jones said. "It came so much out of my memory, so exact. Just like I was a radio or something and zooom! I didn't have to do any rewriting. That's a wild experience. You know you've really been touched. But it becomes increasingly difficult to do that: it becomes more complicated. *The Slave* is much more complicated and finally I wasn't ready for it yet. It's okay, I respect it. But the complexity has to be worked on."

In his plays, there is the sense of the frightening abyss between black and white, the violence, complete involvement in saying something meaningful today.

"In New York," said Jones, "I have a lot of friends, Larry Rivers, Willem de Kooning, people who say you shouldn't get involved in politics. People say, 'Just stick to your poetry.' There's a constant argument: 'Why are you getting involved?'

"You have to be involved, whether you say you are or not. I'm black. I have to be involved. When I walk down the street, a man doesn't say, 'There goes a cultured nigger.' He says, 'There's just another nigger.'

"All the white friends I have, people I really genuinely love, probably only one or two understand what I mean. I was having an argument with Edward Albee one night and he kept calling me Chinese because I was praising Mao. I was praising him because I think he's a wise man—and Edward said, 'You talk like you don't trust me.' I said,

'There's only one white man in New York I really trust—that's Allen Ginsberg. I trust him and love him completely in that sense.' And Allen and I argue all the time. Edward thought I was putting down white people, but it wasn't that at all.

"The most valuable writing is by outlaws like Ginsberg. The reason I always associate with people thought of as 'beats' is that they're outside the mainstream of American vulgarity. The thinking of *The New York Times* is finally what the so-called cultivated American thinks of as being valuable expression. I edited a book of prose called *The Moderns*, and one of the great values of these writers is that they talk about the Americans who have no vested interests in maintaining some finally invalid image of what America really is.

"It's the whole thing: the whole civil rights thing again. The majority in America are satisfied with what they think America is. But there's a part that isn't. The Negro. That's why things are so difficult for the Negro writers. Because the others, the whites, don't want to credit their version of the world. If they credited that, they'd shoot themselves.

"America is not a white, middle-class country in toto and that's why we are getting ready to be blown up. It's the same thing as asking a comfortable white, middle-class man to describe what America is and asking some poor ghetto Negro. Finally, we are talking about two different Americas. If they really admitted that, finally, they'd admit they are evil people.

"The parallel between Nazi Germany and America—about what's coming. They'd be frightened if they thought about it. All these white people saying, 'I didn't know you were suffering.' The majority of whites think Negroes enjoy being poor and suffering. The middle-class German Jew with a vested interest in Germany was in the same position as the middle-class Negro like Arna Bontemps, who says, 'It's all right. It'll be all right.' Well, maybe it will, but maybe it won't."

August 23, 1964
San Francisco Chronicle

Maya Angelou

She gave up her own bitterness in 1965.

Sonoma County

*A*nd Still I Rise is not just the title of Maya Angelou's theatrical production at the Oakland Ensemble Theater. It's the embodiment of her feeling about life: to look at it honestly, humorously, without despair and to speak softly—but hopefully—with steel at the core.

She has a few lessons to offer from her own rites of passage. At seven-and-a-half, she was raped. At sixteen, she had an illegitimate child. At forty-two, she was named Chubb Fellow at Yale University, following the likes of Dean Acheson and Dean Rusk. Not bad for a tall, skinny black girl whose mind was captured by Shakespeare and Dostoyevsky, but whose body briefly skirted the lower depths of prostitution and drugs.

Later, Angelou told it like it was with incredible buoyancy in her own best-selling remembrance of things past: *I Know Why the Caged Bird Sings* and *Gather Together in*

My Name. The third volume of the autobiography that she shamelessly hopes will earn her the title of "The American Proust" is called *Singing and Swingin' and Getting Merry Like Christmas*. An afternoon with Angelou at her rambling Sonoma County home makes it clear that her merriment is irrepressible. It is an irresistable quality in someone who can't help looking majestic—even barefooted and busy turning out a luscious onion quiche. Her booming laugh surfaces while the deep voice pauses on occasion and lifts into the lines of a spiritual:

"Green trees a-bending

Po' sinner stands a-trembling . . . "

"Now THAT is poetry," declares Angelou.

And Still I Rise, which she conceived and directed, traverses the stages of life in poetry— her own and others—shifting deliberately and almost imperceptibly from one plateau to another. Basically, it always reflects her own indomitable good humor, even though there are brief plunges into tragedy—as in Richard Wright's lines on a lynching.

To those who find it confusing as the ensemble moves from youth to love and work and old age, she says, "The truth is that people transit and don't know when they do so. You knew when you were a child and then you're way into being a youth and you don't know when it happened despite the rituals in Jewish, African, and Asian cultures. Those things simply symbolize the transition.

"On stage, I wanted that flow. I wanted to create atmospheres that would shade and hold poetry so that, unless someone knew it, they couldn't tell where one poem began and the other ended. Most human development is of such a subtle nature that's artificial or melodrama if those changes are too abrupt."

Asked why there was no place in the production for the poetry of LeRoi Jones, she chose her words carefully: "I preached LeRoi before his conversion and said for years, he was one of America's greatest poets. I was remiss in not including him. It's damn difficult to be larger than one's prejudices."

The bitterness that transformed the poet Jones into the politician Imamu Amiri Baraka was like the bitter quality she gave up in 1965. It happened when she was teaching at the University of Ghana and Malcolm X visited there.

"That is one transition I can put my finger on," she said. "I was ready to put down people who were not as black as I was or as enraged as I. Malcolm was very good to me and lectured me as if I were a younger sister. He said the most powerful weapon created was not the H-bomb or nerve gas but a concept written down by Machiavelli, which is separate, rule, divide and conquer.

"He taught me don't put down the person because you're ready to go into the streets and he may be an Urban Leaguer in a tux. The money raised at a dance can help put a black student through school. There's a strata for every person as long as the struggle continues.

"I have decided for myself that the easiest way to teach is not use bluster. Now someone else may come along and need to have the fist balled up all the time. Okay. I don't want to put that down. I just say it's not me.

"I'm trying to be a poet and that means in the way I live, in the way I respond to other human beings. To myself, to my work, to maintain my marriage and be a good mother and a doting grandmother. My grandson, Colin Ashanti, is six months old and oh, dearie me, he is *so* gorgeous."

In her roles as grandmother and writer, she is very consciously emulating and paying tribute to her own Grandmother Henderson, a giant of a woman, who—by herself—raised two sons in Stamps, Arkansas, and then had to take over the upbringing of Maya and her older brother.

Angelou got up to demonstrate how Grandmother Henderson stood erect at 6'2" with her arms locked behind her back. "She would stand as if she knew something so wonderful that no one could touch it. It seemed that a piece of steel went down her head right through her body and she could not be moved."

She died before Angelou could tell her how much she loved her. "The Old Souls" section in *And Still I Rise* is one measure of her feeling.

"People do live in direct relation to their heroes and most heroic for me are the old blacks." She paused for a long, low murmur of awe and wonder. "How much they take and have taken and painful it must be, having swallowed one's pride—it must be awfully lumpy—to make enough to feed us . . . "

She broke off, searching for the right words. "They laughed when they weren't tickled and scratched when they didn't itch and it's come down to us as Uncle Tom-ing. How painful for them to become objects of ridicule by their own."

Angelou noted that the Paul Laurence Dunbar poem "We Wear the Mask" is for people "who have taken so much gaff. I'm joyous that the time has come when the young are saying, 'No more! Don't do that to me!' but if we don't tip our hats to those who took so much, we're denying a rich part of our heritage."

August 17, 1976
San Francisco Chronicle

Donyale Luna

She dreamed of being Snow White.

San Francisco

"A s a man thinketh in his heart so is he," say the Hebrew sages quoted in *The Tibetan Book of the Dead*, now high on the reading list of Donyale Luna. There is another quotation from Buddha: "The phenomena of life may be likened unto a dream, a phantasm, a bubble, a shadow, the glistening or dew or lightning flash: and thus they ought to be contemplated."

Their words may help in contemplating the phenomenon of an astonishingly tall and skinny black girl from Detroit who dreamed of being Snow White, conceived of herself as somehow related to the pale glow of moonlight, blossomed on the cover of *Harper's Bazaar*, and will soon be seen as God's mistress in Otto Preminger's movie *Skidoo*.

"It's a very funny story," said Preminger, telling how he met Luna, his latest discovery, at a party in New York for Twiggy. A stunning Negro model whose face had the hauteur and feline grace of Nefertiti approached and invited him to a showing of a film by Andy Warhol. Preminger suggested they come to his office instead. Luna and Warhol arrived with a half-hour screen test for a Mod *Snow White*. It was Luna's script, her idea of "big camp" to play a towering Snow White with thirteen hippies as dwarfs.

"She showed great talent," said Preminger. "Warhol just sat there with his black glasses, never saying a word. I offered drinks. He said, 'I don't drink.' I asked if there was anything else I could get for him. He said he would like some amphetamines. I didn't have any, but I did have some diet pills. He emptied the pill box, ate them all, and still didn't say anything. The next morning Luna called and asked if I would have lunch. 'What do you want to discuss?' I asked. 'Business,' she said. 'I thought you might want to finance a Warhol film.' I said I didn't finance films; I *direct* them. She said, 'Oh, you direct too.'"

Preminger laughed heartily. That seemed to be the end of the matter until work began on *Skidoo*, Preminger's first comedy since *The Moon is Blue*. As he summed it up, the story involves the "confrontation of hippies with the establishment, but the establishment are gangsters who consider themselves very respectable and are proud of our society." Jackie Gleason plays an ex-gangster who retired seventeen years earlier and lives with his wife, Carol Channing, in the sumptuous, stuffy suburbs south of San Francisco. Groucho Marx will play God, the name used by the gang leader who calls Gleason back into service. Faye Dunaway had been cast as God's mistress until she decided to buy out of her contract with Preminger.

As a replacement, the director thought of Luna for the part of the oversexed mistress who continually cheats on God. To Preminger's horror, when Luna arrived from Rome to take up his offer of a three-year contract, she was wearing a blonde wig and blue contact lenses. "And she brought a young man who turned out to be German. He had more hair than anybody I'd ever seen. An actor. Her fiance."

Preminger looked merry throughout this recital between film takes at a wildly rococo, ivy-covered, turreted mansion. It was not significant that he had hired a Negro for the role. "Any attractive woman could play it," he said. "I just thought of Luna, a hunch. The color doesn't mean anything. Call a character God and everything becomes a little unreal. His mistress becomes unreal. His mistress happens to be a pretty Negro model—just like Luna has a German fiance."

Preminger deepened the dismal feeling I already had about meeting Luna, whom other reporters had found secretive, mysterious, contradictory, evasive, mercurial and insistent upon her multiracial lineage—exotic chameleon strands of Mexican, American Indian, Chinese, Irish, and last—but least escapable—Negro. What must it be like for a girl to grow up and up and up—finally, 6' 2"—not white, not black, in Detroit?

One story had her real name as Peggy Freeman, and said she never mentioned her father. In Detroit, a reporter wrote that she was born Peggy Luna and her father was a Ford Motor Company foreman. In fact, her birth certificate lists Nathaniel and Peggy Freeman as her parents, and Ford has no employment record for such a man.

One fact was clear: photographer David McCabe had changed her life when he spotted her in Detroit. She was leaving a rehearsal of a local TV show in which she was to perform. He asked if she was a model and suggested she go to New York. Instant success at age eighteen. The editors at *Harper's Bazaar* couldn't believe their eyes when she walked in. They immediately had her sketched for the January 1965 cover and later rhapsodized that Luna had the "tall strength and pride of movement of a Masai warrior."

What very few people knew was how desperately she must have needed those very qualities. The same month she made *Harper's* cover, Nathaniel Freeman met a violent and tragic death. He had been a "brutal" man, one of Luna's relatives told me, and that unhappy, scrawny little girl had withdrawn early into a private world. "She was a very weird child, even from birth, living in a wonderland, a dream. 'We'd say, 'Peggy, these things aren't true.' Maybe that's why she was so good in drama class." Or maybe "acting was in her blood," an inheritance from a beloved Irish grandmother before her marriage to a Negro decorator.

Luna had a brief, unhappy marriage in New York ("a gigolo, she's found quite a few of them, they hitch right on to her"). When her year-long contract with Richard Avedon expired, she fled from New York, where she had found "they said beautiful things on one side and stabbed you on the back." Soon she was sending out invitations to her marriage to Maximilian Schell—but it never took place. A Danish photographer was her 'fiancé' in London and Paris while she quickly became the hottest model in Europe. A London magazine burbled: "The beautiful thing about Donyale is that she is a Negress . . . the completely new image of the Negro woman. Fashion finds itself in an instrumental position for changing history, however slightly, for it is about to bring out into the open the veneration, the adoration of the Negro . . . "

So here is Luna, about to break into the movies at this momentous time in her life. She swoops in late, an incredible sight in a black velvet, purple silk-lined cutaway jacket, bell-bottomed trousers, a vivid yellow turtleneck sweater, enormous pink jade, amber, glass, and silver rings on eight fingers, a round gold "caste" mark on the forehead. Her fiancé, Georg Willing, formerly with the Living Theater in Berlin, shows up later in an identical black velvet suit with a white open shirt, revealing a necklace of silver medallions inset with ivory scarabs, three jeweled rings on his left hand, a brass Moroccan bracelet on the right. His brown hair is worn shoulder-length and bangs fall over his forehead. Luna's black hair is brushed tightly off her face and neatly tied in back. Her eyes are adroitly slanted with makeup, but the bright blue contact lenses mask her reactions as effectively as Georg's sunglasses mask his. When she takes the lenses out, her eyes are a warm—but wary—brown. His turn out to be blue, intelligent, somewhat self-questioning, masculine.

Luna's voice is low and vaguely foreign, some never-never-land lilt picked up in London, Paris, and Rome. Rome, so full of "love," compared to the "chaos" here. She is happy, rather elegant, so long as the talk is safely impersonal.

"I'm a very sentimental type," she says. The rings are from people who gave her happiness or were made by ancient gurus who could read the future. The gold caste mark is "for fun, pure fun. I think life should be gay, amusing, not ordinary. When I'm being funny I say, 'It's my third eye.' It's with the Buddhist religion. Not all monks acquire a third eye. When a human being reaches that state—they can actually fly. It's called levitation." She is vague about whether it's Buddhism or yoga that appeals to her. No matter.

"It gives me peace of mind."

Gently encouraged by Georg, she finally admits that she has taken LSD, but won't specify how often. "I think it's great," she adds defiantly. "I learned that I like to live, I like to make love, I really do love somebody, I love flowers, I like the sky, I like bright colors, I like animals. It also showed me unhappy things—that I was stubborn, stupid, selfish, unreasonable, mean, that I hurt other people . . . "

"No, you don't," Georg interrupted softly.

"No, I didn't hurt them, but I could make them feel better. It showed me that I lived in a dream world and I didn't know how to get out and I didn't know why. I'm in the dream world very rarely now."

Her sudden fame was "very, very tough," but she went into it willingly. "For the first time, people said, 'Oh wow, she's beautiful' instead of, 'Oh, wow, she's a freak.'" Now she is writing her "Cinderella" story from the age of seventeen, "when I came out into the world, until twenty-one" for a book, *Luna by Luna*. She insists that Luna is the name of her "real, real father." And she will be billed simply as Luna in *Skidoo*.

At twenty-two, Luna says she finally knows what she wants: "I want to fly together with the man I love. I can have that without money. Money really isn't it." If destiny makes her a star, "that's groovy; if it doesn't, it won't change anything." She's not worried about working with Preminger because "I think he's strong, direct, and honest and I dig that honesty. He's a fantastic moviemaker. He really blew my mind, made a mark in my head with *Exodus*. I flipped when I heard I was playing God's mistress. I thought that was the grooviest role in the world. In everything else, they only wanted me to be myself, a model. For the first time, I can be someone I always wanted to play, a sexy, seductive type of gangster girl. Now it's even better: *God's* girl."

How does her mother react to that? The glow left her face and her voice was wooden. "She's glad, very glad," Luna said, "but she really wants me to come home." Luna has no intention of having her mother meet Georg or of discussing plans for their marriage. "You can say we *are* married. I don't believe in these things. If people love each other, they are together. You don't need a priest to confirm that. When we want children, we'll go through that black-and-white process. I'm not going to send my children to school. Schools today are idiotic. They tell lies and make them the truth. Schools just bring about a lot of bad complexes. I have them too. Hangups, hangups. I hope I'll be good enough to teach my children myself. I won't do what my mother did to me. Parents deprive a child of the chance to really live a life. A son calls his father and says he's happy because he's living with the girl he loves and the father calls him a 'gigolo.' The child is put down for something he finds happiness in. Like my mother who wanted me to be a nurse."

Did she hope her new job would open up more movie roles for Negro women?

Icily, she replied, "I don't think about that."

"She's white," said Georg, "didn't you know?"

But then Luna reconsidered for a moment. "If it brings about more jobs for Mexicans, Chinese, Indians, Negroes, groovy. It could be good. It could be bad. I couldn't care less."

Pressed, she fumbled for an explanation of her racial background. "My mother is Mexican," she said.

"Luna," I responded quietly, "it's as impossible to be a quarter-Negro in America today as it was to be a quarter-Jew in Nazi Germany."

"That's America's problem," she retorted. "I would feel for any person who got shot down by a machine gun. I would feel the same for a Mexican or a Chinese. I'm not an American. Yeah, I'm an American *on black and white* but I'm me, *I'm me*. When I got out of school, I started seeing and that's when I said, 'Do away with the churches, the police, the government, because it's all bunk.' It does no good at all. It only creates things like Vietnam, Hiroshima, race riots and frustration, confusion and destruction. What I know about America and what I see is a great deal. A lot of things I wish I had never seen because they are ugly and disgusting. They exist all over the world, not only in America, but they're more out in the open here. I could talk for twenty years about the things I've seen in America."

Then she carefully slipped the blue contact lens over brown eyes that had seen more than they cared to see and sauntered out to pose for photographers, just like any other model in the U.S.A.

May 19, 1968
The New York Times

Julie Dash

"My father is in the Gullah tradition, my mother is from the mountains and very proud she is not Geechee."

San Francisco

When Julie Dash was growing up in a Long Island housing project, she used to lie that she ate ham and eggs for breakfast instead of her family's traditional rice and fish. Today she's proud to defy convention and determined to prove that there's more to Afro-American filmmaking than urban violence and ugly sociological realities.

She was once a woman scorned by the Hollywood establishment for her poetic drama, *Daughters of the Dust*. But the film's critical and commercial success in New York has changed the tune of marketing mavens. Her impressionistic portrait explores a

West African Gullah family living on the Sea Islands off the South Carolina coast in 1902.

The New York Times called Dash "a strikingly original filmmaker." *Newsday*'s critic raved over the film: "The breadth of its ambition, the boldness of its vision are reminiscent of the best work by such European masters of cinematic allusiveness as Ingmar Bergman and Michelangelo Antonioni."

The film celebrates six women of the Peazant family as these descendants of slaves prepare a sumptuous beach picnic before their departure for the "promised land" up north.

Nana, the eighty-eight-year-old matriarch, knows it's "no land of milk and honey," but she can't deter the others. Her daughter-in-law Haagar is contempuous of Nana's closeness to her Yoruba roots and superstitions. Her daughter Viola has turned away from "hoodoo" spirituality and become a Baptist. Nana's pregnant granddaughter Eula is viewed nervously by her husband, who thinks the unborn child is the result of her rape by the white landlord. The narrator is the adult voice of that child.

Tensions rise when Nana's long-absent daughter Yellow Mary returns from Cuba, where she has been a prostitute. The other women, all virtuously clad in white, suspiciously look down on Mary and her intimate woman companion.

The fabric of their lives unfolds at a leisurely pace, in an aura of mystery and magic and humor, while the camera revels in the wild beauty of sea and sky. The impenetrable Geechee dialogue—English with a West African accent—is occasionally "translated" in subtitles. Dash deliberately refused to tie everything together in neat narrative passages, but some subtleties of structure defy instant comprehension.

"I was raised on TV and being spoon-fed stories and images with nothing left to chance of the imagination," Dash recalled. That wasn't the way her South Carolina family told their tales, nor was it the style of the European films that began to challenge and intrigue her.

Dash—a tall, handsome woman wearing a headband of orange, green and black over her intricately braided hair—thinks it's time for a change. "As we move forward toward the twenty-first century, it's important to have a major push in terms of black cinema, that we're challenged more, and we challenge the audience more," Dash emphasized. "We have to get away from old notions of how an Afro-American film should look and how it should be structured. That's not a criticism of what other black filmmakers are doing today. All directors have their own voice and to be a filmmaker we all have to be a little weird," she said with a laugh. "We all have something we want to say that we've carried around since our childhood."

She has the memories of her parents who came from different ways of life in South Carolina. "My father is in the Gullah tradition. My mother is from the mountains. She is very proud she is not Geechee because until recently to be called Geechee was an insult. It meant that you were perhaps uneducated and maintained West African traditions and beliefs which are not desirable for people trying to assimilate into the mainstream. Because the Geechee were known as loud-talkers, high-spirited people who loved to argue, the assimilated Afro-Americans would look down on them."

Dash and her older sister used to be embarrassed that they ate rice three times a day when they yearned for the french fries their friends enjoyed. But, that didn't spoil their pleasure when they watched their father cook.

"He was proud of the fact that he was a better cook than my mother. His preparation of gumbo with okra and corn was almost ceremonial. He'd start early in the morning and cut everything by hand. Then he'd put the ingredients into beautiful, colorful mounds. It was important to wait adding shrimp until the last because it would be too tough if it was overcooked. My sister and I would come around bugging him, and he'd put the sticky okra stems on our heads so they looked like green horns and we'd go scare our mother. It was the ritual every time."

The spiritual traditions of the Geechee also were different. "I like to be very careful today talking about 'voodoo,'" Dash said. "'Vodun' came from West Africa. In Hollywood, it became 'voodoo,' something to be laughed at. It implied the coming of zombies, which is all very negative, and the religion and practice is not like that. The day-to-day religion was about ancestor fellowship. Those ancestors who were deceased were very much part of your everyday life. You spoke to them. It's not ancestor worship. They were part of day-to-day existence. When they speak of old souls, it's like a partnership with those in the past."

Dash had planned to become a clinical psychologist, but she developed a curiosity about film after visiting a friend enrolled in a cinema workshop at the Studio Museum of Harlem. "It was a challenge and I like a challenge," she recalled. She began going to the workshops three nights a week. In her junior year at the City College of New York, she changed her major from psychology to filmmaking. "What I learned in the psychology courses was that your ideas weren't valid if you were not speaking in the jargon of the various schools of psychology. Films are just like that, too. For the most part, it's just a continuation of what is already established. If you try to introduce a new thought, people who are supposed to know everything say you don't know what you're doing, if it doesn't fit into their preconceived notions."

When she got into the conservatory program at the American Film Institute, her teachers wanted her to do 'slice-of-life' dramas set in the black ghettos. "The problem for me was, that's where I came from. It's not what I wanted to see. You don't come from a project and want to watch that. The lady who lived above us used to get beat up every night. I could see that every weekend. I didn't want to pay money to see it in the movies."

She started writing *Daughters of the Dust* as a concept for a silent film, but her advisors kept telling her to be more like Martin Scorsese. After two years at the AFI, she found more autonomy at UCLA. She was able to write and direct a thirty-four-minute, prize-winning drama, *Illusions*, starring Lonette McKee as a light-complexioned studio executive who had made it because nobody realizes she is an Afro-American.

She also shot a seven-minute dance film and *Diary of an African Nun*, a thirteen-minute adaptation of an Alice Walker short story.

Dash won a Directors' Guild award for student filmmaking for *Diary*; her three films have been shown worldwide. Universal and Warner Bros. executives said they loved her work, but she was not able to get a studio deal. So she kept employed by making non-theatrical independent films.

Finally, her sample tape for *Daughters*, shot by her husband, Arthur Jaffa, was screened during a weekend retreat for minority filmmakers at Robert Redford's Sundance Institute. Lynn Holst from public television saw it and told Dash she had "never seen anything so sensual, so lush, and so beautiful about Afro-Americans," and she offered to help develop the project.

"She is responsible for this film being done," Dash said gratefully. PBS put up $650,000 for the $800,000 film. The remainder came from the National Endowment for the Arts, a German company, and a foundation in Georgia where Dash now lives with her seven-year-old daughter. A risk-taking distributor got it off the festival circuit and into theaters.

Dash has ideas for three other films about black women. When she makes her next production deals, she is not going to forget the large New York agency people who saw *Daughters* prior to its successful opening. "They said I had no future because I'm not a celebrity director. I wasn't surprised. To this day, I still don't have an agent, but things have changed. Now I'm going to pick and choose."

March 29, 1992
San Francisco Chronicle

5

What are Dissidents Good For?

Miklos Haraszti

"All our societies are velvet prisons."

Budapest

"What are dissidents good for?" asks Miklos Haraszti in *The Velvet Prison*, his "pessimistic" book about artists under state socialism. The answer to that question may come when Hungarians go to the polls March 25, 1990, for their first free parliamentary elections and find Haraszti's name on the ballot.*

When Haraszti wrote *The Velvet Prison*, for an underground publication in 1986, he could not have guessed how prophetic his words would sound just before the 1990 elections: "They [the dissidents] will want their art to play an active social role one day in shaping the consciousness of the culture of the nation. . . . Indeed, things might take such a turn that they become necessary to the culture that today excludes them."

The novelist George Konrad once described his friend Haraszti as "a dissident who mocks himself . . . He is at his best when involved in confrontations: as a civil-rights advocate, anarchist, militant poet, clown, agitator."

In 1989, Haraszti was a "dissident writer in residence" at Bard College in New York, working on an autobiographical novel about the opposition underground in Hungary. Then "politics snatched me away," he recalled in a quick luncheon interview during his campaign for election on the Alliance of Free Democrats' ticket.

After his time out in New York, Haraszti returned to a different Budapest. The book that had got him arrested and put on trial in 1973, *A Worker in a Worker's State*, was officially—and successfully—published late last year. In 1973, he had received a suspended sentence of eight years imprisonment for his caustic, revealing report on working conditions at the Red Star Tractor Factory, but the trial served primarily as a warning to Hungarian dissidents. Earlier, he had been imprisoned briefly a number of times following his first expulsion from the University of Budapest for helping to establish a Vietnam Solidarity Committee in 1964.

Then, a few years ago, criticism of the regime began to emerge in official publications. "The self-liberation of the press is the secret force behind the Hungarian way of going away from communism," Haraszti recalled with considerable pride. He could claim a gadfly's credit since he was one of the editors of the main samizdat journal, *Beszelo*. "The name is a pun, meaning the one who speaks out, and it also means the visiting place in prison."

By 1988, Haraszti commented, "The whole business of culture and the press and, later, radio and TV, got out of hand. When [the premier] Janos Kadar was ousted in May 1988, it was already the result of the press criticizing him quite freely. People's discontent on the street was somehow channelized into the press."

Did he ever anticipate the present situation?

"Yes. Yes." Haraszti responded eagerly in lightly accented English. "I'm quite proud of a prediction I made in 1980 when I published my first printed—not typewritten—samizdat book, *A Belated Introduction to Kadarism*. I wrote that Kadar would fall in the eighties and with that, the most viable form of communism would collapse in this country." **

The new parliament, Haraszti predicted, "would consist of quite a few writers, actors, doctors, but no professional politicians. It will be a parliament of judgment over the past and will lay down the transition to a democratic system and to a market-oriented system.

"A market-based economy is a must if we want to become part of the world and have the fundamental features of democracy like constitutionalism, a multiparty system, rights for minorities, and the rights of self-government for cities."

He doubted whether Hungarian workers would vote with their special interests in mind.

"They know that transition to a market system is unavoidable. They know that most of our enterprises are non-enterprises. They are not productive and they're not viable in a real market. Our job is to make them understand that there's a price we all have to pay in getting rid of the Stalinist economic system. That's different from what will come later, which is the kind of economic policies they will choose."

The issue of anti-Semitism emerged indirectly during November's nationwide referendum on whether presidential elections should precede or follow free parliamentary elections. The Alliance of Free Democrats, concerned about a new consolidation of Communist power if there was a quick presidential election, won an unexpected, stunning victory when it successfully urged voters to cast ballots for free parliamentary elections first.

The front-running Hungarian Democratic Forum, considered by many to be populist and have an extreme nationalist orientation, urged *"real* Hungarians" not to vote. It was not a phrase that needed translation. "These are allusions that work in an anti-Semitic context," Haraszti—who is Jewish—said.

Pointing out that the issue of anti-Semitism is "sensitive and disturbing," Haraszti carefully emphasized: "There is no anti-Semitic party in Hungary. All major opinion leaders and all major parties officially reject anti-Semitism, but some politicians in some parties are making declarations that arouse this kind of sensitivity." Haraszti—who was born in Jerusalem in 1945—was brought to Hungary in 1948 when his parents returned to their native land.

"The Alliance is being attacked for slandering other parties for being anti-Semitic," Haraszti said. "They say we are orchestrating those attacks in America. So therefore I stress we are not saying that whole parties are anti-Semitic, but there are some things in some parties that are quite aggressive. You won't be able to find the word Jewish in an openly anti-Semitic context."

He noted that the party which was not able to control its more bigoted members "officially made very moving gestures when it called upon its followers to go to a village where there are Jewish cemeteries and take care of them because no Jewish citizens are left in that community. They were eliminated in the Holocaust."

Haraszti—who spent a year in Germany and in France, as well as the U.S.—is aware that "all our societies are velvet prisons. Nobody thinks the West is paradise. Nobody thinks it's a perfect society—quite the opposite. It's a sad way of making democracy and giving up the idea of a perfect society.

"But the main lesson we have learned from communism *is* that society is what it is. I'm a fundamental liberal in the sense that it's up to the people to decide what they want. The maximum I can wish to have in a society is freedom to say what I wish and somehow have a system that stops other people from oppressing my wishes and stops me from oppressing other people's wishes. I think this *dull* commonplace of liberalism is such a vividly living thing in Eastern Europe today that it's the ruling force of history.

March 21, 1990

San Francisco Chronicle

* Haraszti served as a member of Parliament from 1990-94.

** In 2005, the fifty-five participating states of the OSCE (Organization for Security and Cooperation in Europe) appointed him The Representative on Freedom of the Media of this inter-governmental organization. The watchdog institute he is heading operates from Vienna, Austria.

William Abrahams and Peter Stansky

"Legends about Orwell accrete like barnacles to a boat."

San Francisco

There's never been a spring like this for author/editor William Abrahams: a floodtide of books. It's exciting enough to celebrate publication of the George Orwell biography *Orwell: The Transformation* (Volume 2), which he wrote with Peter Stansky, but this "tortoise and the hare" San Francisco Bay Area writing team won't have much time for celebration.

Prize Stories: The O. Henry Awards (1980), edited by Abrahams, is coming out, followed in rapid succession by new books he has edited for Pauline Kael, Lillian Hellman, Ann Cornelisen, Evan S. Connell, Alvah Bessie, et al. And Abrahams hasn't yet stopped beaming with pride over his find of 1979: Thomas Flanagan's novel, *The Year of the French*, which won the National Book Critics Circle Award.

Abrahams and Stansky, a Stanford University history professor and author of last year's critically acclaimed biography *Gladstone: A Progress in Politics*, have been receiving almost unanimously rave reviews in England for their Orwell biography. British critic and author V.S. Pritchett had glowing words about them in the intellectuals' Michelin Guide, *The New York Review of Books*. Best of all was a brief note that arrived in the mail: "I found the book compulsive reading," Signed: Graham Greene.

The question is: Are Abrahams' writers a trifle put out because "Billy" is doing his own thing this month?

Chuckling at the thought, Abrahams said, "Fortunately there are no biographers in my group." Also, he keeps his writing distinctly separate from his role as a Holt, Rinehart and Winston editor, one of the most respected in the country.

It was his authors who kept him from buckling down to finish the Orwell biography sooner. The smaller and senior partner is the tortoise of the team anyway. "Peter," Abrahams says, "is brisk, fast, and efficient."

They interview people together, write separate drafts, swap drafts, and rewrite. The final version "really is a mosaic" of both their styles, although friends think Abrahams writes the literary part and Stansky, the history.

The problem in writing a biography, Abrahams complained, "is that you're not only judged by what you yourself have done, but the subject is being judged too. I always get cross because a helluva lot of work goes into writing a biography, and it's amazing how little attention is paid to that."

For instance, there are legends "that accrete like barnacles to a boat" around Orwell, author of *1984*, that caustic vision of the future; *Homage to Catalonia*, the pro-anarchist, anti-Communist, personal account of his own military experience in the Spanish Civil War; and *Animal Farm*, an anti-Russian fable.

"The Orwell myth starts with people who didn't really know him or knew him later," Abrahams said. "It is a myth of his own making. He chose to create the illusion or allowed people to believe that his circumstances were far worse off than they were. The myth suggests he completely cut himself off from his class and that he was a terrifically political man. But his father was a retired civil servant. The boy—Eric Blair was his real name—went to a very fashionable school. It was still a very social England with all its class differences. His family was anything but working class. But he wanted to create the impression that he was this plain-spoken ordinary bloke.

"Well, he really wasn't. Ordinary blokes don't write that way. At first, he knew nothing about politics and didn't give a damn," Abrahams said. "He began to change when he went to Wigan Pier to investigate the lives of coal miners and the unemployed in the thirties. He was fascinated with the poor *qua* the poor. It never seems to have crossed his mind that their lot could have been better."

In their first volume, *The Unknown Orwell*, Stansky and Abrahams uncovered a great deal of new material dealing with the life of Blair before the publication of his first book, *Down and Out in London and Paris*.

"We had so much stuff that had never been used," Abrahams said, "but it in no way altered the preconceived statements made about Orwell over and over again."

The story of Orwell's courtship of his first wife, Eileen (who died in 1945) has never been told. Abrahams and Stansky believe that marriage, described in the new volume, was the third key element in Orwell's transformation, along with his experiences at Wigan Pier and in Spain.

"The one person who got left out until us was Eileen," Abrahams pointed out. "She is a very important force because he was cold. It's that dour English strain that comes through, and she loosened him up. After their marriage, he seems to me to become a very-so-much-nicer person."

They found letters she wrote from Morocco after the Orwells had left Spain. "They were marvelous," Abrahams said. "You can see what a lively and fascinating woman she must have been and how good with him. Of course, he's a master of prose, but he's forever generalizing. It drives me up the wall. You pick up a letter and find him announcing that 'Conrad has to be a genius because no women like him.'"

Abrahams burst out laughing. "I mean—that's a rather odd remark."

Ask the biographers how they really feel about Orwell and Stansky smiles. Why?

"Because . . . " he began when Abrahams interrupted with a warning laugh.

Unperturbed, the scholarly Stansky continued, "You probably shouldn't use it, but I like Orwell more than Billy does, or, eh, I tend to be more indulgent. A biographer should—and I know it sounds patronizing—look on his subject as his children, unless you're writing the biography of a monster. Billy is probably more acute in understanding them. I think I'm more forgiving or takes their foibles calmly.

"If we've succeeded in making Orwell vivid, it's partially because Billy reacts to his subjects as if they're in the room and they are people you like or dislike."

"That's unfair," Abrahams retorted. "I'm very sympathetic to the Orwell whom we have presented in this book—the TRUE Orwell. Which is rather different from the Orwell he chose to present. How can you not be sympathetic to a young writer who is working so hard and is so determined to succeed? What I don't like in Orwell—and it begins to abate as he becomes more successful—is his envy and mean-spiritedness about other people."

The Orwell biography developed out of their interest in the Spanish Civil War. Abrahams, a Bostonian, vividly recalled the pro-Loyalist sentiment he shared when he was an undergraduate at Harvard University and the excitement of hearing about it from Andre Malraux, who had raised an air force squadron for the Loyalists.

Stansky, twelve years younger, growing up in the apolitical fifties in New York City, thought the thirties were much more interesting years. He had been introduced to them through two albums of International Brigade songs, which he loved. Later, his interest in England's Bloomsbury literary group dovetailed with his curiosity about Spain.

In the Yale stacks, he found two memoirs of Julian Bell (Virginia Woolf's nephew) and John Cornford, a young British poet. They both had died fighting in Spain. Stansky wrote his senior thesis on them and Orwell.

At first, Abrahams and Stansky planned one book on all three, but soon found they had too much material. *Journey to the Frontier*, about Cornford and Bell, was their first collaboration. They don't know if they will continue their life of Orwell past the Spanish period. For one thing, Orwell's widow, Sonia, has appointed an official biographer.

For another, said Stansky, "Orwell in the forties does become a cold warrior, a man who sees Communists under the bed. Unfortunately, the whole Cold War aspect is there and it's not an area that interests or attracts us."

"But also, Peter, there is a difference, a rather sinister difference in one of the paperback editions of his work," Abrahams said, pointing out that *Animal Farm* and *1984* are among the most successful paperbacks, selling in the hundreds of thousands of copies. "One foreword quotes Orwell's famous remark, 'Every line of serious work that I have written since 1936 has been written directly or indirectly against totalitarianism and for democratic socialism as I understand it.'

"And in this book prepared for distribution in American high schools," Abrahams noted, "they've left out 'and democratic socialism.'"

May 6, 1980
San Francisco Chronicle

Vladimir Dedijer

"Every political movement which puts aside ethics and morals carries within it seeds of its own destruction."

San Francisco

Vladimir Dedijer is a poet who helped to make a revolution, but refused to be devoured by it. It was a refusal so honest, so dignified, so principled that few who came in contact with him, both within the Yugoslav government and outside it, failed to be moved.

The man who fought the Fascists with Tito, wrote the Yugoslav president's authorized biography, and differed with Tito, was in the San Francisco Bay area to lecture at Stanford University and the University of California. He established the ground rules for the first newspaper interview he has given since he left Yugoslavia in 1959:

"When I am outside of my country, I never criticize my government."

He was a newspaperman himself once, so he said it gently and with a twinkle.

But in his autobiographical book *The Beloved Land*, published in 1961, he wrote: "Yugoslavia will be able to solve its problems, to heal its traditional traumas, only in a world which unites people, not divides them; this can be brought about, not by reducing different cultures to a level of uniformity, but by allowing them to develop in an atmosphere of tolerance and freedom.

"Such a way of thinking may seem emotional, neo-romantic, anti-political—but this is the way my heart beats. To think or act otherwise would be to betray the best years of my life."

There is little bitterness in this man who stood by his wartime comrade Milovan Djilas, former vice president of Yugoslavia (despite their political differences), when Djilas was tried and sentenced for writing critical views of the regime in the foreign press.

"In my view," Dedijer said at that time, "a Communist should be first of all a human being, and every political movement which puts aside ethics and morals carries within it the seeds of its own destruction."

Dedijer—who had been present at the founding of the United Nations in San Francisco—received a suspended sentence, was ousted from the Yugoslav parliament, and for a while eked out a meager living by writing for foreign scholarly periodicals.

I had met him briefly while he was "in the doghouse" in Belgrade in 1959. There was an indefinable quality of integrity and courage about this rugged and quiet man. Political realities forced him to be suspicious of a stranger, but it was clearly apparent that it was an unnatural reserve for an uncalculating and generous person.

He is a rebel still, although now his life is devoted to writing and contemplation, and he has both anger and contempt for intellectuals who become spokesmen for any country's power structure.

Since he left Yugoslavia with his family in 1959, he has taught and done research at Manchester University and is a fellow at St. Anthony's College, Oxford, on leave now for a year to do research at Harvard University.

At Harvard, Dedijer feels, the intellectuals are "too much identified with power. In England, they are poorly paid and more independent toward the government.

"This balance between a state and society is important. The role of the intellectual should be corrective of the functioning of a state and a counterbalance."

Before the war, Dedijer had been a reporter for the esteemed Belgrade newspaper *Politika* and had translated into Serbo-Croatian O. Henry, Mark Twain, Pearl Buck, Kipling, Galsworthy's *Forsythe Saga*, H.G. Wells, and Sidney and Beatrice Webb.

"There was always this dichotomy within me," he said. "I'm a little bit of a kind of poet—although I look like a butcher—a poet and revolutionary. I'm primarily moved in everything by my emotions.

"Now what I'm doing is the best part of my life. I do lots of contemplating. I put things on paper and admire what I have written and the next morning I look with horror and cynicism at what I have written and start again.

"Even when I was a Partisan," Dedijer recalled, "the best part was walking through the mountains, looking at the stars and thinking."

A Partisan colonel, he was wounded three times; his wife Olga, a surgeon, was killed by the same bomb that wounded Tito. ("I declined to make any critical statements against Tito while abroad," he wrote, "because whatever our differences, we have so much more in common. I cannot forget the days of the war when I was at his side almost daily, witnessing extremes of horror and suffering . . . I could never forget that the bomb which killed Olga at Sutjeska wounded Tito also.")

After the war, while still recovering from a severe head wound and feeling guilty about his wife, who had given her life for the Partisans although she did not share Dedijer's political beliefs, he met his present wife, Vera.

He described the ensuing conflict in his book, asking: "Ought a man to keep sorrow to himself? Does emotional torment, which has no outlet, bring him to death? To suffer in silence—is this the most difficult of all?"

"Vlado" Dedijer is a symbol of courage to many people, but to carry out this role while suffering tragedy and personal loss can be an almost insupportable burden to a man who knows what is expected of him.

With $500,000 in royalties from his biography of Tito, he established a hospital bearing Olga's name in Niksic. In 1963, he visited her grave, a grave he had dug with his own hands on Mt. Romanija.

Following his political difficulties in 1955, Dedijer, who is also a lawyer, decided to "sharpen my mind" by writing *Philosophy of Law*, a book that dealt with military conventions during a war: capitulation, surrender, the influence on the law of historical forces. His *Sarajevo Assassination* is a study of the Bosnian populists who killed Franz Ferdinand.

A knowledge of their struggle came early to young Dedijer. His uncle had been a member of the secret society Young Bosnia, and a friend of Gavrilo Princip, whose act of assassination set off the first World War. Dedijer's father, a member of the first Bosnian parliament, had also been involved in their activities.

"As a child, their deaths tormented me," Dedijer said. "This group of assassins were poets and revolutionaries at the same time, a perfect combination. Because a poet is always a rebel and always tries to find new forms to push society to greater perfection." Young Bosnia was influenced by Walt Whitman. The American writer had been translated by Ivo Andric, a member of Young Bosnia's literary society and winner of the 1961 Nobel prize for his *Bridge on the Drina*.

144

"Their basic inspiration came, however, from Serbian folklore and poetry that sang the right of resistance, the right of tyrannicide," Dedijer said. "Bosnia had no liberty under Austrian subjection and they felt violence was justified against a system of violence."

Now Dedijer is working on a book about European resistance during World War II—resistance to the Nazis by Catholics, Communists, and Jews. He will return to Stanford to lecture on Hannah Arendt's book, *Eichmann in Jerusalem*.

"May I make a sweeping statement about her?" he asked.

"The U.S. culture has been tremendously influenced by the contribution of German Jews. Einstein is a symbol not only of a great scientific mind, but one who understood the problems of human misery. Hannah Arendt is for me a complete denial of this great Jewish inheritance. She has assimilated so much of the Bismarckian mentality that she rejected what was best in the Jewish way of life—the right of resistance.

"If you connect her report on the Eichmann trial with her new book *On Revolution*, you see that she rebels against the concept of the Jews as an oppressed minority. She is basically a conservative republican who denies the underdog the right to revolt today. She can only see one side of the American revolution. She skips over the revolutions in Africa, Asia, and Latin America. Her mentality is one of defending the establishment and the fixed order. She doesn't see the miseries of other people. She doesn't see the poverty that is growing in the world, the tremendous differences between the poor and the rich nations. Her mind is cool; it gives a woman without a heart for the underdog."

During the war, Dedijer recalled, when all the Sephardic Jews in Belgrade were gathered together for the final extermination, a young Jewish Communist could not bear the thought of living with all her people gone, and she gave herself up to the Nazis. Dedijer was shocked at her suicidal act, but after the war when he learned that nine out of ten of his own friends had perished, he understood her sad decision.

"I am here defending the idea of martyrdom," he said. "The martyrdom of those six million Jews cemented the future of all others because it became then a question of conscience for every man with a heart."

When Dedijer finishes his book on resistance, he said he had only one wish:

"To go back to our mountains, and be a shepherd. There is such a beauty there. In no place is the grass so soft, the colors so intense. I have done what I wanted to do, written what I had to write. I don't like this high type of materialistic civilization. I'm basically a conservative peasant. I'm like an eel. They are born in one place and travel far away, and when they get older, they come back to their place of birth to die."

August 11, 1963
San Francisco Chronicle

Norma Barzman

"Cossacks come in all different shapes and sizes. They don't have to be on horseback."

Beverly Hills

The sunny two-bedroom apartment in Beverly Hills is ablaze in color, paintings of purple and pink cows, a film poster of *The Boy with Green Hair*. No swimming pool like the one at the posh Mougins estate near Cannes. No friendly neighbor like Pablo Picasso. And now here's Norma Barzman, mother of seven, grandmother of six. Her husband of forty-seven years is dead and so are most of her many lovers. She's living alone and relishing it. Jubilant, she cries, "I finally feel that I'm the mistress of my own life!"

And what a life it has been. She talks about it, restlessly walking around the living room, pointing out the artifacts and posters salvaged from precious collections. Her old pal, blacklisted screenwriter/director Abe Polonsky, kept nagging her to write her memoir, yelling all the time, "'And you either do it honestly! Or you don't do it at all.' Abe screamed at me," she said, not at all abashed. "I think I bring this on with men. They love to shout at me!"

It wasn't easy, even after years of therapy, but Norma Barzman laid out her life with breathtaking frankness in *The Red and the Blacklist*. *Red* printed in red on the book jacket and red on her name. Revealing how a rich Jewish girl—a Radcliffe College dropout for a quicky marriage—and a Hearst journalist—became a Hollywood Communist, threw a lemon-meringue pie at a poor, Jewish, sexist screenwriter and married him.

In 1948, with careers underway and two babies to support, the Ben Barzmans were nervously awaiting the possibility of being called to testify before the House Un-American Activities Committee. To stay or flee, that was the question. Ben Barzman's mother, who had fled anti-Semitic pogroms in Czarist Russia, told them to go. "'Don't hang around like the Jews in Germany when you see what's coming, when you see the Cossacks,'" Norma recalled 'Mumma's' advice. "Ben told his mother, 'They're not Cossacks. They're U.S. Congressmen.' His mother retorted, 'Cossacks come in all different shapes and sizes. They don't have to be on horses. Go!'"

When Norma Barzman tells this story to the crowds at her 2003 book-signings, it's more than a matter of ancient history. She cites two ominous cases: the Dixie Chicks, whose songs were boycotted even after the lead singe, Natalie Maines, from Lubbock, Texas, apologized for saying she was ashamed that President Bush is from her home state. And the firing of Ed Gernon, executive producer of the CBS miniseries *The Rise of Hitler*, after he gave an interview to *TV Guide* comparing Americans' patriotic acceptance of the Iraq war to the crazed militaristic climate in post-World War I Germany that helped Hitler's rise to power.

"We have to elect candidates who won't be terrified to say the frightful things that Bush is doing to this country," she tells the audiences. "It's true that I fled the other time. Ben had already written *The Boy with Green Hair*, and we went to England to make *Christ in Concrete*, but we knew damn well this was a way of going and getting out without waiting for a subpoena. This time I don't feel like leaving, even though my children urged me to come back to France. Maybe I'm already blacklisted in a certain way." She wonders whether she hasn't been invited to talk about her book on any major TV or radio programs because her outspoken views are still not acceptable. She *could* just talk about Sophia Loren, Charlton Heston, John Wayne, Marilyn Monroe, Anthony Quinn, and all the big names she knew, but that wouldn't stop this exuberant woman from saying what she *thinks*.

And she tells plenty about how the Barzmans and other blacklisted writers and directors survived exile in Europe, about why so many had been drawn to the left during the depression, during the Civil War in Spain and her ultimate disillusionment with the Soviet Union as a beacon of hope in a world that needed it.

What Norma Barzman needed was recognition and support for her burning desire to write on her own, novels, screenplays, whatever, not just to be an adjunct to Ben, who resented and resisted her attempts at independence. Some in the audiences at her readings wanted to know if all the blacklisted were Communists, but others were keen to hear about her affairs, and (oh lord!) who was the best lover. "The affairs I cited," she says, "are part of what I feel is the story of a woman's struggle for her identity and for her own writing career. Love-making has very little to do with what you do in bed or the size of a man's penis. It has to do with who treats you like a human being and respects you."

Still, there was a moment of self-censorship. For the first time in a long, rambling, ebullient conversation, Norma looked uncomfortable. She said she had finished the first draft of her manuscript and realized she had left out perhaps the most painful episode in her relationship with Ben. It was 1955 and she was writing less and less for herself when she was offered a paying job with an international agency whose owners knew her work as a volunteer analyzing books and plays for their screen possibilities. "I went home and I was very excited. I told Ben 'I've got the dream job.' He said, 'You're not going to do it.' I thought this time I'm going to stand up to him, but he said he would tell the agency not to hire me. I hadn't written about it at first because I was so ashamed that I didn't stand up to Ben. From that moment, I fell apart and there is a history of having more children and having affairs that didn't mean anything. It was frustration and feeling there was no way to strike out." Despite everything, she never really wanted a divorce, even though she was financially independent.

Before Ben died in 1989 after a ten-year-long, agonizing illness, Norma asked if he forgave her. The affairs meant nothing, he said, but he didn't forgive her for not letting Picasso use the studio on their Mougins estate as his engraving workshop. Not, she had argued successfully, while three of their little kids were running around happily unrestricted on the grounds.

As for the now-grown offspring, she said, two of her sons had "to divorce themselves completely, disengage themselves, as if it were a book by someone else and enjoy it for all the things it was." The others hadn't read it at the time we talked.

There had been rewarding, challenging, exciting, and depressing times during the Barzmans' thirty-year exile in Europe, with Ben writing more than twenty scripts, including *El Cid*, *The Fall of the Roman Empire*, *He Who Must Die*, *Time Without Pity*, and *Chance Meeting*, some with the help of Norma. And she wrote the screenplays *Never Say Goodby*, *Luxury Girls*, and *The Locket*. Together they collaborated on a novel, *Rich Dreams*, originally called *The Writer*, a satire on novelists like Harold Robbins whose books were full of sex, drugs, mone, and violence.

148

Perhaps the funniest experience was waiting for Sophia Loren and Charlton Heston to spark an erotic glow in *El Cid*, and perhaps the weirdest for a former Communist like Norma was to hear *El Cid* producer Sam Bronston speak lovingly about his uncle Lev, Lev Bronstein, aka Leon Trotsky, a name anathema to all true believers.

When the Barzmans returned to the United States in 1978, Norma began writing columns on aging for her old boss Hearst's newly merged paper, *The Los Angeles Herald-Examiner*. She had no interest in writing a memoir until Polonsky started nagging her. She had just finished a novel that wasn't published and was starting another, but Polonsky—best known for writing and directing *Force of Evil* and *Tell Them Willie Boy Is Here*—insisted that her story was part of film history and should be told. When she read memoirs by her blacklisted friends, she realized that most of them didn't reveal much about themselves and how they really felt during their ordeals.

Busy writing for herself, Norma emerged from her attempt at a political cocoon in 1997. Her friend, blacklisted Paul Jarrico—who had been fighting to get film credits restored for the blacklisted—persuaded the Motion Picture Academy of Arts and Sciences to loan their theater for one night on the fiftieth anniversary of the 1947 HUAC hearings. Historic. One thousand people turned out to hear representatives of four Hollywood Guilds—Writers, Directors, Screen Actors, AFTRA (American Federation of Television and Radio Artists), and the Producers Association—apologize formally for going along with the blacklist. Driving back home to Ojai the next day, Jarrico died in an automobile accident. Furious that the *Los Angeles Times* didn't print a word about the meeting, Norma called the executive editor, who said the paper had already featured articles about the fiftieth anniversary of the blacklist and it would run an obit on Jarrico, but Norma insisted, "If this story about the Academy event happened when I was a young reporter, it would have been a great story for page one!" He protested. She won. Page One.

Then came 1999 when the Academy planned to present Elia Kazan with an Oscar for Lifetime Achievement. "Lifetime achievement?!" snorted Norma. "I wouldn't oppose Oscars for his work, but what was his lifetime achievement? By informing, he destroyed the lives of about twenty-three wonderful people who were his friends in the Group Theater.

"I couldn't stand it," she recalled. "I phoned about 1,000 people, raised a lot of money, got ads of protest in *Variety* and *The Hollywood Reporter*." She was also there with a picket sign outside the Oscar ceremony. Inside, her good old friend, Sophia Loren, jubilantly called the next day to report that fewer than a third of the audience stood up and applauded Kazan while others sat on their hands. (It was actually the Kazan episode that triggered Polonsky's push for the Barzman memoir.)

It still wasn't all politics with Norma. She told me she was busy writing a romantic novel about a woman visiting Cremona, Italy, the city of Stradivarius. Nobody knew why the town had become the center of great violin-making. When Norma visited there in 1973 and again later, she discovered the answer to the mystery. "But *Cremona* is actually about the evolution of a woman in her forties with a college education, married, with children," the novelist said. "She has an affair with a young violin-maker, and it's the first time she has an egalitarian relationship. I brought her down to earth and she's quite a different woman at the end of the book."

When she talked about the "novel," the heroine sounded suspiciously like Norma herself. Her editor was suspicious too. "Norma," he insisted, "*This* is a memoir!" So, in a last fact-checking phone call, Norma was pleased to announce the new title of her forthcoming memoir: *The End of Romance: Love, Sex, and the Mystery of Violin* and was delighted to note that she was fifty-three, not forty, when it all happened in old Cremona, Italy.

Ah, the strains of Fritz Kreisler's "Liebesfreud" wafting through the air!

2003
Unpublished

Kathy Acker

"The idea that women exist to please men is almost relentlessly my subject."

San Francisco

Halloween, the night before the interview, was a spooky time to dream that Kathy Acker was really a man. Why not? After all, throughout her novels, the author's omnipresent first-person narrator is a chameleon, a slippery change artist, shifting mercurially from male to female, gay to lesbian, engaged in confounding encounters with Genet, Hawthorne, Hegel, Persian poets, Artaud, Robert Louis Stevenson, Dickens, and other literary ghosts.

Acker's books, declared *The New York Times*, "have proven as difficult and disordered as the mad world from which they spring: a rock'n'roll version of the *Critique of Pure Reason* by the Marquis de Sade as performed by the Three Stooges."

So who *is* Kathy Acker? I carefully sidestep the clutter of motorcycle gear leading up to her book-swamped San Francisco apartment. Her Art Institute writing class is at the Bearded Lady Women's Café. What manner of woman is writing graphically about sex and menstruation, incest, and the search for buried treasure in her new novel, *Pussy and the King of the Pirates*?

She is tiny, perched in a chair against a stuffed gray shark and a teddy bear. Atop one bookcase are zoids, the Japanese toy monsters she assembles. Her brown eyes are warmly welcoming, and she fields questions about such punk manifestations as her pierced eyebrows, an amethyst-pierced tongue, several hoops on each ear, hair cropped closely to a blonde fuzz. Over jeans, a long-sleeved green and gold shirt hides tattoos of cats, flowers, and a fish. Her smile has a whimsical flash of gold, the remains of a temporary cap affixed when, as a kid, she tried to fly like Superman and fell flat on her face. At forty-seven, she says she is "too cheap" to have it covered.

She never cared about appearances, Acker says, much to the irritation of her mother, a wealthy New York German Jew who "desperately wanted to be part of WASP society."

When her mother was three months pregnant, her husband left her. A year later, she married a "gentle, sweet—and rather stupid—man" who went into her family's glove business. At age eight, Kathy learned he wasn't her real father—whom she has never met. When Acker was thirty, her mother committed suicide. That act is obsessively re-played in her ten novels, particularly *My Mother: Demonology*. Kathy contends that the references to her mother are the only autobiographical threads in her work, despite the confusing appearance of "I" in many guises in *The Childlike Life of the Black Tarantula, I Dreamt I Was a Nymphomaniac: Imagining, The Adult Life of Toulouse Lautrec, Blood and Guts in High School, Great Expectations, My Death My Life by Pier Paolo Pasolini* (included in *Literal Madness*), *Don Quixote*, and *Empire of the Senseless*. They have been published in at least half a dozen other countries.

Pussy, King of the Pirates takes two girls from an Egyptian whorehouse to an un-Stevensonian island where they fight with female pirates over buried treasure. It is a kaleidoscopic story involving dreams and a re-telling of the Shiva myths.

"There's nothing autobiographical about the incest in *Pussy*, Acker says. "It's my way of seeing patriarchal society. You're basically in an incestuous relationship, if not with your father, then with patriarchal power. It's a metaphor for me, but it's reality for a lot of women."

As for the graphic scenes of sex and menstruation, Acker says those themes were triggered by her perception of the United States when she returned in 1990 after eight years in England. Disliking the British class system, she had romanticized America as a free-spirited populist country.

152

"What struck me was the backlash against women. Abortion was up for grabs. There was even a backlash within feminism. I figured there was a way in which women freaked [some] men out. What they hated was the idea of women's bodies. This is simplistic, but a woman's body somehow signified the bringer of death to them that they, the kings, couldn't last forever. And menstruation became a big thing for me because it's what every woman does and it's taboo to talk about it. My mother went through convulsions when I first got my period. I was taught it was something awful and dirty."

It was the relationship with her mother that incited her early rebellion. "I didn't fit in. I wanted to hide in libraries and museums. My parents wanted me to be social."

She felt close only to her glamorous grandmother. "I adored her. She was totally into culture." She would take Kathy to the Museum of Modern Art, where the girl was fascinated by the "moon-drenched sort of decadent late surrealist" paintings of Paul Delvaux and his *Phases of the Moon*.

Acker's introduction to avant-garde art, poetry, and cinema began at fourteen when she met P. Adams Sitney, then nineteen. He was an editor of *Film Culture*, the chief voice of the independent American filmmaker.

"He would lecture me about the poetry of Charles Olson and I didn't understand a word," Acker says. She began to understand cinema when she met filmmakers Jonas Mekas (*The Brig*), Jack Smith (*Flaming Creatures*), and Stan Brakhage (*Dog Star Man*). "I was their mascot. They loved me. That's where I wanted to be. I led two lives until I went to college. Then it stopped."

Her parents' support also stopped when she was eighteen. She began writing poetry and studying the classics at Brandeis; her papers were graded by Roman Jakobson, the pioneer linguist and formalist critic, who shared her interest in the Latin poet Catullus. In 1965, she followed Herbert Marcuse, the charismatic Marxist inspiration of the counterculture, to San Diego State. Later, she spent two years in a PhD program combining classics and philosophy at CCNY and NYU.

Acker is the name she retains from her first youthful marriage to a fellow college student who is now a San Francisco attorney. Her second husband was the New Wave composer Peter Cooper. She says she's bisexual but is currently involved in a long-distance romance with an Australian man, a journalist/academic.

Her characteristic literary use of "I" was inspired when, as a student at San Diego State, she worked as a stripper in a vaudeville house. There she listened in amazement to the other women's stories. "I wanted to write about them, but didn't want to do it as journalism because it would be very cold and I would seem to be looking down on them."

Instead, Acker wrote up their experiences in the first-person and sent them to a magazine recommended by her friends. She got a form rejection, but her friends received a letter from the editor saying that Acker was "absolutely insane and should be in an institution." Acker realized the editor must have believed that "I was all those people, changing gender. And I thought, 'My God, how powerful a weapon is the use of the word I.'"

Acker's penchant for the first-person also stems from her interest in voodoo. Traveling in Haiti, Acker watched a religious ceremony whose participants were possessed by spirits. She thought it made fabulous theater. "The idea that one's *real* identity doesn't reside where we think it is but is what is open to spirits—when the *loa* possesses one—I'm sure that informs a lot of my books. When I copy other texts, when I use Faulkner, for instance, I feel that he is talking to me, he's possessing me."

The model for Acker's first book was William Burroughs. "I went through the experiments he did: in seeing the relation between words and contexts, especially political contexts." Her debut book, *Politics*, which she self-published, is half poetry and half prose. It is "very much" based on ways that Burroughs wrote, says Acker, and he has been "extremely supportive" of her work. *Politics* was republished in 1991 in a short-story collection she whimsically entitled *Hannibal Lechter, My Father*.

For years, she had supported herself in meaningless jobs, from cookie-seller to secretary to ticket-taker. Then, in her mid-twenties, Acker's in-laws offered to finance her for one year while she launched her writing career. At thirty, she began writing art criticism, book reviews, and magazine features. Grove became her first commercial publisher in 1983.

She doesn't take umbrage when asked why she writes so many sexual scenes, some of which verge on pornography. "I'm sure my privileged background has something to do with it, and the fact that my first jobs were in the sex industry. I think I see the world through a sexual lens, like Genet," she says. "The idea that you exist to please men—that is almost relentlessly my subject. But what if it isn't true? In the early days of feminism, it was about 'we're powerful,' 'we're going to have decent lives.' There was no mention of sexuality. They talked about women being demeaned. I came out of an all-girls school and I thought, 'What do you mean? No one is demeaning *me!*' It took a few years in the working world to get it. I'm in the generation that rebelled against feminist dogmatism. I wanted not only the possibilities for decent lives, but I want to transform sexuality and make it something that isn't negative."

Early on, Acker was influenced by conceptual art. "I became interested in problems of plagiarism and appropriation. Artists my age were working with appropriation. It was a reaction against modernism, against the idea that as a creator you're god: the one who decides everything."

Now Acker illustrates her books with line drawings that range from genitalia to the intricate maps in *Pussy* delineating *Pirate Island*. She has written a screenplay and a play and maintains ties to the underground music scene. Her friends have been artists, musicians, and theorists.

"I'm a bit of a hermit and don't see a lot of people," notes Acker. But she misses the stimulation of New York's cultural life. Her desire to travel was satisfied when a Lila Wallace grant sent her to various American states to give readings. But the cut in arts funding has nearly eliminated that gratification.

She's taught at the San Francisco Art Institute for six years, challenging students with the work of the French feminist Helene Cixous, author of *Three Steps on the Ladder of Writing*. Acker is enthusiastic about Cixous' "incredible interpretation of other writers. Her method of reading them is like having a vision."

Now Acker is yearning for a vision beyond the San Francisco Bay. She's been feeling as imprisoned as her literary hero, Genet. "I'd give my right eye to go across North Africa and wind up in Egypt," she says. "I'm interested in Semitic culture. I think it's my way of feeling Jewish. My relation to being Jewish is not straightforward. There's very little in me that *is* straightforward."

December 11, 1995
Publishers Weekly

John Henry Faulk

Beating the Blacklisters.

San Francisco

Anybody who thinks they know John Henry Faulk from watching *Fear on Trial*, the televised play about his successful libel suit against the blacklisters—or what Leadbelly, the folk singer, was all about from the movie of the same name—hasn't heard the gospel truth.

John Henry sure sounds like a Southern cracker at his cornpone worst playing Texas governor Pat Neff in *Leadbelly*, about the black singer, but he is something else again close-up: full of 'ole honeys' and 'darlin's' and 'ole sugah's,' but not much escapes that one good eye of his, and those sweet-talkin,' down-home stories are full of pizzazz and vinegar.

He used to tell Texas tall tales on CBS radio before he was fired in 1956 for being on the blacklist profitably circulated by some right-wing vigilantes, known as AWARE, Inc.

Faulk was the only actor to sue AWARE for its charges of communism. When he finally won the suit in 1962, the original damage verdict was reduced to $175,000. Later, his former wife, Lynne, who had supported him politically during the trial (contrary to the film *Fear on Trial*) successfully sued CBS for its distortions of her role.

It wasn't until CBS produced *Fear on Trial* that Faulk began to get TV offers again. In the intervening nineteen years, he took his humor to the college circuit, worked his farm at Madisonville, Texas, and dug in and studied every last word of the Continental Congress debates on the Bill of Rights, the first ten amendments to the Constitution. It was a revelation of just how precisely the Founding Fathers had understood the vital importance of protecting free speech and a free press.

"Now that the TV movie projected me out as some kind of hero—which I'm not—I'm havin' a time, darlin,' layin' it on the line all around the country about what the First Amendment means," Faulk drawled.

It was Faulk's own father who had laid the groundwork for John Henry's convictions. He was a poor sharecropper who became a civil rights, anti-trust attorney in Austin, Texas.

"Daddy used to run for governor on the Eugene V. Debs Socialist Party ticket. He ran twice around 1908 or thereabouts. In 1933, he took me to the county courthouse to show me his party platform, and every single damn thing was in the Democratic platform in 1932," said Faulk, who was in San Francisco to entertain union members at COPE's regional convention with his jibes at the Republicans—and, incidentally, talk about his old friend Leadbelly. But Daddy came first.

"Daddy was a Mason, a pacifist in World War I, and taught Bible class at the Fred Allen Memorial Methodist Church until the day he died. He was a free thinker, took a little bit of something from Emerson, Jefferson, Spinoza, Marx, and Jesus and balled 'em all up, but he believed in the Bill of Rights. He was an anti-racist at a time when just the murmur of it brought a charge of 'nigger-lover.' Most of his peer group thought he was a little bizarre, but they loved him. This is America, darlin'!

"He was a saint among the Jewish community in Austin, because he really believed in the Judeo-Christian ethic. Daddy's point was: 'Who brought the idea of justice into being?' Judaism. 'Who brought the idea of confronting your accuser?' Judaism. Daddy's favorite prophet was Isaiah. I hear those echoes and they inspire me."

Like his friends, the folklorists John and Alan Lomax (who discovered Leadbelly in a Louisiana prison in 1934), Faulk went around the South from 1939-43, recording black folk songs and sermons. (The records are in the Faulk archives at the Library of Congress and the University of Texas.)

"Those black preachers told me the story of what the Exodus was really about," Faulk noted. He proceeded to orate his own Seder service in that tradition.

"The Reverend Tanner Franklin—he couldn't read nor write, but he could preach a marvelous sermon on Moses getting Pharaoh to let his people go. The struggle out of darkness into light is the eternal struggle of man. It's what life is about."

Faulk continued his recording, he said, "until I went off to save America from Hitler," but only the Red Cross would take the one-eyed volunteer, and he was stationed in Cairo.

"Since Mama was a good Methodist lady and wanted me to see where Jesus was born, I went to Tel Aviv and Jerusalem, and then I got involved with the people on Kibbutz Brenner and got the dream of Israel then. In '43, I found Jews and Arabs living together in warmth and respect, even though the British Army was trying to set them against each other. It was kinda like the poor whites and blacks of the south who realized someone was exploitin' them both."

After the war, entertaining in New York at hootenannys with Leadbelly and Woody Guthrie, he'd perform cameos of southern types, reminding people that "half the population of the south is living in conditions like the ones that had prevailed in Germany. It's one thing to rail at Hitler and another thing to be self-righteous. The twenty-four-hour experience of the blacks in the south was not unlike the fate of the Jews in Germany.

"Governor Pat Neff," said Faulk, getting back to his role in *Leadbelly*, "he was the essence of Christian goodness of that day. He was the essence of all that was the matter with Texas. I'd known him and Daddy'd known him. He didn't pardon Leadbelly out of the goodness of his heart. He pardoned him because he thought, 'That old nigger sings purty good.'

"'This script is crazy as hell,'" Faulk told Gordon Parks, the director. "This wasn't the way Huddie was. He couldn't have looked *defiantly* at the governor. That would have been the end of him. They'd have beat him to death that night. He sang that song asking Governor Neff to let him go free with all the servility, all the urgent ingratiating way he knew. Huddy's genius was survival.

"I told Gordon, 'You're creating something that may appeal to militants today. Huddie had to turn his anger on his own people. He knew he'd be hanged if he acted differently.'"

In the film, Leadbelly tells the elder Lomax he doesn't want his lifestory put in the Library of Congress. Actually, Faulk recalled, "Huddie said, 'If you get me out of here, I'll be your chauffeur.'

"At that time, in all southern prisons, blacks could get paroled to white men. It would take them off the prison rolls and many farmers got their field hands that way. So Huddie was paroled to Mr. Lomax and Alan. They introduced him to white audiences, and he would sing and talk at their lectures.

"Huddie was a powerful genius and a great man who lived in that horrible never-never world in which he had no legal rights or identification before the law. He survived it all by using all the devices of his wit.

"He was the first one that explained the sex thing to me. Those young progressive girls were falling all over him and Huddie told me, 'It's a funny thing that talk about white women needing to be protected. When a white woman comes near me, it drains all my sexhood out because it meant death, death, death to me.'"

April 18, 1976
San Francisco Chronicle

Jean Genet

PHOTO BY JERRY BAUER.

"It's not because the Panthers are black that I'm at their disposal."

Palo Alto, California

Jean Genet, the distinguished French writer whose passionate commitment is to the imprisoned and the outcast, came to the San Francisco Bay Area in April 1970 to speak for the Black Panthers and to offer a bleak view of white America.

A press conference on the Stanford University campus started quietly enough. The guests were late and there was time to become acquainted with the serene-looking woman in slacks who opened the door to the Women's Club. She was Miriam Cherry, organizer of the Stanford Community against War and Fascism, co-sponsor of the public meeting that night for Genet and the Panthers. She has also been for the last fourteen years a Sister of the Holy Cross, assistant to the Newman Club chaplain on campus, and so involved with her work in black ghettoes that she has written to the Pope for a dispensation from her religious vows because life in a convent has become insupportable for her.

She knew little of Genet, who—in a French prison—wrote *Our Lady of the Flowers*, the brutal, homosexual, scatological, and astonishingly lyrical account of the erotic fantasies of men in prison. Genet was saved from life imprisonment as an habitual offender only by the intervention of French writers, headed by Jean-Paul Sartre, who later "sanctified" his life and work in an extraordinary book, *Saint Genet*.

As a child of ten, Genet had been accused of stealing and soon drifted into becoming a thief, spending his adolescence in reformatories. He escaped at twenty, joined the Foreign Legion, deserted, and, at twenty-one, learned that his real mother had left him at birth.

"Abandoned by my family," he wrote, "I found it natural to aggravate this fact by the love of males, and that love by stealing and stealing by crime or complicity with crime. Thus I decisively repudiated a world that had repudiated me."

For ten years, he drifted around Europe, but in Nazi Germany, he was repelled by the real criminals of our time. He felt he was in a "nation of thieves . . . if I steal here, I accomplish no special act that could help me to realize myself. I merely obey the habitual order of things. I do not destroy it."

He returned to France, where he spent the war years in and out of prison, discovering himself and his world while writing about it .

So enter Jean Genet, now fifty-nine, author of *The Balcony*, *The Maids*, *The Blacks*, *The Screens*, plays filled with rituals and riddles, confounding paradoxes of the roles men play out in fantasy and in fact, hurling discomfiting visions into the faces of the audiences, "les justes," the righteous of society.

He is small, bald, in rumpled clothes that look cast-off and slept-in. He was accompanied by David Hilliard of the Black Panthers and a young secretary impressed into service as interpreter. As he faced the three white women reporters from the "establishment" press, his demeanor was quiet, courteous, thoughtful, considerate, broken only once or twice by a sharp demand for instantaneous and precise translation.

He had first met members of the Black Panther Party in Chicago while on assignment for *Esquire* magazine to cover the police at the Democratic convention. (Without a U.S. visa, he had flown to Canada and got someone to drive him over the border.) His magazine report, dealing almost exclusively with the anatomy, real and fantasized, of the Chicago men in blue will never make any New Left anthology on the subject of Cop as Pig.

Recently in Europe, Genet said, "A Black Panther asked me what I could do about the extermination of the Panthers by the police, and for that reason I came to the U.S."

A few years ago, he became interested in the Muslims "because theirs was the first violent reaction against the imperialism of the United States. Before, the blacks had always been preoccupied with evangelical ideas. The blacks I knew twenty years ago had a strong religious system. Malcolm X was the first one to propose a complete break between all the accepted ideas of the white and black worlds."

"Do you support the idea of two separate worlds now?"

"Not at all. Of course not. For 200-300 years, the whites tried and succeeded in convincing the blacks of their inferiority and helped the evangelical Christian moralism which asked the blacks to respect the white man, the master and private property, and hope for a reward in the afterlife. The one man who reacted most vigorously was Malcolm X. The Black Panthers have summed it all up. They are not proceeding with this evangelical moralism. The Black Panthers have started a revolutionary struggle whose point of departure begins in the black community of the United States and includes and should include the entire population of the U.S. If the Panthers were not a revolutionary movement, they wouldn't interest me. It's not because they are black that I am at their disposal; it's because they are a revolutionary movement. They have a theory about the world: It's time to finish seeing blacks with a paternalistic view. Personally I consider myself their comrade in arms. My aim here is to speak to white students who are not already convinced and to be an honest witness for the Black Panther Party."

When did Genet begin to think of himself as a revolutionary?

"It is not a question here of my personal intellectual progress toward the revolution, the problem now is to defend Bobby Seale and the Black Panther Party."

What is the feeling in Europe about Bobby Seale?

"They are much more aware than the American students and professors. There is a tremendous ignorance here. The ignorance is extraordinary."

When he and the Panthers speak to students, Genet said, "They seem interested, but I have the feeling that American students are very far from revolutionary preoccupations except for several exceptions. I really have the feeling that American students are about to do exactly as their parents. I don't believe there is a big gulf between them. They listen to the Panthers and amuse themselves. Of course, some traces remain in their consciousness, but I do not have much hope. The educational system in America is such that it prevents students from seeing the real revolutionary problems."

Sister Miriam asked, "Will American students then choose a system of fascism?"

"American students will have to choose between American fascism and internationalism; they will choose fascism. This is a racist country, a fascist country that wants to be the master race of the world and the white children dream of continuing what their parents began."

As I fumbled a question about violence, Genet sharply told me to rephrase it concisely. I asked, "If you believe the revolutionary feeling among students is so low, what do you think of the violence used by groups like the Weathermen?"

Hilliard started to answer; tension suddenly filled the quiet room. Genet, his face furious, raised his voice in anger. "If a minority of them have used what you call violence, it is the last argument they have left. It is because of YOU," he stormed looking directly at me with unchecked hostility, "the American press. You don't do your job of informing people. I hope you will have the professional conscience necessary for your profession that is so exalted every place in America to publish what I have said."

I tried to explain that there are many honest newspapermen who are very concerned about the inadequacies of the press, but he curtly declared, "I am not interest in your personal confessions."

Interrupted Hilliard, "She is saying she is more concerned about her job than the lives of black people."

A dismal silence replaced the tension. Finally, to restore the atmosphere of a polite, conventional press conference, Genet was asked for his observation of the black ghettoes.

"I went always with members of the Black Panther Party. I'm going to tell you what I saw in New Haven and Boston. In apartments occupied by the blacks, not necessarily offices of the Panthers, I saw apartments where they have to have barriers of steel across the windows, to barricade themselves with iron. THAT's what white Americans have done to human beings. That's what white hatred provokes in the lives of black men. I've also seen the fact that the danger of the threats are so great that in rooms occupied by four men—I won't say where—men sleep right next to their guns."

A look of pain and sorrow crossed his face. "I have seen written on the house in white crayon the inscription. 'F--- you.' You can be sure it was written by a white man's hand. In my eyes, white America is the White House. It is the same thing."

The conference broke up. I tried again, feebly, to say, "You must understand there are whites . . . "

"You," Genet cut me off savagely, "must understand there are blacks . . . "

April 5, 1970

San Francisco Chronicle

Joseph Strick

It takes a certain chutzpah to tackle Joyce, Miller, and Genet.

Paris

It takes a certain chutzpah to tackle James Joyce, Henry Miller *and* Jean Genet, but Joseph Strick's brinkmanship in introducing those controversial authors to the screen brought him a Persistance of Vision Award at the Czech Republic's Karlovy Vary International Film Festival in 2003.

In announcing the honor, the festival noted that the director "is one of the great, largely unsung, heroes of this [American independent] cinema. His daring in choosing difficult literary themes and his social and political commitment are unique." Notable among the features are Joyce's *Ulysses* (1967) and *Portrait of the Artist as a Young Man* (1977), Genet's *The Balcony* (1963), and Miller's *Tropic of Cancer* (1970). As for his social/political commitments, in 1970, Strick won an Oscar for his documentary short *Interviews with My Lai Veterans*, about the massacre of Vietnamese civilians by U.S. soldiers.

The seeds of Strick's cinematic vision were planted early on when the sixteen-year-old youth read Joyce's *Ulysses* and decided that he wanted to be a director. "I knew I was in the presence of something extraordinary. I didn't understand everything in it, but I got enough to know that re-reading it, I'd get more and more. And I thought of it as a movie because it was so cinematic."

The book had been smuggled into the states from Europe by his Polish-born father "because that was the thing to do in those days," Strick told me at his Paris apartment, near the Luxembourg Gardens. The comfortable rooms were filled with an eclectic collection of art, including many pieces from New Guinea. Although we had known each other slightly years ago in Philadelphia where Strick and his first wife, Anne Biberman, were actors at the progressive New Theater, he enjoyed berating me for not paying attention to him until the award was announced. (I remembered seeing the name Strick on truck trailers his father had manufactured and thinking "Joe!" without connecting the director with his own work.)

The father's success was legendary before his son's. He had arrived in the U.S. on a cattle boat in 1914 and was sent to work in a steel mill in Pueblo, Colorado, eventually inventing a multiple nail-making machine during World War I and a tubeless pneumatic tire. He invented a system for sharing the load in heavy-duty trucks so that tires would not blow out and built his first truck trailer in 1935. He had gone back to Europe twice to try to convince his siblings to leave Poland, but eventually only two brothers were saved from the Holocaust out of a family of eleven. By 1951 when he died, he was the largest privately owned truck-trailer manufacturer in the world.

Joe, one of six children, had no intention of entering the family business. He went to UCLA in 1941, thinking that physics would win the war, but he had no talent for science and volunteered for the Air Force, training as a pilot, but eventually becoming an aerial photographer. When he got out of the service, he tried to get a job in the film business in Los Angeles, but work was done by people in "company unions." He was hired as a copyboy at the *Los Angeles Times* and advanced to Assistant to the Telegraph Editor, but he thought he was underpaid so he went on to a job at the *Valley Times* as the makeup editor. Finally, he saved enough money in 1948 to start shooting at night and on weekends.

But how to become a director? Strick asked screenwriter Ben Maddow for advice and he was told, "'You have to learn what it is to be extraordinary. Why don't you get a camera and go out and start to shoot?' I bought a war-surplus bomb-spotting camera and began to film the muscle men and acrobats who hung out in Venice. I brought Ben the stuff from shooting on the beach and he said, 'My God, you've made a film!' and I said, 'Oh?!'" *Muscle Beach*, co-directed by Irving Lerner, was released as a short and shown in competition at the Cannes Festival and all over the U.S. and Europe with the Jean Cocteau film *Les Parents Terrible*.

Reminiscing over the years, Strick talked about some of the memorable circumstances and people in his life: the unforgettable Genet, the thief and notorious ex-prisoner who became a world-famous writer; the way *Ulysses* was banned for thirty-three years in Ireland; about *Tropic of Cancer*, starring Rip Torn, Ellen Burstyn, and even Miller himself—"a love, a darling guy, a very sweet guy"—and how controversy was there almost every step of the way.

Strick wanted to film Genet's play *The Balcony* about a revolution that takes place in a brothel when all the real holders of power have been wiped out with the exception of the police chief. The initial electrifying production in which the brothel customers act out macabre fantasy roles, mocking man and society, aroused violent controversy.

"The only reason Genet and I got to work together was that he was attracted by my idea that we would shoot *The Balcony* in a film studio, which is essentially a brothel. I said, 'All film studios are brothels,' and I told him a couple of stories about Hollywood people in the studios. So he set forth to write the treatment. He wrote every morning and we'd meet every afternoon to discuss it. And that went on for two months. It was a marvelous experience. He was a very brilliant and marvelous person, very, very nutty, very. Special, a wild person."

Strick met him for the first time in Milan in 1962 because Genet didn't dare go into France. In 1948, when he was sentenced to life imprisonment, a petition of famous writers won his freedom. He knew if he robbed again in France, he would be imprisoned again. When Strick and his interpretor were going to their initial appointment with Genet, they saw a short man with his hand out. "I was about to say that I don't give money to beggars and that would have blown it because it was Genet and that's the way he would shake hands!"

He told Strick what his modus operandi was. "He said he would cruise until somebody picked him up, take them to a secluded spot, and when their pants were down, he would rob them. That's the way he made his living. And he said, 'And every now and then they will say, 'Do me anyway.' He would even steal from people's homes who had offered him hospitality after he became famous."

Genet had been hired by *Esquire* to report on the Democratic convention in Chicago in 1968, but he couldn't get a visa to the U. S., so he went to Canada. "He sashays down the streets in Toronto until somebody recognizes him. And they would say, 'Jean Genet? What can we do for you?' 'Well, actually, you could drive me to Chicago.'"

In Chicago, tens of thousands of demonstrators were in the park when the police invaded. Genet and his interpretor are running with the cops in pursuit. As Genet told the story to Strick, "'If we're caught I'll look them in the eye and they won't hurt us.' So they get caught and the cop's got his baton raised and Genet looks him in the eye and the cop says, 'Oh, fuck off!' And now they're being pursued by four cops and they're not going to be able to look *four* cops in the eye. And they're running, running, running into the student section near the University of Chicago and they run into the foyer of an apartment. And Genet tells the man who answers the doorbell, 'Je suis Jean Genet' and the guy says, 'Mr. Genet, come in. I'm doing my thesis on you!'"

Strick once asked Genet, "How did you become a writer?" and he answered, "I was in the prison library one day and I picked out a book by Proust, I read a paragraph and I knew then I had to become a writer." Still incarcerated, he went on to write *Our Lady of the Flowers*, which was smuggled out of prison and privately published, sometime in 1942. Publication led to his acceptance in French literary circles where he became the subject of Jean-Paul Sartre's mythologizing *Saint Genet: Actor and Martyr*.

No matter how famous Genet became, he was never forgiven by Strick's second wife, Martine, a French paleobotanist, for an interview he did three weeks before he died of cancer. Genet had said, "The most beautiful day of my life was the day France fell." But his personal story of being abandoned as a baby in front of a church and raised in brutal foster homes could not make up for that interview because Martine had lost her father, a physicist, on the third day of the war.

The Balcony, starring Shelley Winters, Peter Falk, and Leonard Nimoy, was a success. Strick had been able to make it as a result of the financial profits of an earlier film, *The Savage Eye*, starring Barbara Baxley and Gary Merrill, a docu-drama about a woman who goes to Los Angeles for a one-year divorce and sees the city through her depression. Written by Ben Maddow, it cost only $65,000 and made three times the negative cost in the U.S. alone and won four international prizes.

As a result of *The Balcony*'s success, Walter Reed, the backer, said they'd put up all the money for *Ulysses*, doing it as a partner in a British firm that was a consortium of six companies, including the Boulting Brothers, who said it would never pass censorship because the script had words in it that had never been heard before in cinema. Strick entered into a financing contract requiring the film to pass British censorship. After some financial hurdles, they finally got the money. The film with sixty speaking parts cost $450,000, and it made its entire cost back in one London cinema.

"With that," Strick said, "I thought I could do anything." Nevertheless, there was still trouble to come. The British censors demanded twenty-nine cuts in Molly Bloom's monologue, which Strick refused to do. When it was shown at the Cannes Festival, the festival director masked out twenty-nine subtitles with the proclamation that "There are certain things that can be read but not heard." In Ireland, a government official said that if the film were cleared for showing to "any class" of Irish audience it would bring "discredit" to the government.

But long before there was Joyce's Molly Bloom, there was Aristophanes' women's festival play *Thesmophoriazusae*. After Strick directed Aristophanes' prematurely pro-feminist play in Cork, he decided to resubmit *Ulysses* to the censors. The film was then shown in Ireland for the first time in February 2001.

With the success of *Ulysses* in other parts of the world, Strick didn't have any problem getting the rights to make *The Portrait of the Artist as a Young Man* after John Huston, who had owned the cinema rights, failed to raise $500,000 for it. When Huston's rights lapsed, Strick got them and made the film for $300,000.

At last report, Strick was still busy, shooting a film on sex selection. Of his career, Strick said, "I always wanted to do the best work of which I was capable, and that led me to a refusal to accept the dictates of producing entities which really wanted to make their versions, not mine. So I have only made fifteen movies, but I'm responsible for those, since I don't budge without the final cut. Now I think we're on the verge of a great upswelling of talent since movies can now be made with tourist-sized cameras and everyone will be able to shoot."

2003
Unpublished

Anne-Marie Mieville

PHOTO BY JUDY STONE.

"We wondered why we were so committed to the Palestinians that we weren't looking at struggles at home."

Rotterdam

Nearly everyone knows the name of Jean-Luc Godard, who had a revolution-ary impact on European filmmakers, but finally there was a chance to meet Anne-Marie Mieville, his companion and colleague for thirty years. Honored at the Rotterdam Film Festival in 2001 with a retrospective of her own work, she shed an unexpected light on her relationship with Godard. It began with a mutual interest in the Palestinian movement in 1969, moved on to introspection about their own Eu-ropean society, then to philosophical and personal human problems—and lately to the sight of a gloomy Godard in tears!—in her film *We're All Still Here*.

168

Mieville's own films and some she made with Godard were presented at the Pacific Film Archive in Berkeley in 2002. The programs began with *France/tour/detour/deux/enfants*, a series of television shows that present a funny and frightening image of France through interviews with two children and others who are asked such existential questions as "Why does the cleaning woman gets paid, but mother does not?" The series continued with her most ambitious feature, *Reaching an Understanding*, co-starring Mieville and the morose Godard. The program concluded with the "vicious and plaintive" 1995 film *2 X 50 years of French Cinema* and *The Old Place*, a 1999 essay on the status of the fine arts at the end of the twentieth century.

At Rotterdam, sometimes speaking in French through an interpretor and sometimes in English, Mieville quickly disposed of her early years. At eighteen, she left her native Switzerland for France. In Paris, she used to sing a lot and made two records under her married name of Anne-Marie Michel. She had a daughter who is now thirty-seven and a short-lived marriage, long enough to make her say never again to the wedded state. She has five grandchildren although one would never think it to look at this svelte and savvy woman. She and Godard share homes in Switzerland and France.

"I met Jean-Luc in Switzerland at the beginning of the seventies, not in the world of cinema, but in the world of activism. In Paris, I had been a member of a militant group involved with the Palestinians and for a short while in Geneva. In '68 Jean-Luc had gone to Jordan, Syria, and Lebanon with Jean-Pierre Gorin. They thought they were going to make a very triumphalist film about the Palestinians to be called *'Till Victory*, the title taken from an El Fatah slogan. That project began when the Arab League approached Godard to make a film about displaced Palestinians to counteract the pro-Israel impact of *Exodus*.

But after *'Till Victory* was shot came a series of events—Black September in 1970, followed by many Palestinian airplane hijackings and subsequent government reprisals. Most of the people they had filmed were dead and the documentary was stillborn.

Two years later the filmmakers wanted to see what could be retrieved from the original footage and they began work on *Here and Elsewhere*. "We wondered," Mieville explained, "why we Europeans were so committed to Palestine that we weren't looking at the struggles taking place at home and we wanted to present that. We wanted to ask the question, 'Who are we? What are we doing in our own countries? Why are we becoming involved in struggles elsewhere?' After years of militancy, we wanted to look at our personal perspectives and ask ourselves about our own positions. 'What am I saying? Why am I doing this?'"

Starting with *Here and Elsewhere*, Mieville worked with Godard as co-director, co-writer, editor, and art director. However, she said she has not been influenced by him and his style. "Rather his approach has helped me to find my own path and my own freedom." In doing so, she has focused on women's place in today's world and the interplay with the men in their lives.

The complexities of the Mieville-Godard relationship are hinted at in the moving third part of *We're All Still Here* in which Godard and Aurore Clement play a married couple tangled in their individual needs and desires. It is more autobiographical than *Reaching an Understanding* (also known as *After the Reconciliation*) in which two men and two women flirt, joust, grumble, and attack each other in a dazzling verbal display, replete with quotations from Martin Heidegger, the German philosopher, and R.D. Laing, the British psychoanalyst.

"We have different definitions of reconciliation," she noted. "The first idea that comes to mind is when people argue and fight and afterwards try to have a reconciliation, but that wasn't my idea. The characters are trying to reconcile themselves with the world, with the fact that in the world things are transient. Things appear and disappear. They're also trying to reconcile themselves with themselves. But there's also the idea in the prologue of reconciliation in the liturgical sense. It's a holy space that has been violated, almost a religious space that hasn't been respected and in the prologue there's an attempt to re-sanctify, to re-create, to repair this holy space. Although this space sounds very Christian, I myself am not. I'm using these words to try to express it."

She said she had not planned at first to cast herself or Godard in the film. "I didn't want so much to work with him again because his name is sometimes very hard. Some people would think it's a publicity stunt. But when Jean-Luc read the script, he liked it very much and wanted to participate in the adventure. I wasn't so keen. I looked for other actors, artists, musicians, writers, but at the end Jean-Luc was the best with the words, with the sound, so I decided 'Okay, you can come and join us.' I made him work a lot."

How did he take your direction ? "He found it 'formidable.' [He loved it!] We would come and pick him up, take care of him and he was so happy just to say his lines and not be responsible for anything else."

How did you make him cry? "He is a very good crier. He cries easily. He also cries when he goes to see other movies—like Wajda's *Man of Iron* and *The Conductor*, starring John Gielgud."

Since shooting *Reaching an Understanding*, she said they don't always argue. "We've learned to share the good times that are especially linked to our work and not so much to be bothered by the bad times that each of us are involved with."

But is he easy to live with? "It's not easy to live with anybody," she replied crisply. "But with age and time we've learned to know each other. We've learned that we can allow ourselves this space."

July 28, 2002
The Oakland Tribune

Krzysztof Piesiewicz

PHOTO BY JUDY STONE.

The script asks why a beautiful, clever woman wanted to plant a bomb. Why?

Karlovy Vary, the Czech Republic

Film buffs familiar with the *Decalogue*, the great Polish updated version of the *Ten Commandments*, know the name of its director Krzysztof Kieslowski, but few realize it was conceived by Krzysztof Piesiewicz, an attorney who was the originator, co-writer and close collaborator on the director's last seventeen productions. As a lawyer, Piesiewicz had spent five years defending Solidarity dissidents and had intimate knowledge of police interrogations and the manifold manipulations in judicial systems.

The two Krzysztofs who worked together on *Red*, *White* and *Blue* (liberty, equality, fraternity) had planned another trilogy, but Kieslowski died of a heart attack at fifty-four before they finished the script for *Heaven*. Piesiewicz completed it and went on to write *Hell* and *Purgatory*.

Kieslowski never planned to direct the new trilogy, Piesiewicz said through an interpretor, at the 2003 Karlovy Vary International Festival. Tom Tykwer, the German director of *Run Lola Run*, eventually became the director of *Heaven*. The script went through mind-boggling linguistic metamorphoses: Polish, French, German, English, and Italian. Cate Blanchett, the Australian actress, and Giovanni Ribisi, an American, star in the film, which was shot in Italy.

Although Piesiewicz (who had contractual approval rights) professed to have been pleased with the film there was a sense of unspoken regret in his voice. There were undertones of sorrow, love— and humor—when he recalled his unique association with Kieslowski. "His death was a loss not just for cinema, but for humanity," he said. At fifty-seven, Piesiewicz's face looked as somber as Kieslowski's when he had to endure journalistic questions.

Piesiewicz never wanted to be an attorney. As a student, his passion was trying to understand the roots of totalitarianism, both Nazism and Communism. Nevertheless, he became prominent when he started practicing criminal and family law in 1975. Soon, he was greatly influenced by Harvard professor Lon Fuller's books theorizing that law is not just an instrument to govern, but has to embody real moral values. "When I realized this, I started to join the movement against the Communist regime. I began defending people from the opposition and slowly I became one of them in 1980."

Piesiewicz became acquainted with the cinema director through a client, Hanna Krall, a Jewish novelist who wrote about her experience of being hidden as a child during the war by a Polish family. (She would later inspire *Decalogue: 8*.) Krall knew that Kieslowski wanted to make a documentary about how martial law cases were handled in court, and she suggested that the two men meet.

"Krzysztof and I intended to talk for half an hour," Piesiewicz said, "but we talked for hours and hours and continued talking about everything for the next sixteen years. I was trying to convince him not to do his film for two reasons. One, they wouldn't let him in to film the place where important things are going on. Secondly, you can't see the real drama in a courtroom because everyone is playing a role. The real drama is spontaneous."

However, when cameras were finally allowed into the courtroom, they both learned, to their surprise, that the judges—who may have had history in mind—were afraid to be recorded passing unjust sentences. The presence of the camera almost invariably helped the defense.

Six months later, Kieslowski asked, ironically, if Piesiewicz wanted to become an artist. "I didn't know what it meant to be or not to be an artist. I just smiled and a short time later we started to write a script, *No End*. How did we get to the point of working together? Now, years later, I think he decided there was a child-like naiveté in my personality because I believed I could go with him anywhere, especially a court, and convince Communists that they were not right."

No End was inspired by the death of a legal colleague. In the film, the ghost of a young lawyer (a kind of pure conscientious spirit who couldn't really survive under Communism) observes the world after martial law. Meanwhile, an older attorney, resigned to compromise, takes over the defense of his client, an opposition activist. And in the end, the lonely widow walks away to join her dead husband.

"We didn't want to make *No End* about martial law," Piesiewicz said. "We wanted to show particular people and who they are inside. The film was very strongly attacked by the Communist authorities. It's the only Polish film that described the atmosphere and drama of that time. The trauma of martial law extinguished the marvelous fire inside people who were in opposition to the regime. *No End* reflects my personal experiences, not my facts." But it is a fact that in the first two months of martial law, Piesiewicz lived in different places every day because he was afraid of being imprisoned in an internment camp for intellectuals.

Now a Polish senator, Piesiewicz looks back on those dangerous years and says, "Sometimes there is a moment in human life that we touch paradise on earth, and for me that was the first few years of the Solidarity movement when there was no difference between doctors, lawyers, and workers." He observed then how strength of will and heart overcame bullets and tanks, but the conflicts and suspicions among friends engendered by martial law are still sometimes reflected in Poland today.

As very young men, Piesiewicz said, "We touched everything. I was defending bandits and heroes and Kieslowski made fantastic documentaries, but he came to realize that documentaries had barriers that didn't meet his artistic needs. You can't intervene with a camera into the intimate world of human beings. It's barbaric to try to enter, but you can with fiction. And I had similar problems in my work as a lawyer. I was not so much interested in what man had done, but why? What happens to a human being? What should we do with him? Why does a human suddenly become an animal?"

That human question also resonates in the *Decalogue* that had been inspired by a fifteenth-century painting which Piesiewicz saw as a boy. It was titled "Decalogue" and divided into ten parts with particular themes of the Biblical injunctions in those times. Piesiewicz wondered how they would apply to Poland under martial law.

"The churches were full of people and I was curious how they would decipher the *Decalogue*. Did people become religious or political? These were the paradoxes of our times." In the end, the filmmakers decided that politics would play no part in the human dramas they portrayed.

Politics also didn't play a part five years ago when the two Krzyztofs began work on *Heaven* and terrorism had not yet become front page news. "The script asks why a beautiful, young, clever woman would plant a bomb," Piesiewicz said. "And in the end we love this woman. I know that terrorism is not good. It's more than not good. It's a dramatic immoral situation in the world. But why do beautiful young people make this a big problem? It's a big question, 'Why?'"

October 2003
The San Francisco Examiner

6

Are We European or Asian?

Alev Lytle Croutier

"Looking at Turkey through a telephoto lens."

San Francisco

Like Turkey, her native land, forever split between East and West, Alev Lytle Croutier is still trying to integrate those two parts of herself. The San Francisco author uses fiction to bridge that divide in her two novels, *Seven Houses* and *The Palace of Tears*.

She left Turkey when she was eighteen, with a scholarship to Oberlin College in Ohio, but her adolescence had been marked by that division. For years, living in Istanbul, she took the ferry across the Bosphorus from her home in the Asian sector to the European side to attend an American-sponsored school.

In the mid-nineteenth century, the Suez Canal offered a new link between East and West a crossing that provides the setting for *The Palace of Tears*. The story follows the travels of a French winemaker lured to the Orient by a miniature portrait of a beauty with one blue eye and one yellow eye. When he finally finds her in a sultan's palace, he converts to Islam, changes his name, and eventually becomes a wealthy gunpowder manufacturer. The novel was inspired by a family tale told to Croutier by her paternal grandmother.

That same grandmother—who had grown up in a family harem in Greek Macedonia, then part of the Ottoman Empire—also triggered Croutier's curiosity about the cloistered lives of the women in the imperial Topkapi Palace in Istanbul. Her ten-year pursuit of that mysterious, elusive community, so romanticized in European art, resulted in her first, handsomely illustrated, non-fiction book, *Harem: The World Behind the Veil* (1989), translated into seventeen languages. Croutier then wrote the nonfiction *Taking the Waters*, an exploration of hot-spring spas.

Her most recent novel, *Seven Houses*, characterizes a prodigal daughter's return to Turkey as a moment of reconciliation with the past. There were some early indications that Croutier, also a kind of prodigal daughter, would find a world outside of national boundaries and be able to reconcile her own divided allegencies. Even her name held a portent of sorts. Born in Izmir, one of the towns in *Seven Houses*, she was christened Naile ("one endowed with everything") Alev ("flame, passion") Aksoy.

Croutier spoke affectionately in a low voice about her mother who taught her to read when she was five and about the work habits she absorbed from her father, a labor lawyer. When she was seven, a children's magazine published a story she wrote about a boy standing at a fork in the road and debating which fork he should take.

"Years later," she said, "when I thought about it, I believed I was seeing the future of my own life—that I would always be standing at the crossroads of East and West and wondering what my life would have been like if I hadn't left Turkey."

When she was eight, her parents left for a year's study in Michigan, while she stayed in Izmir. The months she spent in the care of her maternal grandparents "turned out to be one of the most fascinating times in my life," she recalled. "It was a Fellini-esque childhood because the circus came to town, and I spent my time hanging out with tightrope walkers and clowns. I saw them without makeup and frills, and I was curious about their lives. I became close to a woman who was the inspiration for the singer in *Seven Houses*, and I memorized all the obscure songs I heard then. They are also in the book."

At eleven, Alev began her first year of intensive English studies; she was determined to speak without an accent. Accomplishing this helped her to win a college scholarship. But after college and after some years living in Asia (where she worked in film), Croutier found herself reluctant to return home.

"I felt oppressed at the thought of going back to Turkey, and I still do. There's always that tightening feeling, if you behave outside the prescribed way. It is a function of class, it is a function of society. It is a function of a country which went through a reform instantly (with Kemal Ataturk's decrees for modernization) instead of developing gradually. It's a very schizophrenic country, caught in that state of metamorphosis—of not going East or West and wanting both."

So she again turned west, moving to San Francisco where she began writing screenplays. Of her many scripts, only *Tell Tell Me a Riddle* was produced. Then in 1979, she entered the world of publishing, helping to found Mercury House in San Francisco. After eight years as executive editor, she gained the confidence to write *Harem*.

In trying to imagine the story for her novel *The Palace of Tears*, she realized she could incorporate the Frenchman into her grandmother's Scheherazade-like story, although it would have been impossible for a Turkish girl to meet a foreign man at that time. Then recalling the "double dreaming" that appears in many Sanskrit and Persian tales, she found her literary device. (One of the stories on this theme involves two people who are apart, having a simultaneous dream about the other—and the search for the loved ones begins.)

Her research into the 600 year-old culture of the Ottoman Empire began to fascinate her and change her thinking. "In the twentieth century's process of modernization, we turned away from the cultural patrimony of the Empire," she said. "It was necessary because if we glorified the Empire, it would have prevented progress, just as Russians had to deny the heritage of the czars before the revolution could take place."

Writing *Seven Houses*, brought her closer to her Turkish heritage, making the theme of reconciliation very important to her. "It helped to free me to write about other things, but I still ask myself if I'm always going to write about Turkey. The answer is, I don't know. A lot of inspiration still comes from Turkey." (*Seven Houses* has become a best-seller in Turkey.)

"I'm learning so much about Turkey from a perspective that's unique. Writers who live there, like Orhan Pamuk, look at it with a close-up lens, and I'm looking at Turkey with a telephoto lens.

"Having been an expatriate for more than thirty years, I haven't grown up with the changes that would have made me part of the Turkish literary machinery. I'm a foreign writer to the Turks, and I'm a foreign writer to the Americans. I write in English and get translated into Turkish.

"It's an odd position and in a way difficult, because I don't belong anywhere."

November 8, 2000
The San Francisco Examiner

Orhan Pamuk

"I'm anti-fundamentalist. That's the main danger here now."

Istanbul

O rhan Pamuk is nothing if not ambitious. All he wanted to do in his novel *The Black Book* was to write a huge, richly textured, narrative that would capture the schizophrenic angst of Istanbul, a city in a country straddling two continents. He thus joined the search for an answer to the perennial Turkish question he defines as "Are we European? Or are we Asian?"

Earlier in his career, with his third novel, *The White Castle* (1991), Pamuk had merged two themes: a culture in the mysterious process of change and men in the mysterious process of changing identity. These themes emerge again in *The Black Book* (1994).

What better way to explore such mysteries than with a mystery?

In *The Black Book*, a lawyer, Galip ("Victorious"), searches for his missing wife, Ruya ("Dream"), and her half-brother, Jelal (a reference to the famous Sufi poet, Jelaled-din Rumi), a newspaper columnist and Galip's idol. The chapters alternate between Galip's third-person "investigation" and Jelal's first-person meditations, with each chapter preceded by quotations ranging from Sufi mystics to Lewis Carroll and Isak Dinesen. Two assassinations—and 300-odd pages later—we are no closer to a solution of whodunit or why, but Galip has taken on Jelal's persona, churning out words of wisdom for the next day's fishwrapper. And the reader is left with a Golden Horn-ful of literary puzzles to ponder.

At the age of thirty, Pamuk began to earn a formidable reputation in Turkey with the publication of his first novel, *Cevdet Bey and His Sons* (1982), which traced the lives of a wealthy Istanbul family over three generations in this century. Pamuk refuses to let his debut effort be translated, but a pirated edition exists—in Syria. His second book, *The Silent House* (1983), is a modernist novel about three unhappy siblings living with their dying grandmother after the 1980 military coup. The story is sifted through the consciousness of five narrators and was compared by some critics to the multiple-perspective works of Virginia Woolf and William Faulkner. It has been translated into French, Greek, and Italian.

In *The New York Times* review of *The White Castle*, Jay Parini hailed Pamuk as a "new star risen in the east . . . worthy of comparisons to Jorge Luis Borges and Italo Calvino . . . a storyteller with as much gumption and narrative zip as Scheherazade." John Updike, in *The New Yorker*, took a dimmer view of Pamuk's "post-modern atmosphere of fantasy and cleverness." In the novel, a seventeenth-century Venetian scholar is enslaved by Turkish pirates and given to a Muslim master. They resemble each other as closely as twins, and they eventually swap identities while inventing a super-weapon, a putatively fantastic war machine designed to destroy the enemy's white castle and fulfill the Ottoman dream of conquest. Updike criticized the unsuccessful machine as "vagueness on wheels . . . a kind of Rorschach test into which we read what we can . . ." Calling it a "brilliant, yet enervated, novel," Updike proposed that Pamuk "in his dispassionate intelligence and arabesques of introspection suggests Proust, but without that writer's sharp rendition of his memories."

As a sign of his growing popularity, Pamuk's *The New Life* (1997), a "visionary road novel," was published in Turkey in an unprecedented first edition of 50,000 copies with 35,000 sold in the first ten days. The book is a bow to Dante's *La Vita Nuova* and, Pamuk says, "it has affinities to German romanticism." The protagonist is a twenty-two-year-old youth who reads a book that changes his life.

The Black Book sold 70,000 copies, an "unbelievable" response in Turkey, Pamuk told me when we met at his book-lined study in the old cosmopolitan neighborhood of Nisantasi, whose sights, sounds, and smells are vividly rendered in the novel.

"Initially, there were huge media attacks on me. The controversy went on for months, and I enjoyed it!" the tall, lean Pamuk declared in lightly accented English, with an impish look that his spectacles can't hide. "They criticized my long sentences and my style. Then they moved to another level, talking about post-modernism. Then there was a political response from leftists and fundamentalists. The fundamentalists claimed that since I use some basic Sufi material, I'm mocking it. I don't take that seriously. Then, I've been criticized for not being a proper Kemalist." (The reference is to Kemal Ataturk, who established the secular Turkish republic in 1924, changed the alphabet from Ottoman Arabic to Latin, founded a system of public education, outlawed the fez, gave voting rights to women.)

Pamuk doesn't take that charge seriously either, but he believes that it's necessary to know a little Turkish history in order to understand the complaint.

"The Turkish left has a very Kemalist tradition," Pamuk noted. "In a way, they want to protect the state because the state has been a progressive westernizer, but in a way it's an anti-democratic force in Turkish history. All the westernization attempts have been made by the state itself, not by the civil society. So the Turkish left found itself in a dilemma. If you want westernization, you should defend the state, while on the other hand, leftism is meant to be anti-state. Politically, I'm on the left, but that doesn't mean much. I'm anti-fundamentalist. That's the main danger here now."

Pamuk pointed out that he was the first person in Turkey to defend Salman Rushdie when the Ayatollah Khomeini issued a death sentence on the author. Most Turkish intellectuals, explained Pamuk, whether conservative or leftist, hesitated to become involved in the controversy. "It's not because they are afraid," he said. "They think if the issue accelerates, we [writers] will lose. I don't agree, but I see their point."

At any rate, Pamuk has never been an outspokenly political writer. "I'm a literary person," he said. "Ten years ago, my friends used to criticize me for not being political enough. During the military coup in 1980, I was sitting here feeling guilty. Years before that, fascists and communists were killing each other in the streets. I stayed at home and wrote books. I always felt guilty because my friends were putting themselves in danger."

Pamuk grew up in a wealthy, secular household, headed by his grandfather, an engineer who ran a factory and made a fortune building railways. Theirs was a typical Ottoman home with relatives on every floor. The atmosphere gave Pamuk a feeling of freedom and the opportunity to indulge his bookish and artistic interests. "My father and uncles—they were all civil engineers—spent twenty years wasting that money," Pamuk said. "Then my father got involved in politics and taught at the university."

Pamuk's grandmother taught him to read before he started school. She also recited "almost atheistic" poems to him. "In my childhood, religion was something that belonged to the poor and to servants. My grandmother—who was educated to be a teacher—used to mock them. Now with the rise of the fundamentalist movement, it's the revenge of the poor against the educated, westernized Turks and their consumer-society life."

For the last twenty years, Pamuk added, "the Turkish economy has grown immensely, but the division of this wealth has been unjust. The poor are very poor and the two or three percent of Turks are very rich. Now the ruling elite has lost the culture that once held everyone together. The identity of the ultra-elite is now so westernized that they're not Turks anymore in that [cultural] sense. Their TV, their shows, the way they openly enjoy their life, paved the way for the rise of ultra-fundamentalism."

The White Castle may have been a reaction to the omnipresent question of identity. "I was trying to make a game of it and to show that it doesn't matter whether you are an easterner or a westerner. The worst way of reading—or misreading—the book would be to take very seriously the ideologies, the fake consciousness, the stupidities that one has about these notions. The problem of east or west has been a huge weight for Turkish intellectuals. More basic issues are reduced to this easy question. Also it's a very nationalistic question, and I don't like it."

In *The Black Book*, Pamuk's goal was to invent a literary language that would correspond to the texture of life in Istanbul. "I wanted to make you feel the terrors of living in this city, but not to describe it realistically. Imagine yourself walking in the streets of Istanbul, or crossing the Golden Horn on one of the bridges. Think about the images you see. All these sad faces, the huge traffic, the sense of history—more than 2,000 years of history—with Byzantine buildings converted into factories next to kitsch billboards. All this shabbiness. The book takes place just before the 1980 coup, when people were dying in the streets. I wanted to convey the idea of hopelessness, the idea of despair."

To weave that texture, Pamuk drew upon obscure stories he unearthed from traditional Sufi literature—largely unknown to the Turkish public—from the Arabian Nights, folktales, anecdotes, and murders written up in old newspapers, "Believe it or Not" columns, and scenes from American and Turkish movies.

His character/protagonist Galip's trip through an ancient underground passage filled with mannequins, past and present, of mountebanks, peasants, impersonators, soldiers, sinners, sages and scribblers, might also serve as a metaphor for the Ottoman culture, largely submerged after the language reform in 1924.

"The book has an encyclopedic side," Pamuk noted, "with all kinds of trivial knowledge about the past put together in a way that's not realistic but gives a sense that Mr. Pamuk is doing what Joyce has done for Dublin." He declared, however, that he was not "literally" inspired by Joyce.

As for the persistent theme of the doppelganger, Pamuk insisted, "that's not hardcore Pamuk." Language comes before theme on his agenda, but he admires others who have played with that idea. He has read Freud and Jung on the doppelganger themes "for fun," but he's never been in analysis himself. "I'm a straight Turk" he grins.

Did he ever want to be someone else? "That's a good question, and I take it very seriously. Yes, I have. I think writing is trying to be someone else. All the nineteenth century classical realists in effect impersonated the characters they invented. Let's say that creating a character is to be in the position of a double: to put oneself in another person's place."

184

As a youngster, he painted, then decided he would apply his artistic skills to architecture. But he dropped out of engineering school to start writing. Later, he earned a degree in journalism from the University of Istanbul. Living at home with no need for an outside income, he wrote diligently from age twenty-two to thirty. With the success of his first book, he married, although his rigorous schedule doesn't seem to offer much time with his wife, Aylin, and their three-year-old daughter Ruya (yes, named after the shadowy character in his book.) He writes every day from 11:00 P.M. to 4:00 AM, sleeps until noon and resumes work from 2:00 to 8:00 P.M.

Pamuk said that when he began writing he felt very unsure of himself. Four months at the Iowa Writers Workshop, however, convinced him that "being a writer was a very normal thing in America. So I got rid of some of my tension." He wrote more of *The Black Book* in Manhattan, while his wife worked on her PhD dissertation at Columbia.

About ten years ago, he began delving into Sufi literature, drawing on it for some of the more recondite yarns he spins in *The Black Book*. He also has some fun with them. He enjoys quoting Sheikh Galip, the eighteenth-century mystic poet who advises, "Enigma is sovereign, so treat it carefully." Enigma is certainly sovereign in Pamuk's realm. And Galip returns in *Black Book*.

Pamuk's got a sense of humor about his complex style. When I mentioned having had an interview with Juan Goytisolo, Pamuk laughingly commented, "He's more obscure than I am!"

Translating Pamuk isn't easy. For *The Black Book*, he turned to Guneli Gun, an Ohio-based Turkish-American novelist. The translation took two years. Since Turkish is an inflected language with the verb at the end of a sentence, Gun had to change the order of Pamuk's clauses and put them in logical and colloquial English while retaining his intricate effects. She told me that she would occasionally spend an entire day translating one of Pamuk's half-page-long sentences, working "until there was snap and style and sense to it." Luckily, she said, "Orhan doesn't worry about his holy word."

But Pamuk does savor the "holy" words of Sheikh Galip: "Enigma is sovereign, so treat it carefully."

December 19, 1994
Publishers Weekly

Postscript: In September 2005, right-wing Turkish prosecutors attemped and failed to put Pamuk on trial for telling a Swiss newspaper that "Thirty thousand Kurds and one million Armenians were killed in these lands [Turkey], and nobody but me dares to talk about it."

Pamuk had approached the political implications of that problem most directly in 2004 in the mesmerizing novel *Snow*. *The New York Times* reviewer called Pamuk "great and almost irresistibly beguiling."

7
Latin Beat

Juan Goytisolo

"It was always my objective to change the literary language of Spain."

Madrid

Language, sensuality, and subtle social concerns are inextricably linked in the novels and essays of Juan Goytisolo. Now the tangled roots of those passions are laid out in the first volume of his autobiography, *Forbidden Territory*. In a style alternately convoluted and frank, he describes the "intimate civil war of my sexuality and language."

He was a child of the Spanish Civil War, irrevocably stamped by its horrors, but his creative inspiration derives from Spain's Golden Age to which Jews and Arabs made tremendous cultural contributions before being expelled by the Inquisition.

Calling Goytisolo "clearly the great commander of modern Spanish prose," Carlos Fuentes wrote that "all of Spain's rich, golden threads now appear in the hands of Goytisolo, directed by his rebellious intelligence. He goes a long way to undo what the Catholic kings did back in 1492: They discovered a new world and sealed Spain off. Goytisolo discovers that all worlds are both old and new and dangerously open."

"It is very important to see your own culture by the light of other cultures and your language by the light of other languages," Goytisolo said during a brief stopover in

Madrid in 1989. He was en route from his home in Paris, where he lives with his wife, Monica Lange, a French novelist, to Morocco, where he spends half of each year. "I follow the rhythm of the storks," he said. "Winter in Marrakesh and Europe in the spring. It is the most beautiful rhythm of life."

His experiences in the United States—teaching Spanish literature at New York University, Boston University, and at La Jolla—also contributed to his international outlook. He is a slight man, almost frail-looking with somber blue-gray eyes and a reserved face except for the prominent nose that seems to assert his uniqueness.

Goytisolo's serious demeanor gives no clue to the wild satirical humor that dominates his fragmentary, plotless novel *Landscapes after the Battle* in which the author/protagonist joyfully envisions the takeover of Paris by former Arab and African colonists, tilts a sharp lance at noble causes and their fashionable bourgeois sympathizers, and fantasizes himself playing the role of the Rev. Charles Lutwidge Dodgson on the trail of compliant, pre-pubescent little vixens. It is a cheerfully pessimistic view of the apocalypse with little of the love-hatred for Spain that animates his other novels, *Marks of Identity*, *Count Julian*, and *Juan the Landless*, which attacked Spain's social, political, and linguistic orthodoxies.

"If you live in your own country, you don't have other points of comparison," Goytisolo said. "If you have many points of comparison, you can discover what is original and what is imitation. It was always my objective to change the literary language of Spain."

The critic V.S. Pritchett, comparing Goytisolo to James Joyce, Malcolm Lowry and Samuel Beckett, wrote, "He is fully worthy to be considered among the major innovators of our time."

Goytisolo's autobiography, *Forbidden Territory*, is a somewhat difficult but always compelling account of his boyhood in a pro-Franco, Catholic family, enriched by the wealth of ancestors in the Cuban sugar industry. Interspersed with stream-of-consciousness chapters questioning his impulse to autobiography, when so many personal details can be found in his novels, Goytisolo tells of his developing political and sexual awareness and his introduction to the world outside Spain.

"To say that I did not choose the [Spanish] language, but that I was chosen by it, would be the simplest way of conforming to the truth," Goytisolo notes, explaining why he writes in Spanish, although he was born in Catalan-speaking Barcelona. His mother, who was killed in a Fascist air raid when he was seven, and her parents had spoken Catalan, but his father, of Basque descent, insisted that Spanish be the primary language of their three sons: Juan; Luis, also a novelist; and José Agustin, a poet.

In Madrid, the brothers were treated like Catalans and in Barcelona, like Castilians, ostracized by both sides, "and yet enriched through this mutual rejection by the precious gifts of mobility and rootlessness." As a result of his wanderings, Goytisolo writes, "I would soon become that rare species of writer not claimed by anyone, alien and opposed to groups and categories."

Goytisolo said that he probably would not have written *Forbidden Territory* if he had been French or English. "There are magnificent autobiographies in those countries, but in Spain, they don't exist. Spanish autobiography was always to make a very beautiful image of the author. They talk about the private life of others but never the life of the writer. For me, that's not biography."

Some Spaniards—more men than women—were shocked by Goytisolo's revelation of his homosexuality, the instinct that drove him to seek sexual satisfaction with Arab laborers. Yet that same instinct impelled him into a study of Arab culture, history, tragedies and injustices. There is nothing sensational in his approach to the subject. "In Spain," he said, "there is grand hypocrisy and grand exhibitionism. Salvador Dali is the best example of that. You pass from hypocrisy to exhibitionism. I tried to make my way without hypocrisy and without exhibitionism."

Almost equally shocking to his father was Goytisolo's attraction to the underground Communist movement in opposition to the Franco government. Goytisolo eventually found himself repelled by the ineptness and illusions of the Spanish exiles he encountered in Paris and by the "mass meeting" mentality he observed in Castro's Cuba that seemed too similar to those imposed under Franco.

Although he is inclined to turn his back today on political involvement, he signed a full-page ad with 170 artists, actors, and writers, an open letter to Castro, calling for a plebiscite on his regime and the release of political prisoners. Goytisolo is also an advocate of a Palestinian state, but linked to the right of Israel's existence. He sees that position as of a piece with his defense of the Jewish-Arabic tradition in medieval Spain, pointing to the disastrous effects when both cultures were suppressed. "By the end of the seventeenth century, Spain was a cultural desert."

When Goytisolo went to Paris in 1965, full of ambition and the desire to shake loose the shackles and shadows of Franco's Spain, his friendship there with Jean Genet changed his life.

"I never met anyone like him," Goytisolo remarked, "I always say that humanity for me is Genet . . . and others. When I was very young, I tried to promote myself. For me, it was very important: success, and to meet important persons. After Genet, I realized that writing was what was important to me. Writing to express myself. Maybe love and the sexual life and the other things—social relations and the literary life—are not important at all. I changed completely. I look for authenticity. I look for what is important to me, not to play a social role and that kind of stuff."

January 22, 1989
San Francisco Chronicle

Juan José Campanella

"We wanted to escape the cliché of Latin American cinema showing miserable situations and miserable people."

San Francisco

There's more to that title *Son of the Bride* than meets the eye. It is, in fact, the director's gently humorous homage to his Alzheimer-stricken mother, who was never able to fulfill her dream of being re-married in church.

Juan José Campanella, whose Argentine production was one of five Oscar nominees for Best Foreign Film in 2001, didn't seem at all nervous about the outcome when he arrived in San Francisco just before the big Hollywood event. He said he wouldn't mind *too* much if Bosnia's *No Man's Land* won—which it later did.

He's just happy that *Son of the Bride* is Number One at the Argentine box office, drawing more crowds than *Harry Potter* and *Lord of the Rings*. Campanella's film co-stars the great actress Norma Aleandro as the mother whose memory has failed and Hector Alterio as her devoted husband, in their first film together since the devastating drama *The Official Story*. In that 1985 film, she plays a mother who is distraught when she learns that her adopted daughter is the child of one of the thousands who "disappeared" during the military dictatorship.

Aleandro herself was in exile for seven years during that grim period, but she is legendary for her extraordinary career in film and the theater—she "aged" from eighteen to eighty in Vargas Llosa's one-woman drama, *The Lady from Tachna*. She is also a script writer, playwright, and author of several books.

"I was very afraid to approach her because it's a small part," Campanella confessed, "and I had an image of an old-fashioned prima donna. But we sent her the script and when I called her, she immediately said, 'Come over to my house.' She was lovely and amazing. She knew Ricardo Darin, who plays the son, because they had worked together. The only question was who would play the father. When she heard it would be Hector, she agreed. She was only concerned because she had to say some foul words. Just reading the script, she didn't realize that the quality of self-censorship is lost along with memory in an Alzheimer's patient. So I said I would like you to meet my mom."

During their visit to the nursing home, Aleandro had a very loving reaction to his mother. "She said she saw something in my mother's eyes that would make it a challenge to play her. 'This would be the most difficult thing I've done in my life, but if it works out, it would be the most rewarding.'"

Campanella, forty-two, said the film was the process of a lot of conversations with Fernando Castets, his writing partner, about their own lives, and they kept changing their views in long hours of café philosophizing. They were obsessed with the idea of a character who had experienced failures but still had unrealized dreams. However, they still didn't have a story.

"One day, my father told me he wanted to marry my mother in a church even though she had Alzheimers. The church originally refused to perform the ceremony because she had been divorced from her first husband. My father had been an important oil engineer, but after handling the distribution of oil in the seventh largest country in the world, all he thought about after she became ill was taking care of my mother. He cared for her at home for three years, and it was an emotionally terrible time for him. And then she was in a nursing home for five years before she died. It made me wonder why I worry so much about my career."

Gradually, the fictional narrative took shape. Rafael (Ricardo Darin), the main character, is having a middle-life crisis with both his ex-wife and his girlfriend, while trying to keep his retired father's restaurant functioning without any help from the banks, his suppliers, or the government. His father's decision to re-marry in church helps to galvanize him into new actions. "We wanted to talk about the political reality of Argentina, the sell-off of the country, the disillusionment of the middle-class, and the collapse of the banking system. We thought of the restaurant as the perfect metaphor for that."

At the same time, Campanella, a fan of Billy Wilder and Frank Capra, wanted to keep the film's comedic edge. "We wanted to escape the cliché of Latin America cinema showing miserable situations and miserable people. This was a movie that sort of threw people off because it combined popular appeal and good craftsmanship. In Argentina, people just saw it as a very real film and didn't mention its social implications." However, abroad—with Argentina's economic and political crisis deepening—everybody asked about that aspect.

Although he was too young to have been directly affected by the military dictatorship, Campanella said, "The big lesson for me was how we should not allow any government to take charge of the media. Truly, truly a lot of people didn't know about the atrocities going on because most of what we know is through newspapers, and newspapers are telling you a completely different story."

Choosing his words with a trace of his characteristic humor, Campanella said that the first film "that knocked me off my feet was *Singing in the Rain*." He was fifteen and his mother had to drag him to see it because he wasn't interested in musicals. It was the first time he even thought about making a movie, but his parents insisted that he learn something that would bring in an income—like engineering. He entered engineering school, but at night he started studying film as a hobby. "At that school, I saw a thirty-two-year-old print of Capra's *It's a Wonderful Life*, and I had no idea movies could move you in such a way. To me, it was a serious psychological thriller. Later I learned it was a comedy, but I don't think I laughed once, and it completely changed my outlook. I saw for the first time the use of fantasy in a serious piece. Seeing a thirty-two-year-old movie that could still affect me even though I didn't understand the language, I thought that's really what I want to do. It became a process of how do I tell my parents that I want to drop out of engineering? Three months later when *All that Jazz* opened, I never went back to the university."

Campanella graduated from film school in Buenos Aires and then got a master's degree from New York University. For the last nineteen years, he has lived in New York, where he wrote and produced a play, *Off-Corrientes*, wrote television scripts, and directed two films, including *Same Love, Same Rain*, which he wrote with Castets, and which helped him to get financing for the $1.5 million *Son of the Bride*.

"I realized I found my voice in Argentina. I knew exactly the sense of humor and what to tell the actors. While filming, we realized something was brewing and we wanted to say that only the love of the people and a sense of community would help us through. Three months later, an older woman went into the street banging on an empty pot to show she couldn't put food in it. Her action triggered a massive outpouring of the middle-class, which knocked down two presidents in eight days. The Argentine Congress is impeaching all nine justices of the Supreme Court." The children of the 'disappeared' are now in their twenties and want to annul the laws that gave amnesty to the military. "It's still an open wound for them," Campanella said. "It's a very exciting time."

April 11, 2002
The San Francisco Examiner

Lucrecia Martel

"It was absurd that for a country with such a history of horrors, Argentina has no horror films."

San Francisco

An Argentinean Chekhov? A miracle-worker? Altman-esque? A subtle David Lynch? A transcendent Jane Campion?

Critics are having a tough time trying to categorize Lucrecia Martel, writer/director of *The Holy Girl*. Her protagonist, adolescent Amalia, is bedeviled, caught between sexuality and spirituality, while her divorced mother yearns to fulfill her own erotic needs and a doctor visiting their hotel home for a medical convention provokes troubling questions and answers.

There was a glint of humor in Martel's brown eyes as she awaited yet another interrogation to explain what is hinted at in her portrayal of the mother-daughter relationship. Martel's film may be elusive, but she was only too willing to talk as she sat curled up in a hotel chair during a visit to the 2005 San Francisco Film Festival. It was a long road that took her from the repressive Argentine military dictatorship to reliance on an all-protective father, to a lost feeling of "divine abandonment," finally to grasp the reins of her own life and "make a commitment to the rest of society."

Although Catholicism is the thesis that runs throughout the film, nobody in Martel's family was extremely religious, she said through an interpreter. Born in 1966 in Salta, "the most class-conscious conservative area of northern Argentina," she attended a private Catholic school with civilian teachers whose attempts at theological indoctrination were "often superficial and the atmosphere was repressive rather than reflective." Her father, a paint store owner, and her mother had their own ways of dealing with Catholic theology. On his side of the family, Martel said, "They were mostly atheists and believers in science. My mother had an unconventional, anarchical, populist religious feeling, but it was not associated with the church."

It was a crowded household with two sisters, four brothers, turtles, lizards, toads, and pigs. The family didn't bother with mundane pets like cats and dogs. The second-oldest sibling, Martel thought of animal husbandry as a career , but she was also interested in astronomy. Although she had the use of a video camera when she was fifteen, she wasn't at all interested in becoming a filmmaker. She made a lot of home movies, but she was mainly intrigued by the dialogue she overheard and the attitudes of her siblings. Later, whispered words and oblique gestures would play a vital role in Martel's understated style.

Fed up with private education, she went to a public university in Buenos Aires still without any clear idea of what she wanted to do. A major in communications led to a course in animation, which in turn stimulated an interest in filmmaking. She was working on a dissertation about architecture in horror films when her advisor died and Martel dropped out of school.

She had been studying mostly Hollywood horror films like *Night of the Living Dead* and *The Last House on the Left*. "The genre of horror films is very conservative," she explained. "At the same time, they describe very well the spirit of certain time periods and during the sixties, seventies, and eighties, they changed quite a bit. For example, when AIDS made an appearance, a whole series of films showed something horrible and hidden inside the body, and this horror is transmitted from person to person. It's absurd, in a way, that for a country with such a history of horrors, Argentina has no horror films."

After making a number of "unimportant television documentaries," Martel began to feel that "filmmaking was where you could make a commitment to society. That may seem like a very odd remark, but it's a very generational way of thinking in Argentina because—after the dictatorship—my generation couldn't find a place to feel really committed."

Hollywood films in the eighties didn't seem to offer any models because they "emphasized personal improvement and personal growth in a neo-liberal approach. But I was more interested in the way people from my region tell stories to each other when they take naps at siesta time, the different kinds of stories I heard from my mother, father, and grandmother."

In her first feature film, the acclaimed 2001 *La Cienaga* (The Swamp, a town in northwest Argentina), Martel explored the lives of two bourgois families who drink too much and look down on their Indian servants. She didn't see them as mean-spirited, but rather as "people who feel a little bit lost and abandoned and don't have a clear idea of what their lives will be like."

For Martel, "A film is not a story, it's not a whole series of intellectual ideas, but an emotional process. It's a very special feeling I had and one that I perceived in the area where I grew up. I could sum it up as 'divine abandonment,' but I don't know how that sounds in English. It's about a society that takes on its whole moral structure with the thought of a father that protects you from a moral point of view. But then you get to the point where you don't have a sense that father is *really* protecting you. And finally you have to take the reins of your own life. And that is the moment when you make your commitment to people."

In the case of *The Holy Girl*, desire is thought of as something that comes from the divine and how that runs up against all the moral traps and traps of society. Amalia always seems to be listening for the voice of God to explain her role in the divine plan while hearing erotic gossip from her best friend. She tries to cope with the new sensation she feels after one doctor rubs up against her in a crowd. While fighting her own aroused emotions, she decides it is her vocation to redeem the doctor.

"In spite of the good intentions that Amalia may have in terms of salvation, when you take into account a whole moral framework of prejudices, those good intentions could turn into something nefarious," Martel said, but leaves any further explanation up to the film viewers.

"In the area where I grew up, the whole perception about sexual experience is so extraordinary and so special that it would seem to be coming from the divine. Or the supernatural. It's not the religious tradition of repression, exemplified in that rather negative aspect of mysticism that deals with self-flagellation, but it's closer to the tradition in which the mystics identified religious experience as being very close to human desire.

"I want to make it very clear," she said emphatically, "that I am not interested in the whole topic of sexual repression or guilt or any of those things. That always comes up and that is the wrong reading of my film."

When *The Holy Girl* opened in Argentina, Martel was afraid "that people might think I was taking sexual abuse lightly or that I might not think of it as something important, but the response was far more interesting than that. More complex, more thoughtful, less attached to the more typical superficial reading that people do when a film deals with a religious topic. That was really a nice surprise!!"

May 13, 2005
The Oakland Tribune

Federico Luppi

PHOTO BY JUDY STONE.

"Argentina was the worst military dictatorship in the Western Hemisphere."

Buenos Aires

A controversial Argentine film that became a pawn in the hands of left-wing guerrillas *and* right-wing Peronistas kept Federico Luppi on the blacklist for eight years, but it didn't prevent him from eventually becoming Latin America's most famous star and recipient of a Lifetime Achievement award at the Los Angeles Latino International Film Festival in 2003. Audiences had the opportunity to see Luppi's most famous films, including *Rebellion in Patagonia*, the one that wreaked havoc in his life.

Since *Rebellion* is now ancient history, he was able during an impromptu 2002 interview in Buenos Aires to talk with a certain grim humor about the perilous days when he stayed on the run to avoid capture by the Argentine military, which was engaged in hunting down and killing many actors, writers, and trade-unionists.

In person and on film, Luppi embodies a quality of gracious authority whether playing the doctor in John Sayles' *Men with Guns*, a beleaguered physician-administrator in an orphanage during the Spanish Civil War in Guillermo Del Toros' *The Devil's Backbone*, or a Uruguayan hijacker determined to de-rail Hollywood's acquisition of a treasured locomotive in Diego Arsuaga's *The Last Train*.

His masculine charm, enhanced—rather than diminished—by age (sixty-seven), makes Luppi an object of seduction in George Sluizer's *The Stone Raft*. "TWO women!" he exclaimed with a rather triumphant chuckle. "They practically raped me!" He also can't resist a philosophical chuckle when recounting the number of cinematic deaths he's endured. "That's the story of my life," he jokes.

As for his new honor, Luppi said that "it is more than I deserve, but it makes me happy because it places me in the ranks of previous recipients . . . and makes me feel solidarity with the Latin world."

His Lifetime Achievement award came at an auspicious turn in his career: he was about to direct his first film, *Steps*, in Spain (where he has lived for the last few years). *Steps* follows three couples whose friendship changes after the attempted coup d'etat by Lt. Col Antonio Tejero Molina on February 23, 1981, who unsuccessfully marched fifty Guardia Civil into Parliament to stage a military uprising. Based on an original script by Susana Fernandez Abascal (Luppi's wife), the story revolves around how the coup and subsequent affirmation of democracy affects the personal lives of the three couples. (Before making the film, Luppi wrote about the fear he felt in his new role as a director. "Sometimes I wake up bathed in sweat, and to go back to sleep, I cross my fingers real hard until they hurt." When the film was finished, Luppi noted in another email that it was "a passionate and totally enriching experience.")

Directing was not something Luppi contemplated when we talked in Buenos Aires.

"My dream from my childhood was to be great at drawing," he began in a mixture of lightly accented English and Spanish, while joyfully recalling his early love for comic books like *Flash Gordon* and *Tarzan*. Later he was to fall in love with American literature. He ticks off the names: "Dos Passos, Hemingway, Faulkner, Caldwell, Kerouac, and many others."

Born in a village in the north of Argentina, his father, a farmer and a butcher, wanted him to be an architect.

"At one moment, I thought I would be an architect because from time immemorial, architecture and drawing are very related. Great sculptors are often wonderful draftsmen. There's an old saying that if someone cannot draw very well, he cannot paint. All the great painters were also very good draftsmen. In the literary world, if a writer cannot understand the magical charge of the word, he cannot make literature. All this is to explain why I adored drawing."

However, he was sidetracked into law school for one year. "I didn't love it! But I was influenced by American TV and fascinated by the idea that one could convince juries by acting, not by the law, but by the magic movement of the word."

When he discovered less-magical aspects of that profession, he dropped out. A chance visit to a theater rehearsal soon led him to study acting.

Before long, he had his first little theater job playing a Nazi colonel in a production about Janusz Korczak, a Polish educator who dedicated his life to protecting Jewish children in the Warsaw ghetto during World War II and went to the concentration camps with them. (That true story was made into a controversial film by Andrzej Wajda.) Luppi loved the part because the colonel was not a one-dimensional character. "He had deep and painful issues of conscience."

Issues of conscience were very much on the minds of Argentinian artists and writers who lived through the turbulent days of Peron and the successive military coups that followed his ouster in 1955. For a few years, Luppi was able to work in the theater and on TV, but then in 1973, he starred in *Rebellion in Patagonia*.

During a rare moment of liberalization, director Hector Olivera had received permission to make the film, which portrayed the army's extermination in 1921 of hundreds of striking workers on the huge landed estates of rural Patagonia. Many of them were European immigrants with an anarchist outlook. Luppi played Facon Grande (Big Knife), a brave gaucho who has become an independent teamster. He is enlisted to organize farm hands because of his moral authority and his reputation for siding with the underdog. He was to die before the military's firing squad.

By the time *Rebellion* was finished in April 1974, the military mind considered it a threat to the government. Left-wing guerrillas were using a print of the film to train new recruits when the right-wing military "kidnapped" it, Luppi said. Those connected to the film were considered supporters of the extreme left-wing. Luppi was blacklisted for eight years and moved from one place to another to avoid capture. Olivera couldn't make any new films. It was the period that became known as "the dirty war" when 30,000 people were estimated to have been "disappeared."

"It was the worst military dictatorship in theWestern Hemisphere," Luppi said. At least, the Nazis—"with their Teutonic rigor"—kept records of what they had done. In Argentina, "they worked in a perverted and sadistic way because they hid everything they did at night, without witnesses. They invented the 'disappeared.'"

Luckily, around 1976, a Spanish producer invited Luppi to Madrid to star in a play, *The Great Eye-Opener*, about a married couple in the painful end of their relationship. The trip abroad also provided a different kind of eye-opener for him. Not only was the proposal a safety net for Luppi, keeping him away from Argentina's military junta, but he was excited to observe the collapse of the Franco dictatorship. It was during a complicated transition period as Spain was moving away from the Fascist regime toward democratic elections. Luppi found the atmosphere as "fascinating and attractive as a Hemingway novel."

But after a year, he returned to Argentina because he was worried about his two children—then five and six years old, who were living with his ex-wife. "They were safe, more or less," he said, "but the dictatorship didn't respect any kind of relationship. You might be the one they were looking for, but they would get your sister or your friend."

Those years still take a toll on him. Luppi responded pessimistically when asked in an e-mail how he felt about the newly elected Argentine president Nestor Kirchner's plan to throw a vigorous, fresh light on the long-dormant issue of the 30,000 "disappeared" during the "dirty war."

"I feel a large part of my soul is deadened," he replied. "The lies and moral and financial deceit of the political leaders and functionaries of my country have been so numerous and so despicable, that, frankly, it has become difficult for me to attach any credibility to the new president's initiatives. I don't deny either the good faith nor the willingness of Mister Kirchner to embark upon such a laborious task; but for many decades Peronism has shown itself to be full of contradictions, duplicity, and irresponsible morals . . . a permanent source of corruption and thuggery. For many, many years, it has been the dominant and majority ideology in Argentina and that, with the help of military coups and the ineptitude and mediocrity of the Radical Party has cast the country into total ruin. I do not accuse the new president of this, but if he wants to return some measure of faith to the people of Argentina, he must effectively break with the accomodationism and self-serving policies of the Party . . . I wish him well."

Earlier, reflecting on the situation in the world today, Luppi had talked about hating "the business of war hidden under the blanket of a crusade for freedom. None of us can stop feeling the horrors that we are living in, but we need in our soul dreams of utopia. You can't live without dreams. How can you live without love, without wine, without potatoes, without films? There's something in the world that goes beyond the oppression of the business world and the cruelty of money. We need to touch each other, to embrace and to smell and to dream. It's very important because if that's not true—POW ! you would have to shoot yourself!"

July 23, 2002
Los Angeles Times

Maria de Medeiros

"In Portugal, I didn't think we had heroes and we do!"

Montreal

Not every actress can casually quote Plato to the effect that "the transmission of knowledge is always an affair of love, although it might not be physical," but intellectual depth is only one aspect of what makes Maria de Medeiros special. It's not every tiny beauty who can write, direct, and act in a film like *April Captains*, based on the incredible, true, peaceful uprising of Portuguese soldiers against their country's fascist dictatorship. It's not every little woman who can map out a film like a battle plan and get thousands of real soldiers to snap to attention with nary a macho murmur in the air.

"How does she do it?" I asked her husband, Agusti Camps, at the 2000 Montreal World Film Festival, where Maria was on the jury. "She's a general!" he replied with a laugh. She's also the mother of Julia, who's got bright eyes and a beguiling air of self-assurance for a two-year-old who made her movie debut in *April Captains*.

De Madeiros' shy exterior masks a quick-witted intelligence and rare sensitivity; she may not have the commanding profile of a Gen. George Patton, but she certainly showed the genes of a diplomat when she was cast in her first international hit as the novelist Anaïs Nin in Philip Kaufman's *Henry and June* (1990), in which two women competed for the love of Henry Miller. At 5'1", Maria confessed she was a little intimidated when she met her co-star, Uma Thurman, a languid six-footer, playing June, Anais' competition for the attention of Henry Miller. "I thought the best thing would be to say how I felt. What I actually said was that I told my friends she must be the most beautiful girl in the world, and I was very surprised when I learned that I would work with her. It was a way for me to let her know she could trust me. I wanted her to understand I would never be against her."

Maria may have picked up some diplomatic pointers from her father, a musician who was briefly the Portuguese cultural attache in Vienna, where she lived for her first ten years. She was nine when the soldiers who had been fighting in Portugal's unpopular African wars launched their successful one-day revolution on April 25, 1974. "My parents were euphoric," she recalled. "They were jumping around in the apartment. I don't think I had ever seen them that happy, and I realized something very important had happened. Funnily enough, I was brought up like a little Austrian child, so I liked order. I liked things to be clean. To be proper. Then I went to Portugal, where I had been born, and it was the biggest mess, so I thought everything was horrible. All I wanted was to go back to Austria and forget about that revolutionary time. It took me maybe three years to realize I had gone through something very important to live in the building up of a democracy."

It helped to make friends whose parents had been active in the resistance to the thirty-six-year-long Salazar dictatorship. Her best friend became Teresa Villaverde, whose mother had been engaged to Maria's father when they were teenagers. Teresa went on to become a director, and Maria won a Best Actress award at the 1994 Venice Film Festival for her role in Villaverde's dark drama *Tres Irmaos*.

Her career has been divided between theater and film, between Portugal and Paris (where she still lives). At a French school in Lisbon she was profoundly influenced by a philosophy teacher who was also instrumental in developing Lisbon's National Theater. While she was still his student, she performed as Electra in Aeschylus' *Eumenides* and as Jennie in Brecht's *The Rise and Fall of the City of Mahagonny*. She spent a year at the Sorbonne in Paris studying philosophy (which she loved), but drama school became more appealing.

"I was terribly lucky," she said. "I got work very quickly, always in leading roles." The first one was as young Cleopatra in Corneille's drama, *La Mort de Pompee*. Then she did *Elvire-Jouvet 40*, a famous play based on real drama lessons taught by actor Louis Jouvet before World War II. He had been coaching a talented young drama student in the role of Elvire, Don Juan's wife, in Moliere's play, but when the actress finally triumphed, she was denounced as a Jew, ending a promising career. De Medeiros toured in the play for three years all over the world.

In 1991, she also made her directorial debut with an hour-long film, *The Prince's Death*, based on the writings of Fernando Pessoa, a drama that had previously been a big hit in the theater. Both directing and acting as Salome gave her confidence to forge ahead with *April Captains*, an idea she had since she was twenty-one, which took ten years to realize. She had thought about making a war film when she saw Robert Aldrich's *Attack* (1956), a re-enactment of the Battle of the Bulge. "It was so strong, incredible, incredible." Another film, *Paths of Glory*, gave her an idea of what she could explore as a woman.

But why did she want to make a war film? "It's like who came first, the chicken or the egg?" she responded. "In Portugal, I didn't think we had heroes and we do! The way the soldiers took over without any violence was so civilized, so human. There aren't many examples of that, and they didn't seek power afterwards."

Most of the material she worked with came from the diary of her main character, the *April Captain*, Salguiero Maia, who served in the bloody wars in Portugal's African colonies, Mozambique and Angola. "Then he and all the other soldiers decided 'no more of this' and they made the revolution in a totally pacific way. Maia went with grenades in his pockets, and he was ready to blow himself up like the kamikaze if it was necessary. He was absolutely a hero during those twenty-four hours. He became a key participant in the overthrow of dictator Marcelo Caetano, who had succeeded Salazar. When it was over, Captain Maia went back to his barracks and stayed there for fifteen years. He had no political ambitions, and I thought that was really extraordinary."

The film starts, as the revolution did: with a song, *Grandola*, which was outlawed during the Salazar dictatorship and played on the radio to signal the beginning of the military coup that toppled the regime. De Medeiros plays the role of a young teacher/journalist who bridges two worlds in conflict. In the film, her brother, a minister of the Gaetano government, supports the old regime, whereas her husband—who has just returned from the colonial wars—is sympathetic to the mutinying army captains, but his wife no longer loves him because of his service in the army. She is involved with a long-haired boyfriend who had been a political prisoner. Two groups of men are followed: one takes over the barracks to march toward Lisbon with the tanks—although the city streets were not built for tanks. "They have trouble getting in, and they don't know if they must stop at the red lights or not!" she said. "The other group takes over the radio station, and they keep the country informed during the next twenty-four hours."

204

De Medeiros' mother, a political journalist who had interviewed many of the real soldiers, liked the *April Captains* script, but had one reservation. "The only thing she didn't like," Maria said, "was the woman's part. She wanted me to develop it in a better way."

She originally wrote the leading role of Capt. Maia for Joaquim de Almeida, a famous Portuguese actor, but because it took ten years to make the film, he was then too old. It was important for her to have the soldiers be as young as they were when the revolution occurred. So Joaquim became the character who puts the events in perspective. "He's like a Cassandra—a tragic character, who only sees bad things."

Many people thought she would never make the movie. "They just laughed at me." But eventually she raised $4 million in a co-production deal with France, Spain, Italy and Portugal and won the cooperation of the army for the nine-and-a-half-week shoot. "Funnily enough," she said, "I was very attacked by cinema critics on historical points, but I was defended by historians, who liked my interpretation of the events, and *April Captains* was accepted by the army. The army people were wonderful. They absolutely trusted me. They never saw anything wrong with a woman directing the story, and for the first time in my life, I never felt any machismo."

2000
Unpublished

Postscript: In 2002, while pregnant with her second daughter, de Medeiros took on the role of inquiring reporter with *J t'Aime Moi Non Plus*, a documentary she shot at the 2002 Cannes Film Festival, in which she asked critics and directors to analyze their relationships to each other. Said director Ken Loach, "It's the relationship between a lamppost and a dog." And British critic Alexander Walker explains why he never walks out on movies before they're over: "Like a prostitute, I never refuse a client."

Carlos Saura

"Goya is part of the past, present, and future."

Montreal

Carlos Saura still remembers the bombs that terrified him during his childhood. For years, the director tried to circumvent censors and to re-create the horrors of the Spanish Civil War and its aftermath through the memories of his fictional characters. But for him, nothing compares to *The Disasters of War*—those incisive engravings by Francisco José de Goya y Lucientes that stripped all battlefields of false heroics, laying bare the savagery, brutality, and anguish that consumed the combatants.

Introducing *Goya in Bordeaux* at the 1999 Montreal World Film Festival, Saura, sixty-eight, demonstrated a warmth and humor that delighted his listeners, even as he declared his serious intentions.

"The fact that this film is set in the past does not mean it has no relevance in the present," he said. "Goya is part of the past, present, and future. Think of the events in

Kosovo not so long ago and you can find the same images, the same tragedy, the same horrible events. Goya was a visionary, an artist who had not only the power to open a world and see byond that, but to do it with imagination that helps you to go beyond realism."

There is a direct relationship between Saura's thoughts about Goya and about the Spanish Civil War. "Goya was portraying something very much ahead of his time," Saura said. "I don't know any painter who has covered so extensively, in art, the business of war, the emotions of war, the details, the stupidity that surrounds us. It's extraordinary work."

In Saura's film, the eighty-two-year-old Goya (Paco Rabal) is living in exile in Bordeaux with the last of his lovers, the much-younger Leocadia Zorilla de Weiss (played by Saura's wife, Eulalia Ramon). Goya recounts the events of his life to Leocadia's twelve-year-old daughter, Rosario (Daphne Fernandez), who reminds the viewer of other simpatico youngsters in many of Saura's films that are obsessed with children and their memories of war.

A native (like Saura) of the province of Aragon in northern Spain, Goya witnessed his country's imperial decline from the enlightenment of Charles III to the corruption of Charles IV's court and the confrontation between liberalism and tyranny under Ferdinand VII, which forced Goya to end his life in exile. We see the dashing young Goya (José Coronado) display his love for the seductive Duchess of Alba (Maribel Verdu), who enraged Queen Maria Luisa by also attracting the attention of the queen's playboy lover, Manuel Godoy. We witness the changes in Goya's life and art after a mysterious illness leaves him totally deaf. In a spectacular scene, Saura presents a dramatic staging of *Disasters of War* with La Fura del Baus, a popular Catalan action-theater group.

Saura has been preoccupied with Goya ever since he saw the artist's work at the Prado Museum in Madrid. To learn more, Saura studied that artist's paintings, drawings, and engravings, quoting his words: "I see neither line nor color, only shadows moving back and forth." That comment, according to Saura's late brother Antonio, a highly respected artist and a Goya expert, was the clearest statement he knew on the subject of modern painting. Goya—with his free-spirited etchings *Los Caprichos*, which savagely satirized the court and the church—is considered a precursor of that art.

"Goya has pursued me my whole life," Saura said. "I've always felt a powerful attraction for his paintings and his personality, and both are still a mystery to me."

Saura wanted to make his film years ago, but it wasn't possible. "Sometimes you really have to fight hard for projects," he commented obliquely, "but if you really want to do something, you will succeed."

Another key influence on Saura's life was filmmaker Luis Buñuel who also came from Aragon. Saura was a child when he met Buñuel because his mother, a concert pianist, knew Buñuel's family. (Saura's father was secretary of the treasury in the last

Republican government before the Civil War.) Saura began his career as a photographer specializing in music and dance subjects, an interest that later culminated in his 1980s collaboration with dancer/choreographer Antonio Gades on the dance trilogy *Blood Wedding* (a ballet film based on the Federico Garcia Lorca play), *Carmen*, and *El Amor Brujo* (Love, the Magician).

When Saura took his first feature, *Los Golfos* (*The Urchins*) to the Cannes Festival in 1960, he saw Buñuel, who had been living in Mexico since 1947 and persuaded him to return to Spain to make *Viridiana*, a film that finally outfoxed Franco's censors.

"I felt the similarities between us," Saura recalled. "We looked at life in a special way with a sense of humor. It's difficult to explain. We looked at it with irony and cruelty but at the same time with affection and friendship."

They agreed, Saura has said, about the personal suffocation caused by Spanish religion, education, and family life. "Film to me was a way to do gymnastics of the imagination to escape." He likes to quote Buñuel's phrase that "imagination is innocent." In one's imagination, Saura expanded, "you can kill anyone you hate." This desire to escape the socio-political realities of Spanish life—and the censors—was expressed in Saura's tendency to mix real and dream worlds and to move back and forth in time in his films. In his next production, Saura revealed, he will explore the complex relationships among Buñuel, Salvador Dali, and Federico Garcia Lorca, poet and playwright.

With *Peppermint Frappe* (1967), Saura began his personal and professional collaboration with Geraldine Chaplin that lasted through the seventies with *Cousin Angelica* (1973), *Cria Cuervos* (1975), *Elisa, My Love* (1977), *Blindfold* (1978), and the comedy *Mama Turns 100* (1979), which was nominated for an Academy Award.

As Saura moved from metaphorical political themes to more personal ones—as in *Elisa, My Love*, about the relationship between a father and daughter—he attempted to define his political views.

"I am afraid of the eagerness shown by every established power to set up repressive machinery, that obsession with classifying, defining every one," Saura said. "We all live in police states full of files, and the saddest thing is that when those ideologically closer to us are in power, they will also try to control people's lives, education, and information."

September 19, 2000
San Francisco Chronicle

Guillermo del Torro

"A perfect match to do a ghost story in the middle of a much-larger ghost story, the Spanish Civil War."

Toronto

Guillermo del Torro has been fascinated by ghosts and monsters ever since he was a kid in Mexico, but when he grew older he became intrigued by true stories about monsters of another sort—the Fascists who won the Spanish Civil War. So yes, there is the ghost of a murdered boy in his new film *The Devil's Backbone*, but the orphanage that youngster haunts is a metaphor for the war outside its walls.

"It was quite a horrifying war," del Toro said at the 2001 Toronto International Film Festival, "because it was brother against brother, father against son, full of family conflicts. Many who escaped the Franco regime came to live in Mexico, and a lot of them took positions in the Mexican cinema as directors, writers, and critics. One in particular was a good friend of mine, Emilio Garcia Riera, who escaped from Spain with his mother when he was ten and eventually became the most famous Mexican film historian. He guided me to other people who could tell me about the war and to books about it."

Del Toro, who won international fame with his first feature, *Cronos* (a Mexican horror movie with a grandfatherly vampire and an oddball sense of humor), said that the characters in his new film represent the different factions in the civil war. The children are the offspring of Spanish Loyalists. Dr. Casares and Carmen, the peg-legged school director, are "wonderfully idealistic and brave and strong and not in complete contact with reality," del Toro said. "And Jacinto, the young caretaker, is youthful, greedy, and strong. He has a huge class conflict and is only able to articulate how he feels by violence."

A bulky figure with a still cherubic face at thirty-seven, del Toro was born in Guadalajara, where his father had an automobile dealership. Today, he is married to his childhood sweetheart, a veterinarian, and they have two children. But when he was growing up, he felt absolutely alien to the rest of the kids. "I was very thin, very pale, very quiet." He was obsessed by monsters and sin. Since his mother, an artist who believed in "white witchcraft," traveled a lot, he was raised mainly by a devoutly Catholic great aunt he called his grandmother. He adored her even though she made him walk to school with bottle caps in his shoes, presumably to strengthen his spirituality. "My grandmother turned me into the Catholic Church, which I later abandoned completely. I'm an ex-Catholic. I used to say I was an atheist, but I don't anymore because I truly believe, once a Catholic, always a Catholic. It's not something you can brush off. "

He became disillusioned with religion when he was thirteen and saw a heap of discarded fetuses in the morgue of the local hospital. "I understood then that there was no God," he said when he was promoting *Cronos*. Still, that image stayed with him and shows up in the row of bottled fetuses, immersed in rum, a pseudo-medicinal drink for the superstitious, in Dr. Casares' laboratory. When he first conceived the idea of *The Devil's Backbone*, it would have been set in Mexico as "a horror film, purely moved by Catholic imagery," but he abandoned that notion when the locale was changed to Spain.

The film is set toward the end of the Spanish War and about six months before World War II. "It was the first Fascist conflict in Europe," del Toro says, "and a trial for so many weapons and so many things. The orphanage becomes a place that seems to be away from the war but has the war right in the middle of it, even metaphorically, with a huge bomb outside that never exploded. I felt it was a perfect match to do a ghost story in the middle of a much-larger ghost story which was the war. "

Del Toro doesn't think World War II could have been averted even if the United States, England, and France had taken more aggressive intervention in favor of the Loyalists and the Republic, "but it could have been been very different." He based his opinions not only on the pro-Loyalist books that came out in the fifties and sixties, but on recent histories "that have a more balanced point of view in a way. What seemed at first an easy-to-define conflict was not like that, but quite complex. However, I do think it was also the death of an ideal. I believe that the Republican government at that time was quite progressive and before the war was taking enormous steps toward equality and a rational beautiful society, but it was sadly interrupted."

The ghosts of that era have still not been exorcised, del Toro learned while filming in Madrid with the co-production team of El Deseo, formed by the director Pedro Almodovar and his brother Agustin, who agreed with the Mexican filmmaker's approach to his subject.

Marisa Paredes, who plays the widowed Carmen, torn in anguish between her sexual needs and her love for the impotent Dr. Casares, was most recently seen in Pedro Almodovar's *All About My Mother* and Arturo Ripstein's *No One Writes to the Colonel*. For Dr. Casares, del Toro turned to Federico Luppi, the Argentinian actor who starred in *Cronos*.

Del Toro calls Luppi "one of the last true leftist gentleman. That's a contradiction in terms in a way since the concept of a gentleman is totally bourgeois, but he is absolutely a leftist gentleman. He is a very political guy and coherent in his beliefs. He stayed in Argentina during the most conflicted years. He was never a political prisoner and never among the 'disappeared,' but he was severely interrogated by the secret police. He was always very brave and knows the Spanish Civil War story perfectly."

Not surprisingly, the war was very ancient history to the youngsters in the production, but as the filming progressed, they began reading about it and would come to del Toro and say, "Franco did this and Franco did that." They saw about 400 children before they finally cast Fernando Tielve as Carlos, the brave and sensitive new boy who is harrassed by the old-timers in the orphanage. "His instincts as an actor are very good," del Toro said. "I gave him a heavy monologue, and he memorized it in ten minutes. Most important, he received and executed instructions, which I find key with kid actors because their attention span is somewhat smaller, so you have to give them very specific emotional and physical tasks. Inigo Garces, who plays the bully Jaime, has been in a number of Spanish movies, but he said something to me in the middle of the shoot which was very beautiful. He said, 'I think in this movie I have really become an actor.'

"This is a story with a ghost," del Toro said, "but it's not just a horror film out to scare you. It's much deeper and sadder than that. I would like people to come out of the theater with a feeling of nostalgia and loss. Everybody has a ghost behind them."

July 23, 2003

The San Francisco Examiner

Arturo Ripstein

PAZ ALICA GARCIADIEGO AND ARTURO RIPSTEIN. PHOTO BY JUDY STONE.

"Art, I always understood, was convulsive, never nice or lovely."

Park City, Utah

There's an ironic personal history behind the scenes of *The Beginning and the End*, an Egyptian family novel transposed to Mexico by film director Arturo Ripstein and produced by his father, Alfredo.

The film, based on the acclaimed novel by Nobel Prize-winner Naguib Mahfouz, describes the gradual disintegration of a family after the father dies. The mother, her daughter, and two sons all make sacrifices to assure the education of the third son, but their worthy intentions are finally self-defeating.

The Ripstein father-son reunion as a team nearly thirty years after their first collaboration had all the elements of a black comedy, to hear Arturo tell it with dry, deadpan humor when the film was screened at the 1994 Sundance Festival.

The grizzled Ripstein and his elegant screenwriter wife, Paz Alicia Garciadiego, fell in love with Mahfouz's novel and thought it could fit easily into the Mexican scene. "Paz" was fascinated by the guilt-ridden personalities of all the characters.

"Guilt is very rooted in the Mexican culture," the screenwriter said. "It's not only inherent in Catholicism, but it's characteristic of a country which lost half of its territory in two defeats. If you put that in a very macho society, Mexicans have a sense of guilt that they're never good enough."

"It's the brutal inhumanity of the Mahfouz characters that appealed to me," Arturo Ripstein added. "It's very immediate and very deep at the same time with a masterful structure."

The couple gave Mahfouz's novel to Alfredo Ripstein as a birthday present, and after Alfredo read the novel, he decided to buy the rights, much to Arturo's dismay. "I remembered my horrible experience making my first film with my father. It was Gabriel Garcia Marquez's original script, *A Time to Die*. I had gone to my father for financing and he said no. After I threatened to kill him or myself, he agreed, but only if I did it as a Western, which he could sell to Germany. We had to dress the characters as cowboys—which I didn't like at all, but at the time Mexican Westerns were big in Germany. Still, my father didn't sell it to Germany until years after I made other films. After that, we didn't talk to each other for many years."

As a producer, Alfredo "liked upper-middle-class families—very sensible, very legitimate, very wise . . . and very disgusting," Ripstein said. As a young man, Arturo had realized other possibilities when he saw Luis Buñuel's ambiguous *Nazarin*, the story of an unworldly priest whose Christian acts lead to disaster for himself and others. "My need was to be on the side of art," Ripstein explained, "and art I always understood was convulsive, never nice or lovely or to make you feel that your life was good."

At eighteen, Arturo became Buñuel's personal assistant for *The Exterminating Angel*. "From Buñuel, I got only one idea: never betray yourself either by trying to do more than you can do or telling stories that are not in your gut. Be true to whatever you think you need to do and forget the whirlwinds of commercial influences."

Ripstein took that advice and went on to become the most prolific Latin American director without any undue bowing to commercial considerations. Perhaps his most accessible recent film was *No One Writes to the Colonel* (2000), his third collaboration with Garcia Marquez. He also worked with other major Latin American writers, including Carlos Fuentes, Manuel Puig, and José Donoso. In 1978, Puig adapted Donoso's *The Place Without Limits*, the first Mexican film that dealt seriously with homosexuality. "It was a thorny subject to portray openly," Ripstein noted. "It was fun to watch in the theaters where you could sense the erotic aura. So when the moment came for a kiss between the male characters, the audiences in Mexico went nuts. The same thing happened in Spain, but it became one of the most popular Spanish language films."

1994

Unpublished

*　*　*　*

At the 2003 San Francisco Film Festival, Spain figured again in Ripstein's *The Virgin of Lust*. Although the Arturo Ripstein-Paz Alicia Garciadiego productions have usually dealt with sexual obsessions, there is a new twist in this complex plot that features a Mexican waiter—with a porno collection and an unrequited passion for a prostitute—who dreams of becoming a hero by assassinating Francisco Franco.

"This is my first film that has such a political statement," Ripstein said. "All the political statements in my other productions are devious, occult, and hard to get by. They're clear after you see the whole work. But this film is manifest."

It is also "excessive," he acknowledged, "but we wanted a confusing plot to begin with. We wanted constant ambiguity and ambiguity is excessive. It is very difficult. We're all accustomed to very clear-cut, precise narratives, but we wanted to go for a film that included imagining what went through each of these characters' hearts."

Originally, Spanish producers had suggested that the Ripsteins make a film based on a Max Aub story, reflecting his personal experiences, about Spaniards who fled Franco's Spain and found refuge in Mexico, a country they didn't understand. However, "Paz" thought it would be more intriguing to explore the theme of exile by showing it from the point of view of Mexicans who found the Spaniards very strange.

"So this is a film about reality and obsession, about reality and desire," Ripstein explained. "It is about a Mexican waiter who is tired of listening to Spaniards who want to kill Franco, and he volunteers to do it."

The Spaniards who escaped from Franco's Spain became the first political exiles in the twentieth century, he said. "Since then, the world has become a world of exile in every latitude for whatever reason. The whole world is a diaspora now. Nothing is pure, intact, anymore. It can't be. We're becoming a very small world, and it belongs to all of us. So we shouldn't forget that we belong anywhere."

2003

Unpublished

Isabel Allende

PHOTO BY JUDY STONE.

"My life is about ups and downs, great joys and great losses."

Sausalito, California

Isabel Allende was shocked the first time she saw the relatives she had recreated in her 1983 novel *The House of the Spirits* up there on the screen, larger than life.

"Look," the Chilean novelist said, hurrying over to a bookcase and bringing back framed photos of her grandmother and grandfather. "Can you imagine Meryl Streep and Jeremy Irons playing *them*?"

Don't be misled. Allende loves the movie version of her best-selling novel—which stars Streep and Irons—and she is someone who wouldn't mince words if she didn't. That much is evident during an interview at her studio in Sausalito, lined with Allende's books in twenty-seven languages, black Chilean folk pottery, and crafts from Morocco, China, Mexico, India, and Thailand.

214

Small and graceful in a pearl grey velveteen tunic over black slacks, Allende, at fifty-two, is not at all taken in by the hype around the film. But she does tell people, rather impishly, "Don't buy the book. Wait for the movie."

Her richly detailed work, streamlined to movie-length proportion, traces the fortunes of the eccentric Esteban Trueba family in Chile, very loosely based on her own family from 1926 through 1973, when a military coup overthrew the elected democratic government and killed the president. Although not named in the book or the film, he was Salvadore Allende, the author's uncle and brother of the father she never knew.

When Isabel's father deserted his wife and their three young children, her mother, Francisca, returned to her parents' home, but it soon became a sad place. "My grandmother died when I was very young," Allende said, "and my grandfather [who inspired the character of Trueba] mourned her for the rest of his life until he died at 100."

Her uncle, the leftist president, and her conservative grandfather were politely correct to each other when they met at family functions. To little Isabel, Salvadore Allende was just another uncle, but she adored her grandfather. "I was his favorite grandchild. We were very, very close." The little girl needed his affection because her mother was often sick. "I resented the Catholic Church for excommunicating her because she got a divorce. I rebelled against that kind of hierarchical, patriarchal, authoritarian, male-chauvinist society."

Indeed, she claims she disagreed with her grandfather on practically everything, but recalls, "We loved each other so much, it didn't matter. When I became involved with feminism, he was shocked. When I became involved with socialism that shocked him. Then I left the Catholic Church when I was twenty and that shocked him, but I loved every single wrinkle on his face."

Even after she left home, married, and began writing for magazines and television, their relationship continued. After work, she would have a cup of tea with him every day. "He would tell me stories and I have a good memory—only for stories!—so when I wrote *The House of the Spirits*, all those stories just poured out. He made part of his money in mining and also owned land in Argentina and Chile, but he sold it at a bad moment. I'm sure that—unlike Trueba—my grandfather never raped or murdered anybody, but he *was* a very violent, self-righteous man, intolerant in many ways but a *wonderful* character for a book, a sensational character."

Allende was working as a journalist in Santiago when the military coup occurred in 1973. (By then, her mother was happily remarried to Ramon Huidobro, appointed ambassador to Argentina by Salvador Allende.) "Only when my uncle died, did I realize he was a man of historical dimension, that he had become a legend. I saw the bombing of the Papal Palace. I did not imagine he would be killed at that moment. A couple of hours later, the producer of my TV program told me that her husband, a fireman, had put down the blaze in the palace and saw the bodies. I still didn't believe it. The military censored the news, so I called my stepfather in Argentina. He already knew. Everywhere else in the world, they knew Allende was dead."

She was the last person in her family to leave Chile. During the first year of the military junta, she was still able to write a successful play and two musicals. Then in 1974, her mother and stepfather narrowly missed being killed by a car bomb in Argentina. They hastily left with fake passports, no money, "and were quite desperate" until finally resettling in Venezuela.

When Isabel learned of the bomb blast, she was too scared to go on living in Chile and decided to leave "for a few weeks." Later, her first husband, a Chilean chemical engineer, said it was not wise for her to return. Six weeks later, he joined her with their daughter and son in Venezuela. The thirteen-year exile took its toll on their marriage. They were divorced while she worked at odd jobs, including the administration of a school.

It was during this exile in Venezuela that she learned her grandfather was dying, and began a letter to him recalling his stories and assuring him that she would keep his memory alive. That act—which grew into *The House of the Spirits*—freed her from a seven-year writer's block that had taken hold after she left Chile.

When *The House of the Spirits* became an international bestseller, she followed up with *Of Love and Shadows* and in 1988 with *Eva Luna* and became a popular figure on the lecture circuit. In 1987, she met and married William Gordon, a tort lawyer who heard her lecture—and, shades of her grandfather!—was always getting strangers to tell him their life stories. The son of an eccentric preacher, Gordon was raised in a Mexican-American barrio in Los Angeles and inspired her novel, *The Infinite Plan*.

Hollywood producers who wanted to film *The House of the Spirits* began wooing her, but she was reluctant. Danish director Bille August was told she wasn't interested, but, undiscouraged by her negative response, he flew to San Francisco, rented a theater, and called again to say that he wanted her to see his *Pelle the Conqueror*, starring Max von Sydow. "I said to Willie, my husband, 'Well, he's here so we have to see it.' After twenty minutes, I was so impressed. It had that contained passion and a cool Scandinavian treatment of the passion, which I loved." (*Pelle* won the Academy Award for Best Foreign Film in 1988 and the coveted Palme D'or at the Cannes Festival.)

After the screening, Allende and August met in a coffee shop for twenty minutes. "He was very understated, very unassuming, and didn't promise anything he wasn't sure he could do," she said. "He could see this long, complicated, crazy book made into a two-hour movie . . . Also, the political element was clear.

"He told me that elements of magic realism and the supernatural in the book would not work in a movie. Every time it's been tried, it looks grotesque, so you have to be very light-handed about that. He never talked about a big production. I always thought it would be an art movie with a low budget. When it started to grow and grow and ended up being a $6 million production, I was surprised."

After so many tumultuous changes in her life, there isn't much left to surprise her, but whatever happens, it almost inevitably finds a way into a new book.

"My life is about ups and downs, great joys and great losses," she wrote in a 2000 essay. "My writing comes not from the happy moments, but from struggle and grief . . . And the greatest of all my pains was in 1992, when my daughter Paula fell in a coma and a year later died in my arms." (While caring for her, Allende wrote *Paula*, in order to preserve the memory of her daughter.) "I write," Allende noted in her essay, "to understand my circumstances, to sort out the confusion of reality, to exorcise my demons. But most of all, I write because I love it! If I didn't write, my soul would dry up and die."

March 4, 1994
Toronto Globe and Mail

Alejandro González Iñárritu

"Does God's light guide us or blind us?"

San Francisco

Alejandro González Iñárritu knows that success can make a person crazy or stupid, whereas failure may result in wisdom.

The first-time director of two acclaimed films in which happenstance plays a major part, was cautious talking about the luck he's been having when he was in San Francisco to promote *21 Grams* and looked back on his first feature, *Amores Perros*. "I'm successful now," he said in a typical torrent of words, "but I'm very conscious that at any moment I can go out. I'm conscious that there's something you can't plan. It happens."

Life, the Mexican filmmaker said, "is basically just a series of accidents," showing that the "free will we supposedly have is very limited." Two automobile accidents trigger the mysteriously intertwined relationships in both tantalizing films. "Life is defined by the kind of accidents you have and how you behave afterwards," he said. "Some people are cowards, some freak out, others are paralyzed." (Both Alejandro and his scriptwriter, Guillermo Arriaga, drew on their own experiences surviving car crashes—one as the driver, the other as a passenger. A different type of accident sets off events in the director's next film, *Babel*, which takes place in Morocco, Mexico, the U.S., and Tokyo.)

In *Amores Perros*, two men and a severely injured dog are trying to speed past heavily armed thugs. The resulting crash kills one person, hurts another, and leaves the dog on the roadside. Octavio (Gael Garcia Bernal), the dog owner, wants to escape Mexico City's slums with Susana (Vanessa Bauche), his brother's wife. And an injured super-model, the mistress of a married magazine editor, faces an urban nightmare.

The English-language production *21 Grams* plays with time and fate involving a rough ex-con (Benicio del Toro) with religious tattoos, a woman (Naomi Watts) who wants to murder the man whose van killed her loved ones, and a math professor (Sean Penn) who may be dying. As their destinies begin to evolve, subtle notes of possible redemption underline both productions.

González Iñárritu was only five when he was introduced to the perils of happenstance: his wealthy father went bankrupt, losing his family's bank holdings and land. "He had nothing," González Iñárritu said. "When I say nothing, I mean nothing. But my father's failure as a businessman helped me a lot. He was the best example of 'never, never, never give up,' and he was my inspiration. Because I'm aware of that, I'm scared of losing success. So I'm living in fear of failure and I work harder and I'm stubborn and I'm more of a perfectionist."

Growing up, he said, he learned lessons on the street that no film school could teach. For instance, later he knew how to mollify a bunch of tough armed youngsters who threatened to hold up production of *Amores Perros*. Although Alejandro's family lived in a middle-class neighborhood, his pals were street kids from a nearby poor area, and he hung out with a gang that broke windows and and threw eggs at cars. "I planned all kinds of things," he recalled. "I was terrible but not in a bad way. It was one of the most beautiful times of my life."

However, he also faced his first class conflict. He was still attending a rich private school because his mother had pleaded with the principal to allow her children to stay there at a reduced tuition. While expensive autos traveled easily up the hill to school, their old overheated car was always breaking down, to the shame of Alejandro and his siblings. Meanwhile, his good-natured father coped gamely with the new circumstances: he'd wake up at 4:00 AM to collect fruit and wood to sell in the marketplace.

"My life has always been in pendulums," Alejandro said, summing up his adolescent experiences. His conflicts continued when he was sent to live at his maternal grandmother's house when he was thirteen. He hated the change because he was left without his old gang, but soon he began playing tennis with a rich neighbor and became like a part of his family, loving their success. Training hard to emulate his friend, he entered a tennis tournament, but was devastated when he lost in the first round.

His response to the loss was to persuade a seventeen-year-old girlfriend from a rich family to escape to Acapulco with him on money he got by stealing his mother's gold chain and selling it to gangsters. When the teenagers each called home later, Alejandro's father was amazingly understanding, but her father called his daughter a whore and swore that he would kill the fifteen-year-old culprit if he continued to see her.

Whatever happened, listening to music was always Alejandros' escape and it led to his first real job as a DJ with a three-hour "provocative" radio program and then to writing and directing promotional spots for a television station.

But as he was becoming very successful professionally, in 1996 he faced the tragic death of his first child, a son who died two days after his birth. Fighting his desire for revenge against the doctors, González Iñárritu faced the paradoxical realization that the best moments in life are sometimes sabotaged by unforeseen events. His depression deepened his need to do something more worthwhile with his life and his goal was to make a feature film.

Life took a better turn in 1997. Another son was born, and Alejandro's desire to direct returned and he began developing a script. He invited Guillermo Arriaga to join him in the project about a man involved with dog fights. *Amores Perros* took more than three years to come to fruition, but then it was an Academy Award nominee for Best Foreign Film in 2000.

The film reflected some of Alejandro's personal experiences: in the first episode's escape attempt of Octavio and Susana, and the second part about the mistress of a magazine editor, was inspired by a real episode in the life of a friend. Some personal recollections also show up in Arriaga's work. He owned a stray dog when he was nine years old. To his surprise, his pet turned out to be a killer, always winning fights against the other dogs. When the family moved next door to the office occupied by the Mexican president's wife, the ferocious dog bit her bodyguard and then escaped. Eventually, when Arriaga was eighteen, someone stole his pet and put him in an animal refuge.

Alejandro and his wife, Maria Eladia, wrote the title *Amores Perros*. But the English version *Love's a Bitch* doesn't quite convey, he explained, that the film shows "love as tender and animalistic at the same time."

For González Iñárritu, *21 Grams* was a far more personal production with its many religious references and questions. He considers himself a "spiritual person," a non-practicing Catholic whose mother was a "classic guilty Catholic" and his father, a non-religious conservative. As for the pseudo-scientific title, it is simply a metaphor for the weight that persons carry when someone close to them dies. In a way, the film asks the question that the director wrote at the end of his contribution to a collaborative film on September 11: "Does God's light guide us or blind us?"

"How do you answer that?" the director demands passionately. "It's a big conflict I have. I was thinking about a lot of things that I have been going through," he said. "The loss of my kid and the way I relate to the character of the ex-con in *21 Grams* who wonders 'Why does God do these things to me?'" On the good side, he believes God provided him with a van, but on the bad side, the van accidentally kills a father and his two children.

"But God doesn't have anything to do with him," González Iñárritu said. "So all the good things in life are because God wants it but all the bad things God has nothing to do with it? For me, religion takes part in my intellectual debate, not in the emotional one. At times I am very mad at Him—like I think, What's going on? Who's guilty? Who allows this kind of pain and tragedy to happen? Like that tsunami thing. It makes me feel horrible and angry. Those kind of things shake my faith. There's no religion, there's no intellectual, there's no brain that can explain it. Nobody. Sometimes you just have to accept the fact that we are blind. At the end you believe or you don't believe, but I feel connected to something bigger that I can't explain."

2003
Unpublished

Manuel Puig

"If you stay, you'll be killed."

Rio de Janeiro

Night after night, in a Buenos Aires penitentiary, Molina, a thirty-seven-year-old homosexual window-dresser, re-creates movie magic for his Marxist cellmate, Valentin. Molina's inimitable way of spinning out melodrama—with loving attention to all the details of sets and costumes, the characteristics of the stars, and the convolutions of the plot—reflects the lifelong obsession of Manuel Puig, the distinguished Argentinean novelist whose original ambition was to be a movie director.

Puig had hesitated about letting Hector Babenco option *Kiss of the Spider Woman* because he was disappointed with other films based on his work. Later Puig gave the director "full freedom to create the script I wanted." Still, Puig helped Babenco and scriptwriter Leonard Schrader with the final draft for the film that starred William Hurt as Molina, imprisoned for the corruption of minors, and Raul Julia as Valentin, a Marxist labor organizer arrested during an automobile strike. Molina's tales of glamor and intrigue are stories within the film.

Puig—a slight, handsome, elegant man—talked with dry humor about the origin of Molina's tales during an interview at his light and airy bachelor flat in Rio. Ten years ago, Puig left Argentina following threats on his life. He lived in Mexico and New York before settling in Rio three years ago. His study is filled with plants and contains copies of his novels in twenty-four languages as well as his books on film: *The Silent Clowns, The Swashbucklers, Gods and Godesses of the Movies, Hedda and Louella, The Films of Lana Turner, Harlow, The Art of the Great Hollywood Portrait Photographers*, and *The Story of Italian Cinema*, to name a few.

Puig's dark eyes light up with the passion of a true movie buff when he mentions his videocassette collection of seven hundred films. There is boyish excitement in his voice when he talks about the German silents and Garbo movies he would like to obtain. The novelist's witty, satiric, and nostalgic references to Hollywood illuminate the drab and desperate lives of his characters in *Betrayed by Rita Hayworth, Heartbreak Tango*, and *The Buenos Aires Affair*. Critics have compared Puig's dazzling, innovative work to that of Joyce, Nabokov, and Faulkner.

"I wanted a discussion on roles in *Kiss*," Puig said. "What is a masochist? What is a sadist? What is a user? I wanted a story in which a sadist would become a masochist and a user would become the used. I wanted to explore the basic dynamics of human behavior and show that sometimes a person becomes trapped in a role when there are possibilities of being many other different things, and if just circumstances would allow, he would change. At the same time, the book is very much about the Argentina of 1973. There was ideological repression and social repression. I wanted to put those two things together. The rightest government was suspicious of any leftist ideology, and the leftists were puritanical in the sexual area. The repression was expressed in different ways. What I mainly wanted to talk about was the possibility of people changing."

Kiss was never published in Argentina, although Spanish-language editions could be found in bookstores there. Puig's position as an independent socialist was considered suspicious. "I had no party to protect me," he said. "There were moments when people warned me to leave the country, saying, 'If you stay, you'll be killed.'" His family continued to receive such calls even after he left Argentina.

Years earlier, it had been Puig's feeling of vulnerability that led to his intense involvement with film. "When I was very young, I found that movies were my things," he said. The rest of the story can best be told in his own words.

"I grew up in a small town in the Argentina Pampas. It was very remote. A dry plain with absolutely nothing. It was far away from the sea and far away from the mountains. People who are born there and die there without ever leaving don't know what nature is about. The place is the *absence* of landscape. It was really tough. The only place where I felt safe was in a movie house. There was one theater. They showed American movies mostly. Monday, there were serials, plus a B Columbia or Republic picture. Tuesday, there was a revival of an Argentinean movie. Wednesday, a B American. Thursday, a woman's picture. Friday, the day for the maids, there would be a second revival of an Argentinean movie. Saturday, an American film. Sunday was the premiere of an Argentine film or a super production from America. I went every day. I felt that outside this small town, everything was like in an American movie. I didn't like the Argentinean movies becase they sounded too much like reality.

"MGM movies were the most unreal," he continued, "so they were my favorites. The more they were unlike my small town, the better I liked them. The musicals were my favorites. I thought in real life people would sing and dance at certain moments. My supercolossal favorites were *The Great Ziegfeld*, *The Great Waltz*, Ginger Rogers and Fred Astaire. But before them came Eleanor Powell. The Rogers-Astaire films had a certain irony; they didn't take themselves seriously and I *wanted* them to take themselves seriously. That's why I preferred Eleanor Powell.

"When I went away to school in the early forties, Buenos Aires was an unbelievable town. It was the kingdom of show business. It was a haven for refugees from Europe. You could see films from all over the world. (This was before Peron, who came in '46. Then everything became more problematic.) I saw German musicals and French heavy drama. There was a tradition of film consuming. We were getting B-films to Z-films from everywhere. I was very curious about them all. By then, my favorite stars were aging and I couldn't accept their replacements. During my childhood, it was the stars I loved, the MGM ladies—Garbo, of course, Norma Shearer, Luise Rainer. Even Greer Garson. Up to Garson, I was *totally* devoted to MGM."

By '46, Puig saw the emergence of Italian neorealism and the importance of directors like Rossellini and De Sica. "I was particularly impressed by Clouzot because he was very flashy. I was totally dazzled feeling the presence of the director. I remember Clouzot's *Quai des Orfevres* (1947). It was called *Jenny Lamour* in America. A detective murder story. I thought directing was my thing, but my parents wanted me to study more. I took up philosophy and studied languages furiously because I thought without languages nothing was possible. I wasn't interested at all in Argentina. I had a terrible repulsion for the place. All that had started in the movie house."

In 1956, Puig left Argentina because he had a scholarship to Cinecitta in Rome. "I had that strange, maybe unconscious, feeling that abroad everything would be like in MGM musicals. The minute I arrived in Italy, I knew that things were not so.

"I became chummy with Nestor Almendros. I was studying direction; he was studying photography. I was twenty-three; he was twenty-five. We were both of Spanish-language origin, and we *hated* dubbed films. We couldn't accept them, and in Italy there was nothing else. In Cuba too, when Nestor was growing up, they used to get all the foreign films. He had seen everything.

"The Italians looked on us as 'those people from underdeveloped countries.' But we knew much more about films than they did. They resented that. They had that prejudice: 'Coming from Buenos Aires, did you ever *see* a film?' They didn't know that Buenos Aires was a thousand times better. Even after the war, the Italians would get the more commercial American films and that was all. French films they would show for one, two days; there was no market.

"I liked the beginning of neorealism when there were creators behind it. Then it became just dogma and very far-fetched. It's crazy; nobody has written about that. Zavattini became the theoretician. The filmmakers were left-wing; they used causes, but they didn't serve the cause well. Some of them used it for their own advancement. The filmmakers had a terrible dislike for America. They were right about colonialism: what Reagan is trying to do now with El Salvador, that type of thing. But then the Italians considered Hollywood as totally reactionary: hedonistic without the least social consciousness. Everything that was Hollywood was wrong. At the same time, Hollywood knew about storytelling. So storytelling was considered wrong. To consider that there were ways of telling a story better than others, that was reactionary. A film had to live only by its soul, its social meaning. No structure was to be taken into consideration.

"Really, it was terribly castrating. I knew that this awful tyranny of the critics was wrong. I agree with democratic socialism, not the Soviet Union's kind of thing, but the arts, I thought, should never be submitted to political custody."

Puig stayed in Rome for a year and then went to Paris. "*Cahiers du Cinema* had started. Art houses were showing old MGM films. They were *rescuing* things. By then I was not sure about anything," Puig recalled. "When I arrived, *Queen Christina* was playing. In Italy that would have been considered diva stuff, star stuff. In Italy, they considered star a four-letter word.

"By then I was already writing my first scripts, but they were all copies of the films of my childhood. There was always a bit of *Rebecca* or *Wuthering Heights* or *Smilin' Through*. While writing, I felt enchanted because it was like seeing them again, but I was not enchanted when the work was finished. Friends told me to write about the people I knew best. Soon I found that my stories were nourished by an accumulation of details and repetitions. The first script I tried to do in a different way became my novel *Betrayed by Rita Hayworth*."

Puig continued to develop his own narrative style in *Blood of Requited Love*. A spirit of fantasy and wish-fulfillment pervades the conversation that appears to be taking place between two former lovers. At times, their exchange simply seems to be carried on in the mind of the man. Puig brilliantly uses his favorite device of dialogue to express both character and narration.

One character, Maria, at twenty-five, is trying to recall her past love affair with Josemar, who wooed her at the tender age of twelve and deflowered her at fifteen, leaving more or less permanent scars on her nervous system. Josemar, an electrician/mason floundering in his trade and facing the loss of the house he expected to inherit, recalls the past with shifting inventiveness.

Puig based Josemar's character on a bricklayer from the poverty-stricken Brazilian backlands, who was doing work in the novelist's flat. "He was somebody who couldn't face reality at all," Puig said, "but he looked like the most well-adjusted person. He started telling me stories about his life. The tragedy of his life was all symbolized by the loss of his house. Through telling the stories, he got what he had lost. I told him to find a house, and I had my lawyer arrange to give it to him. I didn't give him the money, because he had a very crazy way with cash."

In *Eternal Curse on the Reader of These Pages*, an almost surrealistic dialogue takes place beween an elderly Argentine writer-in-exile who has lost his memory after years in prison and a drop-out American professor, his acerbic, paid part-time companion. The professor was based on a New Yorker, "paralyzed mentally," whom Puig met while living in Manhattan in the sixties. "I found him very strange, but he was full of clues for me to understand New York. I asked him the most intimate and challeng- ing things. He objected to the questions, but agreed to answer. After this work, he changed a lot. It was fantastic therapy for him. I didn't expect such an improvement in him. Before, he only wanted to do menial jobs, but then he went back to teaching and research. It was the most fantastic collaboration!"

The time for talk was over. Puig got ready to leave for his morning swim. First, he stopped a block away to ask his parents which movie they'd like to see that evening from his fabulous collection. "I like being near the beach," he confided. "I love living in Rio because it's a resort and a city. I love to disappear there. Part of my work as a writer is just to be a pair of eyes and ears."

October 14, 1984
San Francisco Chronicle and
American Film

Salma Hayek and Julie Taymor

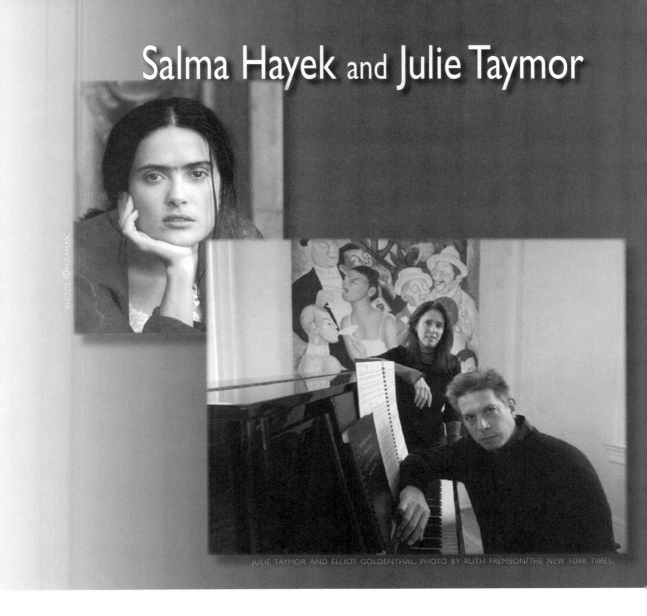

JULIE TAYMOR AND ELLIOT GOLDENTHAL. PHOTO BY RUTH FREMSON/*THE NEW YORK TIMES*.

"Perhaps Frida *might change the way people see Mexico and the Mexican people."*

Toronto

It took a formidable female triumvirate to celebrate the true meaning of love and loyalty in *Frida*: Salma Hayek, the determined actress; Julie Taymor, the visionary director, and Frida Kahlo, herself, the crippled artist who turned her pain into paintings.

228

Before the triumvirate of women came a man: the towering Mexican muralist Diego Rivera, the Don Juan who truly loved his irrepressible wife, Frida. Their complex relationship touched a chord with the artistic companion-collaborators of Hayak and Taymor. At the 2002 Toronto International Film Festival, Hayak pointed with pride to the man who finally whipped a difficult script into its final shape: her boyfriend, the actor Edward Norton.

And Taymor, the remarkable impresario of Broadway's fabled *The Lion King*, said she was "profoundly" affected by the Kahlo-Rivera romance. "Loyalty and fidelity as subject matter is so great, especially for Americans who vilify our ex-president for his smarmy little affair. We've a lot to think about what true love is and about transcending the dark parts of affairs." The romantically reflective Latin musical score was constructed by Taymor's companion, Elliot Goldenthal.

Initially, both Hayek and Taymor were horrified by the thought that each other's men might become essential to the production. For seven years, Hayek had fought to get *Frida* into production. But twenty-five drafts of the script by four writers still didn't satisfy her, and the deadline was looming when Norton—who never got writer's credit—came to the rescue.

"Edward did nine drafts. He would write at night and would work all day on a film he was doing," Hayek said. "I was mortified because he was working so hard and we didn't even have the budget for another writer. When I told Julie that Edward offered to write the script, her first reaction was, 'Oh, my God. The boyfriend! What if we don't get along! What if I don't like what he does!? And I'd have to deal with a personal situation!'"

Hayek burst out laughing. "And when I hired Julie, they told me that Elliot Goldenthal was going to do the music. And I go, 'Oh, my God, he isn't even Mexican and he's been living with the director for twenty years. What if he doesn't understand Mexican music and I'm going to have to deal with the director!!'"

The actress didn't know that in their first collaboration, Goldenthal and Taymor had traveled to isolated places in Mexico to learn how to adapt *Juan Darien*, a haunting Uruguayan tale of "savagery" versus "civilization." Expressed through music and visuals with the only words sung in Latin and Spanish, it became known as a "jewel" of musical theater. Goldenthal had met Taymor as a designer when a mutual friend praised her work as "just as grotesque" as his music.

"Grotesque" also describes Kahlo's explicit and surrealistic paintings of her tortured body. They are complemented by Taymor's magical skeletons and masks. "Frida loved the macabre humor in the Mexican appreciation of death," Taymor said. "She wrote, 'Death danced around me.'" The Mexican celebration of death was very similar to what Taymor had observed during her four-year stay in Indonesia, which she calls the "seminal experience of my life."

The once-precocious child from Newton, Massachusetts, who began acting at eleven and studied mime in Paris at sixteen, got a fellowship at twenty to study visual theater and experimental puppet drama in Indonesia and Japan. She was deeply moved by Indonesian theater in its original function as a religious experience, as a mediator between spirits and people, as a socializing event—and also how it could be used as propaganda. She went on to create her own theater with Javanese actors and masked dancers.

Taymor's visual style in both *The Lion King* and the film *Titus* captured Hayek's imagination. "I wanted to make *Frida* in a language that I considered was Frida's first language—a visual language." Hayek is a vision herself, voice rising and falling with excitement, fingers keeping up a rhythmic beat as she explains her passionate involvement with the subject.

There's still something mischievous in the girl from Coatzacoalcos, Mexico, whose last name reflects her father's Lebanese descent. When she was twelve her pranks reportedly got her dismissed from a Louisiana boarding school, but she eventually surprised everyone by opting to study international relations at the university in Mexico City.

Nevertheless, transported as a kid by the movie *Willie Wonka and the Chocolate Factory*, she couldn't give up the dream of acting. She served her apprenticeship in such films as *Desperado*, *Wild Wild West*, as well as Mike Figgis's *Timecode* and *Hotel*, before taking on her current role as co-producer and star. She had become fascinated by Frida when she was fourteen and a friend showed her photos of the artist's paintings. She was both horrified and haunted by them and determined to do justice to the artist's life.

"I wanted to show Frida's vivacious, colorful vision of the world and what I found was that every time Julie has a visual approach to something, she takes you to a place where you've never been before because you could never imagine the images she comes up with. And that's what Frida did in her art because you've never seen anything like it."

Although Frida Kahlo faced horrendous circumstances, Hayek said, "She not only took the best part of it, but she would do it in an interesting way. From pain she created art and poetry. From Diego's affairs, I think she found freedom. I think she found unconditional love when she married Diego. She probably thought he would change for her but when that didn't happen, she made it work for her. She was hurt but instead of crying, she enjoyed it. She had a lot of men (including Trotsky, the Russian revolutionary), yet Diego was the love of her life. The film is not about people falling in love, but about people staying in love.

"What I learned from this is that true love, unconditional love, only comes when you are able to accept a person exactly who they are without wanting to change them or without judging them. At the end, sex became such a miniscule part of life, so

230

unimportant, since they were partners in so many ways—in political beliefs, in artistic beliefs. They both wanted to change the world, but most importantly they grew together and learned to love each other exactly as they were and they were partners until the very end."

And perhaps, she said, the film "might change the way people see my country and my people. It might open their minds. It might be a little grain of sand in the direction of a way that integrates culture and people who have the courage to be different like Diego and Frida."

November 1, 2002

The San Francisco Examiner

Walter Salles

"Che said what he thought and acted accordingly. That kind of integrity is very rare."

San Francisco

After Walter Salles, director of *Central Station*, was hailed as the person who could revive the moribund Brazilian cinema, Robert Redford asked if he would consider making a film about Che Guevara's youthful trip through Latin America.

Salles thought the offer was extremely tempting, "but on the other hand, it was also sacred territory. Sacred because it had to do with a man who changed the very nature of my continent."

He finally agreed on condition that it be a Spanish-language film with Latin American actors and non-actors. Five years later, after innumerable trips retracing Che's journey and research consultations with his widow, Aleida, and their four grown children in Cuba, *Motorcycle Diaries*, starring Gael Garcia Bernal (the celebrated actor in *Amores Perros*, *Y Tu Mama Tambien*, and *21 Grams*) finally bowed to great acclaim in Argentina, Brazil, and the United States. It is based on Che's memoirs and *Traveling with Che Guevara* by Alberto Granado, his twenty-nine-year-old companion, a biochemist. They started out on Granado's 1939 Norton 500 motorcycle until it broke down. Then they made their way in dire and funny circumstances, determined to complete the journey. Years later, Granado finally completed their adventure by establishing a hospital in Che's name in Havana.

On tour in San Francisco promoting *Motorcycle Diaries*, the soft-spoken Salles, wearing a T-shirt picturing a motorcyle, laughed and wanted to make it clear that wasn't the vehicle featured in his film.

In a strange way, Salles and Che had something in common. The son of a Brazilian financier and diplomat, Salles lived in the United States and France from ages two to eleven, but he always had a severe case of *saudede*, Portuguese for a longing for what one cannot have: in Salles' case a longing for Brazil, a country he didn't know. Che, a twenty-three-year-old Argentine medical student from an upper-class family, seized the chance to explore the rest of his continent and began then to learn its darker side. Over the course of eight months and 8,000 miles in Argentina, Chile, and Peru, Che and Granado met homeless miners, riverboat prostitutes, and patients in a leprosarium in the middle of the Amazon.

Salles' "longing for Brazil" took on cinematic form in *Central Station*, which also involved a long journey of discovery into that country's bleak northeast. The unlikely traveling companions were Josué, a homeless boy, and Dore, a dour woman who tries to help the youngster search for his father. Dore bitterly writes letters for the illiterate in Rio de Janeiro's railroad station and throws them away at home. Shortly after she wrote Josué's mother's letter to her faithless husband, she was killed in a traffic accident and Dore reluctantly gave the boy shelter for the night. Her transformation in the course of the journey brought new honors to Fernanda Montenegro, often called Brazil's greatest actress, and to the film, which won the Berlin Festival's prestigious Golden Bear award.

Despite her experience, Montenegro had to learn a few things from Vinícius, the former shoeshine boy who had never even seen a movie before playing Josué. After interviewing and testing 1,500 kids all over Brazil, Salles met Vinícius at the Rio airport early on a rainy day when the boy had no customers—and no money for breakfast. He asked Salles for a loan and promised to return it when Salles returned from São Paulo later in the day. Instead, Salles said he'd lend the money if the youngster would do a screen test. The boy asked if he could bring other shoeshine kids so they could have a chance too.

"Vinícius brought such an honest and direct way of interpreting the part that he created the necessity to de-theatricalize all the professional performances," Salles said. "Fernanda had to reconsider everything she had learned."

Originally, Salles had written a twenty-thirty-page story outline and then brought in João Emanuel Carneiro and Marcos Bernstein, "two very young writers who had never done a feature script before. In Hollywood terms, you would never do this—trust two unknowns—but in Brazil we had to." The script went through several treatments before Salles got a break—a call back from Redford's Sundance. Scripts had to be submitted in English, but with the deadline three days away, Salles had sent the Portuguese original. Of the 2,000 screenplays submitted, his was the only one not translated.

"You're lucky," the Sundance caller told him. "We're paying for the translation." The script won the 1996 Cinema 100 prize of $300,000 and Salles started filming eight months later. It had not been easy for Salles to begin making films. After the glory years of Brazil's brilliant, innovative Cinema Novo in the 1960s, the country went through such chaotic economic and political turmoil in the eighties and nineties that people said, "Brazilian cinema is dead."

Salles had begun haunting theaters when he was a youngster in Paris, and he frequently saw two or three films in a row: the French New Wave, some films by Antonioni and movies by Scorsese and Coppola. "Living in France was somewhat an ordeal," he said, "but it gave me access to films that you couldn't see in Brazil at the time. Many were forbidden under the military dictatorship. The impact when I saw the Cinema Novo work was enormous and unforgettable. The imprint is still there. Cinema Novo put a Brazilian face on the big screen for the first time. It was a shock to discover not only our own reflection, but what came with it—almost the promise of a viable country, the creative, multi-cultural, ethnically diverse, pluralistic country."

Brazilian film production still was in a long fallow period—until Salles and a group got together in the spirit of Cinema Novo in 1994. "We had one thing in common: a great desire to do films—specifically about Brazil and about the moment it ceased to be a country of immigration and became a country of emigration."

With economic disaster threatening Brazil in 1990, thousands fled to Portugal only to meet new hazards. That theme became the subject of *Foreign Land*, Salles' first feature, co-directed by Daniela Thomas. In it, three Brazilian emigrés in Lisbon became enmeshed in a murky, unpredictable web of drug sales, gem-smuggling, and murder. The low-budget, black-and-white film, shot in four weeks on three different continents, became a festival hit from San Francisco to Rotterdam, heralding a resurgence of Brazilian cinema.

When Salles started to make *Central Station*, he never realized how it would have the emotional voltage it has now. When they shot in Pernambuco, about 2,000 miles from Rio, they enlisted the help of some 700 men and women who had never seen cameras before. Many times they were invited to share food with people who had barely enough to eat. Then, on the last day of shooting, some came out of their houses to say goodbye and began to sing *The Song of the Pilgrims*, which asks for protection. Soon all 700 were singing and crying.

"It was very difficult and very beautiful at the same time," Salles recalled. "The beauty of film is the possibility of learning and sharing. We learned so much from these people."

Salles recounted a similar experience when he was making *Motorcycle Diaries*. "We all ended up meeting persons and seeing situations we had not seen before, and everything made us understand much better what our roots were."

Salles also felt very privileged to be able to get closer to Che, the man behind the myth. "I was surprised to see how much he went beyond the limits of his own social class. I was surprised to understand that he not only confronted what one would call North American imperialism, but he also confronted Soviet imperialism, and he wasn't afraid to do so. I also understood better his caustic, self-deprecating humor. We admired the fact that Che stayed faithful to himself from the beginning to the end. He said what he thought and acted according to what he said, and that kind of integrity is very rare in the world."

September 11, 2004
San Francisco Guardian

Eliseo Subiela

PHOTO BY JUDY STONE.

"To analyze a film from the point of view of being sexist in today's world is as dogmatic as to analyze it from a Marxist view."

Palo Alto

Eliseo Subiela, who made a documentary inside the Buenos Aires insane asylum at the age of seventeen, can't explain why he was attracted to the idea of insanity but it was all tied up with the belief that social criticism in film could change society.

Twenty-eight years later, nothing had changed when Subiela went back to the hospital in 1989 to film *Man Facing Southeast* in which a man from another planet, a Christ-like figure shows his solidarity with the other patients. Since that time, poetry and prostitutes, love and death, fantasy and reality, all infused with gentle humor, have figured in Subiela's unique body of work.

He talked about survival under the dictatorship and contemporary political correctness while on a visit to Stanford University, after winning the best film award for *The Dark Side of the Heart* at the 1992 Montreal International Festival. In this surrealist tale, the protagonist is Oliverio, a young poet hungry for love, but easily bored after sex. So he ejects each femme of the moment from his bed and into oblivion. That is, until he meets Ana, a poetry-loving whore in a cabaret and they make love so strenuously that they start levitating over the city and Oliverio admits she has enlightened the dark side of his heart. The film is not only about love, Subiela said, "but about the fear of loving," a fear the director has recognized in his own life. Although nobody called the film macho in Argentina, that reaction surfaced in the U.S. and Canada.

"I think of all my films, this is the one where the female character has the most presence and isn't dependent and passive," Subiela remarked mildly. "I believe that to analyze a film from the point of view of being sexist in today's world is as dogmatic as to analyze it from a Marxist point of view." Subiela, a quiet charmer, has the unassuming air of a modest man who constantly questions himself and has not come up with any easy answers.

Dark Side was inspired by the work of the great Argentine poet Oliviero Girondo. "For a long time I dreamed about translating his poetry into film because his writing has fiery, explosive images," Subiela explained. His dream somehow coincided with visits to Montevideo, Uruguay, to make commercials that would support his growing family. "It was a very dark and difficult time on both banks of the Plata river because there was dictatorship on both sides. There were hardly any young people left. Those who hadn't 'disappeared' went to the United States. I went to a cabaret where I could talk about poetry and politics and met a woman who knew a lot about poetry. She was a kind of prostitute without being a vulgar prostitute. I became friendly with her, more or less. We couldn't get to be close friends. She maintained her distance. If I had taken her into the daylight, everything would have changed. That is why in the film, Ana says, 'Never look at a whore in the daylight.'"

There were serious doubts about how the film would be received, but young people loved it and made it a hit. For Subiela, one of the most satisfactory reactions was the way all the poetry quoted in the film, including work by Mario Benedetti and Juan Gelman, sold out.

When times were very difficult for Subiela, a story about his father helped him to carry on. His orphaned father had left Spain in 1932 at the age of twenty-five and was supposed to be met at the port in Argentina by a priest who never showed up, but he managed to cope by himself in the new world. Although he was a frustrated orchestra conductor, he eventually became the manager of a wine warehouse, and he introduced Eliseo to art through literature and music. "The normal course for an immigrant was to want their children to become doctors or lawyers, and he never pressured me to do this," Subiela said, still grateful for his father's encouragement. With the teenager mad about movies, his father approved the idea of making a documentary about the asylum and gave him the money to go ahead with the project.

Subiela thought he must have been pretty close to being insane himself because he couldn't cope with the world around him in Buenos Aires. He spent nine months filming at the institution and the administrators never realized what he was doing, "but the patients asked me a lot of questions. I think they mistook me for some very sophisticated lunatic." A journalist who saw the film helped to get it on TV and introduced Subiela as someone different from other young people who spent their time dancing or "up in the clouds." Paraphrasing a line from William Faulkner, the journalist noted that, "between pain and nothingness," Subiela "has chosen pain." When the film with its strong criticism of the hospital was shown on TV, the administrators still didn't understand how he had done it.

There was more than enough pain and hope to go around as youthful rebellions shook Paris in 1968 and reverberated in Argentina. Between '68 and '73, Subiela made several short films anonymously against the dictatorship, but they don't appear in his filmography, including one about throwing molotov cocktails. Recalling it, Subiela burst out laughing and buried his head in his hands. "It was hell to make, but it was a poetic film and had its beauty. The explosions and flames had an apocalyptic quality that I liked. It was very naïve of me to be making those films because people who had done less paid for it with their lives. If I had been found out, I wouldn't be here talking with you today. It's also part of the recent past that one wants to forget." Many of those films have been lost, but to Subiela's surprise, the molotov cocktail one surfaced in a German archive.

Subiela's own ideas have changed with time about *Man Facing Southeast*. In the film, Rantes, a new patient at the hospital, insists he has come from outer space to study the human brain. He informs the skeptical psychiatrist that he has chosen the hospital as the only place to tell the truth and protect his mission. The film plays with the idea that the unknown man may be Christ. "Rantes was crucified in a way because he stopped eating after being injected with a depressive drug. At the end all the inmates are waiting for him to return. They don't want to believe he has died. I think there have been Christs who have returned. Che Guevara and Martin Luther King were crucified. These are people who proposed changes to make society a better place to live in. What I'm going to say is very polemical, but today I realize that Christ probably achieved more profound, lasting, social change than Che because Christ approached it through love and Che looked at it through struggle and controversy. So I admire people like Gandhi more than Che, but I admire Che as well."

After toying with the idea of resurrection or redemption, Subiela took on the theme of reincarnation in *Don't Die Without Telling Me Where You're Going* (1995), in which a lonely film projectionist whom nobody believes in meets a woman in his dreams who reveals that he was one of cinema's early inventors in a past life and she has been his companion through centuries of reincarnation. "Death is not final," Subiela believes. "It is only a mutation. What renders us truly immortal is love."

Finally, Subiela reflects on growing old in *Despabilate Mi Amore* in which friends in their forties who lived through the dictatorships have a reunion and must come to terms with their lives and their loves.

But while those last two films were still in the talking stage when we met, Subiela also had another one in mind: *The Life of Tortoises*. "It has to do with the life of people who wear a shell on top and bottom to defend themselves from love," Subiela said with a smile. "And I'm always working on myself to make myself more fragile and get out of my shell . . . "

1992
Unpublished

Andrucha Waddington

PHOTO BY JUDY STONE.

"This is the old Brazilian cinema coming back."

San Francisco

Andruch Waddington was fascinated but not fazed by the possibility of making a film based on the true story of an earthy woman who lived with three husbands and her children in the poverty-stricken northeast corner of Bahia in Brazil.

Complicated family relationships were nothing new for the director of *Me You Them*, which won a rave review in *The New York Times*, calling it "an unexpected delight" and praising Waddington's direction "as seductive and sinuous as Gilberto Gil's score."

With a name that indicates British and Ukrainian ancestry, Waddington, thirty-one, is heralding the rebirth of Brazilian filmmaking squarely in the path-breaking light of Cinema Novo (New Cinema), which flourished in the sixties.

In 1995, after a long drought in film production, Waddington—who had been making commercials and music videos—saw the opportunity to direct a movie, but for six months was unable to find the right story.

In the meantime, he made his first feature, *Twins*, a simple psychological thriller, as a trial run for future directing. "Then, suddenly, I was at home in Rio on a Sunday night watching TV, when I saw the real woman, Marlene da Silva Saboia, talking about her life with her three husbands," Waddington said, with boyish enthusiasm on a visit to San Francisco.

"She was so powerful. She looked like the actress in the film, but smaller and thinner. I immediately got airplane tickets for myself and a script writer to fly to where she lives, and we did a huge interview with her—although at first she said she didn't want to be interviewed. I wanted to investigate how a woman in such a macho culture managed to deal with that situation."

When Waddington and the writer returned to Rio, they worked for four years on the script, using the archetypes of the three men and the woman who created their own rules to survive. However, the story built into the script was totally fiction. It was not a biographic film and not a documentary. "Is it a comedy or drama or tragedy?" they asked themselves, and debated the ending even into the fourth week of shooting.

The real woman—actually the mother of eight, not four as shown in the film—is now living with only two husbands, because the youngest one was drinking too much and he was sent packing.

For the lead, Waddington starred Regina Case, a former stage actress later known as Brazil's Oprah, who has the voluptuous appeal of an Anna Magnani.

When Marlene, the real "wife," was invited to view the film, she said she would go alone and then decide if her "husbands" could see it. "She sat next to me crying," Waddington recalled, "and then asked if I could make an open-air screening for 15,000 people in her area. At the end, there was an ovation for her with people shouting her name. Nobody complained about her personal situation because she was so powerful, and she said, 'I don't give a - - - - about them. They should respect me. I don't owe anything to anyone. That's my life. Take care of your own life!' Nobody talks about her in front of her—maybe behind her back, but they never insult her."

While her story was unique, Waddington's own family history could inspire a number of scripts. His paternal great-great-grandfather emigrated from England to Bahia. His Ukrainian mother and her family were prisoners of the Germans in a forced-labor camp from the time she was eight until the war ended in 1945. The family emigrated to Brazil, where Waddington's mother married and divorced her Russian husband, with whom she had two children. Waddington's father—a banker turned lawyer/ hotel owner who had three children—got a divorce to marry her.

"And then I was born," Waddington said with engaging spirit. "I have two brothers and three sisters. We lived together for twelve years and they lived together for eighteen years."

As if repeating that pattern, Waddington and his former wife Christiana, an art director who had two sons—now six and eight—share their custody. One child lives with her and the other with Waddington and his present wife, actress Fernanda Torres, and their two-year-old son.

Torres, who portrayed one of the kidnappers in *Four Days in September*, is the daughter of 1998 Oscar-nominee Fernanda Montenegro (*Central Station*).

At sixteen, after practicing photography, Waddington made his first short feature, a metaphorical film about the Brazilian constitution set in a circus. "It was really bad," he said cheerfully. "Even my mother didn't like it."

He decided he'd better learn from an expert and apprenticed himself to Cinema Novo director Carlos Diegues (*Xica da Silva*). Two years later, he became an assistant working in the jungle on Hector Babenco's *At Play in the Fields of the Lord*. He also made some documentaries for Walter Salles, another director inspired by Cinema Novo, and who garnered rave reviews and an Oscar nomination in 1998 for *Central Station*.

Waddington's inspiration for capturing the harsh light of the sparsely populated Bahia backlands for *Me You Them* was the classic Cinema Novo film *Vidas Secas* (*Barren Lives*). Directed in 1964 by Nelson Pereira dos Santos and inventively shot by Luis Carlos Barreto, *Vidas Secas* was an unsentimental portrayal of two inarticulate peasants in that inhospitable climate.

When *Me You Them* was finished, Waddington held a private screening for Barreto and Diegues. "I told them that I was inspired by *Vidas Secas* because it was about human beings against nature and this is about human beings trying to survive by themselves, about friendship and compassion and how many things you have to give to get what you want."

His guests cried watching the film and said, "This is the old Brazilian cinema coming back."

March 16, 2001
The Oakland Tribune

Nettie Wild

PHOTO BY JUDY STONE.

Asking Subcomandante Marcos the tough question.

San Francisco

She learned how to train Arab horses with Bedouins in the Egyptian desert, groomed thoroughbreds in Ireland, escaped howitzer fire in the Philippine jungle and ate "beans and rice, rice and beans" for eight months with the Zapatista National Liberation Army in Chiapas, Mexico.

Nettie Wild is an undauntable soul with a heart engaged in people's struggles for a better life—and a bubbling laugh that demolishes any stereotype of a documentary filmmaker, even though she dresses the part in blue jeans and ragged denim jacket. If she's proud of anything—although she doesn't put it that way—it's her determination to ask revolutionary leaders "tough questions." At forty-seven, the tall, slim, Vancouver director was in the San Francisco Bay Area to promote her film, *A Place Called Chiapas.*

The production is a dramatic account of the eight months she spent in southern Mexico recording the life and battles of the guerrilla army under the leadership of the mysterious Subcomandante Marcos. She also depicts Bishop Samuel Ruiz Garcia, who has worked for thirty years to bring peaceful change to Chiapas, and the Mayan villagers terrorized by right-wing paramilitary death squads.

Wild had just finished making *Blockade*, a documentary about a conflict in a Northern Canada logging community in which native and non-native peoples were battling over land when news of an uprising in Chiapas hit the headlines. On January 1, 1994, the Zapatistas took action to dramatize their demands for control of their lives and land. They chose that date because it marked the first day of the North American Free Trade Agreement, which they call "a death sentence for the Indian peoples of Mexico."

"My antennae were already quivering," Wild said, laughing at her own words. "Because it was quite apart from the free trade issue. This was action by indigenous people, compared to other uprisings and revolutions in Latin America that were Marxist-Leninist."

Wild had already been through enough drama to last a lifetime. Her parents were resigned to her youthful forays abroad. But filming guerrilla armies was not exactly the future envisioned for her by her father, a British journalist who had covered and admired Gandhi's non-violent campaigns for years, or her mother, a one-time opera singer and Nixon sympathizer.

A play Nettie had created with the Communist New People's Army in the Philippines was interrupted by Ferdinand Marcos' armed forces, and she felt fear for the first time while on the run in the jungle for four days. She returned later to film the $550,000 *The Rustling of Leaves*, the complex story of the dilemma faced by the guerrilla army with the election campaign of Corazon Aquino. Aquino won, but, according to Wild, "the wrong revolution won," with the military and large landowners still essentially in power.

The 1994-95 stories about the Zapatistas that were flooding the Internet stirred Wild's activist juices. "It was not the usual leftist, dogmatic stuff. They were very political in the good sense of the word. They had humor and portrayed the people involved." Then for a while, there was no communication from Subcomandante Marcos.

What finally caught her attention was a story on the Internet, probably written by Marcos, "a master at manipulating the media." It dealt with events about a year after the uprising when the Mexican military made a run into the jungle to grab the Zapatistas and their sympathizers. As the villagers of Guadalupe Tepeyac were starting to escape, the women began lugging a statue of the Virgin with them. The men who wanted to run away faster urged the women to leave the Virgin behind. The women were adamant, saying, "No! She's our patron saint."

244

"In that story," Wild said, "you get the whole works, that the people are poor and they will have no home to go back to. And in the midst of this huge crisis, instead of giving them a political lecture, Marcos waited for the villagers to decide what to do."

When Wild first went to Chiapas in June 1996, her hard-won success with the Philippine documentary had enabled her to raise $870,000 for the new film. In it, she wanted to explain who the Zapatistas were. "I was aware of an official conflict between the Zapatistas and the Mexican government, as well as the efforts of the bishop to mediate between the two for a peaceful solution. Then I started to realize there was a whole unofficial war during the time of the supposed cease-fire. It took place outside of the official conflict zone. Anybody who was sympathetic to the Zapatistas was being hit very hard by a paramilitary group. Encouraged by the bishop and human-rights workers, we started to film these hidden communities."

At first, she thought that the conflict was too complicated to tell. "I was having enough trouble coming to terms with the 'official' story, which was at an impasse," she recalled, "but these other people were being terrorized and killed like the refugees I filmed from the village of Jolnishtie. The Mexican media were too frightened to cover the story. It became clear to me that there was nobody to protect these civilians. The church was too frightened to send in priests, and the Zapatistas couldn't defend them because it would mean breaking the cease-fire."

She had to ask Marcos the tough question: "When civilian people support you, like the refugees from Jolnishtie, what can you do to support them? It looks to me as if they are very much on their own." Her attempts to get an interview with Marcos had gone unanswered; Wild finally asked her question at a press conference. Angrily, he gave what she calls, "a politician's answer" and sent word that her requests for an interview were denied and "she knows why."

Wild said that put her out in the cold for two or three months. "I had only planned to stay for four months and I stayed for eight. I wondered if I had created a security risk by asking that question at a strategically wrong time. If the questions we were asking Marcos were difficult, the questions we directed to government and the paramilitary groups were much more difficult, and we were paying for it with our Mexican crew being attacked."

Finally, near the end of her stay, Marcos sent word that she should be in the village of La Realidad on the Day of the Dead. "Knowing his sense of drama, I figured he would show and I sent notes saying if he did go there, it would be nice to come in the daylight." Marcos came as the light was fading and she had to set up gas lamps for the interview. He leaned against a tree and watched them work for forty minutes.

"Then he took the interview into a time, space, and thought which—for us—really amplified the movie. He speaks a very profound, poetic Spanish and getting the nuance from that is a little like Haiku. When he started talking about himself, he opened up and told what it was like as a city person with a university background coming into the jungle. He said that initially it was a nightmare. He talked about the incredible loneliness of being an outsider, about coping with the bugs, mud, and the weather, about being kept alive by indigenous people and about how death eventually takes on an entirely different meaning."

Then, perhaps somewhat scornful of Wild's outsider status, he asked how long she had been in Chiapas. She started to say "seven months," but Marcos interrupted. "You still have a lot to learn," he replied, "I've been here twelve years and I'm barely starting to understand."

June 11, 1999
The San Francisco Examiner

8

Means and Ends

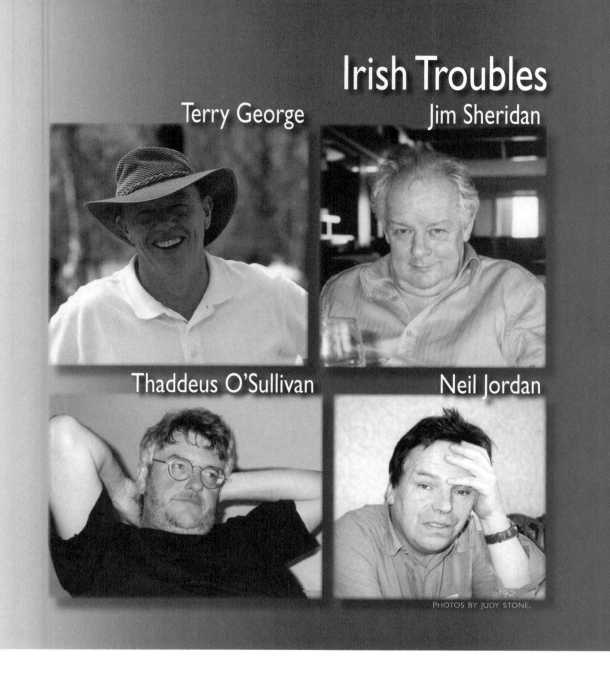

Irish Troubles

Terry George   Jim Sheridan

Thaddeus O'Sullivan   Neil Jordan

"Sometimes the means for justifiable ends are so corrupt that the ends are no longer worth achieving."

May 23, 1998 — *The Irish north and south voted overwhelmingly in favor of the peace referendum.*

July 12, 1998 — *Three Catholic Quinn brothers—ages seven, nine, and ten— were burned to death in Ballymoney, north of Belfast, in an arson attack police attributed to Protestants.*

Aug. 15, 1998 — *A car bomb set off by the dissident "real IRA" exploded in the town of Omagh in Northern Ireland, killing twenty-eight people and injuring 220.*

Feb. 18, 1999 — *The Ulster peace effort is deadlocked with the IRA refusal to disarm before the peace agreement is fully carried out in May 2000.*

March 3, 1999 — *Two Protestant militia groups, the Orange Volunteers and the Red Hand Defenders, opposed to the peace accord, have been banned by the British government because of continued involvement in sectarian violence.*

An evocative look back at the terrors and traumas of the Irish people, as well as their humor in the face of adversity, was presented in an Irish series at the Pacific Film Archive in Berkeley in 1999.

Two of the most powerful productions were *Nothing Personal* (1995), a riveting drama on the tragic trap of sectarian violence in Belfast; and *In the Name of the Father* (1993). Starring Daniel Day Lewis, *In the Name of the Father* is based on the true story of the Catholic "Guildford Four," falsely imprisoned for fourteen years for the IRA bombing of a British pub in 1974.

My interest in the Irish "Troubles" dates back to a few trips I made to Ireland after "Bloody Sunday" on January 30, 1972, when British paratroopers shot dead thirteen Catholics during an illegal anti-internment rally in Derry. Fatal retaliatory actions by the IRA proceeded apace.

Observing the hatred expressed by the two communities, I still remember my feeling of horror at the sanctimonious words on a Protestant marching-day banner: "If God be on our side, who can be against us?" And the delight of a little Catholic boy singing a ditty about boiling Orangemen (Protestants) in oil. Burning took a different toll in Ballymoney.

The charred bodies of Jason, Nark, and Richard Quinn were discovered early in the morning of the final event at the 1998 Galway Film Festival. The audience had been prepared to give a boisterous welcome to an older Quinn brothers' collaboration, *This is My Father*, starring Aidan, directed by Paul, and filmed by Declan. It fell into a sobering silence when Paul referred movingly to the three little Quinns (no relation) who would never experience the joy of working together.

Two other filmmakers, Terry George and Jim Sheridan—who have collaborated on three films about the "Troubles," *In the Name of the Father*, *The Boxer*, and *Some Mother's Son*—put in brief appearances at the festival and reiterated the way they have turned around an old maxim: "The end justifies the means."

George, co-writer of *In the Name of the Father*, directed by Sheridan, declared, "Jim and I say that sometimes the means for justifiable ends are so corrupt that the ends are no longer worth achieving."

There's a ring of personal experience in that observation for George, who served three years in Long Kesh after he was arrested, at age nineteen, in a car with an armed passenger. George, a Catholic, grew up in a Protestant neighborhood of Belfast, until their house was attacked in 1971 and they were driven out into a Catholic ghetto.

"Nationalism never appealed to me," George said. He now lives with his family in New York (and in 2000 became the co-producer of *The District*, a TV police series set in Washington, D.C., and later wrote and directed *Hotel Rwanda*.)

George said he believed that the division in Ireland "was a political aberration and was the root of all the problems. And I didn't like the [bombing] tactics the Provisional IRA engaged in. I think what's going on now is the last throes of the old sectarian Unionism where the Protestant majority was the dominant political force in northern Ireland. That domination was based on the suppression of the minority and is rapidly being eroded. There's no love lost between the two communities, but given the instability of the peace process, it's going to take decades to break down that distrust. At least the parameters are being set up now."

Sheridan, fifty, a native of Dublin who got emotionally involved with the northern troubles when he saw people getting killed on Bloody Sunday, takes a pessimistic view of the American reaction to Irish films, based upon observations he made while living in New York City. (That experience became the basis of his semi-autobiographical 2002 film *In America*.)

"They [the American Irish] left the place the Catholics came from 200 years ago," Sheridan said, "and they don't want to go back to it. They don't want to pay attention to it. They just think it's ignorance and the past, which is exactly what it is. And I don't think they're very interested in it as entertainment while we might think of it as the kind of film that's important for our country."

Thaddeus O'Sullivan, a native of Dublin, doesn't mince words when he talks about *Nothing Personal*, originally called *The Fanatic*. It's set in Belfast in 1975 during a brief truce between the pro-British Loyalists and the IRA. An apolitical Catholic father (John Lynch) and his children are caught in the violence unleashed by his childhood friend, a Loyalist leader obsessed by revenge against the IRA, and by his aide, a psychopathic killer.

"I don't have sympathy for the Republican side. I don't have sympathy for the Loyalist side," O'Sullivan told me. "The reason I made the film is because I was very upset by the fact that so many innocent people died on both sides. I focused on the people who are not interested in the politics, but would like to have peace."

By showing that suffering is the same for everyone no matter which side is favored, O'Sullivan was inspired by Gillo Pontecorvo's *Battle of Algiers* (1965) about the Algerian freedom fighters' battles against the French colonial forces. "The lives of innocent people were sacrificed to both ideologies," O'Sullivan pointed out. "As a study in terrorism, *The Battle of Algiers* had no match."

The intensity of Irish feeling was vividly demonstrated when O'Sullivan took his actors to Belfast so they could absorb the atmosphere. In a Protestant bar, one drinker remembered seeing Lynch portray an IRA man in a movie, called him a "provo," and punched him. "It could have led to something more serious," Sullivan said, "so we got out of there as fast as we possibly could."

They shot the film in Dublin because it's difficult to get insurance for a production in the north. Despite the calm location, "Everybody began to feel the emotional effect of the material and were very upset," O'Sullivan said. Still, a young Belfast Protestant girl turned out to be a real trooper. She is Jeni Courtney (the young star of John Sayles' 1994 *The Secret of Roan Inish*.) "Jeni was deeply disturbed during the re-enactment of the scene in which she is shot," O'Sullivan said. "She cried and went away for a bit and then came back. After we did it three times, she left for half an hour with a nurse, and I told her she wouldn't have to do it any more, but she felt the responsibility and came back for more takes. She was incredibly tough and very determined."

O'Sullivan said he wanted to make a film that says people should build on what they have and not to be torn apart by sectarian violence. "I wanted to make a film about what went on in the streets, because when you're in the street and somebody puts a bullet in the back of your head, there's no debate. You're gone. I wanted to give some physical sense of being surrounded by this trap all the time and nobody quite knows what's involved. It's a real physical fear."

Fear takes different forms in two other films. Pat O'Connor's *Cal* (1982) sensitively portrays the anxiety felt by a melancholy youth (John Lynch) who suffers from guilt for having been involved in an IRA hit against a Royal Constabulary officer. He is drawn to the policeman's widow (Helen Mirren), who is as trapped by circumstances in the troubled north as Cal is.

Neil Jordan's impressive first film *Angel* (1982) features a saxophone player (Stephen Rea) who witnesses two gangland-style murders in the north. After tracking down the mobsters, he eliminates them one by one, and begins losing his sanity.

When *Angel* opened, intellectuals in the south hated it, Jordan told me. "They thought it was a betrayal of the nationalist position. But in Anderson town, the Catholic area in Belfast, a lot of people loved it because they didn't see it as about politics, but as about the effect of violence on your psyche. It was bizarre. What you get a lot of in Ireland are people trying to shed their bourgeois background, and they want to imagine they're behind this great nationalist struggle. I was abused in the press and spat at in public. People I knew quite well wouldn't speak to me for years. It was a very extreme reaction."

Rea, who has played three IRA men, appears as a sympathetic policeman in Jordan's 1996 film *Michael Collins* about the 1916 rebel leader who invented modern guerrilla warfare. "Everyone likes to blame everything on the IRA," Rea, a northern Protestant married to a formerly militant Catholic, told *The New York Times*, "but they have only emerged because of a much deeper problem."

Born in Belfast, he says, "It's a very dysfunctional place. Everyone is maimed to some extent when they come out of that society. But like all dysfunctional families, you don't see it until later."

March 11, 1999
The San Francisco Examiner

Gerald Hanley

"The Irish people have been through every stage that colonialism can produce."

Dublin

The first question that Jomo Kenyatta put to Gerald Hanley back in 1962 was, "Where do you come from?"

"I said, 'I've just come from Ireland.' Kenyatta—who later became president of Kenya—turned to the Kikuyu elders in the room and he said, 'This man has come from a country that has known every aspect of colonialism. You name it, they've seen it. The Irish people have been through every single stage that colonialism can produce.' The elders were amazed to learn that there were white men who had been colonized."

In Kenya that year, the Masai bush telegraph carried the news about the "curious white man who went about stopping old men and asking questions about times so long ago that only a few could remember."

Mindful of the ancient Gaelic oral tradition, Hanley wanted to help preserve Masai racial memories before it was too late. He couldn't catch up with one ninety-year-old Masai who covered the mountains and marshes like a twenty-year old, but finally Marieni Ole Kertell came to him and told him about the past that exists only in the keen memory of a few elders. "He was a marvelous man," Hanley said. "He was a warrior before the white man came. He's seen the whole thing happen: the coming of the white man and the going of the white man."

The transcript of that unique interview is in the appendix of Hanley's fascinating autobiographical book, *Warriors and Strangers*, as well as a very special find, the two "lost" agreements of 1904 and 1911 in which the Masai *loaned* their land to the British in exchange for being let alone to go their own cattle-grazing way. From the vantage of his return trip to Somalia and Kenya in 1962, Hanley offers a compelling look at the gallery of characters he has known—tribesmen, settlers, colonial officials, soldiers—during some traumatic times of transition in East Africa.

The book is infused with what is immediately striking about Hanley himself: his unquenchable curiosity and generosity toward other people, sympathy without sentimentality. I met him three or four times in Dublin; invariably, he was encouraging someone or other to write, praising a new author's first-born novel, offering helpful, unexpected insight into the other fellow's project. A friend of his showed me a cherished old photograph of Hanley looking like a cross between Omar Sharif and Ronald Colman when he was a "British" Major in the Irish Fusiliers—but he was never seduced by that role: "I was an *amateur* officer. I never forgot I was descended from potato-eaters."

He's a large man with a voice so soft and gentle and civilized when he talks about ancient cultures, old religions, and new revolutions that it's difficult to imagine him as a lion-killer, but he was, once upon a time before he started to think it all out.

Hemingway himself took along Hanley's second novel, *The Year of the Lion*, when he went on safari in Ngorongoro, Tanganyika, in 1953. Later he bought ten copies in Nairobi and told the amazed bookseller to have Hanley call him if he stopped by. When Hanley did, Hemingway said, "C'mon down, kid, the wine's open."

In a fragment of his *African Journal*, Hemingway tells of reading *The Year of the Lion* very slowly "because it was such a good book, I didn't want to finish it . . . an excellent book and very inspiring when you were in the lion-hunting business."

A British critic, John Davenport of *The Observer*, once commented that Hanley's "masculinity reminds one of Hemingway, but emotionally he is more mature." Hanley himself was touched and pleased when he read the Hemingway journal. "He liked the part in my book where the lion charges." "I'd love to think I had something to do with that," Hemingway told Hanley.

Hanley was off on a long flow of reminiscence. It was the eve of his first visit to the United States and he was looking forward to a big bash with his nephew, playwright William Hanley (*Slow Dance on the Killing Ground*), and his niece, the actress Ellen Hanley. He was eager to learn what made America "break out" ten years ago, fascinated by Malcolm X, wondering how Alex Haley traced his African ancestry, curious about how young American blacks feel about the freedom of Africa, wishing that they in particular would read his *Warriors and Strangers*.

He wanted to check out the validity of his theory that dialogue is the American way of revolution: "When there is a scandal in America, they *do* sit around and discuss it. They *do* print the Pentagon Papers. I'm not too wide-eyed, of course," he added happily, but he was obviously filled with zest for the next adventure as he must have been when he set out for Africa at nineteen, a poor kid from "Irish Liverpool."

He had been born there in 1916, that fateful year for the Irish. He was the son of a Dublin printer, descended from a long line of Dublin printers. He had to leave school at fourteen because he couldn't afford to continue, became a steelworker, slinging a sledgehammer for four pence an hour, but he also started writing at sixteen.

"There were four brothers, but only one got an education—Francis, a linguist, who teaches Russian at a Benedictine monastery in London. James, the eldest, is a very good writer. He writes about the sea. He's a better writer than I am—he's a *writer's* writer."

It was James (*Another World*) and his friend, the writer John Cowper Powys, author of *Wolf Solent*, who set Gerald up with a job in Africa as a helper on Willie Powys' 200,000-acre ranch on the slope of Mt. Kenya.

"You lived like the Africans lived. I lived in a grass hut. We had 10,000 head of wild cattle, 20,000 sheep, lions, zebra, game. It was not like any other form of ranching. It was very tough, there were diseases by the hundreds. The first thing I had to do was learn the language, and the only way I could learn it was from the Africans. The tribal Africans influenced me enormously. They made me think like mad. There are two kinds of strangers—those who never learn the language and don't want to know and those who are fascinated. I was fascinated. So I learned the tribal language Maru and the lingua franca called Kiswahili, and of course, I learned the customs of the tribe. It was a doomed world, a world that's dying. I recognized that quite quickly in 1935. You could see that the next few generations would not be the same."

The experience left him with chronic malaria, incurable nostalgia, and the stuff for a number of novels. In England, some critics compared him to Sir Richard Burton and E.M. Forster. Not only is he a superb storyteller, but his novels provide sharp, unrivaled insight into the breakup of great colonial empires by showing the "colonizers and the colonized" as complex, unromanticized men and women under the impact of revolutionary change.

"There is a place every man belongs to forever," he told me. "Mine is East Africa. It's a very strange place. Once you've lived there, you never get over it. You can't describe it, but you try. You *long* to describe it perfectly. Isak Dinesen got nearest. Nobody else but Dinesen has got that feel of why you like Africans, of why you learn to respect them, why you want to know all they can tell, once you learn the language, once you've gone into their minds. Then you realize that something's going to be destroyed and they're going to destroy it themselves, the Africans. They want civilization. Once the tribal world comes in touch with it—like Ireland in the seventeenth century—they're hooked. You start to adapt or die."

Brought up "soaked and indocrinated" in Irish nationalism, Hanley said that, when he first went to Africa, he was "very conscious of the fact that you can't own anybody else's land. I knew that. I knew the white man couldn't keep a chunk of Africa unless the black man wanted him to."

Then World War II changed the whole scene. Although the Irish Free State was neutral, the Irish clinging to Wolfe Tone's old slogan that "England's difficulty was Ireland's opportunity." Hanley enlisted—as did 250,000 other anti-Fascist Irishmen. "You know we all wished we'd fought in the Spanish Civil War and didn't. I joined the British Army because politically I felt quite deeply."

He spent the war years in Somalia and Burma with the 11th East African division. "It was quite strange. The whole division was African. We even had a Congolese medical unit. It was pretty shattering for the Africans to meet modern warfare in a country like Burma. When an African from an obscure village goes into a modern war with bombers and planes and guns and tanks, it was quite a shock. We lived on rations from parachute drops, and the Africans had the same rations as the white and Indian troops. When they came back from the war, they had finished with their tribalism and they became politically interested. They realized who they were and they could never go back to where they were. The people who had joined up were no longer the people they had been. They had adopted all kinds of new habits and of course they wanted a new Africa and they began to work for it."

He recalled one incident at the end of the war that illustrated that feeling. "Three white men were waiting to be flown back to Europe and one of the African soldiers who thought all white men were rich said to me, 'You're going back to Europe to all the goods, cars, and all that. We're going back to a tribe.' They didn't like what they were going back to because it was a poorer life than in the army. 'I said, 'You don't realize it. You're going back to *land*. You have land. They're going back to work in factories and they don't want to. They'll be lucky if they get jobs.' They were staggered by this. They were infected. Once you're got a wrist watch and cigarettes, you want to have it all—you want TV—and I'm for that."

The "infection" in all its varieties fascinated him. Twenty years after the Burma campaign, Hanley wrote *See You in Yasukuni*. "It is about the only Japanese soldier I ever saw surrender, the only deserter from the Japanese army. No Japanese unit ever surrendered, they all committed suicide. But this was a little Japanese who had worked for the Americans and he was infected. He knew that the Emperor wasn't a god and that when he was killed in a battle uselessly, his soul wouldn't go to a place called Yasukuni."

Hanley confessed that he used to be sentimental. "I went to Africa because I thought it was peaceful there. I'm not sentimental now because I realized the Africans didn't want that. A lot of people want a lot of things for a lot of people which will keep them nice and quiet, but it's what people want themselves that's important. It took me a long time to discover that."

What made him realize it?

"Well, Chri . . . I have to think. Probably in Somalia for the first time. I said to an old chief, 'What do you want?' He said, 'I want to be well-governed, but I want to be left alone.'

"That's it, isn't it?" Hanley exclaimed, nodding his head. "That's it! What's interesting about man is that not only does he want good for other people, he wants to be *known* to have done it for them. In other words, to stay there, to govern them, being daddy. I don't think he should do that. Fascinating, this longing to be remembered for being daddy."

And Big Daddy has a lot to answer for. In 1945, Hanley kept a curious eye on African soldiers viewing a film about the liberation of Belsen with its "bulldozed hills of corpses." "I watched the African soldiers when the lights went up and I am certain that many of them were looking at us, the white men, with a strange new kind of eye. They were as appalled as the rest of us by the scenes in Germany, but they had an extra reason for puzzlement, and perhaps they knew that until the white man could manage his own anthropoid passions, he should stop feeling superior to blacks merely because he was a white man."

Mau Mau itself, Hanley believes, "was a scream of anthropological rage, a puzzled and bloody turning upon the Christian varieties of religion which the white man themselves did not bother with."

The true story of the Mau Mau has not yet been written, of that he was certain. "I have reservations about all those 'revolting' old tribal customs we heard about. It was to the interest of the white man at that time to denigrate the African. Even now, they like to hear about revolting customs. I'm not satisfied about the revolting rituals of the Mau Mau. I'll tell you why. I was given a printed document by a British officer—an intelligence report—and I know the kind of mentality who wrote this, I know it well. He described a ritual involving a mixture of menstrual blood and semen that took place at a spot called Kibirichia, and he calls it a 'Kibirichia cocktail.' Anyone with the mentality to be smart about something as sad as that—IF it was true—can make you cynical. Further, I'm not convinced because the Kikuyu are a very fastidious people and they had a very strong moral code. Now it's true that the Mau Mau wanted to destroy that moral code to make another kind of Kikuyu, but I'm not convinced about these rituals. That war was a shattering thing for the Kikuyu people. The Kikuyu weren't supposed to be able to fight. They were never recruited as soldiers, but they fought and the score at the end was 10,000 dead Kikuyu to thirty-three white men. So I'd like to read more about the Mau Mau, an authoritative book."

As for the religious and tribal warfare that erupted in India and Africa after independence, "How could an Irishman 'preach' about that?" he asked.

"The north of Ireland is like an iceberg melting. It was a frozen area. If the Catholics, we'll call them Catholics—the minority who are really representatives of the original race who were occupied by the settlers—if they'd been black, it would have been much more understandable to the world, this struggle in the north. It was about some people who feel superior to the people they live on top of. Some people need to feel superior. There must be niggers or wogs or yids or wops or paddies—in order for some people to feel comfortable. Well that's finished now. Of course it's very painful when it ends. It's like the Negroes in the States. Whites didn't want to live next to black men and now plenty of black men don't want to live next to white men. I think it was inevitable, but it's very sad.

"Islam has got one thing in it—it doesn't give a damn what color you are. I was very touched to learn that Malcolm X was shattered to find, as he was introduced to all the Muslims on his way to Mecca, that he knew nothing about Islam, when he met white Muslims, grey Muslims, yellow-haired Muslims, blue-eyed Muslims. There are all kinds of whiteys and there are all kinds of blackys and brownies. Malcolm finally realized you just can't hate whitey really, and I think he got shot for that."

December 1972
Ramparts

David Hanly

Most upsetting were the Irish-Americans who came up with easy solutions to the Northern problem.

San Francisco

He did not look or act at all like that run-of-the-mill, glad-handing, unctuous Chamber of Commerce type: this scraggly, carrot-bearded, disconcertingly keen-eyed fellow showing off Ireland to the likes of Jimmy Breslin, Pete Hamill, Leon Uris, Charles McCabe, and sundry others.

Little did they dream that David Hanly was packing it all in, absorbing every jot and tittle of their ways while downing huge draughts of Guinness and a Paddy or two far into the night and arguing the fine points of American politics, life, and literature with them. Serious he was, but an occasional gap-toothed, irrepressibly wicked smile might have been an early warning signal that a real writer was lurking under the skin of the public-relations man in charge of America for the Irish Tourist Board.

Now this very angry, young (thirty-four) fellow tells exactly what he was thinking all those years about the changing shape of Ireland and United States in his brilliant, incisively witty, first novel, *In Guilt and in Glory*. It is a trenchant look at the complex, difficult reality of Ireland, as Hanly takes the reader along with a U.S. TV team preparing an in-depth report. A black anchorwoman and an Irish-American columnist are key figures on the trip, guided by government representatives from the Irish Board of Welcomes.

"Those visiting Americans introduced me to my own country in a lot of cases," Hanly acknowledged in San Francisco. He was not about to reveal which of the traveling Americans has achieved further immortality in his novel. "It was nice to observe Ireland through their eyes and to be wry about it when they were gone back. I learned a lot about America from them and on my seven visits here."

Hanly, one of six children in the family of a bacon-firm accountant in Limerick, has tender, angry, and grateful memories of his education at a Christian Brothers school. That educational system has been a "whipping boy" for years because of its severe disciplinary measures but Hanly refuses to join the attack.

"There would have been no education for me without them. I was a scholarship boy. We couldn't have afforded secondary school if I didn't get the $50 yearly scholarship, and there were only ten. It's all free now, but it wasn't then. The $50 paid for the books, the tuition, and some money left over is what made the Christmas every year."

There was no money for a university education, but Hanly made up for the lack with "voracious" reading. He soaked up the great Irish writers and Shakespeare. But the ones he studied for style were the moderns: Evelyn Waugh, Scott Fitzgerald's *The Great Gatsby*, Thornton Wilder, Nathaniel West, "anything by Gore Vidal" or early Capote, John Cheever, Bernard Malamud, and John Updike.

His love affair with the United States started when he was fifteen. "I will never forget it. One night, I was going home from the Redemptorists—a Catholic confraternity of men which, at the time, had 15,000 devotees. I'm glad to report they have only 1500 now, which is what they deserve. They don't even deserve one. Nevertheless, coming through the back streets, outside this doctor's door, I saw a *Time* magazine in the garbage can. I had never read words put in such a fashion. My father got me a subscription and I read it for years, growing to know far more abut American politics, literature, traditions, and history than most. No! No! I do not mean that my view of the U.S. has been based on *Time*. I'm telling you how it started."

For a few years, he worked for the Irish *RTE* (television) *Guide* and later wrote "appalling" soap operas before joining the Tourist Board.

Two years ago, he quit, moved his wife, Carmela, and their three children to the Wicklow mountains and settled down to write novels.

He did not denigrate his public-relations work, but eventually he came to "abhor the humiliation the job involved." Many of the Americans are still his friends, but he chafed at dealing with those "who were really inferior in mental ability, with absolutely no reflection, no sensitivity, and yet in their own areas in the U.S. they were revered."

Hanly said he could not comprehend that phenomenon. "San Francisco is particularly blighted. New York is too, but San Francisco is a village to a great extent. This aspect is something I find enormously attractive, but the results are sometimes repellent: the awe and reverence, the unconsidered awe in which various people are held in this town . . ."

The ones who upset him most were Irish-Americans who came up with easy solutions to the Northern problem. They ought to give it more thought, less talk, he suggested, looking every inch the indignant Irishman in his handsome green Donegal tweed suit.

"It's offensive to an Irishman who has to live there to hear an American Irish say, 'Ah, s---, man, we have the answer: we'll get rid of them.' It's rubbish. Their anxieties and reactions are based on hatred. They hate the British because they think the British are responsible for everything that's wrong. There's a certain amount in that. I happen to believe that as long as the British stay, it can't be solved. I think one of these days, the Northern province will break up. There will be no British there at all."

Finally, he is blunt about the North. Abrupt. "There is no solution. None whatever. It will probably be atrophied out of existence."

It isn't only the northern impasse that bothers Hanly. "There are horrific dilemmas. Pollution of everything. Ecological pollution. Pollution of thought, of language, of feeling. Yeats said it all, 'Things fall apart, the center cannot hold, mere anarchy is loosed upon the world.' That's what I see: the death rattle of the Western world.

"One can't but be terrified of the nuclear bomb or terrified of the loss of the word 'disinterested,' for instance, since there is no American who uses it properly, any more than they now use the word 'gay.'

"Ugh, God," he exclaimed, "how por-ten-tous this is going to sound. The important words are discipline and responsibility. I think discipline has completely broken down in the educational field: 'It's all right if you don't know it. It's all right if you don't learn it.' Like Diane Keaton said in *Annie Hall*: 'I'm more in touch with my own feelings.'"

Hanly looked exasperated. "I can't understand people saying things like that. What are they talking about? Where is the sense of personal responsibility for your own thoughts and your own actions? It doesn't matter what other people think. You have to lie on your own pillow at night and answer to yourself.

"Maybe the ability to do this comes from being brought up in a strict Catholic way or a strict Jewish way. It doesn't matter which one. They've lost all that when they say

'She's hassling me' or 'She's laying one on me,' or all those obnoxious phrases. She's not. Stand up on your own two feet and look after yourself and bear your own problems. Not that when things break down you go to a shrink."

These are not just idle words. Hanly has tried to apply them when his full-time writing brought strains to his own marriage. It is a subject that he will not discuss since he despises the attitude of many Americans, "that whatever happens in private should be known about in public. I think this is a dangerous and deadly philosophy and goes back to the psychiatrists who are adjuring people to let it all hang out. Which is rubbish and nonsense and they ought to be shot. There is such a thing as privacy and privacy, is a good thing.

"Everybody I know here has been to a shrink. It implies to me that jettisoning of responsibility for yourself. It implies that guilt is a bad thing. Guilt is a wonderful thing. In my book, one young man says he loves what Americans would call his hang-ups and inhibitions, guilt and the rest of it."

That character speaks for Hanly. "I'm so grateful for the Catholic Church to have hammered the s--- out of me when I was a child because there can be no art without conflict. No true art, I think. If there's no guilt, where are you? It is implicit that in a world without guilt, there's no moral stance whatsoever."

February 22, 1979
San Francisco Chronicle

Conor Cruise O'Brien

An undiplomatic diplomat.

Los Angeles

"It is no accident that the white man is the hero of Peace, the black man of Freedom," writes Conor Cruise O'Brien in the introduction to *Murderous Angels*, his brilliant, witty and provocative play on the Congo. The play had its world premiere in 1970 at the adventurous Mark Taper Forum of the Los Angeles Music Center, showing its relevance beyond the Congo.

In the play, Cruise O'Brien contends that Dag Hammarskjold, the exalted mystic who was Secretary-General of the United Nations, deliberately refrained in the interest of world peace, from preventing the murder of Patrice Lumumba, Prime Minister in the new Congolese nation, an act that precipitated his own death in a mysterious plane crash.

For Hammarskjold, Lumumba was a potential threat to peace; for millions of Africans, he was a martyr in the cause of Freedom. Peace and Freedom are the murderous angels. "For the white man," Cruise O' Brien notes, "the thought of the destruction of civilization is far more terrible than for the black man. It is the white man's civilization . . . "

The harsh realities of the Congo case are hardly disputable. The white man's civilization there meant brutal exploitation of the natives in the extraction of the extraordinary riches of that country. The Congo's Katanga province is loaded with a multitude of minerals from copper and cobalt to uranium. All the uranium that went into the atomic bombs dropped on Japan came from Katanga. Peace and freedom were the noble abstractions, icons of reporters and pundits, but control of this wealth was the hard reality, generally ignored by the world's communicators. To keep that control in one way or another, Belgium was the least prepared of the great powers in Africa to grant its colony freedom and independence.

The stuff for an economic tract? No, the real stuff of drama for a playwright with the insight, knowledge, sophistication—and courage—to explore the way the mysterious manipulations of the mighty control men's destinies. Cruise O'Brien not only has these qualities, but the power and skill to take extremely complex issues and personalities and generate unique theatrical excitement.

By trade, Cruise O'Brien is a diplomat, an undiplomatic diplomat with an irrepressible tendency to blurt out the truth as he sees it, an independent mind, a novelist's eye for character, a deadly sense of the comic, and the candor to recognize publicly his own mistakes. He is now a Labor member of the Irish Parliament.

As one of the Irish delegation to the United Nations, he had been selected by Hammarskjold to represent the Secretary-General's office in Katanga in May 1961 to apply the Security Council's resolution aimed at ending Katanga's secession from the Congo. Hammarskjold's deportation of Moise Tshombe's foreign advisers, arrest of foreign officers, and use of force against the Tshombe regime provoked strong protests from Britain and Rhodesia, which in turn led to Hammarskjold's fatal flight to meet with Tshombe in Rhodesia.

Cruise O'Brien's own role, described in his superb book, *To Katanga and Back*, is omitted in the play. In the book, he brings to life the whole wily cast of characters, somber and hilarious, as well as the weird, bloody attack on some U.N. staffers, including Maire MacEntee (who later became his wife).

In the play, he concentrates on Hammarskjold and Lumumba, using real names to preserve "the shock of recognition" in a frankly political drama. Yet, the author warns, calling on Aristotle for classic sanction, that these are not "real people: they are imagined characters, with the names and some of the attributes of real historical figures, placed in a dramatic situation matched as closely as possible to the historical situation of these figures." That delicate distinction is difficult to comprehend quickly and has already been challenged.

In one scene, a film clip of Ambassador Adlai Stevenson underscores the subtle hypocrisy of the official polite regrets over the death of Lumumba (by Tshombe's men), compared to the real anger over the subsequent anti-U.N. black demonstrations that erupted in the Security Council.

It is clearly Hammarskjold who intrigues Cruise O'Brien. He is intent on finding the "missing" political key to the intense religious mysticism in the Secretary-General's diary, published posthumously as "autobiography" under the title *Markings*. Hammarskjold's acknowledged sense of divine mission in the pursuit of peace, his vanity and narcissism are all explored in this portrait. There are also references that some will consider gratuitous, to homosexuality and a discreet, though totally fictitious, relationship is implied with his black assistant.

Under enormous pressures from Britain, France, and the Soviet Union and most fearful that the Congo would become another Spain or Korea, Hammarskjold is seen as compromising, even lying about important U.N. actions and deliberately withholding U.N. protection that might have saved Lumumba. If the dramatic assessment appears harsh, Cruise O'Brien ameliorates it by commenting in the introduction: "If we condemn what he did, we must at least keep in mind the possibility that we might all be dead if he had acted otherwise. I do not myself think this is probable . . . "

February 10, 1970
San Francisco Chronicle

9

The Veiled Society

"Iranian cinema is probably the most extraordinary phenomenon of the last ten to fifteen years."

—Alberto Barbera, consultant to Italy's National Museum of Cinema

Azar Nafisi

PHOTO BY JUDY STONE.

"Literary discussions opened a window to life in Iran."

Washington D.C.

The way Azar Nafisi's rebellious hair kept slipping out past the confines of her government-imposed hejab (scarf) was no small matter to the Iranian guardians of Islamic morality, but they couldn't cover up her stubborn insistence on the power of imagination to make people free.

Today at her office in the School of Advanced International Studies at Johns Hopkins University she can laugh, albeit grimly, about the trouble her slippery scarf kept causing her, but it's no laughing matter in Iran, where the question of a woman's hair is still a most sensitive issue.

That subject of the hejab or veil crops up constantly in *Reading Lolita in Tehran: A Memoir in Books*. In her vivid account, Nafisi writes of the secret private class at her home, where she taught seven English-speaking young women the works of Nabokov,

Henry James, Jane Austin, Saul Bellow, F. Scott Fitzgerald, and Flaubert, among others. "Those works of the imagination were the windows to the world they couldn't have," Nafisi said.

She also drew on their own Persian tradition with the example of Scheherazade, the beauty who outwitted the murderous king. But Scheherazade survived because the king couldn't resist her stories. "They showed him a world full of color and controversy and contradictions. My argument was that this is the third domain of the imagination that no government can take away from you and through that third domain Scheherazade saved the kingdom."

Literary discussions with her special students also opened a window to life in Iran, not just to unmentionable subjects of love and sex, not just to killings, disappearances, torture, and fear during the Iran-Iraq war, but to the way people were "deprived of the right to be an individual."

At twenty-nine, Nafisi was the youngest professor in the English section of the Persian Literature and Foreign Languages department at the University of Tehran and had only been teaching for a year. She and her husband had returned to Iran in late summer, 1979, right after the Islamic revolution, idealistically hopeful of democratic changes.

She had gotten her PhD degree from the University of Oklahoma with a doctoral dissertation on Mike Gold, the radical author of *Jews Without Money*, and the proletarian literature of the 1930s. At Oklahoma, she had been involved in the Iranian student movement opposing the Shah, but during her last year in the United States she had become "deeply disenchanted" with the groups, dominated by extreme Marxist-Leninists. "A lot of the people in opposition to the Shah were just as bad as people in power, sometimes worse."

When she went back to Iran, she hadn't intended to become politically involved in the turmoil that erupted at the originally secular university and resulted in its closure. "But I discovered that I was existentially involved," she said. "Because if I were a woman, if I were a teacher, if I were a writer, I could not agree with the closing of the university. "

Recalling a big public meeting arranged by the Committee to Implement the Cultural Revolution after the universities were closed down, Nafisi was one of only three faculty members who refused to wear the veil there, and she spoke up on that question. "I said that we wanted the freedom of choice. My paternal grandmother was told under Reza Shah that she had to take off the veil. For a few months she refused to leave home because the veil was an article of faith for her, but I didn't think I should be forced to worship that way. Rather ironically, I said I would never wear it. However, after the meeting, a woman who later became head of the English department told me I was foolish 'because tomorrow you will be forced to wear the hejab to the grocery store.' But I told her 'the university is not a grocery store.'"

Nafisi herself had an impressive tradition to live up to, she indicated with the animation and warmth that must have inspired her students. She came from a family of "natural-born rebels" including "women of knowledge, either writers or university professors." Her outspoken mother, who constantly opposed the Shah, was a member of Parliament. Nafisi's popular father, a poet who became the youngest mayor of Tehran, was imprisoned for four years under the Shah. He was eventually exonerated of everything except "insubordination."

"It became a way of life for me after that," she said. She would remember that charge when she read Nabokov's words: "curiosity is insubordination in its purest form."

Nafisi was to instill curiosity and imagination in her students at the University of Tehran, but as Islamic fundamentalism took hold, she was eventually expelled, despite the support of even the traditional Muslim students who used to challenge her. She was out of university life for about seven or eight years, but by 1990 she was able to get her passport back and go abroad for talks and conferences.

"Every time I returned from my travels I had to report to the Ministry of Higher Education. They insisted that I wear the veil abroad and, of course, I refused so we always had this horrible discussion. The government wanted to polish its image so the fact that they would let a woman go and talk about Jane Austin and Nabokov was a plus for them, but on the other hand they wanted to control you and I would always stay out of their control."

During that time, she was also writing about literature. Her first book, on Nabokov, was published in Farsi in 1994. The chapter on "Invitation to a Beheading," which involved the relationship between the individual and the totalitarian state, appealed particularly to the young. "What I wanted to prove was how the fight against tyranny in Iran is very individual. It's about our hearts and minds." The most reactionary paper in Iran attacked the book, calling Nabokov a "dissident formalist." That only made it more popular.

Near the end of the Iran-Iraq war, Nafisi returned to teaching at the University of Allameh Tabatabaii and confessed that she was able to do a few "things that were a lot of fun." She brought outside speakers on psychiatry, abstract art, and films to packed public events.

To her surprise, Abbas Kiarostami, director of *Where Is the Friend's House?* (1987) who had been maintaining a public silence, agreed to appear at the first program. Long before he achieved his present international acclaim with the Cannes prize-winning *The Taste of Cherry* (1996), he was known for films raising questions that left the answers to the viewer's imagination.

"Kiarostami said he would not make a speech, but wanted the students to interact with him. Someone would ask, 'What is the symbolism here?' and he'd say, 'What do you think?' He also showed them a private screening of his film *Homework* (1989), which was then banned by the Ministry of Higher Education because it was a critique of how the schools were run. In it, a classroom visitor warns that the Iranian tendency to punish rather than engage a student's imagination will "produce an indignant, cheerless generation susceptible to any mental problem."

"*Homework* had an amazing effect on my students," Nafisi recalled, "because they said, 'This is how we're being taught, not allowed to think on our own. We are expected to learn things by heart and to repeat it.' Kiarostami was not appearing as an authority figure. He wasn't trying to be political, but he was teaching us a lesson in democracy: 'Think on your own and don't accept what the authorities say.'"

Eventually outside speakers were banned, and by 1995 Nafisi submitted her resignation to the university. For two years it wasn't accepted, but she refused to return. Meanwhile, she taught her seven students at home, listening to their problems and even revealing a few of her own.

When she, her husband, and two children left Iran in 1997, she decided to write her *Lolita* memoir because she thought that, although Americans could understand reports of killings and torture, they didn't comprehend the impact of the Islamic state for depriving its citizens of all ordinary pleasures. "That is why they hate this government. I wanted readers to realize that no matter how different people are culturally, everybody wants life, liberty, and the pursuit of happiness. Who doesn't want to be happy? And can you be happy if you're flogged for wearing nail polish? Iranians are often portrayed in the media as wanting a moderate form of Islamic rule. Well, it's not that they don't respect their religion, but they want to be free."

2002
Unpublished

Tamineh Milani

PHOTO BY JUDY STONE.

"Many ideologies wanted to get rid of the Shah and have a democratic system, and it ended up with the Islamic Republic."

Cairo

Tamineh Milani, the internationally famous Iranian director of *Two Women*, who recently served seven days in prison on shadowy, unsubstantiated charges, still does not know the outcome of her unprecedented case. She has apparently become an unwitting pawn in the ongoing struggle between the liberalizing policies of President Mohammed Khatami and powerful right-wing fundamentalist forces.

Milani's new film, *The Hidden Half*, just won a top prize at the 2001 Cairo International Film Festival for the artistic way she dramatized events in 1980, the year after the Islamic revolution. The hitherto taboo subject touched a raw nerve in Iran. In those volatile days, determined to make the universities Islamic, fundamentalist forces tried to get rid of all opposition by imprisoning people thought to be dissident and executing some. Other opponents of the new regime escaped from the country.

That ugly situation comes into public focus for the first time in Milani's film. A wife played by the luminescent Niki Karimi appeals to her husband, a judge, to dig deeply into the case of a woman he is about to try, by telling him about her own youthful past. She confesses to her activism against the Shah during college and her attraction to a married intellectual with a wandering eye, played by Mohammad Nikbin (Milani's husband).

In an exclusive interview here, Milani talked for the first time about her arrest. Her husband (who is an architect) translated while she listened closely with occasional passionate interruptions. When the conversation seemed to get very serious, their frisky five-year-old daughter, Gina, cuddled up to her mother. When Milani was arrested, Gina was told she had gone to a film festival in London, but after three days she seemed to understand what was going on and insisted on being with her father all the time.

Oddly enough, Milani's problems started one month after *The Hidden Half* was shown in Tehran theaters and continued to be screened even after she was in prison.

Late in August, four men went to the couple's office looking for her and then proceeded to the filmmaker's home, confiscating hand-written notes and scripts. They told her, "We have permission to arrest you" and after fifteen minutes they took her, accompanied by her husband, to the revolutionary court, which is under the control of fundamentalists. Ordinarily it would have been possible to post a bond and leave, but the judge wasn't there, so they couldn't release her and said they had to take her to another place. Her husband was not allowed to accompany her.

She was taken to a single cell and for several days was not allowed to mingle with other women prisoners. When other inmates finally met her, they all rallied to her defense, giving her fresh clothing, volunteering their shower time for her—and suggesting she make a film about their plight.

"Every day for five hours, I was questioned about my movie," Milani said. "I was accused of doing things against national security and collaborating with anti-revolutionary groups outside of Iran. It is one of the most dangerous accusations they can make, and the sentence is the death penalty."

After the judge saw the film, he realized there was nothing against the law in it, but speculation grew that her case was being used to discredit the Ministry of Culture and Guidance (Ershad) which had licensed *The Hidden Half* and to intimidate other independent directors. The rumor was that some unsuccessful filmmakers with powerful connections were responsible for making life difficult for filmmakers like Milani and Jafar Panahi, whose film *The Circle* is about women who had just gotten out of prison.

Meanwhile, Milani's husband, Nikbin, did not go to the press with the story because the deputy minister of Ershad was working hard to get Milani released. At the same time, concern was rising at the Montreal and Venice festivals about Milani's fate, petitions were being circulated in her support and questions about the case were being raised in the press.

At two press conferences, President Khatami said he had checked with the information ministry and was told she had no record of anything bad in her background. He said he knew her personally, that she was a very good citizen and he was amazed at her arrest. Later, the Ershad minister Masjed Jamee appealed to Ayatollah Ali Khamenei, the supreme leadership, who ordered her immediate release.

"We were extremely worried," Nikbin said. "The court had charges and accusations but didn't have any documentation. Two hours after she was released from prison two groups came from the judiciary office. One came to our home and took whatever they wanted and another group of five started searching our office again. They took pictures, videotapes, handwritten notes, film books, and scenarios. At the office, they took my architectural material and contracts, which I need for my work."

Following Milani's release, she and her husband tried to get the case closed and the return of their belongings. "They have not given us a direct answer about when we'll get them back, or what's going to happen," Nikbin said. "It's an open case right now."

Knowing she was dealing with a controversial subject, Milani said she wanted to make the film because she thought it would be in line with President Khatami's proposals to start a dialogue on the past in order to renew the country.

"We need to see what happened to those people the year after the revolution," Milani noted. "I was in my first year of architectural school. There were many diverse political groups wanting to get rid of the Shah and have a democratic system and it ended up with the Islamic republic. How can we judge a teenager then who emotionally wanted to do something for the country and may have been attracted to a left-wing group? Many people left the country at that time for various reasons. Some wanted to become engineers or doctors and saw that they would become nothing here. This is the story of their lives. They'd love to come back to Iran, but they can't."

The film has been watched with extraordinarily intense silence, followed by tears after the screenings and thanks to Milani for opening up the subject, Nikbin said. "Until we get rid of the anger some people feel from those days and release that negative energy first, we can't really be united."

October 26, 2001
Los Angeles Times

Babak Payami

PHOTO BY JUDY STONE.

"*I wanted to draw on the contradictions and absurdities of modern life.*"

Toronto

I t's no wonder that Babak Payami felt like a tightrope walker when he was directing a feature film called *Secret Ballot* in Iran. The title alone is enough to send shivers down the spines of the fundamentalist rulers of that country and to provoke cynicism among the young people who have voted hopefully by secret ballot for democratic reformers only to have their aspirations crushed by the authoritarian Islamic mullahs who hold the real reins of power.

A citizen of both Canada and Iran, the stocky writer-director seemed sanguine enough about the prospects for his off-beat absurdist comedy when it had a lucky pre 9/11 screening at the Toronto International Film Festival last year. After all, he had just won the special jury prize as best director at the Venice festival. But now, a year later, although the production has received mostly favorable reviews in the United States, it has still not opened in Iran.

Reached last week by telephone in Tehran, where he is preparing his third feature, Payami refused to speculate on the reason for the delay in a theatrical opening. He noted that Jafar Panahi's controversial *The Circle* has not been banned, but two years later, it has still not been shown in Iran.

Like Panahi, he insists that he is not a political person and he was not endeavoring to make a political film. Still, different interpretations—or misinterpretations—are possible for the strange spectacle of a gung-ho young woman in an all-enveloping chador who is determined to get everyone on Kish Island to cast their votes in her huge ballot box while the armed soldier assigned as a guard observes her in wonderment.

So do most of the residents on the sparsely populated island in the Persian Gulf. And she only has a few hours before her 5:00 PM deadline to convince people to vote for two candidates out of ten on the ballot. For what positions isn't clear to us or to the hard-to-find residents. But she has a pitch for every skeptic: the voting process helps countries improve, the election can bring a new water system, herds would prosper. She's only slightly taken aback by an elder citizen who will only vote for God or by a strong-willed matriarch who doesn't want any interference in governing her own realm or by a young mother who insists that the election worker is more interested in politicking than in people's problems. And when she tries to get the soldier to drive past the red light on the only traffic post in the desert, the man—who is not as naïve as he looks—says, "You've been talking about the law all day long and now you want to break it!"

Payami, thirty-six, said he was inspired by a short film, *The Test of Democracy* by Mohsen Makhmalbaf, one of Iran's most prolific directors. His film was a short pseudo-documentary about a director who abandons his set in order to cover the elections three years ago. While Makhmalbaf was filming, he went to Kish. When he came back, he called Payami and said, "I shot this really crazy scene about a girl in a full chador who has an election box in her hand and is dropped by parachute into the sea." Not only did Makhmalbaf agree with Payami's suggestion that he would like to expand that idea into a feature, but he also proposed Nassim Abdi, a young journalism student, for the leading role.

From the start, the production was plagued with problems: monsoon-like rains that totally destroyed the sets they had built, the whole crew had attacks of flu, and the first person cast as the soldier couldn't take "the pain and agony" of the filmmaking process. Just before Payami was going to return to Tehran to find someone else for the role, he liked the sound of a man's voice who was arguing with a friend. He had him tracked down and hired Cyrus Ab, another non-professional.

For his film, Payami "wanted to draw on the contradictions and absurdities of modern life, about the necessary illusions that are created in our society to manufacture consent among the masses. This was basically my dilemma and not just about Iran. I felt this way even when I was not living in Iran."

He had grown up in Tehran, the son of an oil-company attorney, but he left Iran in 1971 during the Shah's regime and attended American international schools in different countries including Afghanistan—sojurns that eventually made him fluent in Dari (an Afghan language), Turkish, German, and English as well as his native Farsi. His longest stay was in Toronto, where he has lived since the eighties.

In a way, his film is an homage to the romantic comedies of the forties in which opposite characters—like the election agent and the soldier—are so much focused on working against each other that they fall in love. The film also reflects a bit of the old silent cinema. When the director of photography asked how he could get a comedic undertone into the visuals, Payami referred him to the straight-faced comedy of Max Linder, the French silent star who influenced the development of screen comedy, humor that sometimes borders on the tragic.

"For me," Payami said, "the comic and the absurd elements in the film were like that stick the tightrope acrobat holds in his hand to keep his balance. I didn't want to be judgmental about Iran. Not that I didn't want to. I felt I shouldn't be. But I didn't want to be ignorant of the specific nuances of the situation in Iran. I know that it's a very sensitive subject, and I did not want to be unfair or political about it. I didn't want to turn the other way as much as I wanted the film to be universal and have global relevance, but I felt very strongly about how I saw the situation in Iran and how I could portray it."

The New York Times review questioned whether the director's intentions were incredibly calculating on behalf of the Iranian theocracy and the token democratic reforms that the mullahs have permitted or incredibly naïve. Payami declined to comment on the article, but he noted that the critic's negative remarks were based on his erroneous assumption that the Iranian army provided the filmmakers with a transport plane that dropped the large ballot box by parachute to the island. In fact, Payami said, "I had a camera crew waiting to shoot some airplane footage and later digitally added the ballot box dropping from the plane."

Finally he hopes that audiences will get "at least what I got from the film: The need to talk, understand, and appreciate differences. The deeper and farther I went to the margins of society the more my respect for the people grew. I realized how much we can learn from them."

August 23, 2002
The San Francisco Examiner

Siddiq Barmak

"The Afghan people understood that the U.S. supported the Taliban when they first came to power because of oil interests."

San Francisco

Ever since Siddiq Barmak was five-and-a-half years old and saw *Lawrence of Arabia* in Kabul, he was obsessed by the mysteries of cinema, but when he finally got the opportunity to study film, he faced a double crisis. At eighteen, he had a "horrible time" trying to decide whether to attend Moscow's prestigious film school while the Soviet Union was Afghanistan's enemy. Also, as an only son whose father had disappeared, he didn't know how he could leave his mother alone.

Barmak, forty-one, talked about that youthful conflict the day after *Osama*, his first feature won the Golden Globe award for Best Foreign Language Film. On a promotion tour, he was in great spirits, having just phoned Kabul to tell his wife and three children about the prize and was amused because they wanted to know how much the gold weighed.

280

The honor was worth more than any weight in real gold for Barmak, whose goal was to focus the world's attention on the horror his country had endured under the Taliban's rule. All the indignities the Afghans suffered seem summed up in *Osama*, which portrays the stark fate of one twelve-year-old girl. With no men to care for them, her widowed mother and grandmother cut her hair short and dress her in boy's clothes so she can find work to support the family. Harrassed by skeptical kids who sense her real identity, she is protected by one boy who tells them she is called *Osama*. The worst torment comes when she is put on trial by a Taliban court and sentenced to marry an old mullah who has three other wives.

Searching everywhere for his amateur cast, Barmak found Marina Golbahari, the tremulous beauty who plays Osama, when she was begging on the street in Kabul. During the Taliban regime, her father was often arrested because he was a musician, and she lost a sister. Barmak has since helped to purchase a house for Marina's family, and she is acting in a short Afghan film.

Barmak got the initial idea for *Osama* after he himself fled Taliban rule in 1999 and was living in Pakistan for two and a half years. While working on a BBC radio drama aimed at Afghan refugees, he was also absorbing their tragic tales for future use in cinema. Still, he was shocked to read a letter from an old Afghan teacher about a little girl with such a burning desire to attend school during the Taliban regime—even though education was for males only—that she changed her appearance by cutting off her hair and wearing boy's clothes. However, police eventually penetrated her disguise.

Although most of the refugees had no hope for the future, Barmak remained optimistic. "I was sure the Taliban would be removed one day," he declared in faintly accented English. "They were not part of our culture. They were strangers."

Asked how he felt about the American invasion, he said, "I wouldn't call it an invasion, but a fight against terrorism." Barmak is a genial, outgoing man, but there was a touch of anger in his voice when he noted: "The Afghan people really understood that the U.S. supported the Taliban when they first came to power because of powerful oil interests. The oil companies never expected that the Taliban and Al-Qaeda would became a big enemy of the United States." (The secret American negotiations were documented in a book, *Bin Laden, the Forbidden Truth*, by two French intelligence analysts, Jean-Charles Brisard and Guillaume Dasquie.)

In February 2002, three months after the Taliban's collapse, Barmak returned to Afghanistan, determined to raise money for *Osama*. The prospects were dim in that impoverished country until he told his dream project to Mohsen Makhmalbof, the Iranian director, who offered him start-up funds and Iran's Ministry of Culture donated other film and laboratory services worth about $25,000. After shooting began, Barmak got additional help from Japan's NHK, a Japanese TV network, and an Irish production company, Le Brocquy Fraser Ltd. At a screening in Tokyo, the Iranian director Abbas Kiarostami was touched by *Osama*'s haunting depiction of that time and amazed to learn that it was a first feature.

As a youngster, Barmak had began making films without any instruction, eventually learning more from Iranian cinema books and finally becoming a second assistant director at the Ariana film studio when the Russians invaded. Although he wanted to make "guerrilla films" against them, he was tempted by the opportunity to study cinema in the Soviet Union.

He had resolved his youthful conflict about going there when he learned that his father, a police officer under the former monarchy, was safe in Germany and he found a cousin to care for his mother. During six years in Moscow, Barmak said he discovered "another face of Russians. In secret meetings I met a lot of good people, intellectuals, poets, and writers who were against the invasion of Afghanistan. The most important thing they showed me was how I could say something against the invasion by using symbols in my films."

Using symbolism was not like anything he had imagined during his childhood glimpse of *Lawrence of Arabia*, dubbed into Farsi by a Metro-Goldwyn-Mayer agency in Tehran. He had been born a Tajik in a Panjshir village near Tajikistan, but he doesn't like talking about "ethnic divisions because I believe we have to be one country, one unity."

When Barmak's family moved to Kabul, the boy was fascinated by everything he saw, especially that first movie. "It was like a shock for me. More than the big images and the sound, I was attracted by the light coming from behind through a very small hole. I wanted to see what was behind it, and I wanted to find out by myself. After two years I discovered the projection room and I wanted to become a projectionist." He still thinks "that line of light can be moved towards peoples' minds and enlighten them, especially in Afghanistan."

In Russia, Barmak's first student work was a ten-minute anti-war film called *The Wall*. The second, *The Circle*, criticized a young Afghan living abroad who comes as a tourist to explode a bomb in a Kabul theater, ostensibly thinking it was an anti-Russian action but, in reality, he was harming his own people. In *The Stranger*, he showed the misunderstanding between two civilizations by portraying the reluctance of an Afghan farmer to let his wife sing for a stranger who was collecting folkloric music.

After six years in Moscow, when Barmak returned home in 1987, he was eager to create a new Afghan cinema, but it didn't take long before he was in trouble. Although the Russians withdrew in 1989, the pro-Soviet regime of Dr. Mohammad Najibullah exercised strict censorship over all cultural activities. Barmak managed to avoid being drafted by

282

finding radio and TV work. However, his twenty-seven-minute documentary showing ordinary people who had lost their arms and legs in the war between the Mujahedin and the government was shown once and banned. Threatened with being drafted and sent to the front, Barmak fled to join the Northern Alliance force of the legendary Mujahedin commander Ahmed Shah Massoud (*The Lion of Panjshir*), who had become a national hero fighting against the Russians—*and* who was also a big film buff.

"We were trying to build a cinema foundation and started to educate young people who really wanted to make documentaries. We organized a video collection of 500-600 old foreign films, including *Gone With the Wind*, *Casablanca*, Oliver Stone's *Platoon*, and Massoud's favorite, *Spartacus*."

Barmak also made a documentary, *Invasion File*, about Pakistani Arabs who had been taken prisoner by the Northern Alliance. "The prisoners were involved in a very dirty game," Barmak said. "They came to Afghanistan to make it a big center of terrorism and horror. Sometimes they wanted to show they're progressive Muslins, making very big lies to attract young guys to their organization, but they were very sick people looking for special things."

Asked if he is a Muslin, Barmak replied, "I believe much more that my God is a god of peace and love and not for horror or making killing. I believe that all religion was created to make a good, moral society, and gods should create beauty. "

Barmak's own impressive creation came to western attention when Peter Scarlet, then director of the Cinémathèque Française, went to Afghanistan with the blessing of the French Ministry of Foreign Affairs to bring some laughter to the war-torn country. He took about forty videos, including Chaplin and Keaton productions, Iranian animated films, and Kiarostami's early *Bread and Alley*. Scarlet and his wife, Katayoun Beglari, held amazing screenings, including one at an orphanage to the delight of kids who had never seen movies. The audience reactions were captured in a documentary by the American "underground" director Lech Kowalski.

Scarlet found out that when Barmak was in exile and the Taliban were destroying 35mm prints of old Afghan films, nine men, devoted to cinema, hid all the negatives at risk to their own lives. He arranged for Barmak to show some of those old films at the Bologna festival of re-discovered cinema and at the Locarno festival. And when *Osama* bowed at the Cannes Festival, Barmak received the Camera d'Or special mention for best first feature.

Now, despite the resurgence of the Taliban in Afghanistan, power struggles between tribal warlords, and continual day-to-day problems, Barmak plans to make a comedy—more or less—*something* that will project an optimistic light on life at the end of the tunnel and give his people something to laugh about.

February 17, 2004
Toronto Globe and Mail

Abbas Kiarostami

PHOTO BY JUDY STONE.

"We have to accept responsibility for what we create."

San Francisco

Abbas Kiarostami's dark glasses are a medical necessity, but they also serve as a kind of metaphor for enigmas behind his films and poetry. The eyes are hidden and only a sudden dazzling smile suggests the humor and warmth within this director who paved the way for the emergence of Iranian cinema internationally.

He was here to receive the 2000 San Francisco International Film Festival's Akira Kurosawa award for lifetime achievement and to show his new film, *The Wind Will Carry Us*. It was a fitting tribute since Kurosawa considered Kiarostami's films "extraordinary."

With Kiarostami's usual spare, open-ended, and rhythmically repetitive style, the film introduces two filmmakers from Tehran, visiting a remote village in Kurdistan to record a ritual that would follow the death of a 100-year-old woman. While the wait drags on, the frustrated leader, Behzad, holds conversations with a little boy who keeps him informed on the old woman's condition. The title from a poem by the late Forough Farakhzad, the most famous woman poet in Iran, runs: "The wind will carry us away." During a key scene, Behzad sees a young girl, hidden in darkness, milking a cow while he reads in a voice-over from Farakhzad's erotically infused poem. The scene proved so upsetting to the censors that the film has never received theatrical distribution in Iran. The girl is presumably a symbol of repressed Iranian women, whereas in an altogether bracing scene, an independent matriarch in a tea shop slyly puts down a customer's assumption of male superiority.

When Kiarostami, sixty, is bedeviled by too many questions either about the exact meaning of his oblique films or about censorship in fundamentalist Iran, he answers, "I was very much influenced by Kurosawa-san. When he was asked a lot of questions, he answered, 'I don't know. A moviemaker is not a philosopher, but even a philosopher may just have his or her own philosophy and not know how to tell someone else about it.'"

In Kiarostami's film, the boy asks Behzad, "Where do good and evil go on judgment day?' He is told, 'Evil goes to heaven and the good to hell.' Then Behzad twists the answer: "Good goes to heaven and the evil to hell."

"It's a play in his mind," Kiarostami explained quietly through an interpretor, "because he doesn't have any idea where heaven is and where hell is because it's so uncertain and so impossible that it's one or the other."

Asked if his film related to the Koran or existentialism, Kiarostami objected to the question. "Movies are not to tell you one thing or the other. They are a way to start you thinking about different aspects of life.

"Sometimes it's difficult to answer a question when you don't know for sure what your answer will be," he said. "Then your answer should not be interpreted as diplomatic. A person asking the question should be sensitive enough to know if he can say anything more than that. Not to dig too far because that's where he needs to stop. In this case, I really don't know the answer. It takes nine years for scholars to go through the Koran and know what the Koran is saying. I'm afraid of the Koran in a way because there are so many contrasting interpretations. What kind of book is this that has so many different views based on it? I can't say that I know the Koran enough to have a view because it is so diversely interpreted."

Interpretations of Kiarostami's films accelerated in 1997 when he shared the Cannes Festival's top Palme d'Or award for *A Taste of Cherry*. They had begun to be expressed internationally in 1989 after the eight-year Iran-Iraq war when the Locarno festival introduced his third dramatic feature, *Where Is the Friend's House?* Again Kiarostami has taken the title from a poem, Sohrab Sepehri's "Address" in which "...You see a child/Going up a towering pine/ To take out a small young bird from the nest of light./

You ask him: 'Where is the Friend's House?'" It is a question repeated again and again by eight-year-old Ahmad. He has accidentally taken home the notebook of a classmate who was sharply reprimanded for not having done his homework and is threatened with expulsion. Ahmad does not know his friend's address, but sets out on a maze-like journey determined to find him.

Endless journeys or quests are a signature feature in many of Kiarostami's films. His concern for simple people is always apparent but not sentimentalized as, for instance, when a director, played by an actor, tries to find out what has happened to Ahmad and his friends after an earthquake levels their village in *And Life Goes On* (1992). In *Through the Olive Trees* (1994), he explores the quake's effects on a courtship and a film within a film. In the script he dictated into a tape recorder for Jafar Panahi's *The White Balloon*, a Cannes Festival's Camera d'Or winner in 1995, a seven-year-old girl is on a quest to buy a goldfish for her New Year's celebration.

Kiarostami's childhood was similar to most of the children in his films, he said, "not too poor, not too rich," but his father—who had "the spirit of an artist"—was a lover of literature and poetry, so the boy grew up under that spell. "I was a very restless kid and got very little sleep. I still sleep only three hours at a time." Now his restlessness finds some release in travel. He often serves on festival juries around the world, but each time he vows never again because he finds it difficult to make judgments on art. Nevertheless, he cannot fight the urge to travel and get acquainted with the assessment of films by people from other countries. On a far different excursion, he went to Uganda last year to make a short film for the United Nations about children with AIDS: *A.B.C. Africa*. (Martin Scorsese praised it as "a cinematic poem on the human capacity to move beyond tragedy.")

For years, Kiarostami has been writing poetry, but his first collection of haiku-like verse was recently published in Farsi, followed by a French edition. A newer book of poetry was published in Italian translation. In his book of photographs showing trees in all seasons shot over more than twenty years, one can almost sense his paternal feelings for them. ("Trees carry no passport," he has said. "The big things in life, like nature, have no nationality.") The photos share his films' visual poetry. A one-man show of his landscapes was presented at a New York gallery last July, and Japanese and English translations of the poetry, *Walking with the Wind*, have been published.

"What you see in my art doesn't necessarily come only from my family," Kiarostami said. "I'm also influenced by what I can hear over the walls from neighbors in the streets, by the government and traditions. Tradition says that children don't know anything, the adults know more and grandparents even more. So a child doesn't have freedom of thought or get too much to say. It's a very respectful tradition. The teachers are the ones who have responsibility to discipline the children. It's something in the social structure and especially the misinterpretation of religion, of Islam and the Koran. The religious aspect of people's lives indicates how they should think and what they should do, and that doesn't leave too much creativity for people because everything is decided that this is the way it should be." In Kiarostami's documentary *Homework* (1989), the conflict between harsh authority and the youngsters is highlighted when the boys can define the word "punishment" but few understand what "encouragement" means.

After studying art at the university in Tehran, Kiarostami began making commercials and designing film credits, as well as children's books. In 1969, he was invited to help found the cinema department of the Institute for the Intellectual Development of Children and Young Adults. The day he started work there, his first son was born.

When that youngster was twelve and the younger boy was four-and-a-half years old, Kiarostami's wife fell in love with another man, got married, and began living in France.

It was a time of doubly intense turmoil for him as the Islamic revolution had been gathering storm since 1979. He wasn't sure if he would be able to continue making films, and he turned to nature photography as a release in that traumatic period.

"I'm not sure if a good marriage is when you break it and let the other person have freedom or if it's when you try to stay together," he mused. "It was difficult for me, but I understood her situation and agreed to take care of the children. They influenced my work a lot. I learned about life from my sons."

His first short film, the twelve-minute *The Bread and the Alley* (1970) about the meeting of a frightened small boy and a large dog, was the Institute's introductory production. Made with nonprofessionals, it indicated the elements that would characterize Kiarostami's future work: improvised performances, documentary elements, and real-life rhythms. Instead of writing a formal script, he works intensively with his "actors" to achieve dialogue that seems to spring naturally from their characters. Most of his early films dealt with children, but even an educational work like *Toothache* (1980) showed the mark of an artist.

"I do not approve of debasing or exciting the spectator. I do not wish to prick the conscience of the viewer and create a sense of guilt in him." Kiarostami said. He hates narration and literature in cinema. What he likes is to leave a film's interpretation to the viewer, often allowing gaps in the narrative for the audience to explore. He told a conference in Paris: "I believe in a cinema that gives more possibilities and more time to its viewer, a half-fabricated cinema, an unfinished cinema that is completed by the creative spirit of the viewer, [so that] all of a sudden we have a hundred films."

In *A Taste of Cherry*, a man contemplating suicide is trying to find someone who is willing to pour earth on the body in the grave—like a hole he has dug for himself. Driving in the city, he gives a ride to a soldier and then to an Afghan religious student who are both reluctant to help him. Finally an old man agrees. He says he had once thought of suicide, but abandoned the idea when he enjoyed eating some berries. The controversial ending shows Kiarostami, his film crew and a group of soldiers relaxing around the empty gravesite. It was, after all, just a movie.

"The emphasis is not so much on suicide," Kiarostami explained, "but it's the Omar Khayyam type of philosophy that we have a choice whether we want to live or die. We who are alive have a choice as to whether to be alive and since we choose to be alive we might as well enjoy it." He quotes the late Romanian philosopher E.M. Cioran, who wrote, "Without the possibility of suicide, I would have killed myself long ago." Kiarostami adds, "I'm a strong believer that God is kind to us because we have the possibility of suicide. That's one of the kindnesses of God and that's why I'm a believer."

He's also a firm believer in an artist taking responsibility for his or her work whether or not censorship or self-censorship has been imposed. "We can't hide ourselves to say, 'I would have made a fabulous masterpiece if I didn't have all these limitations.' We have to accept responsibility for what we create and not make it sound as if it would have been very different had it not been for outside elements such as censorship. I strongly believe that choice is what we have."

When Kiarostami unexpectedly presented his Kurosawa award to a former Iranian actor, Behrooz Vosooghi, now a San Francisco Bay Area resident, he cited him as a man who had made a choice and lives with the consequence. "He was a very popular, very well-known actor until the Islamic revolution. But he made a choice to leave Iran twenty years ago, and that was career suicide for him. He has not worked for twenty years, whereas other people who stayed and acted in third-rate movies said, 'We didn't have any other choice.' In honesty, we have to stand behind our choices and accept the consequences."

September 26, 2000
The San Francisco Examiner
April 13, 2001
Toronto Globe and Mail

Postscript: When Kiarostami's *Ten*, his tenth feature and first one dealing provocatively with the lives of Iranian women, was screened at the 2002 Thessaloniki Film Festival, he made no reference to the fact that he had been denied a U.S. visa to attend *Ten*'s screening at the New York Film Festival, but his response at that time was gracious. In a letter to festival officials, he wrote: "I certainly do not deserve an entry visa any more than the aging mother hoping to visit her children in the U.S., perhaps for the last time . . . or myriads of other urgent cases. As a privileged person with access to the means of public expression, I feel profoundly responsible for the tragic state of the world, for the betterment of which we the public people have not done enough to ensure. For my part, I feel this decision is somehow what I deserve."

Bahman Farmanara

"I cannot be indifferent when writers and poets aren't published and directors don't get a chance to make films."

Can a "dead" Iranian film director tell the tale of his ten-year "burial," his resuscitation, and a "wake" that didn't happen?

Yes, but the ongoing battle between reformists and Islamic reactionaries is like "walking on ice and carrying a baby in your arms," according to Bahman Farmanara—who wrote, directed, and stars in a film about his "own" funeral, *Smell of Camphor, Fragrance of Jasmine.* In this case, he explained at the 2000 Toronto International Film Festival, "The baby is freedom and democracy, and you have to worry about two things: falling down yourself if you slip on the ice and then damag-

288

ing the baby you're carrying, which is a very precious commodity. So reforms end up becoming like a tango: a step forward, two steps back, and trying to keep your balance."

Farmanara, fifty-nine, kept his balance by a combination of fortunate circumstances: a wealthy father who let him begin his education in England at age sixteen, the opportunity to attend film school at the University of Southern California, and a way out of Iran after the Islamic Revolution, when he spent ten years as a producer and distributor in Canada and the U.S. Finally, in the midst of producing Jean-Claude Lauzon's *Leolo*, he was called back to Iran in 1990 to run his family's textile business. That gave him economic independence, but it didn't stop him from trying to make films. He had been crazy about movies ever since he was a kid, when projectionists would sell him two frames from a film that was supposed to be destroyed and he would collect and swap them the way American youngsters swapped baseball cards.

His financial freedom when he returned to fundamentalist Iran didn't alter the depression he felt when censors turned down every film script he submitted annually for ten years. Even during the Shah's regime, there were early signs that Farmanara was not going to follow official lines. A TV documentary he was assigned to do on caviar turned into an exposé of the poor lives of the fishermen who caught the most expensive food in the world. It was banned and to this day Farmanara exclaims, "I HATE caviar!" However, he later won acclaim as a director for his first feature, *Prince Ehtejab* (1977), about a decadent aristocratic family under the dying Qajar dynasty (circa 1900). The Shah banned his next production, *Tall Shadows of the Wind* (1978), in which a scarecrow multiplies and terrorizes a village. The same film was banned again after the Islamic revolution in 1979 as nervous officials considered that metaphoric scarecrow a threat to THEIR new society.

Sensing a possible change of atmosphere after the election of Ayatollah Mohammad Khatami as president in 1997, Farmanara submitted a new script which was also rejected. With the tantalizing title *I Hate Abbas Kiarostami* (a collaborative bit of Puckishness by A.K. himself and his old friend Farmanara), it featured a fictional character, based on an anti-Kiarostami critic, who works in a mortuary where people talk about many things, including famous directors.

"My tendency is to make political or sociological films," Farmanara said amiably. With a minimum of bitterness and a lot of black humor, he glancingly touches on such issues in his new film as brutality toward women (and some of its causes such as the desperation of the unemployed), bureaucratic nonsense in a cemetery, and the disappearance of intellectuals.

"When you live in a country like Iran," Farmanara said, "you always have to push the limit as far as possible. Any director worth his salt has to start looking around at what is happening in society and wanting to talk about it. I'm one of those people who cannot

290

ignore what is happening on a day-to-day basis. I also have this odd circumstance that I'm running a textile company. I go to the factory on the outskirts of Tehran and I see the workers' lives and how under pressure they are. If one illness happens, their whole savings are gone. I cannot be indifferent when on the intellectual side you see your writer friends who don't get their books published and painters who are not allowed to have exhibitions, poets who don't get their works printed and filmmakers who don't get a chance to make films."

Despite his recognition of the realities, Farmanara was in the grip of a massive depression when his last script was rejected, but he decided to write one about a director who couldn't work and wanted to make a film about his own funeral. "I gave the proposal to them not thinking they would really allow it, but it only took about one week for them to approve the outline," Farmanara said. "They wanted to see the script and after a month and a half, it was approved. Later, I made a joke with them: 'Did you approve it because it was about my death?' but they didn't get my sense of humor."

That decade of cinematic—and civic—silence has its offbeat reflections in the film: Ayedin Aghdashloo's portrait of a Spanish-looking nobleman with tapes across his eyes and mouth; and in the Edgar Allan Poe story, *The Fable of Silence*, that "Bahman" reads to his speechless mother about silent people in a silent city. Aghdashloo was originally supposed to portray the Bahman character, but he pulled out shortly before shooting began and Farmanara took up Kiarostami's original suggestion that he play his own part.

The only objection the censors raised dealt with four scenes in which a white-turbaned mullah reads the regulations governing funerals. Their words were not objectionable in themselves, but Farmanara speculated that "they" might think the scenes could possibly indicate a conflict within the clergy when juxtaposed with a televised speech by President Khatami in which he declares that whenever freedom is forced into an historic confrontation by other forces such as justice or religion, those combative forces are the losers. Farmanara argued with the censors for five weeks, but eventually agreed to a compromise. In the prints for Iranian theaters, the funeral regulation scenes were re-shot with a bearded, non-turbaned, civilian teacher, but the film was permitted be shown abroad with the original footage.

Even after Farmanara's production won eight awards at the Fajr Film Festival in Tehran last year and began to get international recognition, the fundamentalist media tried to hinder its release. As a result, the producers planned to open it without advertising at the worst possible time in December. But they hadn't reckoned on Farmanara's ingenuity.

Following the Iranian custom of printing a notice about where the wake of a deceased person will take place, Farmanara had 10,000 copies of a funeral notice printed with his picture and warning about the burial of the film by right-wing forces. University students put the warnings up all over Tehran, and the film went on to a successful eleven-week run in five theaters.

It's those young people who need attention now, Farmanara believes. "When a country is sixty-five percent below twenty-five years of age, you have a time bomb clicking. You have to create jobs for them, and they want certain freedoms. The right has ruled seventeen years out of twenty to twenty-one. They're not willing to let go of the elements of power and because of that, there's conflict. When a director from Iran says, 'I don't make political films.' I always say that denial is a political act in itself. But I say we cannot ignore what is happening in our country."

August 24, 2001
Toronto Globe and Mail

Manijeh Hekmat

PHOTO BY JUDY STONE.

"I thought of prison as a microcosm of society."

Thessaloniki

A small group of foreign guests at the 2002 Fajr Film Festival in Tehran was quietly waiting in the Laleh Hotel lobby to go to an unauthorized screening of *Women's Prison* when the usually vibrant director Manijeh Hekmat shakily told us that she had just been informed she would be arrested if she went ahead with her plan. Instead, shortly after the festival was over, she secretly managed to show a few visitors her disturbing film, the culmination of a two-year struggle with censors. Several months later, a print surreptiously found its way to Singapore and then on to the Venice Film Festival, where it was acclaimed for daring to dramatize the brutalizing conditions of incarceration over a seventeen-year period from 1982 to 2000.

Since then, *Women's Prison* has been warmly received at festivals worldwide and won the Rotterdam Festival's first Amnesty International award. As occasionally happens, the foreign success eventually led to permission for a cut version to open in Iran. The film describes the changing relationship between Tehereh, a jailer assigned to suppress a prison riot, and Mitra, imprisoned for killing her stepfather in defense of her mother. *Women's Prison* was an immediate hit in Tehran, breaking box-office records and winning the top prize given by the Committee for Cinema in Iran, but that's not the end of the story. Weeks later, an Isfahan cinema showing the film was burned down, *Women's Prison* was pulled off screens in four cities after protests by hardline religious groups, and then the number grew to ten. Finally, as of this writing, it was banned.

Although *Women's Prison* was the first feature directed by Hekmat, it was not her initial encounter with controversy. As a teenager under the Shah, she recalled that "the injustice, conflicts, and the problems in our society bothered me very much. Even though I came from a socially comfortable family, I felt a need to express my feelings and my points of view. I didn't have an extensive understanding of what was going on, but emotionally, I knew something was wrong with the Shah's regime and needed to be changed." The vast discrepancy between the very poor and the very rich disturbed her and she began to participate in protests against the Shah when she was only fifteen or sixteen, despite the disapproval of her father, supervisor of the railroad system in Arak, southeast of Tehran.

"The first three years of the revolution shaped my character and my thoughts," she told me, speaking through an interpretor, at the 2003 Thessaloniki Festival. It was a time when the revolutionary movement against the Shah had brought together a coalition of clerics, middle-class liberals, and secular radicals, all pushing divergent agendas as they vied for political power. "They were the best political years in Iran and I don't think they will ever be repeated. It taught me how to live, work with others, how to think in the right direction and find my own way. We all thought we were going to have something better for our nation, but unfortunately . . . " She didn't finish the sentence.

At first, Hekmat didn't know if she would write about social issues or make films, but when she started photographing with a still camera, she realized that she could record an image that might be too difficult to explain in words. She began working in cinema as a script girl before becoming an assistant director on eleven feature films. Later she produced five features, including the award-winning *The Girl in the Sneakers*. Giving birth to two daughters didn't seem to lessen her productivity . . . or her pride in the younger girl Pegah Ahangarani, who plays three roles in *Women's Prison*: as a political activist who is executed, as a drug addict who is raped by a woman collaborator and commits suicide, as well as a street girl born in prison who leaves and eventually is returned to the same cell.

Hekmat thought of prison as a microcosm of society at large and didn't know if it would be possible to explore that idea in a film without making a purely political statement. A newspaper story that she was planning a movie about prisons resulted in a "pure luck" phone call from the correctional administration's public-relations officer asking for her plans. When she said she didn't yet know, she got permission to visit some prisons and talk with the inmates.

Working with a five-person team, she spent the next two years interviewing about 2,000 prisoners and synthesizing what was learned into the script. She was particularly moved by the plight of women who had given birth in prison, only to see their daughters, unable to cope with the outside world, sent back to prison to have that birth pattern repeated. Hekmat noted that it was not possible to make any generalization about the women she met. "In prison, the law is the law of survival. One needs to act like a bully or be strong to protect and defend herself—which I've noticed is the law of the whole world. The most painful points that I've observed in my research are the laws of Iran. The common problem the inmates share are the laws of Iran."

For instance, she said, some of the prisoners are murderers who killed their husbands because they did not have the right to divorce them. As for the prison administrators, many were appointed right after the revolution without any special training or much education. "They are very tired of their jobs, many like Tahereh [the jailer in her film] have changed their feelings about the work and have their own difficulties."

Hekmat's first difficulty was finding a jail to shoot in, although she had no intention of filming real prisoners. The judiciary authorities immediately rejected her proposal, but after forty-two meetings over three months, she got permission to shoot at the still-functioning Qasr prison, east of Tehran, an institution for men. Other troubles were still ahead. Although she had been in the profession for twenty years, as a first-time director she needed a special permit from the Iranian Society of Film Directors, but was rejected. She finally got the directing permit in the name of her husband, Jamshid Ahangarani, who was the art director.

The script by Farid Mostafavi, who had participated in the research, managed to gain approval from the Ministry of Culture and Islamic Guidance in 1999. "That was the shining year of Iranian cinema," Hekmat commented. "Some of the censors said the Iranian cinema needs this film, but you may have problems with it and we may not be able to support you."

That prediction came true when the finished film had to get final approval from a different group. For a year and a half she struggled, on the verge of a nervous breakdown—she still has to control the tremor of her hands. "I would wait every day from eight A.M. until midnight at the Ministry [known as Ershad], and all I heard were insults. The authorities in charge of prisons wanted to take me to court. The only person who helped me was the Ershad minister Masjed Jamee."

Women's Prison finally opened in Tehran, minus seven minutes. These deletions included the shot of a prisoner being led off to execution and another scene in which the women are smoking. It inexplicably preserved a moment that implied a lesbian sexual attack under the bedcovers. Although *Women's Prison* was daring enough in its references to crime, corruption, prostitution, and drug addiction, it obviously could not describe some of the real horrors that have occurred.

Nevertheless, the production won strong praise for its courage and realism from B., a former very-long-time prisoner who now lives in the United States. B. is a woman who spent most of her youth in prison but remained determined not to submit or go crazy. She felt that she had to find a way to bear witness for those who were unable to endure such brutal incarceration. She has learned that time has not improved the lot of women prisoners, particularly in the smaller towns. And those who once played an active role in resistance to the regime now find an outlet for their energies in artistic endeavors.

Reality was much harsher, B. told me, than the film depicts. In all fairness, if it had tried to show the worst abuses, the film would never have been approved. Although life has changed for B. a graduate student at a leading American university, she asked to remain anonymous when she talked to me about her lost years. Without emphasizing her own role in any way, B. has unforgettable memories of the ordeals suffered by others in what was known as *barzakh*, the state of suspension before the descent into hell. Among them:

- Farzi, who first came into prison in 1981 as a beautiful, pregnant woman, gave birth to a daughter and pretended to be a double agent for the regime, working in a prison group of the Mujahedin, who were opposed to the government. She was released after two years. Later, she was re-arrested in one of the Mujahedin's secret houses in Tehran. Subjected to severe torture, she became a collaborator for the regime and was subsequently repudiated by her husband. Eventually driven crazy, she wound up lying on the bathroom floor for eighteen days, her body covered with worms.

- Zahra, a rebel against the religious views of her family whose members had achieved high government positions, was considered potentially more dangerous than the non-religious. Nevertheless, she spoke her mind directly and went to an extreme left position until she was brutalized into insanity. She was hospitalized, but finally committed suicide.

- Roya, who looked like a beautiful angel, was tortured and insanely began setting imaginary tables for visitors. She thought the torturers had sucked out the contents of her brain and got her to bark and crawl like an injured dog. Torturers in both regimes enjoyed forcing their prisoners to act like dogs and donkeys. Although they were forcibly undressed under the Shah, after the revolution, Muslin guards often avoided touching the prisoners, but both regimes found it expedient at times to unveil, undress, and rape their prisoners.

- Shakar, once the "most responsible and kind" nurse, was changed into a person who inflicted pain on her friends and was in turn beaten by them. But toward the end, she regained her integrity and in court refused to collaborate, knowing that she would be executed.

The distinguished Iranian novelist Shahrnoosh Parsipour, whose work is banned in Iran, wrote her own *Memories of Prison*, based on five years of incarceration both under the Shah and the Islamic Republic. At the time of my interview with her, she was living alone in a book-lined Berkeley garage. As if her incarcerations were not enough, she was later harshly criticized for her novel *Blue Wisdom*, which candidly described the ignorance of married women about their sexual organs, called the vagina "holes" and "curtains," which are pierced after the nuptials.

Sexual proscriptions made a horrible prelude for imprisoned virgins condemned to die. The women were first married to Revolutionary Guards in respect to the Koran's prohibitions against the killing of a virgin—and then executed. This practice was confirmed in the dedication to *Journey from the Land of No*, by Roya Hakakian: "Between 1982 and 1990 an unknown number of Iranian women political prisoners were raped on the eve of their executions by guards who alleged that killing a virgin was a sin in Islam."

Torments such as B. and Parsipour recorded obviously would not have been approved for *Women's Prison*, but Hekmat, that persistent director, plans to make another film exploring the lives of inmates after they are released. Still, when Hekmat recalls the first few years of the revolution when people still hoped for change, she says that the artistic progress of the last twenty years comes from that short period of democracy. "Just imagine if we had a longer period of democracy," she said, ever the optimist. "We could change the world."

2003
Unpublished

Rakhshan Bani-Etemad

"I am criticizing part of our own culture which forgets that a mother is first of all a woman."

"I can't understand what categories like male or female cinema mean. I don't know what women's cinema is. I don't like these kinds of segregation. I have never wanted to participate in a festival of films made by women only. Maybe because I am a woman, I am more aware of feminine sensibility, but I don't approve of the separation between men and women filmmakers."

—Rakhshan Bani-Etemad

Montreal

Nothing in the soft-spoken demeanor of Rakhshan Bani-Etemad, Iran's most famous woman writer-director, prepares one for the forthright thrust of that quotation. The power inherent in those words can only be appreciated in observing the way she shows the personal toll that Iran's patriarchal society exacts from both women and men.

In *The May Lady*, her sixth feature, the tension between a divorced mother and her jealous teenage son, Mani, who objects to her patient (unseen) suitor, reflects the rigorous traditions of a male-dominated society. In her film *The Blue Scarf* (1995), the tables are turned. A wealthy middle-aged widower who falls in love with a generous, free-spirited peasant is tormented by class-conscious gossip and the hostility of his greedy daughters.

When *The May Lady* had its North American premiere at the 1999 Montreal World Film Festival, the director smilingly emphasized that there is nothing autobiographical about the production even though her protagonist, Forugh Kia, is a documentary filmmaker. Forugh's goal is to make a film about an "exemplary mother."

The more Forugh interviews women distraught by poverty, neglect, and injustice—shown in documentary clips—the more difficult it is for her to come to grips with the subject. And, at home, while trying to be an "exemplary mother" herself, she has to deal with her son's suspicions about the man who keeps calling her. Although Iranian law favors giving the father custody in a divorce case, Forugh's mother-in-law intervened in her favor because Forugh had been abandoned by her husband.

"I am criticizing part of our own culture which forgets that a mother is first of all a woman," Bani-Etemad declared, speaking only partly from personal experience. Like her protagonist, she is also divorced and has a fourteen-year-old daughter from her second marriage, to Jahangir Kosari, the co-producer of *The May Lady*.

"The woman in the film is a very conservative character. I am not at all conservative. Forugh finally realizes that she has to approach the man through her own choice and not listen to her son. If she were not conservative, she would have reached this conclusion much earlier." In fact, her decision is handled so subtly at the conclusion of the film that it takes a moment for the viewer to understand her response. Bani-Etemad said it was a very difficult film for her. "I never wanted to make a social manifesto, but I wanted to do a movie that could approach social issues." Her original synopsis was submitted and approved under the (very conservative) Ministry of Culture.

"I wrote it in a simple way so that the authorities would either allow the film or not. When it was completed, I knew I would have a problem of one or two sequences being changed, but the whole film would either be rejected or permitted. After a lengthy discussion, it won approval."

Perhaps ironically, the protagonist in *The May Lady* is named Forugh in honor of Forugh Farrokzhad, who was a poet and filmmaker, the first to speak out for women's rights, questioning macho attitudes and writing about her love affairs. She died at the age of thirty-six in a car accident about thirty years ago.

Bani-Etemad was born in Shiraz in 1954, one of four daughters and four sons of Iran's first chartered accountant, who died when she was nine. As the eldest of those living in Iran, she had to work to pay for her education. Employed for four years as a script girl at Iranian television, she thought she would study architecture, but became so fascinated by the use of images that she soon changed her mind.

In 1979, the year the Shah fled from Iran, she graduated in film directing at Tehran's College of Dramatic Arts. From 1984 to 1987, she directed TV documentaries on consumer culture, the employment of rural migrants in town, and the economic effects of the Iran-Iraq war. At the same time, she began to work as a film director's assistant.

"Women played a great role against the Shah," Bani-Etemad commented through an interpreter. "Different types and different classes of women from the educated to housewives. Others were also affected by the movement. Even women who are not so active are still involved in some very specific periods, such as the Iran-Iraq war, the presidential election, and in some social-political issues. That is the result of the most important experiences they had during the [Islamic] revolution."

One obvious mark of the changes made by the Islamic regime is the mandatory head scarf (the hejab) that all females must wear after eight or nine years old. When Bani-Etemad learned that the photographs being taken were for publication, she put on her scarf. "The hejab is traditional," she explained. "Even mothers wear it at home, but when it is compulsory, I am against that. Now it is a law and I respect that, but how I think about it is a personal thing."

In reference to the political struggles between the more moderate President Mohammad Khatami and the Supreme Religious Leader Sayed Ali Khamenei, she said, "Of course, I am affected by the tensions of my society, but nowadays we can see conflicts in the administration and we never saw such things in the history of Iran. It is one of the most valuable periods that the people are experiencing. Even if the efforts of President Khatami do not lead to victory, the people can not return to the situation they had five or ten years ago. They can't go back to it."

March 10, 1999
The San Francisco Examiner

Mariam Shahriar

PHOTO BY JUDY STONE.

"A metaphor for the loss of identity."

Montreal

It was something like a last-minute miracle that Mariam Shahriar's *Daughters of the Sun* squeaked past Iran's censors and went on to win the first-time director's prize at the 2000 Montreal World Film Festival. Her moving production was a ground-breaking portrayal of women's bleak lives in an isolated carpet factory.

Shahriar, a tough-minded thirty-two-year-old who had studied for years in Los Angeles and Italy, tackled the subject of a woman's identity obliquely. In a country where women (including tourists) are legally required to wear an enveloping scarf (hejab), Shahriar uses hair as a metaphor for womanhood.

In the opening scene, Amangol's father cuts off his daughter's long, luxuriant, black hair, shaves her head, and disguises her as a boy, presumably so that she will be protected when she goes out alone into the world to support her poor family. At her job in the carpet factory, Amangol is in a unique position that becomes precarious when one girl develops a crush on the attractive "male" co-worker. When Amangol eventually leaves the factory, she is seen walking toward the horizon in a long red dress, her shaved head still uncovered.

"I never saw the shaving of the head as a physical thing," Shahriar said. "It became a great metaphor for the loss of identity. What is your role now? How do you find out who you are? It's NOT a cultural thing. Unfortunately, all of us in the world have reached the same level. Somehow women do not have a clear identity. They don't know whether to be a feminist or a humanist or just be a simple housewife. I wanted to say that, aside from our roles in society, we should celebrate our femininity. No matter who you are or what you are, it's wonderful to be a woman!"

None of that impassioned feeling is spelled out in the script, which was originally approved by Iranian censors who later had other things on their minds. They wanted her to cut the first and final scenes, but she adamantly refused. Her reaction was: "Over my dead body!"

The censors said there was nothing wrong from an Islamic point of view with the girls touching each other in their innocent way, according to Shahriar. They objected to the story itself. Since the smitten girl thinks Almangol is a boy, why does she let a "male" touch her?

To comply with those objections, Shahriar cut all the "touching" scenes in one night—which wreaked havoc with the editing—to get it ready for the annual international Fajr Film Festival in Tehran. Then she waited and waited for permission to show it. Persisting in her efforts to see a censorship representative, she was informed that the film came in too late to be scheduled. But the feisty director, daughter of an equally independent mother, retorted that they had looked at the video a long time ago.

In recounting her dilemma, Shahriar offered an unusually revealing glimpse at Iranian censorship.

Finally, a representative of the censors told her that he was the one with the authority to approve her film, but after looking at it for five minutes decided it would not be shown at Fajr. He advised his committee members that they could watch the film but they could not choose it for the festival.

Eventually, she convinced him there was nothing political in the production, and he agreed to give it one 11:00 P.M. screening at a theater outside the festival. "People saw it in the most miserable situation with no subtitles or dialogue list," she said. Nevertheless, Montreal guests wanted to show it at their Canadian festival, but she could still not get permission for its release.

There were objections by those who thought the film showed "too bitter"a view of Iranian society. They also wanted to know why she had dedicated it to the late Ahmad

Shamlou, one of the great Iranian poets who was imprisoned during the Shah's regime and harrassed thereafter because of his belief in the separation of church and state.

It was the election of President Khatami that persuaded Shahriar to return to Iran after ten years abroad. She had left the country during the Iran-Iraq war after hiding out during the bombing of Tehran. She would return on visits, but sensed a "completely different atmosphere" after Khatami became president and she believed she would find new opportunities as a filmmaker.

At the moment there may be uncertainty in the film world due to the recent forced resignation of the liberalizing Minister of Culture and Islamic Guidance, Ataollah Mohajerani. What that will mean for Shahriar's new script is unclear. She called the story she was working on about two Afghan lovers "ten times more controversial" than her first feature. She already had received questions about her use of quotations from the Old and New Testaments in the film.

"I hope," she said, "they don't look at it as advertisements for Christianity or Judaism but will consider it from a humanist point of view."

December 2000
The Oakland Tribune

Bahman Ghobadi

PHOTO BY JUDY STONE.

"I wanted to present a real look at the Kurds."

San Francisco

April 11, 2003, might have seemed a cause for Kurdish celebration when Saddam Hussein lost control to U.S. troops of the oil-rich towns of Kirkuk and Mosul, but for Bahman Ghobadi, a Kurdish filmmaker, it was almost like another chapter in the splintered history of his people. (Those two towns had been left under Baghdad's rule when Kurdish lands were divided after the 1991 Gulf War, while others became autonomous under Western protection.)

Ghobadi had not yet heard the report when he arrived for an early morning interview to promote his film *Marooned in Iraq* in which the harsh Kurdish life along the mountainous Iran-Iraq border is depicted with music and amazing good humor. "I can't smile at this news," Ghobadi said through an interpretor, "because I think it's a foolish war between the United States and Iraq. If the United States wanted to do something [about the Kurds], it should have been done earlier, twenty, fifteen, ten years ago. Then, there was a possibility that war might start between the Kurds and the Turkish people. If the United States achieves its goal now, it won't support the Kurds. I don't trust the U.S. government and the politicians because they're after their own benefits, just like the Hollywood cinema."

He spoke with the knowledge that twenty million Kurds—scattered throughout Turkey, Iran, Iraq, and Syria—are the largest ethnic group in the world without their own state. "In *Marooned* I wanted to show that the Kurds have no place. Movies that depict the Kurds as being very violent give the wrong impression. I wanted to present a real look at them. They're wanderers. To them war is only a game they are used to. But with music and humor, they can tolerate and survive hardship and traumas."

Musicians reflect that history in *Marooned* because Ghobadi didn't want the film to have the bitterness of his first feature, *A Time for Drunken Horses*. In that heartbreaking tale, poor orphaned children try to raise money for an operation on their disabled brother by crossing the border to Iraq under such terrible freezing conditions that their mules have to be fed whisky to get them to work. It won the Camera d'Or for Best First Film at the 2000 Cannes Festival.

Marooned is set sometime after Iraqi planes bombed the Kurdish town of Halabja in 1988 with mustard gas, nerve gas, and cyanide, killing 5,000 men, women, and children in a few minutes. Mirza, a popular Kurdish singer in Iran, learns that his former wife, Hanareh, who was also a singer, is living in a refugee camp in Iraq and needs his help. As he and his two grown musician sons head for the border, they have a number of discouraging—and humorous—encounters before Mirza finds Hanareh ,who has been disfigured and lost her voice in the chemical bombing. In Kurdish, her name means pomegranate, "which can be seen as a metaphor for the Kurds' search for a homeland to hold them together, just like a pomegranate's hull holds the seeds together," according to Jamsheed Akrami, a film professor in New Jersey, who is also an Iranian Kurd.

With a smile, Ghobadi traces his love for movies back to his first taste of sandwiches when he was about six or seven years old, growing up in Baneh, a very poor village in Iranian Kurdistan near the Iraqi border. Someone opened a sandwich shop next door to a theater that showed action films. "Those movies weren't so great," Ghobadi recalled with an almost boyish enthusiasm while doodling away on a napkin, "but if you had the money, you could watch a movie while eating a sandwich with a Coke, and *that* was great!"

A few years later, factional fighting broke out when the Iranian revolution began and Bahman's father, a policeman, smuggled the family out to Sanandaj, which was somewhat safer, but a haven for drugs. To keep the boy out of trouble, Bahman's father enrolled him in a gym where he studied and practiced wrestling for five years.

When he was sixteen he visited a photo lab next door to the gym and was hooked. On a mountain-climbing trip, he shot a roll of film with a borrowed camera and when it was developed, he was told that he had a natural talent for photography.

Ghobadi thought about becoming a photographer, but he didn't have enough money to buy a camera. Instead, he bought a book, *The Cinema of Animation*, and became obsessed with the possibility of making an animated film, to the strong disapproval of his father and the firm support of his mother. Their disagreement became one reason for their subsequent divorce. His mother helped him make a ten-minute 8mm film with a borrowed camera in which cigarettes carried out the action on a box rigged up like a soccer field; the short won a prize at a film festival in Tehran. "That was my start," he said proudly.

About the same time, an office for filmmakers was opened in Sanandaj and Ghobadi became its first member. "What was great about that was instead of two books on cinema, there were ten, all written in Farsi. There were no books in Kurdish or film schools for Kurdish people." Although he was accepted by a university in Tehran and got all the credits for a degree, he never received a diploma and thinks he learned more about filmmaking in the course of turning out about thirty-six shorts than he would have learned in school.

He said that one of the things that made him a filmmaker were the hide-and-seek games he used to play with his father. "I learned about *mise en scene* and rhythm from those games and tricks I used to play on him." The director's father died a few years ago without seeing any of Bahman's work.

"The second thing that made me a filmmaker was what was happening in Kurdistan and the great support of my mother."

When he worked with Abbas Kiarostami on *The Wind Will Carry Us*, Ghobadi convinced people in the Kurdish locations to cooperate with the director, who is "one of the great masters of Iranian cinema." He also "played" an unseen part as the person in a hole. He said he didn't learn anything specific about filmmaking from Kiarostami, but he learned two major things: how you can become really in love and passionate about cinema and also "that I should follow my own path in filmmaking."

When he followed that path in 2004 with *Turtles Can Fly*, *Variety* wrote that Ghobadi "confirmed his place as the poet laureate of Kurdish cinema . . . with an engrossing, nuanced pic about orphaned children in a refugee camp on the Iraq-Turkish border . . . shifting between wrenching tragedy and comedy . . . "

2003

Unpublished

Dariush Mehrjui

PHOTO BY JUDY STONE.

"*Reality is worse than what I show in the film.*"

Tehran

There were unexpected consequences when Dariush Mehrjui had his initial taste of fame with *The Cow*, a dark portrayal of Iranian rural society. When it was smuggled out to the 1971 Venice Film Festival, it became the first Iranian film to win an international prize. More surprising, the ground-breaking work later won an expression of approval from the Ayatollah Khomeini that helped to open an exploratory new path in Iranian filmmaking. Despite that ecclesiastic nod, Mehrjui had his share of "crazy" censorship in the course of a long career that has been marked by five films unusually sympathetic to women: *Banoo* (1992), *Sara* (1993), *Pari* (1995), *Leila* (1997), and *Bemani* (2002). The latter was inspired by a rash of fiery suicides among girls in a desperate response to oppression.

Although *Bemani* was passed over for an award at the 2002 Fajr Film Festival in Tehran, it won the plaudits of foreign guests. As befitting a man with a philosophy degree from UCLA, Mehrjui, sixty-three, seemed unfazed by the jury's rejection when he talked about it in the festival's crowded hospitality suite. *Bemani*, he explained, is a name parents choose when a first or second daughter dies and it expresses the hope that the new baby will stay alive.

He first heard about the suicidal girls of Elam in the remote Elam Province when a friend who had made a documentary about them encouraged Mehrjui to visit their village homeland on the 400 kilometer border with Iraq south of Kurdistan. It was an area particularly affected by the 1980-1988 Iran-Iraq war. As one survivor told Mehrjui, "We are a very miserable people. When the enemy was getting ready to return to Iraq, they would drop all their surplus bombs on us. That's why we had to run away every day."

"What is amazing," Mehrjui noted, "there was no sign of suicide at all during the war. The first year after the war, there were about twenty-five suicides and a year later, about thirty-six and then more and more. When we went there every day someone was putting herself on fire. It's a tribal area with a very closed and prejudiced way of looking at the world. People wouldn't show the girls who burned themselves. They usually hid them. Some lived with their parents, but most of them died." None of the girls were allowed to talk to a man alone, but a few talked to Mehrjui's co-writer, Ms. Vahideh Mohammadifar, who researched the variety of problems they faced.

Those oppressive pressures emerge in three fictional stories told in the film: Madina, a divorced carpet-weaver murdered by her uncles; Nassim, who committed a fiery suicide after her father pulled her out of her university medical class and Bemani, forced to marry her family's landlord, survives an attempt to set herself on fire after being brutally abused. But at the end, the scarred young woman meets someone more miserable than she is: a war veteran whose occupation is washing the dead and who feels that everyone ignores him.

Mehrjui thought there were many reasons for the suicides: a high rate of unemployment, which bred frustrated males as well as women. People were having trouble coping with increased modernization. And men were putting a lot of pressure on the girls.

"Reality is worse than what I show in the film," Mehrjui said, citing what happened to the girl who plays Bemani. Her parents and most of her brothers agreed to let her perform, but one brother was not well informed. When she was returning from an evening shoot, he started shouting at his sister and beating her because she was coming home so late. But there were favorable surprises as well: a university professor who played the part of the father who dragged his daughter out of medical class was broad-minded enough to portray that ignorant man.

Mehrjui had not told anybody in advance about the plot because he was afraid the non-professional performers would start "acting." In addition, hostility and suspicion were rife in Elam about what the filmmakers were doing there. Local newspaper articles attacked them, suggesting that the project was designed to make people lose their faith. People expressed fear that the film would not give a good impression of their community. Toward the end of filming, a script was accidentally left in a house where a scene took place. One of the amateur actors told everybody and there was a radical change the next day. The performers didn't want to go ahead with their roles until they were persuaded to continue by Mehrjui, who explained that the film was designed to help people solve the problems in their community. Even so, on the last day of filming, Mehrjui's male assistants were beaten up.

"The main reason I made the film is that I was so affected by this tragedy going on every day. My God, it was like a silent protest, these innocent girls who cannot protest against the regime. I thought maybe raising this issue would make officials do something economically for the region, and provide some recreation for the people." As for the obliquely happy ending to the film, Mehrjui said, "I didn't want to show these people without any hope."

Although there was no "official" censorship on *Bemani*, when Mehrjui looked back at his former experiences, he said that sometimes the mentality of the censors is ludicrous. "Once I told the censors, 'You look at things as if you're looking with Freudian eyes. You see sexual symbols in everything.' The poster title for *Sara* had her name painted in red and I was told to change the color because it's like a woman's period." He burst out laughing at the recollection. In *Banoo* (*The Lady*), based on a true story but reminiscent of Buñuel's *Viridiana*, a lonely wealthy woman takes in a homeless gardener, his pregnant wife, the couple's runaway daughter, and others, but she learns that her hospitality is not rewarded. The film was banned for eight years; censors complained, "You're trying to show that rich people are good and bad people are the poor and this is an insult to the people."

Asked to compare censorship under the Shah and the Islamic Republic, Mehrjui said, "There's no difference. They're both based on ideological outlooks, constantly dividing things dogmatically into black and white. I was asked to make cuts in some of the films. Some, but not all, were first confiscated and banned."

That banning cycle started with *The Cow*, which showed a poor village thrown into turmoil by the loss of its one cow and the owner's mad obsession with the dead animal. It was one of four Mehrjui films funded under the Shah's regime but then banned for anywhere from one and a half to three years. They included *The Cycle* (1974), about poor people forced to sell their blood, and *Postman* (1971), a re-working of Buchner's *Woyzeck*.

Mehrjui's resistance to that royalist regime began when he was "shooting documentaries like mad against the Shah," including the Ayatollah Khomeini's activities in France. With the downfall of the Shah, Mehrjui thought, "there would be democratic, liberal changes and everything would be more or less civilized." He soon learned differently.

In that brief hopeful moment right after the Islamic Revolution, Mehrjui got state funding for his feature, *The School We Went To*, about a student revolt against a dictatorial school principal. It was invited to the 1981 Cannes Festival, but by then Mehrjui was living in France and the Iranian authorities refused to release it unless he returned to re-cut the film. Even after he made his cuts, it was "butchered" so badly that he took his name off the film—which was nevertheless banned for nine years.

Although Mehrjui had made a feature on the life of the poet Rimbaud in 1983, he was not very happy in France, but he was afraid to go back to Iran. "All the dissidents were abroad. I was very nervous, but I thought it would be a good challenge," he said. "I hadn't done anything drastic except for a few articles I wrote that were not overly critical of the regime. So I took a few valiums and nothing happened."

When he returned to Tehran, then in the midst of the Iran-Iraq war, he made *The Lodgers* (1986) about apartment-dwellers who were fighting with an eviction-determined realtor. It is still considered the best comedy of Iranian cinema, and *Mama's Guest* (2004) won praise for Mehrjui's return to that humorous approach about everyday life. Many Iranians consider *Hamoon* (1990) Mehrjui's best film. It depicts the breakdown of a forty-year-old intellectual as his marriage unravels and his wife screams, "Women have no rights in this country!" That outcry seems to have set the tone for the five films pertaining to women, including *Leila* with its poignant performance by Leila Hatami as a barren wife whose mother-in-law insists on a second marriage for her reluctant son.

Despite all of Mehrjui's productivity, at the 2002 Fajr Festival he mentioned that he still finds his daily life is affected by events in the country. "Last year people were arrested and taken to jail. So more or less you always live in a situation of terror that you may get caught up. If they discover you had a drink or find a bottle of wine in your car—that's a crime. You always fear someone is watching you and you're guilty of I don't know what. Suddenly a few days ago, I heard that two or three film magazines were banned. For no reason at all people are arrested, taken away, and they don't let the families know.

"During the Shah's regime I was summoned by the secret police several times just to tell me very politely that they were aware of what I talked about when my films were presented in Berkeley. The police wanted to show that they wouldn't do anything drastic. After the Revolution, I was summoned by the authorities politely once or twice, but my case is different because luckily the only film that Khomeini saw was *The Cow* and he liked it very much and talked about it. That's why the historians say it created a way for films to be regenerated because cinema had been completely dead. And because my films often have mystical, religious, and philosophical overtones, they think I'm a valuable director."

2002

Unpublished

Majid Majidi

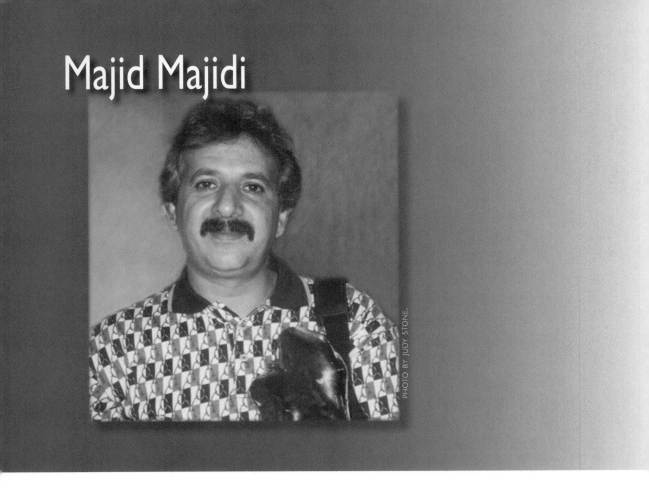

PHOTO BY JUDY STONE.

Haunted by the Afghan plight.

Montreal

Majid Majidi has been haunted by the Afghanistan plight ever since 1992, when he shot his first feature film on the Iran-Pakistan border and saw dead Afghan refugees on the road, hit by cars traveling without lights. In his production, *Baran*, Iran's 2001 nominee for an Oscar, he explores the plight of immigrants in a dismal construction site where a feisty Iranian teenager falls in love with a fellow worker, a frail Afghan girl disguised as a boy. But even as Majidi was savoring the success of *Baran*, he took off in November 2002 to film the life of women and children in two refugee camps inside Afghanistan and began editing 900 hours of footage for a documentary, *Barefoot to Herat*.

A trip to Afghanistan was certainly not on Majidi's mind when he talked about *Baran* at the 2001 Montreal World Film Festival, which awarded him the Grand Prize of the Americas for the third successive year. The production is a considerable departure from his best-known works, the heart-tugging but unsentimental *Children of Heaven* and *The Color of Paradise*. There are no resourceful tots in *Baran*, but its unrelenting depiction of those exploited Afghans would come as no surprise to those who saw Majidi's first feature, the daring *Baduk*, a "Dickensian" tragedy about a teenage Afghani brother and sister who were smuggling illegal merchandise across the Pakistan-Iranian border when they were kidnapped and sold to slave-traders.

Speaking softly through his interpreter, the very modest Majidi, forty-two, said that in *Baran* he wanted to show that "love and affection can put people together, beyond borders and political conflicts."

His empathy for the strangers in his land was eloquently expressed in a note from his diary after he interviewed a prospective Afghani performer for the film: "There is no remedy for the pain of living in an alien land. I have been seeing you for years—waiting in city squares or toiling, as a temporary guest, on construction sites of skyscrapers and towers. Every brick and stone present signs of your hard work. I wish to hear the story of your life, of the devastating war raging in your homeland, and of the pains of leading the vagabond life of an immigrant."

Between one and three million Afghanis live in Iran, making it the country with the largest number of refugees. Because it is illegal for them to work, they seek the most menial and lowest-paying jobs, often taking the employment of Iranians. Despite that, there is less prejudice and tension than is commonly supposed, Majidi said. "Considering the fact that Iran went through eight years of war with Iraq and has a very difficult economic situation, also due to the American embargo, the Iranian people have been fairly open to the Afghans. Of course, there are some Iranians very negative about their presence, but that exists mainly in the country. In general, the more normal people are not aggressive to them."

However, since the Taliban have been driven out of Kabul and other major Afghan cities, Iran has accelerated the expulsion of Afghans and forcibly deported several thousand immigrants in violation of the 1951 Geneva Convention, which bars countries from returning refugees to a homeland where they might face political persecution or physical danger, according to a United Nations report.

The fear they have faced about being expelled by immigration officials is graphically depicted in *Baran*, while other Iranian directors have chosen a different way of approaching the Afghan situation, notably Mohsen Makhmalbaf's *Kandahar*, which explores the condition of women under Taliban rule, and Hassan Yektapanah's *Djomeh*, about an Afghan immigrant's infatuation with an Iranian girl in a rural village.

During a bleak period after the Islamic revolution when Iranian filmmaking was practically non-existent, Majidi said he and Makhmalbaf saw a lot of foreign videos that were smuggled into the country and "worked together in acquiring knowledge." Majidi was particularly affected by *The Grapes of Wrath*. As film production resumed in the 1980s, Majidi appeared in three of Makhmalbaf's early productions, starring memorably in *Boycott* (1985) as an imprisoned revolutionary who is forced to reconsider his early beliefs.

Majidi had shocked his illiterate parents by starting to perform in amateur theatricals when he was eleven or twelve. The second of five sons, he told his father, a truck driver who wanted him to be a doctor or lawyer, that he was accepted at the university's engineering school when in fact he was entering the dramatic department. It was a time when the students, including Majidi, were busy demonstrating against the Shah. When Majidi was seventeen, his father died and the boy dropped out of school to act in theatrical productions and television. Two years later, he made a successful short that was shown on television and stimulated his interest in a filmmaking career.

When he began planning *Baran*, his fifth feature, Majidi knew he wanted to have all displaced persons speaking different languages in the cast and that the Afghani girl would never utter a word, but would have "something strong and tender in her eyes." Hossein Abedini, the lead character who is of Turkish origin, had dropped out of school at thirteen to help in his father's fruit store, when he got a minor role in another Majidi film. But meanwhile, he had lost his Turkish accent and Majidi wanted it back. So Hossein spent three or four months working on construction sites that employed Turks to regain that foreign sound. He later won the Best Actor award at the Fajr Film Festival in Tehran and, with Majidi's encouragement, went back to school at night and is now making plans for college and an acting career.

For more than a month, Majidi searched in two large refugee camps in the desert for a girl who had a spiritual look. When he finally found Zahra Bahrami, he was surprised by her strong personality and how much she knew. She had been brought up in that refugee camp since she was one year old and had never been to a city, but she had seen Majidi act in some old films that were replayed on television.

"With money from the film, we got her a private teacher and bought the family a house in Mashad, where they are now living. And she became a little bit like my daughter," said Majidi who has a seventeen-year-old daughter and a son, thirteen. In November 2002, Majidi went into Afghanistan to make a documentary about women and children in two refugee camps, the Mataki camp run by the Taliban and the Mill 46 by the Northern Alliance.

It was a potentially dangerous undertaking since the Taliban had murdered eight Iranian diplomats and a journalist in August 1998 in Mazar-e-Sharif, so Majidi and his small crew went disguised as Red Cross workers. Even so, three members of the crew were arrested by the Taliban and held for eight hours until Majidi managed to get them released. At the Northern Alliance camp, Majidi helped establish a school by donating 200 pencils and notebooks that would have to be shared by 500 potential pupils.

His documentary *Barefoot to Herat* covers the two trips that Majidi took. The first relates the journey of Afghans fleeing the bombing and war around Herat to take refuge in ill-equipped camps. The second trip took place after the fall of the Talibans in the city of Herat, where city-dwellers talk about their memories and hopes. Forgotten in a nearby camp, 150,000 displaced Afghans barely survive.

"In the context of what is unfolding in Afghanistan," Majidi noted, "if the American military actions bring about the downfall of the Taliban, we should all rejoice, but only if this is achieved without inflicting more harm on the innocent people of Afghanistan. Close to a million Afghani women, children, and elderly will be stranded behind borders and, without any protection, will die of starvation and disease. If this actually happens, how will the collective human conscience justify it?"

July 17, 2002
The San Francisco Examiner

Nelofer Pazira

PHOTO BY JUDY STONE.

Pessimistic about the fate of Afghanistan, her perennially wartorn native land.

Toronto

Three days before September 11, Nelofer Pazira, a native of Afghanistan, was at the Toronto World Film Festival, discussing how it happened that she inspired and starred in a movie with the prescient title *Kandahar* about the search for a young woman driven to suicidal thoughts by life under the Taliban. But now that the world knows about Kandahar, Pazira is still pessimistic about the eventual fate of Afganistan, her perennially wartorn native land.

"I'm feeling kind of sad," she said recently on the phone from Canada, "because we did not have to lose so many innocent lives in America to become aware of the tragedy of another country. So I don't cheer and say, 'great! finally the world is doing something.' I don't support the American war. I feel that a lot of innocent lives are being lost. As human beings we have forgotten what we were supposed to do in the first place. As much as one feels happy that at least women can get out and do what they want to do, but warlordism is still continuing."

In 1989, Pazira left Afghanistan at sixteen with her parents and a younger brother and sister on a grueling, illegal, ten-day trek from Kabul to the Pakistan border. After a year in Pakistan, they finally made their way to Canada, where Pazira was determined to learn English and become a journalist. "What I saw as the big problem in the world I came from was ignorance and power," she said, looking beautiful in an embroidered red Afghan dress and somber as she spoke about her life. "Journalism was for me the best way to struggle against that."

Early on, she understood something about struggle, although she came from an upper-class family. Her mother, one of the few educated Afghan women, was a teacher who had a university degree in literature and journalism. Her father was a pediatrician who had worked for the World Health Organization in India, where Nelofer was born.

"My father was one of a small group of intellectuals at the University of Kabul who followed the ideas of diversity, of parties, parliamentary democracy. He wanted things to change in the country. He was imprisoned for opposing the monarchy by asking for freedom and a free press. Then he was imprisoned when the Communist government began arresting all professionals." Although educated people were leaving the country every day, he felt a responsibility to stay until he became too sick to carry on.

When Nelofer was in second grade, she had learned a lesson in courage and endurance when she used to go with her little brother to visit her father in a Baghlan prison. Her mother was afraid to go there because she was terrified of being harrassed by officials. "The men in government were morally corrupt and they wanted to take advantage of her. They would tell her, 'Your husband is a criminal. Why don't you leave him and marry one of us?'" During one visit to the prison, Nelofer began sobbing as if her heart would break. Her father cautioned, "'I haven't raised you to cry. You must be strong and crying won't do you any good.' Ever since, I haven't cried."

When she moved to Canada, the first letter she wrote was to Dyana, her best friend, who worked in a bank in Kabul until the Taliban arrived in 1996. Two years later, forbidden to work or leave her home, the severely depressed Dyana wrote: "I can't go on anymore. My life has no meaning."

Determined to try to locate Dyana, Pazira headed for the Iranian border, where—concealed in a burka—she tried to cross over into Afghanistan with a refugee family, but they retreated when they learned that the Taliban was torturing their relatives. Back in Iran where she had lived for several months while making two documentaries, she called the prolific director Mohsen (*Gabbeh*) Makhmalbaf and asked for his assistance. She didn't know him, but she was impressed by the vision and compassion she saw in his work, particularly his film *The Cyclist*, which dealt with a destitute Afghan refugee. Pazira was the first Afghan woman Makhmalbaf had ever met and he had plenty of questions to ask her, but he couldn't offer any help at that time. However, almost two years later, he called her in Canada and said he was ready to do a fictionalized version of her search for her friend with Pazira in the main role.

In the meantime, Pazira, twenty-eight, who had a B.A. in journalism, had received an M.A. in anthropology and sociology and was working as a radio and TV journalist in Ottawa.

Acting was more than she had bargained for, but the next two and a half months of production were unlike anything she had imagined. In the film, the Afghan-Canadian journalist is called Nafas—which means "to breathe" in Farsi—and she is searching for her sister. The shoot took place in Iran at a refugee camp on the Afghanistan border. Each person in the small crew had different problems to solve every day. The camera operator was distributing food; someone else gave out medicine.

"I was going house-to-house trying to convince families to let their daughters be part of the film. The people divided along ethnic lines and they wouldn't talk to each other. I was desperate. I was so upset I just wanted to take the heads of these people and bang them against the wall and say, 'What's wrong? Look at what's happening in your country, look at what's happening to you,' but then I began to understand it more from their point of view. They would want to go back but not when people are dying."

In one village, the refugees didn't know what a film was. "We set up a small movie theater and showed some Iranian films with one day of screenings for the men, another for the women. We took about 300 videos to show them. Then we went house-to-house and got a doctor from Iran to examine people. Then we learned they had no running water, no electricity. Before we could even get into negotiations with them, we'd start finding refugees who had just arrived and were dying. We'd have to rush them to the hospital and we'd have to go to the market to buy food to give to some families. One woman came to me and said, 'Would you please tell the leader of our community, the head of a tribe, to talk in the mosque and say it's okay for us to help with the film?' Each tribe had its own mosque. I said I would try and had negotiations with tribal leaders again and again, and they'd promise but wouldn't do it."

The film finally opened to critical acclaim at the 2001 Cannes Festival. And Makhmalbaf went there armed with his extraordinary fifty-one-page document detailing the political, historical, and economic background of that nation's tragedy. It was entitled *The Buddha Was Not Demolished in Afghanistan; He Collapsed Out of Shame*. Five months later, U.S. bombs started falling on Afghanistan.

"It's difficult to say now we've got peace and security," Pazira said on the phone. "One can be optimistic about the prospects of the future, but one has to be realistic about the possibilities of peace, especially since the international force should have been quicker to move in and disarm the population. Instead of that we have actually armed one group against the other and the moment the interests of the Americans are over, they will walk out and there will be more chaos and we won't be surprised if the country will be plunged into another civil war. Because of that, I'm quite fearful about what could happen. We will have to wait and see. It's not an easy task."

January 4, 2002

The San Francisco Examiner

Samira Makhmalbaf

"In New York, I could see all the art and films I never saw before. How can you create something in Iran when you have nothing to see there?"

Thessaloniki, Greece

Perhaps the most important thing to know about *The Apple* is that the fruit symbolizes knowledge and the enjoyment of life in Iran. The Iranian film of that name captures the zestful spirit of its eighteen-year-old director, Samira Makhmalbaf, daughter of the famous director Mohsen Makhmalbaf.

A 1997 television news show about a father who kept his eleven-year-old twin daughters totally secluded behind locked doors ignited Makhmalbaf's intense curiosity. Neighbors had notified authorities that the girls were unwashed, uneducated, and had numerous physical maladies.

"It was so painful, I couldn't stop thinking about it," Samira Makhmalbaf exclaimed in a torrent of English when the film was shown at the 1998 Thessaloniki International Film Festival. "I thought it could be me, my sister. Every father loves his children. What kind of ignorance made him do it?"

Stunned by the criticism that followed the TV news story, the impoverished father wanted to tell his side. So when Samira suggested making a film about the family, the father agreed to appear in the docu-drama with his blind wife, enveloped in a chador, and their two daughters, Massoumeh and Zahra Naderi.

"The father thought he was doing the right thing for his daughters," Samira said. "He thought it was not safe for them to go out on the street. He quotes from an old book that describes girls as flowers that can be faded by the 'sun' of a masculine gaze. You could say their lock-up occurred in that neighborhood because it is poor and has a low culture. But I think this disaster happened because the father believed in such an extremist way. The attitude didn't come from the sky. When you go in that neighborhood in Tehran, there are bars in front of the houses and women are behind those bars. No man is behind bars. When you go deep into that culture, you see all these people believe the same thing the father believes. They're not aware of it, and this is the problem."

Samira's interest in the twins reflects her ongoing fascination with sociological subjects. She said she wanted to see what happens to a human being when all communication is cut off. The uncannily self-possessed teenager, wearing her hejab (the obligatory head scarf), reasoned that "their father believes in something that is quite ignorant, but in a beautiful, poetic way. Ignorance is not all the time ugly. It can be beautiful but damaging. He sees two other girls playing hopscotch and nothing damaged them. But staying at home would have damaged them, as it did his daughters. They would not be completely human."

Nevertheless, she insisted that the attitude which locks people away from communication with other people, other cultures, could happen in any country. "Ignorance can happen anywhere, but you have to find a reason for it and not put guilt on people because that doesn't solve anything."

Makhmalbaf, who had been itching to make a movie since she was fifteen, grew up observing the work of her father, Mohsen, best known in the United States for his poetic *Gabbeh*. A few days after the TV report about the twin girls, Samira borrowed her father's camera, got some of his precious film stock, and enlisted his help as scriptwriter and editor on what was largely an improvisational film, shot in eleven days. (Those two credits have skeptical Iranians wondering how much of the responsibility for *The Apple* rests with Samira or her father. He has declined to comment on his role.) Samira became an instant celebrity and the youngest director ever invited to the Cannes Film Festival.

In an interview, Mohsen Makhmalbaf spoke about the predominance of children in Iranian films as one way of circumventing censorship. For instance, little girls are not required to wear a hejab (scarf). And in his film *The Silence*, he featured a ten-year-old blind boy who works as a tuner of musical instruments "Finally," Makhmalbaf noted, "children are the vision of our dreams. You can only find the hope and passion for life in children."

It is certainly true of his own children. Just as Makhmalbaf left school at fifteen to support his family, so Samira at that age announced she intended to quit school. "It took a long time to make my parents believe I was going to stop because I was a good student. I told my father I'm going my own way whether you accept it or not. I expected him to tell me in five minutes how to be a good director." She laughed, recalling her ultimatum.

The demand for advice eventually brought about a home class in which the father taught Samira and her two siblings art, music, architecture, film, photography, literature, and poetry. She is as proud of her siblings' accomplishments as she is of her own.

Before starting to tell this interviewer about *The Apple*, she burbled with enthusiasm about her little sister Hanna who—at eight—directed her first short film, *The Day My Aunt Died*, which was selected for the Locarno Film Festival; and about her older brother, Messam, nineteen, who worked as a still photographer on *The Apple*.

On Samira's first trip outside of Iran to Switzerland, she only saw the vast differences in the two countries, but she began to study English intensively to communicate better with the people she would meet at the Cannes Festival. Then when she was invited to the New York Film Festival, she realized that friendship there was the same as in Iran and she thought, "I could be born or live anywhere."

She couldn't get over the energy she felt and the art she saw in New York. "It's the only place where strangers can come and feel at home after five days. I could go to museums and see all the art I had only read about. I watched films I never saw before by Fellini and Kurosawa. How can you create something in Iran when you have nothing to see there?"

March 26, 1999
The San Francisco Examiner

10
Middle East

Etel Adnan

SIMONE FATTAL AND ETEL ADNAN. PHOTO BY JUDY STONE.

"The Arab world is infinitely large in terms of space, and infinitely small in its vision…"

Paris

In an age dominated by self-serving publicity and public relations, it is noteworthy that *Sitt Marie Rose* (1982), a 105-page novel based on the true story of a woman abducted by Christian militiamen during the Lebanese civil war, sold more than 12,000 copies without the publication of a single review. The author, Etel Adnan—novelist, poet, essayist, artist, born in Beirut to a Syrian Muslim father and a Greek Christian mother—writes in French and English and says she can only express herself as an Arab through her abstract paintings.

"How then," *The Nation* magazine asked in a 1994 review of her other work, "can one come to an easy definition of Adnan? Is she a Lebanese writer, a French writer, an American writer, a woman writer?"

I knew Etel Adnan first as a cinema buff who eagerly waited in line with her companion/publisher, Simone Fattal, for shows at the San Francisco International Film Festival. Later I learned that she had taught philosophy for fourteen years at Dominican College in San Rafael. I didn't know then the range of her accomplishments: two plays, *The Actress* and *Burning Like a Christmas Tree*; love poems set to music by Gavin Bryars, the British opera composer; author of the French dialogue for Robert Wilson's multi-national, thirteen-language *Civil Wars* opera; and eight more books including *Paris, When It's Naked*, in which her love for that city is tempered by a reality that tears her apart: "Look, look how ugly are the Arab Quarter's pimps, how dehumanized the Algerians who squat in it, how destroyed their women . . . And I consider this monstrous being called Paris to be beautiful." In contrast, two of her poetry volumes carry whimsical titles: *Pablo Neruda is a Banana Tree* (1982) and *The Indian Never Had a Horse* (1985). Not so whimsical is her illustrated, surrealistic *The Arab Apocalypse* (1980) wherein the sun—which "unites the Arabs against the Arabs"—is a metaphor for war.

With the spotlight newly focused on the Arab world, I thought it was past time for an interview with Etel. She and Simone were dividing their time between Beirut and Paris, but kept their Post-Apollo Press office in Sausalito. In 2003, both Etel and I were in Paris at the same time, and we talked in their Paris apartment, filled with Etel's large, colorful paintings, Arabic publications, and Adnan's books in translation in French, Italian, Dutch, German, Arabic, Urdu, Turkish, and English. Her eyes had a mischievous sparkle and her voice was husky as she recalled her past. A handsome turquoise ring was a reflection of her love for Native American art in all its forms.

Her first languages at home in Beirut were Greek and Turkish. She was the only child from the second marriage of her father, an officer in the Ottoman Empire army and the commander of Smyrna during World War I. "He already had a wife and three children in Damascus when he met my mother in Smyrna. She was seventeen, beautiful, and about twenty years younger than my father. As a Muslim, he could marry two wives, but he divorced the first wife after he married my mother, and he settled in Beirut because he didn't want the two women to be near each other."

Such a mixed Muslim-Christian marriage was an "anomaly," Adnan explained. "I felt both rebellious and apprehensive any time an allusion was made to the religious make-up of my family."

Her father had been an agnostic ever since he attended military school in Istanbul, where he was a classmate of Mustafa Kemal Ataturk (who was to become the founder of the Turkish Republic). "My father admired Ataturk. He thought that there wouldn't have been a country called Turkey without him, but on the other hand he thought Ataturk was a traitor to the Sultan. Ataturk wanted to modernize Turkey, but my father, who was not involved in liberal ideas, thought it could be modernized without kicking out the Armenians. He was not anti-religious but he didn't practice the religion. He knew the Koran by heart and would quote it all the time because it was part of everyday life."

He also encouraged Etel to study more than her disciplinarian mother allowed. At the age of five, Etel was sent to a French convent school where Arabic was forbidden. She said she still speaks Arabic with a French accent. "The French nuns were stern," Adnan wrote in her essay *Growing Up to Be a Woman Writer in Lebanon*. "They behaved like colonialists and like missionaries: they had the dual purpose of extolling the virtues of French civilization and the infallibility of the Church in matters of religion. They created for children an authoritarian and dogmatic environment . . . my earlier creative works were the invented confessions of non-existent sins at the confessional."

From the age of seven, Etel loved scrawling her childish words "before I even knew what *writing* was. Words were a comfort for the body and the mind. We didn't have books at home, only the Koran, a German-Turkish grammar, and my mother's book of the Gospels in Greek. When I finished high school, my mother thought that was enough and I should get married."

Instead, at sixteen, with the outbreak of World War II and Lebanon under French rule, she went to work at the French Information Bureau in Beirut, but she was "homesick" for school. Someone suggested an unheard of thing: that she become a freelance student. Adjusting her classes and working hours, she earned two baccalaureates, the equivalent of a junior college degree. In the meantime, with Free French officers, Australians, and New Zealand soldiers flooding into Beirut, she observed how the Allies were "working together and cheating on each other and lying even in their little reports."

Etel said she saw history in the making, but she didn't learn what the war against Fascism meant in Europe until she was twenty-four. She got a scholarship in 1949 to study at the Sorbonne in Paris and met refugees from Yugoslavia, Czechoslovakia, Romania, survivors of the concentration camps. She became friendly with a Jewish Communist in the Resistance whose father had been taken away by the Germans and never returned. She also met her first Americans. "I had no notion of what is America. I asked if there were trains in America!"

In 1955, she arrived at the University of California in Berkeley to study philosophy and became aware for the first time of the Palestinian-Israeli conflict. "I felt sorry for the Palestinians and guilty that I was not conscious of their problems and I became very militant, although I always tried not to generalize the problem because I had Jewish friends all my life. I never thought in black and white. Maybe it's in my nature to see alternate points of view." After two years at UC, she continued her studies in philosophy at Harvard University and returned to Beirut in 1972. While working as an editor on a daily newspaper, she met Simone Fattal, an artist with an appreciation for literature, who was a philosophy student. Simone introduced her to younger people in a Beirut different from the city Etel had known as a girl.

Simone was born in Damascus to a Christian "jet-set" family who moved to Beirut with their importing business. "Her family was upset that she didn't get married and have a conventional life, but they never stopped her subsidies," Etel said. The partnership between the tall, handsome Simone and the Gertrude Stein-like figure of Etel didn't cause any problems. "In the Arab world you can do what you want if you don't make a scandal of any sort. I shouldn't say the Arab world because it would not have been that easy in Damascus, but Beirut is a more open city. If women want to live alone, they have to work. The liberation of women comes from the work force. I didn't grow up thinking of marriage as a shelter.I knew that most married couples didn't love each other. People married out of necessity and social duty. I never romanticized marriage."

Although she has never written about sexual matters, she praised the Egyptian psychiatrist/novelist Nawal el Saadawi, who "tackled that issue head-on." Saadawi is the first person who attracted attention to the problems of Arab women with her book *Women and Sex*, which cost Saadawi her job as director of the Ministry of Public Health in Cairo. Imprisoned in 1980 for her criticism of Anwar Sadat, Saadawi wrote what Etel called "a little masterpiece, *Woman at Point Zero*." That novel was based on the experience of Saadawi's fellow prisoner, a prostitute who killed her pimp and refused to ask for clemency in order to avoid being executed.

Execution *is* the fate of the heroine in Adnan's first novel, *Sitt Marie Rose*. In Paris, Adnan had read a few lines in *Le Monde* about the kidnapping of a well-known woman in Beirut. It was the first time a woman had been abducted. She was a teacher and the divorced mother of three children. Although a Christian, she was militant on behalf of the Palestinians.

In the real story, Rose Marie ("Sitt" is the Arabic word, somewhat like Madame, denoting respect) didn't have a Palestinian lover, but a Lebanese one who was also pro-Palestinian.The Christian Phalangists didn't say they kidnapped her, but that she had disappeared in their territory. For nine months the family didn't know if she was alive or dead.

Etel wrote the novel in six weeks in French and it was published in Paris. But when it was translated into Arabic and made its way to Beirut, it was quickly banned. Adnan lost her newspaper job and began receiving death threats. After she left the country, the English translation became the first work published by Simone, who started her career as a publisher in 1982 with a $10,000 inheritance. The new firm, based in Sausalito, was called the Post-Apollo Press, reflecting Etel's interest in the space experiments Apollo 1 and Apollo 2. Its logo is the crescent moon. Simone got the Bay Area feminist movement interested in the book, and soon it was being ordered by universities throughout the country from Harvard and Yale to West Point. "And," laughed Etel, now an American citizen, "even in Texas!"

Adnan's approach in *Sitt Marie Rose* was unique. Each untitled brief chapter is told in turn in the first-person, starting with Marie Rose, then by the deaf and dumb children in her class, and by the four Christian militiamen who kidnap her under the ambivalent leadership of Mounir, the rich would-be filmmaker who as an adolescent was in love with Marie. There's no ambivalence in Mounir's follower Fouad, "the perfect killer. He suffers from never having killed enough . . . He prefers killing to kissing."

But while expressing the views of all the characters, the voice of Adnan is clear:

- "They [the executioners] are moved by a sick sexuality. It's not that they are deprived of women or men if they like, but rather are inhibited by a profound distaste for the sexual thing. A sense of the uncleanliness of pleasure torments them and keeps them from ever being satisfied. Thus the Arabs let themselves go in a tearing, killing, annihilating violence, and while other peoples, virulent in their own obsession with cleanliness, invent chemical products."

- "The Arab world is infinitely large in terms of space, and infinitely small in its vision."

- "No one seemed to want to admit that cruelty was a part of a moral cancer that was spreading through the whole of the Middle East. That was how Beirut became a huge open wound."

As for Adnan, what is probably her strongest belief:

- "The true Christ only exists when one stands up to one's own brothers to defend the Stranger."

2003
Unpublished

Karim Dridi

"It was important to show something intimate from the Arab culture to French and other Occidental audiences."

San Francisco

Karim Dridi, son of a Tunisian Muslim father and a French Catholic mother, says that his light skin protected him from discrimination when he was growing up in Paris, but it never masked his anger at racist remarks.

His days of boyhood fisticuffs are long over. But his determination to combat the stereotype of Arabs as "terrorists" or "fanatics" is manifest in his richly textured film, *Bye-Bye*, the $3-million tale of two brothers risking temptation in the teeming tenements of Marseilles.

Their parents, who have returned to Tunisia after a family tragedy in Paris, have instructed French-born Ismael, twenty-five, to send the reluctant Mouloud, fourteen, home to them after a brief stay with relatives in Marseilles. Their independent-minded aunt and uncle welcome them warmly, but Mouloud is drawn into the world of drugs and crime by his rebellious older cousin. Ismael, guilty about his responsibility in the death of a handicapped brother, is tempted into a sexual encounter with the sweetheart of his best friend.

"It was important for me to show something intimate from the Arab culture to French—and other Occidental—audiences," the writer/director said during a stop-over at the 1996 San Francisco International Film Festival. "I wanted them to see an Arabic family from the inside, to show they are normal persons, like an Italian or French or Jewish family. I wanted to prove that racism is stupid and it comes from ignorance of the people. I wanted to prove that you cannot generalize and say that all Arabs are bad."

The film's production may have been hastened unwittingly by a "scandalous" remark conservative Paris mayor Jacques Chirac made about immigrant Arab families a year before he was elected president of France. He was quoted as saying, "These people have a bad smell." Recalling that offensive remark, Dridi said, "I made this film to prove that these people can also 'smell' good. That's why I show people cooking and eating meals like any other family."

Speaking easily in French-accented English, Dridi, thirty-five, a slim, quiet man, observed that "Paris has changed a lot" since he lived there from age two to seventeen. Dridi's father, who came from a poor Tunisian family, had received his education in France when he was in the French army. He eventually became an economics professor in France. Earlier, in Tunisia, during the fight for independence, he tried to defend his own country, but it was difficult since he was already married to a French woman, a nurse, and Dridi—who was born in Tunisia—was a baby.

"My father was always against French power," Dridi said, "even though he learned everything from France. Although he is a non-practicing Muslim, he never assimilated. That's why he returned to Tunisia with my mother ten years ago and became a businessman. I was not brought up in any religion. My parents set me free to choose. I don't believe in God so I'm neither, but both cultures gave me a lot."

As a boy, Dridi spent a year in Tunisia with an aunt—who later became the model for the aunt in the film. "My aunt is maybe stronger. She's a professional woman who owns three stores. Arab old men speak loudly, but the real power belongs to the woman. In French and other foreign films, we see Arab women under the control of men. It could be reality, but it's not so simple. We have a lot of strong Arab women."

Living in Tunisia from age seventeen to twenty was difficult, because he didn't speak Arabic well. More important, it was not a democratic country. "There's a strong police force. You don't feel free to speak out or walk everywhere."

After returning to Paris, he pursued his interest in film, which began when he started making Super-8 movies at the age of twelve, shooting members of his family and neighbors. Self-taught, he learned everything by watching the movies. At twenty, he sold his first short to TV. His *Zoe the Boxer* won several awards and a producer's offer to make his first feature. *Pigalle* (1994), set in the red light district of Paris, is a love story between a thief and a girl who works in a peep show. Praised for its kinetic energy, it was a success on the film festival circuit. But with a touch of irony, Dridi calls it a "white film, a very white film." There were no Arab roles.

He is disturbed by the changes he sees in France now. "We have refugee problems and economic problems and new problems with Algeria." After Algerian extremists began planting bombs in Paris, French soldiers were assigned to police the subway. "There are bad moments between the French and Algerian people. I think France will change more and more in a bad way."

When he began researching the Arab community in Marseilles, he learned that the people needed a film like his "because they're only shown as dealers or thieves in most French films. Of course, I have an Arab dealer in my film, but I also have the family, for balance." In Marseilles, the police loved it because no police are in the film.

Dridi believes that problems faced by Arab immigrants and their French-born children are similar to the situation of Mexican immigrants and their children who are born in the U.S.

At the San Francisco Festival, some Tunisian and Moroccan viewers told Dridi they were happy with the film, but they also had some criticism. "One guy said, 'you don't show enough violence against the Arabs.' I said, 'If I put more violence in, the western audience would react against it.' I didn't want to make a film to prove that the Arabs are good and whites are bad. I tried to have a balance. One French viewer from Marseilles said, 'You show only bad white people except for one man.' I told him it's just my vision, and the relationship between the French and Arabs is not so simple."

Two young Moroccan girls who live here complained about the "provocative" behavior of the Yasmine character in *Bye-Bye*.

"We're not like that," they told Dridi. One man said Yasmine was a "bad girl" because she has relations with two different men.

"I told him she reacts exactly like a man," Dridi said. "'You never say that about a male character.' I like her. I really believe in equality in the relationship between a man and a woman. In American cinema, the male power is obvious. They decide. They choose and woman is like an object."

A French journalist in New York asked Dridi if he felt menaced by American cinema. "It's a crazy question," he says, "but it's a fact that cinema has become more and more standardized, like hamburger. And I don't like hamburger. I used to love American cinema—Cassavetes, Coppola, Arthur Penn, Scorsese, Kazan—but now I have pity for it. Tarantino? He should be working at McDonald's. He kills people for a joke and they laugh. It's a bad example for kids."

August 19, 1996
The San Francisco Examiner

Atef Hetata

"As an artist, fundamentalism interests me because of its obvious effect on anybody creative."

Cairo

The main thing to worry about here is getting killed by one of those cars jam-packed every which way on these chaotic streets. To understand that more insidious killer—fanatic fundamentalism—it helped to see *Closed Doors* in 2001 during this twenty-fifth-year celebration of the Cairo International Film Festival.

The Oedipus Complex and an adolescent boy's sexual yearnings become the fuel for fire when a sect leader entices sixteen-year-old Mohamed into the paths of "righteousness" with promises of the thousand virgins waiting for him in heaven. The unusually revealing film offered fresh insight into fundamentalism after the September 11 events.

The film is set during the Gulf War in October 1991. There are some eerie resonances to today's hostilities in an ironic TV scene where a demonstration banner proclaims "Thanks, Mr. Bush, for the liberation of Kuwait."

Mohamed's mother, Fatma, a hard-working divorcee, only wants her son to continue his education and become a pilot(!). Her work as a maid for a wealthy alcoholic woman is made precarious by the husband's erotic advances and her demands on Fatma to spy on him in his private hideaway. One day Mohamed returns from school, plugs in a fundamentalist audio cassette about how women should conduct themselves, listens to the words "No one can save you from the fires of hell," and sees his usually clean-scrubbed mother being made up by a married neighbor who is a prostitute on the side. A virtuous woman, Fatma occasionally assuages her loneliness by having Mohamed cuddle up to her in bed. The boy pleads with her to put on a veil, stay home, and let him support her by selling flowers and kleenex on the crowded streets. As Fatma resists his suggestion and his teacher expresses an interest in her, the jealous Mohamed is drawn more and more to the fanatical advice of the sheik who urges him, as the man of the house, to control her. It leads to a fatal confrontation when Mohamed spots his mother and his teacher in their first embrace.

A first feature film by Atef Hetata, thirty-five, the son of two Egyptian novelists, he calls himself a "Muslin by origin" but emphasizes that he is a "free-thinker." After making three short films, he worked as an assistant to Spike Lee when that director shot part of his film *Malcolm X* in Egypt.

He minced no words calling the Taliban regime "fascist" during an interview here. Although he was initially interested in writing about problems of adolescence, a subject rarely examined in Egyptian films, he also wanted to explore the historical background—the Gulf War. He started writing the script in 1993. "I was against the war," he said. "It was overwhelming the way western forces were concentrated in the Middle East. It created a sort of identity confusion in the region. It happened with the media invasion of the area, which was new at the time. We had a feeling of being crushed."

Hetata was born in New York when his mother, Nawal El Saadawi, was getting her M.A. in medicine at Columbia University. He grew up in an Egyptian family atmosphere of "freedom of movement and freedom of thought." Although *The Net*, written by his father, Sherif Hetata, was translated into English, his mother's work was more famous and controversial. Her experiences as a doctor led her to write in some twenty-four books about the taboo issue of womanhood and sexuality. In 1972 she was dismissed from her position as Director of Public Health after the publication of her first non-fiction book, *Woman and Sex*. She was imprisoned in 1981 for writing against the policies of Anwar Sadat and released after his death in 1982. Placed on the fundamentalists' death list in the nineties, she left for the United States to teach at Montclair college in New Jersey.

Talking about the historical context in his film, Hetata said he could not ignore the fundamentalists, although they don't have the strength today that they had ten years ago following a government crackdown. "As an artist, fundamentalism interests me because of its obvious effect on anybody creative. It's best to talk about extremism and fascism and fundamentalism in all its forms—Muslin, Christian, and Jewish. They all feed each other. But there are different kinds of fundamentalism. There are terrorists and there are fundamentalists who are very rigid people, but they are not violent. There is violence of talk and repression and there is the violence of weapons. I think they are both very dangerous. My film is about the violence of repression and talk."

Closed Doors was never censored, but there was an extreme response to the film. "Many people adored it," he said, "but others were really upset. Some articles accused me of presenting negative images of Islam. Fundamentalists do exist in all religions, but I had to speak about what I know."

2002
Unpublished

11
Family

Jacob Berger

PHOTO BY JUDY STONE.

"I perfectly understand I am symbolically committing a symbolic murder of the father."

Toronto

The age-old conflict between fathers and sons is played out in uncanny ways by Gérard and Guillaume Depardieu on screen in *Aime ton Père*, (*A Loving Father*), the film that represents screenwriter/director Jacob Berger's long struggle to exorcise his own angry estrangement from a famous literary father.

"I perfectly understand that in this film I am symbolically committing a symbolic murder of the father," Berger said in a slight French accent at the 2000 Toronto International Film Festival, speaking quietly about his antipathy *and* admiration for John Berger, a renowned art critic, Booker Prize-winning novelist, essayist, and playwright. Jacob's multi-colored striped shirt somehow hinted at the turmoil hidden under the softness of his voice.

338

"Sometimes Gérard reminds me of my father. He's capable of staying quiet for one or two minutes in front of a huge audience trying to find a word and nobody will dare to interrupt. He has that kind of presence and charisma. My father is completely *made of the same wood*, as we say in French. They drive by motorcycles and marry their women and travel across the world and have an opinion about everything. They never get tired and let the sons step forward and say, 'Let me handle this, Daddy.' Until one day they just die."

Having said that, Berger explained that as soon as he started to write the story, his concern was no longer to be faithful to biographical connections. In the film, Gérard plays a famous writer who is going to be awarded a Nobel Prize when his long-alienated son from a first marriage tries for a reconciliation with him. Berger's aim was to produce something "that was more or less like a detective story, but obviously not with a detective-story element. I worked to have believable characters so it moved away from biography. None of what happens in the film has ever happened to me."

And yet, Berger dissolved in tears at the end of a long scene in which Paul, the writer's son, talks about his drug addiction. "Gérard started laughing at me. 'Look, look, you just saw your life unroll in front of yourself.' He was amused that I was being a spectator at something that was so close and intimate for me. For many years I became a real drug addict, and that experience fed the story, too."

But for ten years after Berger wrote and directed his first film, *Angels* (1990), he couldn't come to grips with a feature that would be a way for him "to step away" from his father. During that time, he lived through the lingering death from AIDS of his first wife, Christina, an actress who played in *Angels*. While trying to shake his own addiction, he made fifteen documentaries on the hot spots of the world: Afghanistan, Russia during the Yeltsin-Gorbachev coup, the first Palestinian Intifada, the Islamic front in Algeria, and ten features for Swiss and French television. He now lives in Paris with his second wife, Noemie Kocher, with their infant son Dimitri. Kocker plays the mother in a flashback scene in *Aime ton Père*.

Born in Great Britain, Berger was eleven when his parents separated. "I was happy. I was thrilled, that meant I'd be rid of my father. My relationship with him was never easy. He was always an impatient, irritable person in my life." However, he always enjoyed the support of his mother, a prolific translator of books by Le Corbusier, Ilya Ehrenburg, Wilhelm Reich, and Trotsky, among others. She was the daughter of a Viennese Jew and a Russian who came from what is called "the small nobility." After the Russian revolution they fled to Harbin, where Berger's mother was born. John Berger, born in England, came from an upper-middle-class Jewish family in Trieste who had converted to the Anglican faith, but he was more at home on the European continent as an unorthodox Marxist.

As a youngster, Jacob played a small part in Alain Tanner's *Jonah Who Will Be 25 in the Year 2000*, written by John Berger. When Jacob returned from film school at New York University, Tanner was blocked in his career and asked Jacob for his input on a new script. "It was basically about himself," Jacob said. "It was about the incapacity of a man to make a movie and needed a woman to find inspiration and energy" to go on working. In addition to working on the *Ghost Valley* script, Jacob played the young man who is sent to find an Italian actress for the film, which co-starred Jean-Louis Trintignant and Laura Morante. It played at the Venice Film Festival in 1989.

When Jacob was finally able to write his father-son feature, he couldn't imagine anyone but Gérard Depardieu, "who would be believable as Leo, a literate, educated, sensitive poet of a man, but at the same time who had the physical emotional charisma with animality, violence, authority."

At first, he couldn't think of anyone who could play Paul, Leo's son. "I needed a boy who's dangerous and somewhat scary." He sent the script to both Depardieus and then set out to find producers until he learned that French producers don't react to scripts. But a few weeks later, both Gérard and Guillaume called and said they wanted to do the movie. "I think what interested Gérard was not only the quality of the story but that he could do it with Guillaume." Prior to their acceptance, Guillaume had had a motorcycle accident that required the first of many surgeries on his leg, which was finally amputated in June 2003.

"Guillaume gets hurt a lot," Berger said. "Because we had such frightening fathers, our reaction to our fears was that instead of running away, we run towards it and that's why Guillaume was constantly getting into trouble. I'm so moved by his pain and his honesty and his unreasonable showing off and his cockiness. When something frightening or dangerous happens to me, I channel that into boxing, and the only reason I'm a good boxer is not because I'm good technically. I'm quite lousy technically, but when anybody hits me, I move on towards them. It takes a lot of energy to stop me."

He spoke of both Depardieus as "being sweet and lovable characters, although they can be monsters and very cruel. They got along very well on the set and that was a good calculation of mine and it worked. Each one was the keeper of the other. Gérard knows about Guillaume's problems—his anger, his anguish—and obviously he didn't want that to happen on the set. And Guillaume knows about Gérard and his drinking and his bad temper, but Gérard—who goes through phases—was never drunk on my set. He was extremely professional."

Although *Aime ton Père* had reunited Guillaume and Gérard, there was an ironic postscript after the film opened in Paris. Both father and son complained about each other in a number of newspaper articles, and Gérard informed the press he would not longer see his son.

As for John Berger, he had still not seen the production when I spoke with Jacob. "He was angered that a film would be made about him, although I said it was not about him but about me. At first he contemplated suing, but my sister and half-brother discouraged him. After he read the script, I got a short, unsigned note saying basically that we have nothing to do with one another."

Despite John's reaction, Jacob said, "I do want my father to see the movie not as a father but as an artist I admire and respect. I want nothing more—if not to be admired, to be respected myself. I don't need legitimacy as a son anymore because I have my own son now. I needed it at one point, but now I want sheer recognition as a fellow human being, maybe as a modest fellow artist."

2000

Unpublished

Postscript: In 2003, *A Loving Father* was chosen as a *Variety* Critics Choice.

Hanif Kureishi

PHOTO BY JUDY STONE.

"My father told me stories about India and the way he and his family were treated by the British."

When *My Beautiful Laundrette* opened in New York in 1985, Pakistanis picketed the theater every Sunday with signs proclaiming "This film is the product of a perverse mind."

And so it is in a way, Hanif Kureishi admitted jauntily at the 1987 San Francisco Film Festival. Kureishi, who won an Oscar nomination for his screenplay about a Pakistani lad in love with his boyhood British pal, said that the protesters hadn't seen the film. "They hated the homosexuality. They heard that it was a dirty picture against Pakistanis. They would say, 'Pakistanis are pure and kind people,' as if the film were saying, 'These Pakistanis are terrible people.' They say there is not one Pakistani homosexual."

342

The odds are that the Pakistanis will be just as horrified by Kureishi's film *Sammy and Rosie Get Laid*, which is directed by Stephen Frears (who also made *Laundrette*). *Sammy and Rosie* features a Pakistani politician accused of having been a torturer and his weak-willed son Sammy, who has an adulterous relationship with an American photographer and can't keep his wife, Rosie, from straying. There are also assorted lesbians and blacks in a London that is burning both figuratively and literally.

If the new breed of British filmmakers is made up of "guerrillas" in the world of cinema, an English journalist wrote, "then Kureishi must be counted as a leading terrorist."

This enfant terrible, born in London thirty-one years ago to a Pakistani father and English mother, had an answer for the protesters. "You want me to do P.R. for you," he told them. "You want to be shown as healthy, wise, clever people, but you're not. The world isn't like that either, and it's not my job to portray you like that."

No matter what they're like, Pakistanis in England are despised anyway, Kureishi said. The Pakistanis reacted as if Kureishi were making their situation worse.

He got moral support from Philip Roth, who had been attacked by Jewish groups who claimed *Portnoy's Complaint* gave ammunition to enemies of the Jews. (Later, in *The Ghostwriter*, Roth—who is Jewish—described having been "giving homage to Goebbels" by his depiction of some Jews.) Roth told Kureishi to take no notice of the attacks.

"He was very protective of me. He said, 'Just write what you like.' And it made me feel better," Kureishi said.

Growing up in a London suburb in the fifties, Kureishi was "the only little brown face in the street. I hated my Pakistani background. I didn't have any curiosity about it at all. I wanted to repudiate it. I always thought it was like some terrible curse that had been done to me. I saw it as a personal problem. I didn't see it as a political problem, a social problem. In those days, being an Indian in the suburbs was a rather exotic thing. Only later it became the worst thing in the world, after waves of immigration and speeches by right-wing politicians."

Although a Pakistani heritage may have been "exotic" to some people, Kureishi recalled that he suffered enormously from the racism and violence. "I remember my mum having to go to school to tell the other boys not to abuse me, but my parents weren't really able to help me. I lived a kind of separate life: my life and the world and my life at home. My parents weren't very aware of it. They shut their eyes to it. They didn't want to confront it. They found it too difficult."

In 1980, Kureishi's feelings about being a Pakistani began to change. Inspired by James Baldwin, Kureishi was writing plays that were soon put on by the Royal Shakepeare company and the Royal Court theater. *The King and Me*, about a woman obsessed with Elvis Presley, got very good reviews, and Kureishi was wondering what to write next. A friend of his pointed out that he was unique in knowing about Pakistani life in lower-middle-class London. "No one's writing about them," he told Kureishi. "That's your subject."

The comment came as a "blinding illumination," Kureishi recalled. "Fifty percent of your work is finding out what your subject is, what your talent is most suited to. I sort of found myself as a writer after that."

Describing his own background in his work helped "to make strong feelings into weaker feelings. I've integrated them into myself. I wasn't able to when I was young. Now they're not like sticking out of my flesh. I've absorbed them."

Some of the ideas for *Sammy and Rosie* came from the atmosphere he had experienced during two three-month stays in Pakistan in 1983 and 1984. Others reflected the awareness he had gained from his father, who came to London after the partition of India in '47 and met his wife in a dance hall.

Kureishi's father hated his job as a clerk in the Pakistani Embassy and found a creative outlet in writing two books on Pakistan, as well as freelance magazine articles. When Kureishi was fourteen, his father bought him a typewriter and told him to "get on with it."

"My father told me stories about India and the way he and his family were treated by the British at that time. There were places they couldn't go. It was whites-only in the clubs, and at the cricket matches you had to lose. His heros were Gandhi, Nehru and Mohammed Ali Jinnah, founder of Pakistan. However, my father thought Jinnah was less sympathetic.

"I grew up on all those stories. I suppose his anger and desire to be defiant and rebellious against the British entered into me in an odd way. It has become support for the underdog because of my own experience growing up and the kind of hatred people had for you."

Trips to Pakistan were important to him. "It was a very moving and developmental experience—going to a country where all these people belong to you and suddenly you realize you knew nothing about them but they know who you are—who you belong to; they welcome you and ask you to live with them."

At the same time, Kureishi was shocked at being in a "theocratic dictatorship and an Islamic one-party state. You're in a country where the army's on the street every day. Where there are no free newspapers. No movies. No organized opposition. You're not allowed to do this. You're not allowed to say that. An unfree country. Yet a country which emotionally one's very involved with."

And in Pakistan, he was on the receiving end of another kind of prejudice because he was half-English. When he was trying to find out to what extent he belonged, "They'd say, 'We're Pakistanis, but you'll always be a Paki.' That derogatory term meant I was not ever one of them entirely."

He disliked "their racism. Their snobbishness. Their lack of concern for anyone but themselves. Their lack of culture. That's why I could never live there."

Asked if *Laundrette* had been shown there, Kureishi gasped. "Good God, no! Never. Never. Never. But it was booklegged and everyone watched it and pretended not to. I've been too nervous to go back. On the one hand, they envy you because you are successful in the West, and on the other hand, hate you for the gay stuff in the film. You've no idea of the strength of their homophobia."

Kureishi is not a homosexual himself. At first, he says the question isn't relevant, but immediately decides that it is relevant since his films have a sexual dimension. "I wanted to deal with homosexuality for formal reasons because it made *Laundrette* work. I had the relationship between the two boys, and it had to be a strong relationship. When I was writing it, I thought the film would really work if they were in love. It was a mechanism for me getting the story going rather than saying, 'I'll write a gay picture.' It just jumped into my mind."

When he was talking to a group about *Laundrette*, a black lesbian asked why there were no black lesbians in the film. "I couldn't think of any reasons. So I thought I'd put them in *Sammy*. Gays are out now. We're on to lesbians and heterosexuals. It's a new age."

Kureishi likes the idea of using humor to say complicated things. "I want to write films about social and political issues that are very serious, but have humor, irony especially, and a lot of sex, filth, and anarchy in them because they're rough and kids will like them. They're accessible. They're not art films. The kids loved *Laundrette*."

On the other hand, *Sammy and Rosie Get Laid* is an attempt to be part of the political debate in Britain. It is an attitude that director Stephen Frears shares, at least in part. According to Kureishi's diary, "Frears is becoming more adventurous and disrespectful of British society, seeing it as part of his work to be skeptical, questioning, doubting and polemical." At the same time, he noted that Frears expressed some misgivings about the "simplistic politics of the film."

But the title *Sammy and Rosie Get Laid* is a joke. "It's intended to be ironic because the notion of getting laid is ambiguous. On the one hand, it has to do with sex. On the other, with being squashed."

A number of elements entered into the depiction of Sammy's Pakistani politician father. Kureishi was partially inspired by Japanese director Yasujiro Ozu's *Tokyo Story*. "There was the idea of the old returning to see what the young are doing and the young being neglectful of them, but Ozu's creation is so lovely, simple, and compassionate—completely unlike my film."

Kureishi was also interested in a biography of Zulfikar Ali Bhutto, first popularly elected prime minister of Pakistan. Bhutto had attended the University of California's School of International Relations with Kureishi's uncle before going on to Oxford.

"Bhutto said, 'I'll either be hanged by my enemies or I'll end up sitting in a London pub again,' and he was hanged. I wondered what would have happened to him if he returned to England when London's on fire. So I conceived of this guy arriving with his suitcases—thinking that London was a civilized, tolerant, book-ridden, and decent place and seeing the streets on fire."

From his time in Pakistan, Kureishi got the impression that Bhutto had a record of torturing his enemies. "But I wanted to make clear the character was not based on him in any specific way. At the same time, I was watching a lot of rioting on TV and fighting in Soweto with police beating up and killing black kids. I wanted to work out in my mind what it was like to do something like that as a policeman and go home to your wife and ordinary life but torture, maim, and damage people at the same time. I wondered, 'What do you say to your wife? What do you do in the evenings?'"

Among the many social issues in *Sammy and Rosie* is a sequence dealing with the eviction of squatters on a block of London wasteland. But in Kureishi's diary, published along with the text of the play, he expresses second thoughts about the depiction of such situations. Kureishi wondered, "Aren't we stealing other people's lives, their hard experiences for our own purposes? Frequently during the making of the film, I feel that what we're doing is a kind of social voyeurism."

December 27, 1987
San Francisco Chronicle

*   *   *   *   *

Seventeen Years Later:

[Kureishi is the author of several books, including three acclaimed novels: *The Buddha of Suburbia*, *The Black Album*, and *Intimacy*. In *The Black Album*, the British Muslim protagonist has an identity crisis when he becomes involved with fundamentalists. Once again, Kureishi said, "It was not too happily received by British Muslims."

Kureishi's film script for *The Mother*, which persuasively dramatizes an older woman's sexual experience, brought critical praise, but low box-office returns in England.

Now the father of ten-year-old twin sons and a six-year old boy, Kureishi unexpectedly learned something new about his own father who becomes the central character in his new memoir, *My Ear at His Heart*.]

One day his London agent surprised Kureishi with a novel by his father, who had died eleven years earlier. "I read it and found some others," Kureishi said at the 2004 San Francisco Film Festival. Although the writing was "a mess," it was informative about his father's life in Bombay. "He claimed it was a novel, but it was clearly a memoir about the end of colonialism. It gave me an entry into his early life. Another was about his education in missionary schools taught by Irish nuns. One book gave me a sense of what is like to be an immigrant in England.

"Oddly enough, I had a very strange experience in reading the second book in which the father had a son and the son is rather a repellent figure. I realized this guy is me, and it's rather wonderful to find yourself drifting into somebody else's novel. There is this boy with long hair, unwashed, face covered in acne, listening to loud music in the bedroom and sprawling around with naked girls up there and the father hates this boy. It's very moving and amusing." Kureishi laughed with evident pleasure. I asked if it was a fairly accurate portrait. "Not in my view," he laughed again. "But I can see his point of view. Yeah. Yeah."

Actually, father and son had a very good relationship. "He liked me and I liked him. I was really the only person he could talk to in the suburbs where we lived. He was not a practicing Muslim. He was part of the Bombay liberal intelligentsia who wanted to get the British out, and he hated Hinduism and he hated Islam. He wanted a secular, united India, but he had no choice after partition. He thought his books were better than mine. He thought my books dealt with drugs and weirdo stuff whereas his were philosophical and deep. He was proud of me and also annoyed. He died after my first novel, *The Buddha of Suburbia*, was published."

Kureishi's English mother had regrets that he didn't quite understand until they had lunch one day and his mother admired the waiter's "lovely" hands. Kureishi laughingly admonished her. "Mother," the unrestrained writer cautioned, "I think you should be more restrained in your vocabulary," but she responded, sadly, that she didn't think "anyone would ever touch her again, apart from the undertaker." The remark made Kureishi think "of a woman in that position who is turned on by a young man and who would act on her feelings."

Kureishi said she was very pleased with *The Mother*, the movie she inspired. He added admiringly, "She's a very randy old girl!"

Unlike Kureishi, who grew up feeling the sting of racism and didn't want to know his Pakistani background, his twin sons (who are "one-quarter Pakistani" and live in a mixed neighborhood), are curious about their grandfather's experiences. "They want to know, 'How come we're brown?' They're interested in the way they happen to be Indian or Pakistani."

Kureishi, who had no use for the institution of marriage, now lives with his girl-friend and their little boy. He wrote a devastating portrait of a middle-aged writer in his autobiographical novel, *Intimacy*. After a painfully critical self-analysis, torn with the love he feels for his children, the writer walks out on his lover and their two sons.

Without specifically referring to *Intimacy*, Kureishi said he would like to "write something about analysis. I'm very interested in therapy culture. I want to know what it does to our vocabulary and our heads." He spent ten years in analysis and figures, "I'm nearly cured. I suffered from a lot of depression, which I no longer have."

2004

Unpublished

Todd Field

An excuse to imagine a marriage.

Montreal

For Todd Field, director of the award-winning *In the Bedroom*, the film was an excuse to examine a marriage.

His first feature, acclaimed for its wrenching understatement, has all the ingredients for melodrama: a passionate affair, suspense, and murder, but what most interested Field was the verbal, emotional eruption between Matt and Ruth, a happily married middle-aged couple.

"For me," Field said at the 2001 Montreal Film Festival "their fight is the most violent scene [emotionally] because Matt and Ruth are in the generation that doesn't say everything that comes to the top of their head. That whole generation has been labeled as repressed or not in touch with their feelings, but the fact of the matter is that they had the grace not to say everything that comes into their minds and other things that were not necessary to say but were implicit. They had never fought that way before."

On the other hand, Field, thirty-seven and the father of three, believes, "Someone my age could have that fight, make up, have dinner, and three weeks later might have that fight again and might have a fight like that a dozen times a year and that's normal for someone my age because—for my generation—words are meaningless. For Matt and Ruth, words mean something, and there are certain things you don't say. They reminded me of my parents very much. There were things that happened between my parents that were private and discussed in the bedroom behind closed doors. That way, there was no theater for children."

Field would have been happy to have had a more intimate relationship with his parents, "but it was more than me missing out on something. I think they missed out on something, whereas my children are people to me. They're completely comfortable talking about anything to us, and I'm the better for that."

Tall, boyish, and refreshingly artless, Field said he was "scared" by all the attention he's been getting since his $1,500,000 production began winning prizes for best film, best direction, and best acting. "I don't think it's something you ever get used to. You feel like a kid who's been given a new bike and the bully around the corner is going to come and take it away from you."

Directorial success is not anything Field had anticipated when he was acting—for Woody Allen, Victor Nunez and Stanley Kubrick. After being in a number of interesting films, Field decided to adapt and direct *Killings*, the short story by Andre Dubus, whose "very brave and elliptical" writing had haunted Field for years. The way Dubus handled the strained dynamics between the husband and wife who live in Maine made Field want to open it up.

Matt (Tom Wilkinson) is a doctor who likes to go lobster-fishing and Ruth, his wife (Sissy Spacek), is a music teacher; they have a college-age son, Frank (Nick Stahl). Ruth hates the fact of Frank's affair with Natalie (Marisa Tomei), an older working-class woman with two children who is divorcing her angry, brutish husband. The subsequent tragedy is the occasion for Field to explore the manifold nature of grief and what happens to a marriage.

Both Spacek and Wilkinson had won numerous best-acting nominations for their previous roles. Wilkinson, a renowned British stage and screen actor (*The Full Monty*), was an unknown quantity to Field, whose original choice for the role had dropped out at the last moment. The director put in a desperate call to a friend in England who knew the script very well. The friend immediately suggested Wilkinson.

Field said, "I had never seen him in anything and when I met him, I thought, 'Wow!' I couldn't imagine anyone else playing the role. He felt like a man, he felt like my father, not like an actor." He also wanted someone well-known to play Ruth. "I thought

Spacek's authority would actually serve in the hierarchy of the marriage, that she would have more power."

As a director, "You don't need to explain everything," Kubrick had told Field when he acted as Nick Nightingale, the pianist, in *Eyes Wide Open*. "Stanley was very open and also very private," Field recalled. "He told me, 'If you start talking about meaning, it's a dangerous thing to do. If you actually give voice, it becomes cheapened and marginalized. If you can, keep it intensely private.' He would never talk about the meaning of something. He had seen me playing a disillusioned dreamer in Victor Nunez's *Ruby in Paradise*.

"Stanley loved *Ruby* and was very curious about Victor's working methods. Actually, Victor worked much like Stanley did—in the size of the crews and the tone of the sets. He, too, would never talk about the meaning of something."

Before he became turned on to acting, Field, who plays trombone and piano, thought he would make music for a living. In fact, it was music that put him on a different path. Woody Allen hired him out of hundreds applying for a job in *Radio Days* (1987). Field's subsequent "Frank Sinatra-ish" rendition of "All or Nothing at All" opened many new doors for him.

The son of a police officer and librarian who ran a small family market when they retired, Field grew up in a rural community outside of Portland, Oregon. He was influenced by his Lutheran minister who visited Israel and came back saying, "If you want to be a good Christian, you must first be a good Jew."

"So we observed all the Jewish holidays in an Orthodox way," Field said, "and I thought that was fascinating. I wasn't interested in being a Lutheran anymore, and I went to Temple by myself. Then I was interested in Catholicism, but I got kicked out of the church because I kept laughing. And then I was interested in Mormonism for a while. The only thing that really stuck was Judaism."

Field showed a quiet amusement talking about his unorthodox search. He even had his son, now eight, circumcised by a mohel "just in case he wants to become a rabbi."

He was thus prepared to encounter the mixed marriage of his future in-laws: Serena Rathbun was one of the daughters of a "blue-blood WASP," and Bo Goldman, Oscar-winning screenwriter of *One Flew Over the Cuckoo's Nest* and *Melvin and Howard*.

Talking about his wife Serena, Field is unabashedly rhapsodic and loving. "She is fifty times more talented than I am. She's a genius. Her versatality is frightening. She can do everything and is the most modest human being I've ever known. She did interior decorating to put me through film school, and she wrote the script for *Nonnie and Alex*."

That short film about how two children cope with the death of their mother was directed by Field as an American Film Institute school project. It went on to win a prize at the Sundance Festival and an Emmy, along with glowing predictions about Field's future.

"It's a beautiful, beautiful film, which is really Serena's doing," Field said. "But she's very private about her work. She gets upset with me when I talk about her to the press." But unlike the Matt and Ruth couple who don't express their feelings in *In the Bedroom*, Field can't be stopped from saying everything that's wonderful about Serena.

December 27, 2001

The San Francisco Examiner

Christina Stead

"The big thing in my life is that I met the right man."

Sydney, Australia

"**I** don't have a room of my own, dear."

At eighty, Christina Stead was explaining—simply and without self-pity—why she was unable to write at the moment. Nevertheless, her statement had an ironic ring coming as it did from this great novelist who had rarely started and finished any of her twelve novels in one place.

In her life, Christina Stead roamed far afield from her native Australia. Yet everywhere she went, her observations about the human condition were sharp, precise, and penetrating. She had an extraordinary range and corruscating wit, whether writing about *Seven Poor Men of Sydney* (1934) or the French world of high finance and prostitution in *House of All Nations* (1938), which was acclaimed as a work of literary genius in the tradition of Balzac.

Stead was as coolly objective and psychologically acute in writing about herself through her character Teresa in *For Love Alone* (1944) as she was in describing the lamentable state of marriage that existed between her bombastic father and harried stepmother in *The Man Who Loved Children* (1940). To many critics, she was that rare humanist: steadfastly remaining on the side of those who suffered oppression and prejudice, but she never let sentiment cloud her caustic perceptions about the complex nature of men and women. Later in life, Stead vigorously rebuffed attempts to canonize her as an early "feminist" writer.

In one of her last—and very rare—interviews in October 1982 in Sydney, Stead told me that she divided her living time among her brothers and sisters, trying not to outstay her welcome at each place. "I run around taking more and more papers to six or eight places. It's very enervating."

I thought of her homeless state, separated from her books, when I learned that she died in Sydney on March 31. At first the death of this extraordinary novelist went unannounced. She wanted no publicity, no memorial service.

Stead always had shunned attention, and I wondered again at having been able to interview her. I think she finally agreed to see me not because I was an admirer of her work, but because I had expressed my appreciation for the massive Civil War novel, *The Copperheads*, written by her husband, the American novelist William Blake, who died in 1968. They seem to have shared an unusually rich, long companionship and marriage. My visit gave Stead an opportunity to reminisce about "Bill," a banker, Marxist economist, and novelist who had hired her as a secretary in a new bank when she first arrived in England from Australia in 1928.

She tells the autobiographical story in her novel *For Love Alone*: how she, renamed Teresa in the fictional work, starved herself for six years to help support her father's second family and to save enough money for the journey to London. She was following a man she had fallen in love with in Australia, although he had given her scant encouragement. He is the "Jonathan Crow" of the novel, but it was her employer who changed her life.

Blake fell in love with her although she was a "living skeleton," she recalled. When we met, she looked very brisk and lively in a smart white slack suit. Her delicate magenta-blue blouse complemented the keen blue eyes, but her voice was soft when she referred to Blake. At first, he took a fatherly interest in the skinny girl and asked to meet her beloved "Jonathan," who "immediately behaved like a cad," she said, recalling the real story behind the novel and mixing the real and fictitious names. "Jonathan thought Bill would take an interest in his career. He was nothing but self, self, self. He said to Bill, referring to me, 'She thinks she's a writer, too.'

"So Bill came back distressed at the way this man acted. He asked if I would let him see something I'd written. Not for publication. I'm a WRITER, you know. (As if to say, 'What does mere publication matter?') The next time I went in to take dictation, his eyes opened wide. He had big brown eyes, and he said, 'It has a lot of PEAKS!'"

Australians who did not know her first works "now make out that I was very depressed or neglected. This isn't true at all because my works were widespread in America and England, translated into French, Portuguese, Spanish, Italian, Swedish, and Danish, but the Australians make up for their gap—I don't blame them. What do I care? I wasn't here. I don't want recognition. I don't care if I never write another word. Or read another word about me. The big thing in my life is that I met the right man who understood and helped me and was impressed, very, very impressed, but that was because he had his mind open for literature in general, which was very European."

Stead can't remember when she began writing. "I was always writing. At school, they annoyed me very much by saying, 'You're going to be a writer.' I thought, 'Lay your hands off me, leave me alone.' I didn't WANT to be a writer, I WAS a writer."

When she wrote *The Man Who Loved Children* (1940), she transformed her father and stepmother—with exceptional originality and power—into two Americans, Sam and Henny Pollit.

"My father was a very handsome man and very sure of himself. A big public speaker. He never prepared his lectures but went on the platform and gave intimate advice to women. About shaving their armpits. He was very shy on the sex problem actually. He knew nothing about it."

Her father was very good in one way, she granted. He was commissioner of fisheries, and he loved science. "We had an immense library. I read everything I could lay my hands on. Darwin. All the flora and fauna. Also Milton. Everything printed on beautiful, thin paper. I read Milton from cover to cover when I was around ten. My father never stopped me from reading. He thought he was a socialist. In fact, he started the first socialist enterprises in this state: trawling. He was very lusty and forceful and he thought if socialism came in, he'd be a top figure. I soon realized, he never studied anything. He was just a baby socialist."

Stead insisted that, although she didn't mind talking about her books, "once I've done them, I've done them. I don't do it for readers or for publishers or publicity. I write because there's a story." As to her discipline as a writer, she also insisted she didn't have any. "The typewriter just tempts me because it's such an easy way of writing."

Stead wrote *The Man Who Loved Children* out of sympathy for her stepmother, who was driven to suicide by repeated pregnancies she couldn't prevent. She didn't see it as an attack on marriage in general. The book is very popular in the U.S., and even the women's movement took it up, which provoked Stead's denial of being a "feminist" writer. "It wasn't written with the intention of attacking marriage, but what can I do by complaining? I was just sorry for my stepmother, who was in a marriage trap."

Stead said she never understood what feminist critics saw in the book and wouldn't discuss the matter beyond mentioning almost off-handedly, "At least in some arts, women have always had a chance."

January 29, 1983
San Francisco Chronicle

Liev Schreiber

"Everything I did was motivated by my grandfather."

San Francisco

When Liev Schreiber dedicated his new film to his Jewish grandfather, it was more than testimony to a lifetime of love and sacrifice. For the spirit of Alex Milgram, born in a Russian shtetl, inexplicably hovers over the tale of the Ukrainian grandfather in *Everything Is Illuminated*, the first film that Schreiber, an award-winning actor, wrote and directed.

Based on the acclaimed, best-selling novel by Jonathan Safran Foer, the film recounts the search of Jonathan, a young American (Elijah Wood) who travels to Ukraine to find the woman who saved his grandfather's life during World War II. He is accompanied by Alex (Eugene Hutz), a would-be Ukrainian translator who massacres the English language, and Alex's grandfather (the Russian actor, Boris Leskin), who claims to be blind, but drives the Heritage Touring car that carries Jewish tourists in search of their history. Along for the trip is the old man's "seeing eye" pet dog, name of Sammy Davis, Junior, Junior.

Wisely, Schreiber used a scalpel to eliminate chapters in Foer's book that explored Polish Jewish shtetl life from 1791 to 1942, and he changed the ending. "The biggest challenge for me," Schreiber said in San Francisco, "was to shift the film's tone." That ranged from the hilarious opening scenes to the somber conclusion, and he didn't mind expressing the thoughts that led to the surprise ending.

While Schreiber was in pre-production and musing over the character of Alex's outspokenly anti-Semitic grandfather, he saw a documentary that strangely, almost replicates Foer's fiction. *Hiding and Seeking* is the true story of a search for the Polish peasants who saved three Jewish brothers from the Holocaust at risk to their own lives. The ancient grandmother, doubled over in pain, clearly remembers the Jews they helped, but grimly notes that they never even sent a postcard after they left Poland.

That documentary stimulated Schreiber's ideas about the contrast between the way those who died in the Holocaust were memorialized and how little thought is given to those who lived and what they had to go through in order to survive. "The very least of which was to deny their faith," Schreiber said. "Spirituality was no longer acceptable if you wanted to stay alive. Beyond that they had to give away children, to point fingers at family members and friends, to lose their identity and other horrible horrible things in the name of survival. When they came to the United States or Israel, wherever, they sometimes defined themselves in a non-Jewish way. There was this self-inflicted anti-Semitism that Jews who survived the Holocaust had to deal with."

Beyond that, Shreiber, a towering figure with a gentle voice, went on without a pause, "I grew up on welfare, on the Lower East Side of New York, and lived in squats. My grandfather, a chivalrous, cultured man who came to America before 1920 to escape anti-Semitic pogroms, worked very, very hard to raise me and support us. He delivered meat from the meat market to the diners. My mother drove a taxi and she made puppets and sold them on the streets. She was an artist and a painter but never made a living doing that. Now she lives in a Virginia ashram, which has given her a sense of well-being in a community that shares interests and spirituality with her. She always wanted me to be proud of my Jewish heritage."

But at the same time, he saw Jewish slumlords who were burning people out of their homes in order to sell their real estate. "I thought, 'Well, I'm a Jew and my Mom tells me we're the chosen people, so how could these people be so cruel?'

"I thought that the Jews who came to America did have justifiable paranoia and fear, and that set off a new kind of [Jewish] anti-Semitism. So I chose to change the ending of Foer's book hoping that the character of the grandfather could articulate some of that and do it in a cathartic way. Alex's grandfather had denied his own Judaism in order to survive and was living in a kind of shame and guilt and tremendous anger. He was quite spiteful and anti-Semitic, but at the same time he ran a business that helped Jewish people find out what happened to their loved ones."

Out of Yale School of Drama for only seven years, Schreiber early on began achieving recognition for the diversity of his roles in movies (a transvestite, a murderer, Orson Welles, a cuckolded husband) and on and off Broadway (*Cymbeline*, *Hamlet* and his Tony Award-winning performance as the abusive salesman in *Glengarry Glen Ross*). In a 1999 *New Yorker* profile on Schreiber, his work drew an unusual accolade from Dustin Hoffman: "He has a kind of wisdom about human contradictions that is beyond his years."

Perhaps Schreiber understood those contradictions as a result of his own extraordinarily difficult, angry, attention-getting thievery in his youth or from the example of his socialist grandfather, who lost his life's savings in helping his often-troubled daughter in the fight against Tell, her wealthy husband, an actor, to gain custody of Liev when he was four. (Long estranged from his father, Liev noted that he and Tell have since reconciled. "My father saw the film at the Toronto festival and was very moved by it," Schreiber said.)

But, the beloved grandfather who was his father figure died at age ninety-three in 1993 when Liev was twenty-five. Since then, Schreiber said with a sweetness of remembrance, "Everything I did was motivated by my grandfather. Every character I played, everything I've written was motivated by him. He was my model of what it is to be a mensch, a man."

He was writing a script about his grandfather when he read *A Very Rigid Search*, by Foer, in *The New Yorker*, which foreshadowed the novel to come. "I felt deeply connected to it," Schreiber said. "He had done in fifteen pages what I had been trying to do in 100 and had done it with humor." He believes Foer is happy with his changes.

And when Schreiber traveled to Odessa to cover the ground in Foer's book, he also engaged in a search for his grandfather's shtetl, called Tomastil, but he never found it. He was warned in advance about what he might expect by Eugene Hutz, the Ukrainian musician who plays Alex.

"'Liev,'" he said to me, 'you'll have a problem in Ukraine because Ukrainians don't want to own up to this story.'"

For practical reasons, Schreiber finally decided to shoot in the Czech Republic. And Eugene, who had never acted before, Schreiber said, gave one of his best performances in a completely unscripted moment. It occurred when Jonathan informed Alex about what his grandmother had told him: that before the war the Ukrainians were worse than the Nazis.

"Eugene gets right into Jonathan's face and he goes, 'Who told you that?' and you can feel the anger and the danger in a character who, up to that point, was just humorous. All of a sudden, he brings a quality of 'don't fuck with me or my country' and he asks his grandfather, 'Eta pravda?' Is it true? And the grandfather is speechless. I thought it was not only terrific acting by Eugene, but very bold, political acting. Like he was taking a standpoint that would not be popular with his own countrymen and played it very articulately and with heart."

September 24, 2005
San Jose Mecury News

Chris Eyre

"Adoptive parents can't give you a culture that's not their own."

Taos, New Mexico

Chris Eyre believes that if he had not been adopted by non-Indians he would never have had a yearning to learn about Native American culture and history.

The result of that drive to understand his own Cheyenne/Arapaho background eventually led to *Smoke Signals*, a road movie filled with deadpan, oddball humor aimed at skewering Indian stereotypes.

Eyre, who directed the screenplay based on Sherman Alexie's award-winning collection of short stories, *The Lone Ranger and Tonto Fistfight in Heaven*, calls it a milestone: the first film to be written and directed by Indians.

It features two very different young men, saturnine Victor Joseph and gabby Thomas Builds-the-Fire, who travel from Idaho's Coeur d'Alene Indian reservation to Phoenix to retrieve the ashes of the father Victor never knew.

"My whole idea is to reinvent Indians on the screen," Eyre said at the 1998 Taos Talking Picture Festival, where he won the Land Grant Award for a promising young director. "There have always been Indians in the movies, but the problem is they work with non-Native directors and writers who perpetuate and write their own history about Indians."

Sure he enjoyed *Dances with Wolves*, Eyre conceded. "It's an entertainment. It's a step in the progression to where we are now, but if you take it from the Indian perspective, I don't need Kevin Costner empathizing or suffering for Indians. It's like all these liberals with massive guilt."

Eyre, a large, jovial man of twenty-nine, speaks fondly of the former Presbyterian minister and his wife who adopted him in 1968 when he was a month old. "There was a period when Indian kids were adopted by non-Indian families. It's harder to do nowadays. I grew up very sheltered in Klamath Falls, Oregon.

"I was protected from a lot of controversial things. My adoptive parents were very supportive about anything I wanted to do, but on the other hand, there was something they couldn't give me. They can't give you a culture that's not their own."

He won't generalize about whether such adoptions are "good" or "bad." "It depends on the family you're adopted into. My parents always told me I was adopted and that I was Cheyenne/Arapaho. If you do adopt a child of another culture, it's important to give credibility to that culture so they don't think it's bad. It's important to make them feel comfortable with their own history, to help them love that part of themselves so they don't feel self-hatred."

His biological family background is complicated, Eyre said with a bit of reluctance. He never met his father, but a few years ago he located his biological mother. Now he has a relationship with her and his biological family. Two older sisters were also adopted and his biological half-brother still lives with their mother.

Because of that split family history, Eyre said, "I speak from two different sides sometimes. But if I had been born and raised in my biological home, I wouldn't have had so much of a desire to learn about Indian history. For that, I'm grateful."

For Eyre, sorting out his Native American history is a lifelong learning process that intensified recently when he began researching a Showtime TV program about the notorious Carlisle (Pennsylvania) Indian School that aimed to assimilate Indian youngsters but succeeded mainly in alienating them and causing some to die of homesickness.

Eyre had a lot of mixed feelings when he discovered the Carlisle cemetery of children who had died there, inscribed with the names of his own Cheyenne and Arapaho families: Antelopes, Thunderers, Springers, and Lumpmouth. He was even more moved by letters in the school archives in which youngsters told their parents they didn't want to speak Indian anymore. Basically, they were saying their parents' ways were wrong. "The letters showed that the kids were feeling self-hatred."

He couldn't help but contrast their bleak experiences with his own youthful memories.

"In high school, I was kind of a nerd," Eyre laughed. "I did a lot of photography. It was the one thing I loved and still love. I thought it was a way into filmmaking, but telling a story in one picture was too difficult. Give me twenty-four frames a second."

At the University of Arizona, he discovered and loved the work of Yasujiro Ozu, whose quiet films about morality and family often resembled still photography. When he went on to New York University's film school, he won the best short film prize with his *Yenacity*, about two Indian kids on the Onondaga reservation who encounter two rednecks on the road.

Earlier, after reading Alexie's *Lone Ranger* in 1993, Eyre immediately wrote a screenplay proposal and sent it to the poet/writer. Adapting four of his stories, Alexie shaped the script into the tale of Victor, whose father had abandoned him years earlier. Eyre and Alexie were both helped to develop the project at the Sundance Filmmaking/Screenwriters lab. Later, *Smoke Signals* won the Sundance Audience Award, the first film to be financed by the Seattle-based Shadow Catcher Entertainment, the name Indians gave to Edward Curtis, the photographer who worked with Native Americans in the nineteenth century. Eyre, who subsequently opened his own production company in New York City (where he now lives), is mum on the film's cost, saying with a grin that it was about 1/100th of the *Titanic* budget.

For Eyre, the theme of *Smoke Signals* is still haunting, as it reveals a father who always wanted to go home and ask for his son's forgiveness, but instead died thousands of miles away. "For Indians especially," Eyre said, "a sense of home is such a strong thing whether you had stability or dislocation."

He was reminded of the unknown Indian woman who stopped him once years ago and said, "It's time for you to go home."

"It didn't hit me until years later, but *everybody* wants to go home."

July 1998
The San Francisco Examiner

Heddy Honigmann

Musical families in exile.

Rotterdam

When people ask Heddy Honigmann where she's from, she answers, "From a lot of countries, a little bit from everywhere. And I think I will die like that." For the record, she was born in Peru in 1951. Her parents were Jewish refugees from Poland and Austria. She grew up hearing stories about the melancholy of displaced persons. She felt somewhat displaced herself, neither European nor Peruvian. She went to film school in Italy, fell in love with a Dutch director, and moved to Amsterdam, where she now lives when she isn't traveling to Brazil, France, Israel, New Jersey—wherever the spirit moves her to delve with extraordinary empathy into the lives and memories of ordinary people, savoring the ways music, poetry, love, sex are tools to their survival.

She has known marriage, motherhood, and divorce, but her zest for life in all its unpredictable manifestations is nowhere more joyously demonstrated than in *O Amore Natural*, my introduction to her cinema at the Rotterdam Film Festival in 1996. In it, she persuades elderly Brazilian men and women to read the erotic poetry of a famous Brazilian writer and to reminisce with astonishing gusto about their own sex/love lives.

362

In Peru, Honigmann had already become acquainted with the poetry of Carlos Drummond de Andrade, translated into Spanish from the original Portuguese. Later in Holland, a very good translator of Portuguese literature brought out the book, *O Amore Natural*, that Drummond didn't want published while he was still alive. "I thought, 'Well, this is such powerful and honest, beautiful, erotic poetry, it's an opportunity to make a film about literature which won't be a literary film. I was very busy making films about love and the physical part of love like in my fiction feature *Goodbye* (1995). I wanted to make the poems to be alive. So how should I do it? What do I want? And I decided to only work with old people because they are much more open. They are not anymore ashamed to talk about erotics and I wanted to make a film about memory—memory about strong sexual experience, memory about love. And sex is a very important part of love."

Memory is also a vital part of her film *The Underground Orchestra* (1997) in which she features musicians from many countries who eke out a living playing in the Paris Metro. It was inspired by the last Peruvian taxicab driver she interviewed for *Metal and Melancholy* (1993). That was about all kinds of new taxi drivers—an actor, a teacher, a lawyer—who needed other jobs during an economic crisis in Peru. "It's a film about how they have to find a different way to survive and they're very creative. The last driver survives with only one memory of a woman he met forty years ago and fell in love with. He never forgets her. She was Italian and he was in England, so their love was impossible. It's really a melodrama. And he has one cassette with music which he always has in the car, music they bought together. And he says, 'That's the only memory I have from her, this music. May I put it on?' And he plays the music. That's the end of the film. The memory of this woman and the music help him go through the day. So music is a very important carrier of memory."

For the musicians of *The Underground Orchestra*, music is the way to survive. "If they couldn't play music I think they would die. I think for the first time I combined a lot of themes which are very personal—the theme of the stranger, the foreigner who doesn't live anymore in his native country and is forced to play music as a carrier of memories and the art of surviving. These things came together in one film."

The documentary developed after she heard a beautiful cello performance of Bach's music when she was walking in the Metro. "When I am sad, there is one partita of Bach—one minute long—I always repeat it ten times and it gives me such a power. It makes me happy, even if it's not such a happy piece." With that in mind, she met the Romanian cellist who was from East Germany and who was very well known before the Berlin Wall fell. He told her his story and she couldn't forget it.

Originally she wanted to make the whole film in the Metro, but she couldn't get permission. So she decided to shoot secretly with a small digital video camera in the trains and at the stations, knowing that, sooner or later, she and her crew would be thrown out.

That gave her the idea of "going upstairs, which would be a reflection of the world" and inside the musicians' homes.

For two years while waiting for the permission that never came, she did research and interviewed the musicians. Most of them were agreeable, "but the Romanian cellist said, 'I don't want to speak about my sadness.' Even one hour before the shooting, he said to me, 'No, I don't want to be filmed.' So I pushed, 'You have to because your story about disillusionment is very important. It's impossible to make a documentary nowdays about this theme without sadness. Sadness is a part of the film, but also humor is and you also have humor.'" Unable to find steady work, he said that the only reason he stayed in Paris was so his son, a violinist, could get a good musical education. Eventually they both appeared in the film.

One week before filming, Mario, the Venezuelan harpist, told her the Zaire musician's story, but he insisted that the man had to tell it himself. "I knew he didn't want to speak about it. So I asked him, 'Could you begin to clean your teeth? Because the first time I met you, you were cleaning your teeth.' He said, 'Yes, no problem.' It's very good to make an interview when somebody is doing something else, because he forgets the camera."

She told him she wasn't doing an interview, but having a conversation with him. "Sometimes I know what I'm searching for, but I don't know the way to get there. I think people talk to me because I'm very curious and open and really interested in the person before me. They are not a *subject*; they are a person. And that's why they open to me. I give my openness. I get this back from them."

1997

Doris Lessing

PHOTO BY OSWALD JONES

"What fascinated me about La Dolce Vita, L'Avventura, and 8½ is that nobody ever has any children."

London

It was impossible shortly after the assassination of President John F. Kennedy to speak with anyone here without discussing that first, but for Doris Lessing the far-away scene had the added impact of a familiar nightmare.

She had grown up in Southern Rhodesia, loving its silence, solitude, and space and instinctively hating its white superiority, all memorably recreated in her first books, *The Grass Is Singing* and *This Was the Old Chief's Country*.

"My part of the world was like Dallas," she told me. "You can't talk about it in any sane terms."

It was a world she would leave with few regrets in 1949 for England, but one that she could not forget. She returned after seven years carrying her notebook of impressions, *Going Home*, with its freshened perception of the pathetic quality of the settlers' life. The poignancy of the racial conflict undoubtedly helped earn her present status of "prohibited immigrant."

The parallels between Texas and Rhodesia were in her mind the night she asked me to dinner. Her twenty-two-year-old daughter, visiting for the first time in many years from Southern Rhodesia, had also invited a Rhodesian friend.

"Of course I haven't been to Dallas," Lessing said, before they arrived. "But this flavor of lunacy that comes from Dallas, I was brought up on it. A white settler in southern Rhodesia, I was brought up to assume the black man was inferior.

"You can't talk with these people," she said. "They live in a mad atmosphere. You have to assume that one day they'll get out of it, if they're not pushed out. No lunacy is permanent. Anyway, economics is against them. I don't think racism is entirely conditioned by economics, but there can't be a state of perpetuity where white minorities deprive the black majority; it doesn't make sense.

"The kind of paternalism, the 'my nigger' attitude which has a certain amount of kindliness in it, the kind of thick-headed possessiveness is what I loathe, the inability to see these people as anything but servants."

The novelist, who has been acclaimed as one of the most brilliant women writers of our time, said that in books by American southern writers, she had found the kind of "unreal loyalties" that were familiar to her.

"I know perfectly good people where I was brought up who will go out and die heroic deaths for unreal things like white supremacy.

"I guess," she added thoughtfully, "that any kind of attitude will breed its heroes. But out there, there are all kinds of rationalizations about it, not simply 'we are the white minority defending ourselves against a black majority.'"

How had she avoided the infection?

"I don't know," she said. "I was reading myself into an education away from my environment. Reading the English classics and the Russian classics teaches you to look at your environment differently."

The introspective girl did not quarrel with her parents—an embittered, one-legged British veteran of World War I and the nurse he married. "You have to have something in common in order to quarrel."

The parents chafed in the wild, almost empty, country of Lomagundi which produced gold, tobacco, and maize—but no fortune—for them, while the girl marveled at the magnitude of the land and the revelations in the glittering, moving stars.

"It's the most incredible landscape," she was saying as her daughter arrived, a blonde version of the mother with sensitive eyes. "It's a great advantage to any continent to be without people. You can walk all day without seeing people." Suddenly mother and daughter both recalled, with almost one voice, "the most beautiful stars!" now lost behind the London fog.

Mother and daughter were happy to be united, but the atmosphere tightened when the Rhodesian guest arrived. She was a pretty, proper, polite young lady, satisfied with herself and her world, a bit excited by a continental fling before going back to the "proprieties."

Rhodesia's most famous woman writer served dinner with a subdued air. She and a "sort-of-adopted daughter," wearing a Committee for Nuclear Disarmament button, listened while we made conversation.

The chocolate pudding eaten, we hastily went our separate ways.

Up in the novelist's high-ceilinged, bare workroom, Doris Lessing still smoldered at what she had glimpsed in—and beyond—her guest, and then berated herself for dramatizing it.

"Why do I care after all these years?" she demanded with all the passion of a person repeatedly wounded by caring too much, about too many abuses, and unable to stop caring.

It is this quality of carrying that so distinguishes her powerful *The Golden Notebook*, a novel that sees, through the eyes of several women, Africa, the left-wing of the forties, the disenchantment of the fifties, the problems of "free and independent" women.

The anger still in her rose as she discussed the reaction to that book. Ignoring the overwhelming praise it received, she asked, "What right do they have to assume that it is autobiographical?" (It was a question that included this reviewer.)

"No one asks why I chose that structure. No one asks about the time thing. It's highly literary in theme. What do they mean when they assume it's autobiographical?"

(An editor in New York had asked, "How can you interview a woman whose work is so autobiographical?")

"I'm so angry, I can't talk about it," she said. "I started a series, *Children of Violence*, ten years ago and they said, 'It's autobiographical.'" (The series included *Martha Quest*, *A Proper Marriage*, and *A Ripple from the Storm*.) "It's very impertinent for reviewers to assume it's autobiographical. It also means the book has not been read with any knowledge of European history. It comes out of that whole tradition. If I get angry about it, I get angry about the whole state of literary criticism today. I got a wad of cuttings about *The Golden Notebook*, and the two catchphrases are, 'It's autobiographical' and 'She hates men.'

"The detachment behind it, the construction of the book, the relationship between the political, social, and sexual attitudes aren't looked at.

"My work is pursued by gimmicks. When I first started writing, they said, 'This is a book about the color bar.' That was the first thing I had to contend with, and now 'She's a Communist' or 'She hates men.' I'm not rational about it really.

"People should look at the ideas in a book, what the author is trying to say. One can say about any book out of Africa, it's about the color bar, and this way you can dismiss many interesting levels. Or say about any woman, this is about her experience, but having said that, you've said nothing really."

She referred to *To Room Nineteen*, a story in the collection *A Man and Two Women*, the sad study of a woman in a "happy marriage" and her desperate search for privacy.

"Did it really keep you awake all night?" she asked me curiously. "Would you like to hear how I got the idea?"

She stretched out on her stomach on the floor, kicking off her shoes, and recounted an incident involving some friends. It had no similarity to the story that finally evolved. She became fascinated again with the true story, murmuring, "I must write that some day."

At the moment, she was writing a film script, *A Woman Without a Man*. "Children are very important in it," she said.

She had spoken about her other children briefly, a twenty-four-year-old son in Canada, and a seventeen-year-old son who lives with her. "But, they shouldn't be written about. It isn't fair to children," she said.

"What fascinated me," she went on, "about *La Dolce Vita*, *L'Avventura*, and *8½* is that nobody ever has any children. Everybody is very rich and has cars and beautiful clothes and nobody has children. It's a world without responsibility, and that's why, fundamentally, it's not interesting. The whole of *8½* went by and not one child. It's just nonsense, isn't it?"

Denmark's *Weekend* had children in it. "A marvelous film," she said. "And the British critics called it 'a little bit of Danish blue.' That sums up what I hate about critics—their cheap smartness. The critic's job is to ask, 'What is this writer trying to do?' And then say if he has failed or succeeded.

"I spent years thinking out *The Golden Notebook*. I started plotting it out ten years ago. It's extremely impersonal and worked-out. I'm not saying it didn't have autobiographical stuff in it, but that's different.

"Usually when you try to write a novel, there's a unified person who tries to write it. *The Golden Notebook* broke that because, in the different bits, I tried to create a different person and I tried to do it by all means. If I faced a gap in the plan for a section to be written by such and such a person, I tried to create that person. You've no idea how difficult that was. I was left with this incredible experience which has changed me really—of trying to change myself into a different person.

"Have you ever tried to go without eating? Well, I didn't want to have a sane person trying to write about two people going around the bend, but I just couldn't do it. I thought, 'How can I get this feeling?' I tried marijuana, nothing happened. I tried getting drunk and that was no good. I tried going without sleep. Finally by accident I didn't eat.

368

"Now I have this recipe for anyone who wants to write a bit high: Get very hungry, very empty, and have just a bit of Scotch. Then I was in fact writing about being around the bend a bit. All kinds of things I was describing weren't mine at all."

Another part of the book required "the easy sentimentality of Salinger—I'm very tough on Salinger"—and when she wrote it, it had echoes of Salinger, just what she wanted.

She thought for a while and said, "It was very ambitious, that book. I wasn't equipped for what I wanted to write. It was too big a novel for me. But I had a pretty good crack at it. That's a very British remark." A smile brightened the rather shy and brooding face.

Does she feel British now?

"I feel myself to be—I feel myself to be part of the landscape I was brought up in and I feel myself to be part of this country as well. Recently by accident, I remembered a lot about Persia, where I was born and lived until I was six. I don't know what I am . . .

"Here you're never alone for a second, but oddly enough, now that you mention it, it's the same thing. You walk around London, nobody knows who you are or gives a damn. But in the middle of the night, you feel the pressure of ten million people like a quiet roar. But I love London because it's extraordinary and improbable. And here in England, there's a phenomenon I don't think you have in America.

"A writer just goes on slogging away to produce books. You go on working away. It's much less exciting than in America, much less money, but I think it's rather nice. Nobody expects anything of you. You don't have to be social. You don't have to be rich. You don't have to get married. You don't have to take attitudes. You can be very private, if you want to be. And I am."

December 29, 1963
San Francisco Chronicle

Jon Robin Baitz

"*Ideas live. Ideas vibrate.*"

San Francisco

The boundary between literature and life is what Jon Robin Baitz set out to explore in *The Substance of Fire*, an acclaimed play that he has substantially altered for the film version.

Baitz's protagonist, Isaac, is still the same: a Holocaust survivor obsessed with the meticulously designed, unprofitable books he publishes, and who remains oblivious to the reactions of his three grown children.

"The reason that this man tries to make these beautiful, perfect works on acid-free paper with hand-sewn bindings is that he's trying to hold on to life itself through these books, and it can't be done," Baitz explained.

The playwright had been toying with the idea for a script about a refugee child who becomes successful in America and reinvents himself. It crystallized when he saw Ron Rifkin play the father in Arthur Miller's *The American Clock*. "A tremendous appetite was visible in Rifkin's character, a combination of humor and sorrow, a combination I love to write. I saw in him the perfect actor for my words."

Baitz, thirty-five, said he has always been fascinated by the way things break down. "The degeneration of the body. The degeneration of possessions. How impermanent all things are. Books in particular struck me as having a peculiar kind of physics, but ideas live. Ideas vibrate. And they serve you if you spent a life with books. The ideas become your partners. You enter into a dialogue that never stops, but they aren't a substitute for real life, and I was acutely aware when I wrote the play that literature is literature and life is life. Although they are parallel to each other in some way, the play came out of a kind of understanding that the two could never marry completely successfully."

The lanky, boyishly intense Baitz, who grew up loving books in a kaleidoscope of cultures—Los Angeles, South Africa, and Brazil—said that there is no resemblance between the rigid Isaac and his own parents, the American offspring of Viennese and Russian-Jewish immigrants.

"On all sides of my family there was a passion for discourse, for questioning conversations, for ideas and a tremendous currency in learning. So I think some of Isaac is a great Jewish archetype, but he's made up entirely of the debate I have with myself—not to mention my own feelings of rigidity and Prussian rigor."

In person, Baitz's quirky eagerness to talk about his ideas is more Jimmy Stewart than Erich von Stroheim. Some of the questions that resound within Baitz reflect the divergent worlds he observed when his father was a corporate executive for Carnation Milk. After a childhood in Los Angeles's protected, "oddly segregated," community, he spent years seven to ten in Rio de Janeiro "where the slums and poverty are right in your face," and from ten to seventeen in apartheid Durban, South Africa.

"Every day of my life," Baitz asks himself, "what does one fight for? What does one accept? How much horror can one live with? Where do your standards come into play? What does discipline mean?"

In South Africa, he said, "I was actually aware of how complicitous I was just in order to get through the day. You're told that all people have the right to the pursuit of happiness, but in Durban you couldn't share a bench with a person of another culture, another color. They could not share with you legally, publicly, a life except in order to serve. So the question becomes, are you living a lie? I was conscience-stricken. It had practical ramifications in my everyday life."

He was reluctant to say more about the South African experience because he has written two plays set in that country: *The Film Society* and *A Fair Country*, about the family of a United States information officer stationed in Durban. *The New York Times'* Margo Jefferson wrote that it is "the best American play I have seen at Lincoln Center for some time."

When producer Ron Kastner—whom Baitz calls "our own little Medici in New York"—offered to bankroll a film version of *The Substance of Fire*, Baitz knew he would have to do more than open up the two-act play. When they ran out of money on the $2.5-million production, Miramax came to the rescue and gave them final cut.

Critically analyzing the play in terms of a necessary rewrite, Baitz observed that the original version was "claustrophobic and very internal as a piece of writing." It was also funnier. In a new prologue, the film sets the scene for what will follow by showing Isaac as a traumatized child, witnessing Nazis making a bonfire out of books.

As an adult years later, Isaac risks ruining his publishing house by continuing to print books about the Holocaust and other non-commercial volumes. The film, unlike the play, elaborates on the lives of his two sons and a daughter who all have a financial interest in Geldhart Publishing. Aaron, the eldest son and a partner in the firm, is now openly gay. He tries to convince his father to publish a potential bestseller written by his lover, and enlists the help of his siblings to influence their father. Sarah, who is caught in her own self-destructive love life, and Martin, a lonely professor of landscape architecture, reluctantly take Aaron's side.

In the play, Baitz observed, "Aaron was limping towards resolving his own homosexuality. He had been at least vocally confused, but he got it all together. He's gay and he's happy and he's working. He's got life and work sorted out. He's the most like me."

For seven years, Baitz has lived with Joe Mantello, an actor and director who just finished directing the film version of Terrence McNally's *Love! Valor! Compassion!* and played Louis in Tony Kushner's play *Angels in America*. Kushner is "quite simply the greatest living playwright," Baitz enthuses. "I'm utterly in awe of him. I think he's a writer that without exaggeration can be compared to Dickens. I don't have nearly his capacity for an enormous canvas. I'm a miniaturist and I'm happy to be a miniaturist, but Tony's tremendous grasp of the metaphysics and the politics and the minutiae of human business is truly miraculous."

Still, for a "miniaturist," Baitz has completed his longest play, with twenty characters in three acts. *Amphibian* is about an American expatriate painter, living in southern Mexico for thirty years. The most unintegrated Indian region had fascinated Baitz ever since he'd begun reading about exploited workers in the jungle novels of B. Traven, one of the "un-commercial" authors published by his fictional publisher Isaac in the original version of *The Substance of Fire*.

In *Amphibian*, the artist is astonished to learn that he's going to be put under a spotlight as a discovered missing link to DeKooning, Pollack, and company. "He's lured back to the States briefly to be celebrated, and his paintings rise in value. At the same time, his village is being bought piecemeal by an American resort chain and destroyed. It's also the focal point of the Zapatistas in Chiapas. It's very interesting what's happening there," said Baitz in the understatement of the day.

March 13, 1997
The San Francisco Examiner

Jeremy Irons and Sinead Cusack

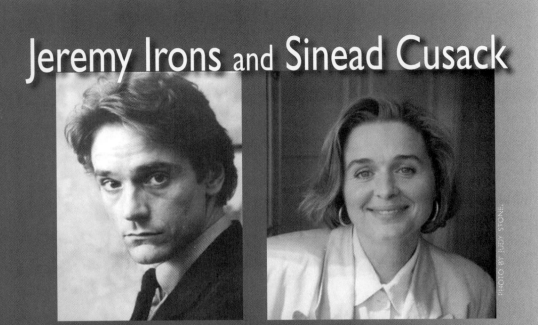

How history puts its mark on private lives.

Toronto

It was not intended as a loaded question, but for a moment Jeremy Irons and his wife, Sinead Cusack, were shocked into silence at the 1999 Toronto Film Festival.

The query was simply apropos of their new film, *Waterland*, in which Irons plays a British teacher trying to convince his skeptical American students that history puts its mark on private lives.

So does the long, strained history of Anglo-Irish relations have any effect on their twenty-year marriage?

With a look of amused dismay, Irons replied cryptically, "It's a long one, this." Cusack plunged right in with her brilliant blue eyes flashing: "We come from two very different traditions with very different attitudes to lots of things, so our marriage is very combative because I'm Irish to my bootstraps. I was a wild child, and as Jeremy will confirm, I stayed wild and will remain so until my dying day."

Soon Americans will have a rare opportunity to see them together on both the large and small screens. Cusack, a famous theater actress in England, stars as Nelly, the young, unpredictable wife of Heinrich Mann (Alec Guinness) in the American Playhouse production of *Tales from Hollywood* on PBS. Irons acts as narrator in Christopher Hampton's drama about famous German exiles in Los Angeles during World War II.

In *Waterland*, directed by Stephen Gyllenhaal, Cusack has a supporting role as the teacher's wife, Mary, whose traumatic teenage abortion haunts her life.

Together, Irons and Cusack play a neat game of verbal ping-pong. The daughter of Cyril Cusack, the famous Irish actor, she said that when she was growing up she wanted to be a saint. Irons said, "I've been nagged at by this saint for the last twelve years to put her in a picture with me."

"That's completely untrue," she countered.

"Everytime a picture is cast," Irons continued, adopting a whine, "she says, 'But *why* Glenn Close? *Why* Meryl Streep? Why not me?'"

"*That* is a tissue of lies," Cusack retorted. "The fact of the matter is that they cast somebody else for the part of Mary that was tailor-made for me. Fortunately I put a sort of hex on this actress, and Celtic witch sorcery went on and she had a conflict of dates and had to bow out."

"When I met this one," Irons noted blandly, referring to his wife, "one of her attractions was that she was Irish and came from a theatrical background and carried with her the mystery, the blackness, and the wildness that the Irish have." He, on the other hand, was the son of a Protestant chartered accountant.

"That's about as strait-laced as you can get," Cusack said. "Jeremy called me Siobhan when I met him, so I hit him."

"I knew she bred dogs, and I love dogs and I liked horses," Irons went on. "I admire good breeding and, looking at *my* antecedents, I thought what my children will need is a bit of Irish wildness."

She, indignant: "Take me for my breeding! A brood mare!"

"In my mother's household," Irons said, "my stepfather who fought in the war, will not go to Ireland. Yes, there are extraordinary vibrations in the society I brought Sinead into."

On the professional side, Cusack mentioned that she had never before observed Irons at work in a movie. "It was interesting to see him ruthlessly in pursuit of a scene like a dog with a bone. He'd shake the thing until he got there, and I respected that attitude."

Later, when her husband was absent, the actress talked about the "wonderful" role of Nelly Mann for *Tales from Hollywood*. "She was a streetwalker in Berlin when the much older Heinrich fell in love with her." Somehow, she got him out of Germany, took him over the Pyrenees to safety, and got them passage on the last Greek freighter that left Europe in 1940.

An anti-fascist writer, Heinrich was deeply devoted to democracy and more famous for a time than his younger brother, Thomas. While the Nobel-winning Thomas was feted in America, Heinrich and Nelly had no money and were virtually starving to death.

"Nelly was desperate. She was a drinker and a wild woman," Cusack said. On Heinrichs' seventieth birthday, she walked stark naked into a dinner party, carrying his anniversary cake and announced that she had sold all her jewelry.

Although the shot of Cusack is discreet, she was squeamish about appearing in the altogether. "I had never done it before, but Nelly was too brave to dishonor her by not doing it. Jeremy was very supportive. He said I looked very nice."

Being a trooper is in the family tradition. Cusack started acting at eleven as a deaf mute in her father's version of Kafka's *The Trial*. Last year, she and her two sisters, Sorcha and Niamh, won rave reviews in Dublin and London for their performances in Chekhov's *Three Sisters*. She played Masha, the rebel, and their father was the alcoholic Dr. Chebutykin.

Cyril's parents had been strolling players. From the age of five, Cyril went to different schools every week. According to Sinead, he would say, "I'm with the actors. Can I come to school?" He did that until he was fifteen and then had two years of formal education. Sinead's mother had been a leading ingenue at the Gate Theater in Dublin until she had five children in quick succession.

"Father always felt rootless, which is why he was terribly keen to root us strongly in Ireland," she recalled. "We were educated through Irish, our own language. I was taught English and math through Irish until I was twelve and was sent to an English boarding school near Dublin." The difference was extraordinary, she recalled.

She changed her given name of Jane to Sinead, the Irish equivalent, because she was determined to retain her Irishness. "My Irish school was coed, which I think is a healthier way to raise a child. To be very suddenly plunged into that very-regimented, formal, claustrophobic, single-sex atmosphere was quite a shock. I never really recovered, but at the beginning, I thought, 'Rather than fight them, I'll join them,' so I decided to be a saint and made all sorts of promises to God about chastity."

She fell from grace when she was fourteen and wrote a play about the scandalous affair between British Minister of War John Profumo and call girl Christine Keeler. "We got half-way through performing it for the nuns when all hell broke loose. My father was summoned home from Paris, where he was filming and I was threatened with expulsion, but my parents begged, cajole, and prayed for me to stay on. After that, I was the black sheep and remained so."

She never trod a careful path, she said, what with "unsuitable men, party going, drinking." She went to England when she was twenty to get away from the "claustrophia" of Dublin. "I came greedy and predatory to London. It was a land of opportunity that didn't exist in Dublin. In retrospect, it's quite damaging to uproot yourself from all that's familiar.

"As I got older in England, I started to yearn for certain attitudes, certain values, certain comforts. Just the way we talk to each other. We're constantly curious, and there is no façade that hides emotions. In England, you might exchange a word with the man sitting next to you about the weather, but that world is alien to me."

She met Irons when he was playing John the Baptist in *Godspell* and she was in the Royal Shakespeare Company's production of *London Assurance* by Dion Boucicault. A mutual friend introduced them at a birthday dinner because she thought they'd be an ideal couple. "She was completely wrong about our being an ideal couple," Cusack said. "Jeremy wanted a total commitment immediately. When he dropped me home, I asked if he'd like to come up for a cup of coffee. He said, 'I warn you, if you do I'll stay for the rest of my life.'"

After three months, they were a couple. Later, when they acted together in *Wild Oats*, she whispered to him one night as she was exiting the stage and he was entering, "I am with child." Irons went on, but he said that his mind was awash with images of school scenes and mortgages. "I wasn't keen to get married," Cusack said, "but five months later, we did."

First, Irons had to undergo a two-year intensive interrogation by the Catholic Church to determine if his youthful, brief marriage could be annulled. "He came to respect the church hugely as a result of that experience," Cusack recalled, but he didn't convert.

Their two sons are raised as Catholics, although she's critical of the Irish Catholic position against abortion. "In my ideal world," she said, "no pregnancy would be unwanted, but we don't live in that world. It is still considered a great sin in Ireland to be pregnant and out-of-wedlock and I think that's a terrible reflection on us. Young girls like Mary Crick in *Waterland* are pushed to such desperate measures that your heart breaks. The abortion choice must be there, otherwise we will go back to the Dark Ages."

October 1992
San Francisco Chronicle

Alfred Hitchcock

What would you like engraved on your tombstone?

Los Angeles

The suspense was excruciating. Where was New York? Why were only Dallas and Chicago coming in loud and clear at Alfred Hitchcock's closed-circuit television press-conference spectacular uniting four hubs of the USA in one grand celebration of his fifty-third film, *Family Plot*? Was it a plot? Had New York failed to pay its telephone bill? Why was there only a faint strangled cry from the Big Apple? Was some mad terrorist holding New York City hostage?

Hitch was taking this hitch very damn inscrutably. Benign Briton to the bitter end. How much longer could he expect to thrill people with bloodless kidnappings and brakeless automobiles and diamond heists in a world that had been hog-tied with suspense by the SLA and mesmerized by Hon. Kamikaze pilot dive-bombing Kodama-san? How much longer? Huh, Hitch?

"We're fighting headlines all the time," conceded the master of fright, folding his arms calmly over his renowned avoirdupois, the very epitome of imperturbability. Going on insouciantly to the next question from the sixty-five live ones assembled at NBC-TV to see the master in the fulsome flesh. Somber and dignified in stark black and white.

In Chicago and Dallas, twenty and thirty purveyors—respectively—of critical opinion could only watch this living legend, in color on a TV screen, and ask remote questions via the big "bird" satellite floating out there somewhere over the equator, under the old silent screen heaven. God and Pauline Kael alone knew what horrors were facing the thirty men and women assembled for this momentous occasion in New York.

Didn't . . . anybody . . . *care*? I silently smothered a shreik.

L.A. kept asking Hitch questions about the symbolism of Blanche's white car. Chicago was burning for comment on the symbolism of staircases. Dallas fretted about the symbolism of Shoebridge and Rainbird in *Family Plot*. Richard Schickel, *Time*'s man at the movies and the L.A. moderator in TV photogenic pale blue, pondered the symbolism of an abduction in a church. (Grace Cathedral, to be precise.) And was Hitch having it on with *The Exorcist* in the seance scene?

No, no, no, no, no, replied Hitch in more or less that order. Staircases are meant to go up and down. Light switches symbolize light. The seance is a seance. He regaled his interlocutors with stories of his meticulous concern for the infinite advance detail, his cool contempt for improvisation. In measured tones that recall the glory of Winston Churchill declaring war on the forces of darkness, he recalled his unceasing battle to vanquish the ever-present threat of the insidious cliché.

Coincidence, on the other hand, is a part of life, he graciously allowed, and a pun—"I had to make the location of the diamonds crystal clear"—may be gracefully indulged.

Nobody noticed the sweat pouring down the brow of one Dominick Azzaro, 6'1", all 195 pounds quivering while he pops Rolaids. Not only is Mr. Azzaro vicepresident of Video Techniques, Inc., which successfully beamed Muhammed Ali from Zaire to the world on closed-circuit television, he is a citizen of Yonkers and, ipso facto, has a vested interest in the survival of greater New York. What *is* going on? The shotgun mikes are dead. Industrial sabotage? New York is out. Down for the count. Once. Twice. It's zero hour. New York, this is your last chance. "Hello, New York?"

"Thees eees Gracila Lecube of Bue Hogar in Argentina." Her dulcet query wafts through the air. Good Grief. It's Buenos Aires! Azzari collapses.

But, no, wait, there's Henry Kissinger's voice coming through. No. No. It's the terrifying tiger of *New York* magazine, John Simon. New York lives!

"Mr. Hitchcock, vot is ze religious symbolism," Simon asks, "of ze vooden cross stopping ze runaway car?"

"Mr. Simon," replies the ex-Jesuit seminarian with a touch of asperity, "I am not *that* religious. I do not look for symbols or messages."

"Mr. Hitchcock?" L.A. was taking over for the finale—"we wish you a long, productive life, but since your new movie is called *Family Plot*, what would you like to have engraved on *your* tombstone?"

The star was startled. The cue hung in the air. "I don't know," Alfred Hitchcock, stalker of graveyards, finally replied, " I guess it would be quote, 'You can see what will happen to you if you aren't a good boy.'"

July 26, 1976
San Francisco Chronicle

Jacques Perrin

"If we protect nature, it will be better for education, for the children."

Paris

For fifteen years, Jacques Perrin lived in a home with no windows, no water, no electricity, and—if lucky—ate chicken once a year, but he remembers it as a "beautiful time" before he knew the value of money. Self-taught, today he's famous as an actor, writer/director, and producer whose films have ranged from politics to the planet's life of insects, monkeys, and birds.

Perrin was at the peak of his career as producer with the fantastic international success of *Winged Migration* when he took time out in the spring of 2003 at his Galatee Films office near the Arc de Triomphe to talk modestly about his life and career in heavily accented English. His kindness to a reporter struggling with an uncooperative tape recorder seemed somehow rooted in a temperament that has always wanted to make life better. With an impressive shock of white hair, he is even more handsome now than he was as the youthful sailor/artist who appeared with Catherine Deneuve in *Les Demoiselles de Rochefort* and as the young journalist in Costa-Gavras' *Z*, the film that also launched his career as producer.

Perhaps those happy, albeit hardship, adolescent years enabled him to be philosophical about the money he lost on *Winged Migration*. Although it made at least $20 million in the U.S., the film went over budget because of technical problems and took four years to make instead of three. "Losing money matters," he told *Variety*, "but it is not the most important thing. If I've anything to leave to my three sons, it is more a lesson in living than money in the bank."

Born in 1941, Perrin got his first lessons in living from his actress mother, Marie Perrin, who saved money in the war-haunted years by trudging ten kilometers twice a week to earn a pittance in a cabaret by reciting French poetry to support him and his two sisters. He adopted her maiden name rather than that of his rarely seen father, M. Simonet, a stage manager at the Comédie-Française. By age fourteen, he had dropped out of school and soon began studying acting, though it always seemed too "passive" an occupation. "You are not at the origin of things. You are not responsible. I wanted something else."

He became involved in "something else," even as he got his first acting role at eighteen playing a French resistance fighter in *La Verte Moisson* (1959). While continuing to perform, he enjoyed his first taste of producing and travel when he worked on a documentary for a few years with a photographer friend. They began shooting "without reflection" as soon as they arrived at airports in Africa, South America, and southern Italy. That documentary, he laughed, "is not in the memory of the history of cinema."

After acting in two Costa-Gavras films, *The Sleeping Car Murders* (1965) and *Shock Troops* (1967), the director offered him a role in *Z*, based on the assassination of a popular Greek physician and parliamentary deputy. After a few months, he told Perrin that nobody—no producer, no distributor—wanted his script for *Z*.

But Perrin, who felt immediately involved in the project, was determined to help the film get made. "We must remember what the world was thirty years ago," Perrin recalled. There had been a coup d'état by the Greek colonels in April '67. France was still suffering from the after-effects of the Algerian war. There were dicatorships in Portugal, Spain, and Latin America. And in May '68, student and worker protests broke out all over Paris. "All the young people were sensitized by what happened in France. So it was for me the first project with an eye on what happened in the world."

He likes to call himself the lawyer for *Z*. "I make all my best efforts not because I want to produce, not to make money, but because it's necessary to make *that* movie in *that* time." A friend, an Algerian director, offered him a co-production deal, and *Z* was finally shot in Algeria. Then Perrin managed to find some French bankers who believed what he said about good contacts in America who would appreciate this "wonderful" movie. "If you make a movie as producer, you must take risks. We'd be in a bad position if the movie was a disaster, but it was not." *Z* won an Academy Award as Best Foreign Film.

Perrin continued to produce winners: another Academy prize for *Black and White in Color* and *Himalaya*, an Oscar nominee for Best Foreign Film. Meanwhile, he acted in more than 100 films, including *Cinema Paradiso*. He disregarded the advice of backers who turned down his film *Les Choristes* about the healing powers of music in a harsh postwar reform school for boys, but it became a surprise box-office hit. And he has embarked on a major film about oceans, involving documentary effects and fiction.

He appreciates the diversity in all his efforts, but he's not about to separate the political from the natural world in film. "What is political?" he asks. "It's to make life better. I think if we protect nature, the oceans, the forests, the animals, it will be better for our education, for the children. I think the planet is not our garden. It's also the territory of the others, of other populations, the animals. More or less we forget that. I think we cannot be good in life if we don't protect the life of animals."

His film *Le Peuple Singe* about monkeys brought him to the attention of two French biologists, Marie Perennou and Claude Nuridsany. They had spent years studying insects, hoping to film them in a "poetic drama," but they needed an imaginative producer. Fascinated by their ideas, Perrin immediately agreed and set about securing 4.8 million francs from private investors and the French Ministry of Culture and Education. *Microcosmos* took five years to make, using their most ingenious device, a computerized miniature robot that carried a camera, permitting high-precision photographs.

For *Winged Migration*, which Perrin directed and produced, five teams were activated to follow bird migrations flying over seven continents. It was a project dear to Perrin's heart. "What if we understood that our borders did not exist," he asks, "and what if we learned to be as free as birds?"

When Perrin makes a movie, he doesn't think of it as a system of production. "It's my choice in life. I can imagine maybe it was possible to have another life. Maybe I have not twenty different lives. It was fantastic to be a producer for the birds for four years. And I love this possibility to open windows in my life."

August 10, 2001
Toronto Globe and Mail

Diane Johnson

PHOTO BY JUDY STONE.

Toujours l'amour.

San Francisco

It was a damp, gloomy Sunday morning, but the rainbow over Diane Johnson's Telegraph Hill home was a two-page spread in *The New York Times* book section: a rave review of her novel *Le Mariage* and an author interview, conducted earlier by telephone from her second residence in Paris.

Any other writer would be dancing with joy at that magisterial seal of approval, but the truth is that she was exhausted. In the midst of a grueling eleven-city book tour, she had a single day's respite in San Francisco and had to be up at 7:00 A.M. to fly north and then back to the Bay Area for a reading.

She hadn't been the focus of so much attention for her first eleven books, including a biography of Dashiell Hammett and a collection of essays, *Terrorists and Novelists*. But then *Le Divorce*, her eighth novel, took off in 1997. There were nine printings, in hardcover and paperback.

Johnson used to buy the remainders of her books and store them in her garage, but there weren't any leftovers for the best-selling *Le Divorce*. Which is not to say that she had gone unnoticed by the literary cognoscenti. She has been nominated three times for the National Book Award and twice for the Pulitzer Prize.

As demure and self-effacing as she appears, she has always been someone to be reckoned with. She wrote her first book as a nine-year-old in Moline, Illinois—a mystery novel involving triplets, inspired by Nancy Drew detective stories. Years later, surrounded by four children (in six years), she wrote her first two "unhappy housewife" novels, *Fair Game* and *Loving Hands at Home*. At the same time she was finishing her doctoral thesis on the nineteenth-century poet George Meredith, and feeling enough empathy for the poet's first wife, Mary Ellen, to make her the subject of a full-length biography, *Lesser Lives*.

With the eye of an artist, she sees through falsity, pomposity, credulity, sexual posturing, and frustration and pricks them with sly wit, but utterly without malice. "I don't think I have much of a slasher about me," she says. "I think that comes from being Midwestern."

Surprisingly, she volunteers, "I am rather moralistic and didactic and I do that in my books." However, the attentive reader has to uncover those qualities in her pithy little sidebars when not distracted by the entertaining mysteries, paranoia, murders, terrorism, medical mistakes, and marital mayhem that crop up in her novels.

Johnson got the opportunity to turn her attention to the differences between the French and Americans when she and her husband, Dr. John Murray, a retired professor of medicine at the University of California, San Francisco, and author of a standard text on chest diseases, decided to split their time between the two countries.

Not surprisingly, doctors appear in several of her novels, notably in *Health and Happiness*, set in a San Francisco hospital. It is not exactly a paean to the profession, but there is a sweetener in the dedication to Murray and "to my many other friends who are doctors, with affection and apologies."

Although Johnson hadn't planned *Le Marriage* to be a kind of sequel to *Le Divorce*, marriages between Americans and the French, with their misconceptions about each other, play important roles in both books. She wanted to title it *Conviction*, but the publisher objected.

"I was thinking about the inevitable clash when middle-class, privileged Americans impose their convictions on other countries. In this case: our convictions against hunting animals came into conflict with the hunting tradition of a French neighborhood . . . and there's a clash of convictions in our society about cults."

The theft of a valuable medieval manuscript called the *Driad Apocalypse*, the murder of a rare-book dealer, and a possible kidnapping by Oregon terrorists get the plot and several subplots simmering. Caught in the whirlpool are Anne-Sophie, a proper but ditsy young French flea-market dealer in horsey artifacts, and Tim, her fiance, a half-American, half-Belgian journalist who is erotically stirred by Oregon-bred Clara, a former movie star. Clara is married to the famous reclusive film director Serge Cray, who is hostile to animal hunts on his vast estate. Clara's passions are ignited by the suave, married Antoine de Persand, a character from *Le Divorce*. There's also a naïve antique-shop owner from Oregon with a link to various cults.

How much of such confabulating comes from the inscrutable life of Johnson herself? In *Le Mariage*, she invented the title of the stolen manuscript, but she notes that a manuscript *was* stolen from the Morgan Library in New York that was reported to have some tangential connection to the bombing in Oklahoma City. Nothing more was ever published about it. And apocalyptic manuscripts were stolen in France, too, but those events didn't inspire Johnson's novel.

"I don't know what triggered the book," she says. "I always had an idea about a Franco-American couple and the things that separated them as they wended their way to the altar. Serge Cray was a compendium of directors I have known. The fact that he doesn't go back to America for years was suggested by Roman Polanski, who legally couldn't return, and by Stanley Kubrick, who didn't go back."

She wrote the script for Kubrick's *The Shining* after he read and admired her evocation of paranoia and horror in *The Shadow Knows*. It is the only one of the scripts she worked on for Mike Nichols, Francis Ford Coppola, and Sidney Pollack that made it to the screen.

Johnson pokes fun at herself in *Le Divorce* when Estelle, Anne-Sophie's novelist mother, complains about all the Anglophone writers who keep turning out books about France. Estelle's sexy purple prose owes a bit to Colette. Johnson admires the French novelist's elegantly sensual sex scenes—though it's "not what greatly interests me," she says. "What interests me is the stuff that they have to go through to get into bed."

April 23, 2002
The San Francisco Examiner

12

G-d forbid that we should use His name

Rolf Hochhuth

"How could our people have killed six million Jews?"

Eschwege, Germany

For a man who has provoked a storm of conscience and controversy in the Christian community and shattered the inviolability of the Vatican, Rolf Hochhuth is surprisingly shy and diffident, but he has the courage to examine the most terrible moral problem of our time: "How does man exercise his responsibility?" The thirty-two-year-old German Protestant and former member of a Hitler youth group was not looking for easy answers or a scapegoat when he wrote his searingly anti-Nazi play *Der Stellvertreter* (*The Representative* in England, *The Deputy* in the United States), accusing Pope Pius XII, Christ's Representative on Earth, of failing to raise his voice, even once, publicly, explicitly, unequivocally, against the murder of six million European Jews.

The question that haunts him, and all young Germans: "How could our people have killed six million Jews?"

He talked about the German reaction in an interview during the 1963 Christmas holidays while visiting his parents in Eschwege, the small town in which he grew up.

Hochhuth is a slender man with a look of pain on his face, the physical residue of a partial paralysis compounded by some inner struggle. A slight imbalance of the eyes compels attention, and the level sincerity in them commands respect. His grave and lovely wife, Marianne, whose own mother was decapitated by the Nazis, acted as translator.

"If I had killed someone," Hochhuth said slowly, "I can never get rid of it, no matter what I do. So I must live with this feeling of guilt and gradually I get used to it. It's the problem of each individual: how he can live with guilt. Whether he gets indolent or superficial. I wrote this book; that's how I lived with it." He paused for a long time and murmured, "But if you measure it [writing a book] against the murder of one child, it is, of course, nothing."

The uproar in Berlin when the play opened in February 1963 under the direction of the famous Erwin Piscator has since spread to Switzerland, Paris, England, Denmark, Vienna, and the United States, where it opened in New York, produced by Herman Shumlin. For the play, Hochhuth won the "Young Generation Playwright Award" of the 1963 "Berliner Kunstpreis" and shared the Gerhard Hauptmann Prize of 1962.

He has been praised as a social conscience, a mantle he wears awkwardly and reluctantly, and he has been damned variously as a Nazi, a Communist, and an anti-Semite.

To those who asked him to refute the charges, Hochhuth replied with quiet dignity, "I will not answer. I want them to judge my play independently of my person. Whoever reads my play and still maintains the opinion that I am an anti-Semite, or Nazi, or Communist, this one cannot be answered."

In all the controversy about the Pope, Hochhuth said, his major point has often been overlooked. Perhaps because the truncated, oversimplified, three-hour stage versions have lacked the moving complexity of the eight-hour original drama, published in the United States as *The Deputy* by Grove Press.

"To me," Hochhuth explained, "Pius is a symbol, not only for all leaders, but for all men—Christians, Atheists, Jews. For all men who are passive when their brother is deported to death. Pius was at the top of the hierarchy and, therefore, he had the greatest duty to speak. But every man—the Protestants, the Jews, Churchill, Eden, Cordell Hull, all had the duty to speak."

It is absurd, he said, that people should accuse him of trying to diminish the guilt of the Germans because he has accused the Pope of silence: "The arsonist does not become less guilty because a fireman resigns in front of a great fire.

"I hope that this play will give a lecture for the future," he said, "because I think the terror against the Jews in our time is only one example of the terror which reigns on earth at all times, in all epochs, in every century. In every nation there are feelings that wait for a Hitler to awaken. In other centuries there was the Inquisition. Nearly all times have known horrible examples that certain groups of men were persecuted in dreadful ways. The Christians in Rome, the heretics persecuted by the Christians. Therefore, I fear that this will never cease. Today there is race persecution between white and black; the persecution of the American Communists by McCarthy and others and the persecution by the Communists. There was McCarthy, on one hand in America, and Ulbricht, on the other, in East Germany and Kadar in Hungary.

"I believe that this play may be a lesson for the future if only people will accept it. A friend asked me, 'Why do you take such pains to write about the Final Solution? In twenty years' time no one will talk about it.'

"I have studied enough of history to know that he was probably right; actually, the victims have always been forgotten very quickly. But in spite of that, I am convinced—not only in spite of it, but because of it, that the play can teach a lesson that is timeless.

"To oppose injustice," Hochhuth said, "one needn't be a moral man. It is enough to do nothing which damages others." (To a critic who asked, "Is this indeed enough?" Hochhuth replied, "It may not be much if you measure saints by it, but for people, it is enough.")

How could a young German grow up under the Hitler regime and retain a moral sense?

Hochhuth was born in 1931 in the little town of Eschwege in Northern Hesse, near the river Werra, now just a few miles from the East-West border, a border that torments the playwright. "You must see the border," he urged repeatedly. When finally we did it was an odd sight. After their heavy noon-day dinners, the West Germans come on Sunday outings, with powerful field glasses, to look at the border. What are they looking for? What do they see?

Hochhuth sees for the Germans a tragic fate, inextricably linked to that of the Jews, and in the border, an almost mystical analogy to the Jewish Diaspora.

Asked if he thought that Germany could ever again be a threat to the world's peace, he replied, "Only in an indirect way. A country of 70,000,000 that is cut into two pieces against nature can never come to peace. The Germans should be forbidden atomic weapons for all time, but they should be given their unity. The occupying powers can stay; they don't disturb us, but the border between the Germans should be removed. One should always think of it and see it. It's idiotic, this border.

"This border in Germany may be the beginning of a Diaspora like that of the Jewish people. I think that German history will become as sad and tragic as the Jewish history. I feel that the tragedy of Jewish history has not come to an end by the foundation of the state of Israel. This small country with a small population in the midst of the Arab world is menaced so terribly. I fear for it . . . And when one thinks of the anti-Semitism in Russia leading to persecution again . . . The Germans and the Jews seem to have the quality of always getting themselves disliked and persecuted."

Hochhuth has refused to let his play be performed in Eastern Europe or in any country where the Church is suppressed by the State, but he wonders if his decision is correct. "When I read now in a leading Jewish newspaper in West Germany that the Jews are actually persecuted in Russia, I ask myself if it wouldn't be important to publish my play in Russia for evidently the Church is less suppressed at the moment than Jewry. A Hungarian anti-Communist in Paris who left Hungary during the revolution wrote that it was great folly not to allow my play to be published in the East. He said the play calls people against all forms of terror, and for that reason the people in the Eastern bloc would understand."

But Hochhuth—who has had offers from Poland, Prague, and Belgrade—said, "I am convinced they would abbreviate it in a radical way and I couldn't do anything about it. I'm afraid the Communists would use if for propaganda against the Church."

He himself had little formal religious training in Eschwege, where his father ran a shoe factory that had been founded by Rolf's great-grandfather. The elder Hochhuth had been an officer in World War I and an officer for three months in the second World War before being retired because of his age. One brother served in the army in Hungary and two cousins died in the war.

In 1941, at the age of ten, like all other boys, Hochhuth became a member of the Deutsches Jungvolk, a Hitler youth organization. When still a boy, he met his future wife, Marianne Heinemann, editor of a recent book of German poetry. Her personal tragedy is nowhere reflected in the serene warmth of her blue eyes, but unspoken pride shines in them when she speaks of her mother. Marianne has achieved a matter-of-fact tone when she tells of the day two Nazis in civilian clothes came to their home in Berlin to take her thirty-five-year-old mother away "for questioning." The ten-year-old Marianne watched as the men found the hidden, forbidden books by authors whose works had burned in the unforgettable bonfires of 1933. Marianne's grandmother, a poor peasant girl who had worked and studied to become one of the first women Social Democrats and served on the Frankfurt Town Council until removed by the Nazis, trembled and sank into a chair. Marianne's mother, tense and pale, tried to summon reassuring words for the child. Nine months later, Marianne was told her mother had died of a heart condition, but years later, she learned of her decapitation in prison. Her father, a former teacher, died serving in the Wehrmacht in Romania, and eleven-year-old Marianne was sent to Eschwege to live with relatives. She and Rolf met in school toward the end of the war.

Hochhuth, trying to recreate the mood of those black, wartime days, said, "To the end of the war, the little boy Rolf wished that Germany would win. My parents did not wish it, and they would never have thought it possible that Germany could win after the invasion of Russia, but of course, they could not tell their feelings or they would have been killed. They heard the English and American broadcasts, even though there was a death penalty for anyone caught listening. My mother entered a restaurant one day and told someone that the Americans were in Brussels. Since the German radio did not announce it until the following day, it was clear she had heard it on the enemy radio. She was denounced to a Nazi organization, but the leader was an old teacher of hers, a good man, and he told my uncle, who later became burgermeister for the Americans, to warn her not to do it again. That time they tore up the report.

"We feared the Russians," he said, "and because of the bombing of the Allies, we hated the Allies. From a propaganda point of view, it was not a good idea for the Allies to bomb civilian centers. As boys of the Hitler youth, we had to pick up pamphlets and leaflets dropped by the Allies. On these leaflets, it was written, 'We are not fighting the German people but the Nazis.' But we boys mocked those words because we saw dead women and children and we were impressed and hated those who had done it. The Americans who attacked Eschwege tried to find the military targets only, and it was only bad luck they bombed the streets near the airport. But the English destroyed Kassel. We saw the town burning from here, and my fourteen-year-old brother had to go there at night to help. The English didn't care where they bombed, but now I understand the English point of view."

Although Eschwege had many Jews living there, by 1941, the last ones were driven out to nearby Kassel and from there to Riga, where they worked in the mines and were later killed. Rolf remembers with grief the act of charity extended by his mother to the Jewish wife of their cousin, a well-known doctor in Wiesbaden.

"A Jew married to a non-Jew was considered half-Jewish, so they were not deported in 1941, but they had to wear the yellow star. My parents invited her here in 1943, we boys were ashamed and wondered what people would think. She was very sweet to us and grateful. She stayed for a few weeks although people wondered and talked in a small town. When she returned to Wiesbaden, she had an 'invitation' to go to the Gestapo, and she poisoned herself. Her husband was asked to help revive her, but he would not because he had promised to respect her wishes about her own fate."

Meanwhile, the townspeople heard from soldiers returning from Russia of rumors that the SS had engaged in mass shootings, but the rumors were all very quiet, very hush-hush.

"We thought it could not be true," Hochhuth said. "It was so ugly and brutal. But in a war, people's feelings become insensitive. The Jews had disappeared from our lives, but we knew from books and school lessons that Jews were described as *untermenschen* and that all other people were second-class. We also knew that the Russian prisoners of war in Germany and the German prisoners of war in Russia were treated badly and died of starvation, but this didn't affect one. Each one of us had his own problems; we trembled for members of our own families."

After the Americans occupied Eschwege, they nominated as mayor Rolf's uncle, a well-known businessman who had not been a Nazi. He appointed the thirteen-year-old Rolf to be his messenger between Town Hall and the military government.

"The first week of the occupation was not very agreeable for the occupied. My parents and others had to leave their homes, but we were relieved because the war was over. My brother who had been taken prisoner by the Americans was released. And then the cruel things of the concentration camps became known. The photographs were shown in the papers, and it shamed and sickened us. We didn't dare to believe . . . "

In the turmoil, he said, "The American army would have won the hearts of the German youth at once if they had treated the German soldiers better. Of course, they made great speeches that the Germans must not for the next 1,000 years have guns, but you must take into consideration that the boys liked soldiers and ships and suddenly they heard it would be forbidden for the next 1,000 years. On the one hand, they understood how guilty they were and the disaster we had brought to Europe, but these were feelings that struggled inside us. And we were terribly afraid of the Russians. We heard about the most dreadful crimes the Red Army had committed in the Eastern Zone, and this was no more Nazi propaganda, but facts. I say all this knowing that we Germans have started with all these cruelties and that 'who sows the wind will reap the storm.'"

The young people today, he said, consume great quantities of non-fiction pocket books about the Third Reich and they ask, "How could it have been possible?"

"The people who were adults at that time and who silently feel guilty do not want to get near these problems. They have made great sacrifices through the war to Hitler. It is not very rare to find German families who have lost two sons, and there is almost no family who has not lost one. I do not want to weigh the victims of the battlefields against the gassed people. I am not trying to make an accounting. Auschwitz was the top in inhumanity. But I will try to make you understand a little more. The old people are tired of torture. They want to be left in peace from politics. And also of the politics of today. One can be glad they come out for elections. But for the young people as truly as I am sitting here, there is no anti-Semitism. They don't know Jews. (One man said, "Jews are like Martians to them.") Towards the Jewish people they feel guilty. 'How could our people have killed six million of them?'"

When the war ended and the realities of daily politics became too complex and confusing to young Rolf, the introspective youth kept to his books and began writing poetry. Then he discovered Thomas Mann and *Buddenbrooks*. It was a great revelation.

"The world of *Buddenbrooks* was the world of my ancestors. The firm my mother came from was also founded in 1797, and the last of the family was no more a businessman, but a sensitive artist. This touched me; the decay of a family fascinated me because I saw it in all the families I knew."

While reading the book, he learned that Mann had voluntarily left Germany because of his opposition to Hitler. "Mann has influenced me most," Hochhuth said. "The early Thomas Mann, his attitude towards life, his humanity, his engagement in politics. I have learned from him that the poet always must be active in politics. That he is also responsible. *The Deputy is* politics."

At the age of seventeen, Hochhuth left school to become a bookseller because he believed that he could come closer to literature and writing than by taking German lessons and studying natural science. After a few years as a bookseller in Marburg, Kassel, and Munich, he fell ill for a year with an undiagnosed illness that left one side of his face partially paralyzed. When he recovered, he still could not work, and he decided to attend the University of Heidelberg and the University of Munich to study history and philosophy.

In 1955, he became a reader and editor for the largest book club in the world, Im Bertelsmann Lesering, and he edited a collected edition of the famous anti-clerical satirist and caricaturist Wilhelm Busch. Among hundreds of caricatures of people and animals, the book included some drawing of Jews, a fact that led to an attack on Hochhuth as an anti-Semite.

"Busch was not an anti-Semite," Hochhuth maintained. "One of his stories is about an innocent Jew who is hanged for a crime committed by Christians. But Busch was anti-clerical, and I have discovered that in certain historical periods, one must be anti-clerical in order to defend oneself."

However, in an edition of Busch for children—his Max and Moritz characters became a model for the Katzenjammer Kids—Hochhuth omitted the pictures of Jews "so that German children would not mock the Jews."

At the same time, he wrote an unpublished novel in the form of letters called *Occupation*, a picture of the last weeks of the Nazi regime and the first month of the occupation. But he was writing more history than fiction, and in studying the documents of the Nuremberg trials, he discovered the strange and improbable figure of Kurt Gerstein, the SS officer who plays a major role in *The Deputy*.

Gerstein had been active as an Evangelical Church youth leader. He wrote and distributed anti-Nazi pamphlets of the Confessional Church until his arrest in 1936. Upon his release, he determined to enlist in the SS and led an almost suicidal double-life there to determine the truth behind all the rumors of genocide. Gerstein finally made his way into the SS "Institute of Hygiene" and was responsible for taking delivery of consignments of Zyklon B, the lethal agent used in the death camps. In August 1942, he set about trying to sabotage the destruction process, and from that time on was "driven without respite" to make the facts known to Protestant and Catholic leaders, including an attempt to reach the Apostolic Nuncio in Berlin. After making a full report to the Allies in 1945, Gerstein's trail disappeared in a Paris prison, and his name has been placed by the Paris Jewish community on their memorial table for the victims of Fascism.

Fascinated by the figure of Gerstein, Hochhuth felt that he was a Christian "of a type so modern that to understand him completely one needs to read Kierkegaard. What interested me was that Gerstein was a Protestant in the most literal translation of that word. I believe that the Christian spirit—as he expresses it—is the real spirit, the form of Christian spirit for our time."

Hochhuth became so excited reading the documents on Gerstein that the drama inescapably began to form in his mind, although he had never before thought of writing drama.

"Then in the autumn of 1958, Pius died," Hochhuth said "In Germany, the newspapers and radio declared that a holy man had died. The Germans loved Pius, whose three closest advisors were German and they called him the German Pope."

But Hochhuth, stirred by Hitler's murder of almost 2,500 Catholic priests, felt that "the holy men were those people who had died in concentration camps and not a man who died in his sleep at an advanced age. Those Catholic priests whom Hitler killed are the true martyrs of the Catholic Church in our time, not the man who personally never tried to protest.

"I saw that this was the tragedy, the tragedy that the Vatican out of reasons of state did not support those members of their own church who sacrificed themselves."

He dedicated his play to the memory of two of them. One was Father Maximilian Kolbe, Internee No. 16670, a Polish Franciscan priest who died in 1941 in a starvation cell at Auschwitz after asking to take the place of a prisoner who was going to be among ten men punished to death by starvation in retaliation for the escape of one prisoner.

He died too slowly for the SS, and they finally gave him an injection to hasten his end. The other was Provost Bernhard Lichtenberg of the Cathedral in Berlin who prayed publicly for the Jews, was arrested and who asked to be allowed to share the fate of the Jews in the East. But he was taken to Dachau and died on the way there in 1943.

Hochhuth's fictitious figure of Father Riccardo Fontana, S.J., who confronts the Pope with the fact of his official silence, is based on the deeds and aims of Provost Lichtenberg, who was concerned with the Pope's response, pins a yellow star on his cassock, and goes with the Roman Jews to Auschwitz.

"I did not discover the fact of the Pope's silence," Hochhuth said. "In 1944, Albert Camus had posed the question: 'How was it possible that Pius kept silence?' François Mauriac asked the same question, as did the Catholic philosopher Friedrich Heer in Austria."

Leaving Germany, Hochhuth went to Paris and London to study all the relevant documents, the ones published and the ones lying unread in archives. Later he spent three months in Rome, living near St. Peter's, studying the atmosphere, talking to Swiss guards, Romans, and Jews who had been hidden in Italian monasteries. He posed a series of questions to one Bishop whose name he will not reveal. After avoiding Hochhuth for weeks, the Bishop finally agreed to see him, confirming the belief of the author in his thesis.

Since the publication of the play a year ago and two books dealing with the controversy, there has been no real answer from the Vatican, Hochhuth said. "If the Vatican had in its archives documents to throw doubt, even only to throw doubt, on my play, they would have found them and published them," he believes.

Shortly before his election to the papacy, Cardinal Montini wrote a letter commenting on reports of Hochhuth's play (cut nearly in half for the theater) to *The Tablet*, the leading Catholic periodical in England. In it, he did not deny the fact of the Pope's silence, but defended the character of Pius and told of his concern for all the victims and fear of bringing on even greater tragedies.

In Basle, Switzerland, where the Hochhuths live with their three-year-old son, the playwright said, "I was visited by a prominent Jesuit father. We talked one whole Sunday, but believe me, we hardly spoke about the Pope. We were mainly concerned about Act 5, 'Auschwitz or the Question Asked of God.'"

The padre told me that another Jesuit, very old, had said in a circle of Church people that the fact that Hochhuth had attacked Pius was not so important and should not lead the discussion away from the fact that I had said inexcusable things about God.

"Pius is a historical figure, one of 260 popes, and his attitude is not enough to characterize the institution of pope-dom, either in its good or its bad sense. But the question for God is timeless, as the atrocities are timeless," Hochhuth said.

He quoted the German poet Trakl: "Silently over the heap of skulls, God's golden eyes open."

"Now for our contemporary sensibilities," Hochhuth commented, "this might have been said somewhat too beautifully, but whether God looks on the heap of skulls or if one says with [Georg Christophe] Lichtenberg [an eighteenth-century physicist and author] 'No invention has been easier to people than the invention of heaven.' This question for God is more essential than the silence of death of the so-called confessional peace that my play has been accused of endangering. That is unimportant to me. Luther once said, 'There must be upheaval in Christendom.' The Christians live much too comfortably today. The Churches have never before been even remotely fed with tax money as they are today, and on top of this, one should leave them in peace? Why?"

Spring 1964
Ramparts

John Duigan

PHOTO BY JUDY STONE.

"One must not love oneself so much as to avoid getting involved in the risks of life."

San Francisco

John Duigan, a scholarly director with a special empathy for non-conformists, came to the San Francisco Bay Area to talk about his new romantic/wartime epic *Head in the Clouds*, but soon the talk turned to an earlier film. He learned to his quiet delight that a measure of justice had finally been achieved in California for the reluctant hero of his film *Romero*, about the Salvadoran Archbishop who was brutally murdered in 1980 as he performed mass.

The assassination of Archbishop Oscar Romero triggered the twelve-year-long bloody civil war that was a fight for justice against right-wing militarism in El Salvador. No one was held accountable for the crime until September 3, 2004 when a federal judge in Fresno found a retired Salvadoran Air Force captain liable in the slaying and ordered him to pay $10 million in compensatory and punitive damages for the killing. Captain Alvaro Rafael Saravia had been living in Modesto, California, but disappeared after learning that a suit had been filed on behalf of a relative of Romero's. The day before the assassination, the Archbishop had publicly confronted the military, declaring in his final homily that "no soldier is obliged to obey an order that is contrary to the will of God" and begged them "to stop the repression."

"This court case is very pleasing," noted Duigan, in soft, measured tones befitting someone who earned an honor's degree in history and philosophy and a master's in philosophy from Melbourne University. "It will encourage people to perhaps seek other compensations for the deaths of thousands of people who have suffered at the hands of right-wing death squads and the military during that period. If there are succesful prosecutions, it might at least discourage in some small way the sort of crimes these people carry out. They can no longer believe themselves to be above the law and to be immune from prosecution."

Although *Romero* (1989) and *Cloud* differ in theme and style, Duigan indirectly commented on the links between the two. In *Cloud*, the idealistic Irish hero (Stuart Townsend) goes off to fight in the Spanish Civil War, even though he's reluctant to leave Paris and his wealthy sweetheart Gilda (Charlize Theron), who is notorious for her frivolous lifestyle, her unusual photography, and her intimacy with the Spanish model Mia (Penelope Cruz).

Gilda eventually learns that "you cannot live in isolation aloft from the political and moral issues of the time, especially when they invade your own space." In his time, Oscar Romero, memorably portrayed in the film by Raul Julia, learned a similar lesson. He had been chosen to be archbishop because the other bishops considered him "weak," apolitical, and open to manipulation. His gentle approach changed after the murder of his friend, a leftist priest sympathetic to the struggle of peasants in the countryside. That killing transformed Romero into a powerful voice against state-sponsored violence. Moments before his assassination, Romero declared that "One must not love oneself so much as to avoid getting involved in the risks of life that history demands of us, and those that fend off danger will lose their life." All the other Salvadoran bishops, save one, had turned their backs on him, even sending a secret document to Rome accusing him of being "politicized" and of seeking popularity.

It wasn't the first time that Duigan's films criticized Catholic church policies. *Sirens* (1993) was ostensibly a sexy comedy, but it dealt with Norman Lindsay, a controversial Australian artist who scandalized the hierarchy with his etching *The Crucified Venus*. The etching showed a naked woman being nailed to the cross by a representative of the Church. "In *Sirens*," Duigan said at the time, "I wanted to make a film about sensuality and repression and the Church's attitude towards sexuality."

He had tackled the issue of non-conformism early on. A British "air force brat," he was born in 1949 in England (where he now lives) and was educated in Australia. He thinks his sympathies for misfits developed as a result of the number of times he had to move with his parents. "By the time I was eleven, I had been to nine different schools. It means that one was constantly an outsider, whether one liked it or not. I went to Australia as an English boy with a very strong English accent and that meant I was a figure of ridicule at the boarding school I attended. The kids were mostly middle-class from farming backgrounds. They tended to be very cruel and to victimize people. I explored that theme, which is loosely based on my boarding-school experience, in *The Year My Voice Broke* (1988) and *Flirting* (1991). In *Flirting*, Duigan introduced two future stars, Naomi Watts and Nicole Kidman.

In two of his earliest films, *The Trespassers* (1976) and *Winter of Our Dreams* (1983), Duigan observed the non-conformists of the Vietnam War era whose politics and personal lives were contradictory, and he was particularly critical of those who became so disillusioned that they failed to continue working for democratic changes.

For a long time, Duigan had wanted to make an epic romantic drama, set between the two world wars, along the lines of *Gone With the Wind*, *Dr. Zhivago*, and *Lawrence of Arabia*. "It's the biggest canvas I've tried my hand at. *Romero* was big in its way, but this is a longer span of time taking place in three countries."

As usual, he began *Cloud* by developing the main characters before thinking about the storyline or the casting. "Gilda's character is informed by the sense that her life is predestined. As she puts it, 'It's lying in wait' for her, yet that's completely at odds with her personality, which is to live life as vigorously and impulsively and spontaneously as possible. She will take on and discard people as she sees fit, but she's intensely loyal to those she becomes close to, and she loves strongly and passionately."

Guy and Mia are political by nature. "They come from working-class backgrounds. Mia's father was a coal miner and anarchist in Asturias when the Spanish Civil War began. Her brother was probably killed in the war, and her leg was broken when she tried to come to his rescue. In Paris she's training to be a nurse so she can return to Spain to join the struggle. Guy, like many intellectuals, feels conscience-bound to go to Spain. Their instincts are to engage with the issues of the day, but they are quite conservative as far as relationships are concerned. They each would like to have a one-on-one relationship with Gilda, and Guy would like to be married to her."

The sequence in Spain reflects Duigan's long-held interest in that war. "It seemed there were very sharply defined issues at work in Spain, which had a democratically elected government that was under challenge from the right wing and the military. I suppose there were also links with the film I did about Romero, which was another civil war between the right-wing and the left-wing guerrillas and where the church was involved nominally and mostly on the side of the military and the government."

As to whether political films have any effect, Duigan said, "It's difficult to quantify, but they certainly inform people and they are part of the social process of change. It's seldom that a film can change people's attitudes, but a film can be part of the national debate. I think *some* films should be political. That's not to say that all films should be political but there's certainly room for that kind of thing just as there's room for comedy and frivolous entertainments."

The latter is obviously not on his immediate agenda. He has already written a script about the experiences of refugees in Australia. It has been a very controversial subject since a boatload of refugees, mainly Iraqis and Afghanis, were refused asylum in Australia in September 2001 and transported to "fly-blown squalor" in camps on the tiny island of Nauru. Duigan's new film may not make any changes in Australia's refugee policies, but it will assuredly create a bit of a stir.

September 2004
San Jose Mercury News

Brian Moore

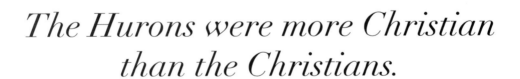

The Hurons were more Christian than the Christians.

Brian Moore, who remembers being beaten regularly while at school in his native Belfast, was amazed to learn that the Native American Hurons could not bear to strike or reprove their children. "'Hit *me*,' they would say, 'don't hit the child.'"

"They were more Christian than the Christians," Moore observed when he talked about his novel, *Black Robe*, the story of a Jesuit priest and a young French boy making their own *Heart of Darkness* voyage through the Canadian wilderness in 1635. The "savages"—as they were termed then—shared in everything, Moore said. "They were polygamous because they thought it was part of their nature. They didn't have jealousy the way white people did."

On the other hand, they were cannibals—the Iroquois being the most fierce. "They drank people's blood, tortured them, and cut their hearts out for religious reasons.

They thought that was a way to capture their victims' spirit. If they didn't, they believed their victims had captured them."

Moore discussed his seventeenth novel during an interview at the 1984 Toronto International Film Festival, where he participated in a seminar of Canadian writers whose works had been made into movies. He had written the film script for his own novel *The Luck of Ginger Coffey* (1960). He talked about how he had suffered through a co-writing experience with Alfred Hitchcock on an original script, *Torn Curtain*, but received wide praise for his TV adaptation of his novel *Catholics*. He adapted *Black Robe* (1985) for the Canadian company that produced *Atlantic City* and *Quest for Fire*. The Canadian approach is preferable to that of Hollywood, the slightly built Moore commented with a glint of humor in his lilting brogue, "since the Indians are now through with Marlon Brando re-inventing their own history."

Moore, son of a surgeon, was brought up in a "very Catholic" upper-middle-class milieu in Belfast. He said he lost his faith at the age of ten or eleven. "I had to keep it quiet for a long time," he said, smiling. He quoted Graham Greene, one of his favorite authors, to the effect that "'Faith is a gift. Some are given it and some are not.' I couldn't quite believe in it, so I identified with the Indians a lot."

Moore, who has lived in North America for thirty years as both a Canadian citizen and resident of Malibu, left Ireland during World War II. After serving with the British Ministry of Transport, he worked as a journalist in Montreal for seven years and quit in 1956 after the success of his first novel, *The Lonely Passion of Judith Hearne*.

Although *Black Robe* seems like a departure for Moore, he says it deals with themes of belief that have always interested him. In addition, he admired the marvelous oral memories of the Native Americans, which he compared to that of Ireland's Aran Islanders. Moore recalled that when he was a child, his uncle, Eoin MacNeill, founder of the Irish League and first president of the Irish Republican Brotherhood, went out to teach the Aran Islanders how to read and write.

With *Black Robe*, Moore said he wanted to "destroy the whole James Fenimore Cooper legend of the noble savage—as well as our total misunderstanding of what these people were like."

Actually, Moore isn't keen on historical fiction because it's usually too long and requires too much research. "I try to write more in the tradition of a tale," he said. However, he claimed to enjoy the challenge of trying to do something he had never done before: establish the sense of an unfamiliar time and place.

He wanted to juxtapose the superstitions and beliefs of Native Americans, which were totally at variance with the superstitions and beliefs of the Jesuits. "And each of them was totally wrong in misunderstanding the other.

"I've used religion as a metaphor for any belief—political or anything. It's a condition most of us share. We believe in something when we're young and lose that belief later. The great question here is that a Jesuit goes to the interior to baptize these people and partly loses his own faith in the process."

The story is brutal, Moore feels. "For instance, the Indians use very filthy language. It was their way of saying, 'I'm not angry. I'm joking.' When the Jesuits asked their word for God, they'd say 'fuck.' The Jesuits had to learn all this bad language in order to know when they were being conned. The Indians were terribly logical in argument. The Jesuits would say, 'If we baptize you, you'll go to Paradise.' And the Indian might reply, 'If I'm baptized and my wife and children are not, then I don't want to go to Paradise.' So there's no argument."

April 7, 1985
San Francisco Chronicle

Michael Tolkin

"*Do you believe in God?*"

New York

Anybody who asks Michael Tolkin if he believes in God doesn't get an answer. Tolkin turns the tables and retorts: "Do *you* believe in God?"

Belief is not a subject likely to crop up in connection with many movies, but with *The Rapture* it's inevitable. The surprisingly suspenseful film deals with the spiritual journey of a telephone information operator (Mimi Rogers). Tied to a head-set by day, she opts for a night life of marriage-swapping and sexual diversion with innumerable strangers. Finally, revolted by her lifestyle, she becomes a born-again Christian only to have fate—or God—play a disastrous trick on her.

The consequence of her conversion provided grist for heated discussions when *The Rapture* was shown at the Telluride, Toronto, and New York film festivals.

"I wanted to make a movie in which there were no villains and no scapegoats and in which the central figure comes to an intense self-realization," says Tolkin, a novelist and former religion major who is making his debut as a director. "I wanted to make a film about man's relationship to God, and to take either side would be in vain."

People ask Tolkin—who appears to be a man of passionate self-assurance—if he's an atheist or a believer. "If you say you're an atheist," he responds, "it's vain. If you say you're a believer, there's a certain arrogance in that. I think you should be very careful about public confessions of faith. If you say it privately, it's one thing, but it's another if you stand up and say I am this or that. Fitzgerald said the definition of genius is the ability to hold two opposing ideas at the same time. I wanted the film to hold two opposing ideas as delicately as possible."

He also wanted to deliver a blow to a trend he believed movies were following in the last ten or twelve years. "They have increasingly discovered that the audience wants to be united in a mob. I wanted the audience not to be turned into a mob. I wanted everybody to be left really within themselves so that people at the end will feel lonely, lost, unhappy, and scared. The standard of tragedy is to make you feel pity for the tragic figure and terror for your own fate."

The tall, intense writer/director was sitting in a New York hotel room trying to explain how he came to make a film so out of step with the mainstream. At the same time, he was struggling, unsuccessfully, to control his irritation with room service that had sent him a cup without a saucer for his Pero coffee substitute.

"If I say a cup," he snaps into the telephone, "do you suppose I could get a saucer as well?" He hangs up and says sarcastically, "'Oh, you want a handle on the cup?!Why don't you make it yourself, sir?'"

It was a neat little diversion from a heavyweight subject, but somehow oddly in character with the author of *The Player*, the ironic Hollywood thriller Tolkin wrote about a disturbed studio executive. Fittingly, it was made into a movie by another Hollywood iconoclast, Robert Altman.

Describing the genesis of *The Player*, Tolkin said, "There was a day when I looked at a studio executive's eyes and saw how bored he was and how right he was to be bored. I thought about how many writers he saw every day, how many stupid stories were pitched, and I felt this terrible sympathy for him. The standard Hollywood novel is about a terribly sensitive writer who is misunderstood by the kind of executives who haven't a thought. I wanted to invert that and explore the soul of an executive facing the writers who are all gnats buzzing around him."

When he was preparing for *The Rapture*, in a similar vein he was irritated by movies in which a born-again Protestant minister was "pictured as a thief, a liar, a hypocrite or a Southern boob." Watching Christian television programs and listening to fundamentalist ministers on the radio, Tolkin said, "I identified with their pain. I felt that their diagnosis of what was wrong with the world was right.

I have a different definition of 'satanic' than the Christians, and I don't believe in a supernatural evil, but I think they've been terribly maligned."

The idea for *The Rapture* came to him when he saw a bumper sticker with the phrase: "Warning: In case of rapture this car will be unmanned."

The evangelical phrase, he explained, "means that when the rapture comes, the driver will be raptured into heaven. If you're behind the car, it will be out of control and you'll have to hit the brakes. Otherwise, you will slam into a driverless car."

Some of the early sexual shenanigans in the film were inspired by what Tolkin observed as a freelance magazine writer when he did a story about Plato's Retreat, a "big orgy swing club" for straight working-class and middle-class couples at the old Continental Baths in New York.

Tolkin said he's upset by what he thinks is the misplaced direction for the energies of about fifteen million people in this country who are born-again Christians. "I think a lot of them have been deluded by their ministers and by the Reagans and Bushes. They are people who are in pain and want the world to be right and they're being manipulated."

Tolkin's own family was "not particularly religious." His father, Mel, a writer for the old Sid Caesar show and other comedy programs, had left Russia at age thirteen because of the anti-Semitic pogroms in that country. He emigrated to Canada, where he met his future wife, whose parents were Romanian emigres.

"My father came from a family that had thrown out most of its ties to orthodoxy before he was born. My mother's father was almost more of a pagan than a Jew. He believed in the life in trees and rocks and water and the sky. It wasn't a typical American household. There was a sort of European darkness to it. I was bar mitzvahed and took Judaism seriously when I was a boy. I've always been interested in religion and always interested in other people's obsessions. My own obsessions are in a way other people's obsessions. I've always been a voyeur, too. What really interests me is what gets other people excited."

Fascinated by the "subcultures" of America, he wrote his first film script about skateboarding in a Vietnamese community in Orange County. The original script for *Gleaming the Cube*, starring Christian Slater, dealt with adoption, suicide, family, and murder, but it was rewritten twice and finally did not reflect what he had set out to do.

Nevertheless, youngsters love the film, Tolkin said. "When River Phoenix was in Florida, he was mobbed by kids who thought he was Christian Slater and wanted to know where his skateboard was."

Tolkin was disappointed by *Gleaming the Cube*, but the money he earned gave him the opportunity to finish his novel, *The Player*. He wrote the film script for Altman and produced the movie as well. Tim Robbins has the leading role, and many movie stars play themselves in it: Julia Roberts, Bruce Willis, Andie McDowell, Angelica Huston, Whoopi Goldberg, and Cher.

"Like a lot of artists," Tolkin observed, "Altman is very complicated and is trying to work things out for himself. People are very suspicious when you're working things out for yourself in a movie. People are very intolerant of movies that don't work exactly the way they want them to. People will forgive a book. They will certainly forgive a painter. They will forgive the ballet. They will forgive a TV show, but if a movie doesn't do exactly what they want, they turn on it almost like a lynch mob and react violently to movies that disappoint or frustrate them. Or leave them feeling in any way strange to themselves."

At the Telluride festival in Colorado, he said, the people who liked *The Rapture* best were from small towns that don't have art houses. "It was controversial and a lot of people really hated it. Others wanted to talk about the emotional ride they had with the movie. They were less insistent on forcing me to say exactly what I thought it meant and to torture me into confessing something that would prove they were right to hate the movie. One woman came up to me weeping because she was so moved. She had been worried that the film was going to make fundamentalists look crazy and it didn't. An editor on a campus *Crusade for Christ* paper said they're encouraging their members to see the movie and see how misperceived their message has become. I think that people who like *The Rapture* can disagree over its meaning, and people who hate the film can disagree over why they hate it, but I think the people who respond negatively to the film are afraid of being overwhelmed by feelings of despair, sadness, and loneliness."

November 3, 1991
San Francisco Chronicle

Franco Brusati

PHOTO BY HAZEL FIELD.

"I can't stand the part of Catholicism that says sex is a sin."

Montreal

Franco Brusati has a soft spot in his heart for outsiders and some very strong feelings about the Hollywood hustle at Oscar time, Soviet censorship, his old friend Franco Zeffirelli, and the Catholic Church's attitude on sex as a sin.

When he attended the North American premiere of his film *My Sleazy Uncle* at the 2003 Montreal World Film Festival, the Italian playwright and director pointed out that all of his prize-winning plays and movies (among them *Bread and Chocolate* and *To Forget Venice*) deal with people "not happy living in any sort of society." In *My Sleazy Uncle*, the Giancarlo Giannini character "believes in all the contemporary myths: success, money, family, and children. His uncle [Vittorio Gassman] couldn't care less."

Brusati was clearly on the side of the uncle, a retired professor and poet, whose lifestyle is a mess and whose sexual curiosity remains undaunted by age. Brusati's own attitude about sex fairly exploded when he talked about his old friend, the late poet and director Pier Paolo Pasolini.

407

A few days before Pasolini was murdered in 1975, he had asked for Brusati's opinion of his most controversial film, *Salo*, set in that puppet Italian republic, which was the last bastion of Fascism at the end of World War II. There, 72,000 people were murdered, 40,000 were mutilated, women and children were sexually humiliated. Utilizing the historical facts, Pasolini combined them with his version of the Marquis de Sade's *The One Hundred and One Nights of Sodom* and made a blistering study of the sexual, cultural, and social perversions of Fascism.

Brusati told Pasolini that the film was "far too Catholic." Pasolini, he said, had a "deeply rooted religious sense and was filled with guilt about his homosexuality. He was a Communist and also very Catholic and he suffered greatly. I told him that *Salo* was like a furious sermon done by a Spanish Inquisitor against all flesh and pain because Pasolini was against himself.

"I am a deeply religious person myself," Brusati declared with his voice rising, "but I can't stand the part of Catholicism that says the sense of sin is related to trash, that sex is the sin. No! That's not true! The sin is not to take care of other human beings. The sin is not to be generous. It's not to think about those who are lonely or lost or unhappy. That is the sin of life. Sex is a joy. Who cares if a boy goes to bed with a boy or a girl?"

Brusati, born in 1923 into a rich and noble family in Milan, feels that his own life was "wounded once and for all" when he was nine and his father left their home. "He was very nice, but he lost all our money, everything, out of stupidity. I felt the lack of the father image, and that affected all my plays. It was a scar in my soul that never healed. My mother had to play the role of both mother and father, and it was not good for my psychological development."

When he read Thomas Mann's story *Tonio Kroger* about an artist "who was sick to death of depicting humanity without having any part or lot in it," the work made a strong impression. "It gave me a feeling of what my life might have been, the life of a man who keeps feeling himself apart." It also gave him a sense of revenge. "I had to be successful and had to recover what I lost when I was a boy. . . . I wanted to win the Nobel Prize and the Oscar and all that in order to please somebody who never accepted it, and that somebody is myself."

Wary of self-deception, Brusati is equally critical of Italian sentimentality and delusions in his work. *To Forget Venice*, which won an Oscar nomination in 1979 for Best Foreign Language Film, dealt with an aging homosexual trying desperately to act younger than he is while beset with the magic and misery of childhood memories at a family reunion. Brusati said he suffered when he went to the Oscar ceremony.

"You can't buy an Oscar," he said, "but you can buy the atmosphere in which you can win an Oscar. The Germans were there with Volker Schlondorff's *The Tin Drum*. The ambassador and the consul were all there, along with a firm especially created to promote the film. And we Italians had a secretary in one small room, calling people and saying shyly, 'Would you like to see an Italian film?'—while the other ones [the Germans] were giving cocktails, parties, dinners. We could not do anything because the producer was bankrupt."

After *The Tin Drum* won, Brusati went to his room "a little bit sad, but then to be a good sport, I go back down for dinner. The secretary to the Motion Picture Academy whispered to me that I lost by five votes. Five votes! I could have thrown the table away! I thought of how a little effort could have changed the vote. I hated to lose."

He suggested that an Oscar for "best publicity-maker in the world" should go to Franco Zeffirelli. Brusati is still angry at Zeffirelli over the script for *Romeo and Juliet*. Zeffirelli claimed it was just a little TV film and there was no money in it, so Brusati said he agreed to write the script for a "symbolic" amount on the condition that he get sole writing credit. The "little producer" turned out to be Paramount Pictures, and Zeffirelli added his name as co-scriptwriter.

"Zeffirelli became rich out of that film," Brusati claimed, "and I never got paid one cent."

The ways of the film world are strange indeed, west and east. Brusati was mystified when he took *Bread and Chocolate* to the Moscow Film Festival in 1973. There Brusati learned that the censors had cut a key scene of a bawdy drag song and dance number in which the Italian immigrant waiter abruptly stops the show, declaring "We have to change things, not sing about them." It was the most "left" line in the film, Brusati said, but each time he tried to find out why it was cut, the subject was politely changed, with the suggestion that he visit Leningrad.

"I hope that things are different now," Brusati said, but he didn't sound very optimistic.

April 10, 1991
San Francisco Chronicle

Nino Manfredi

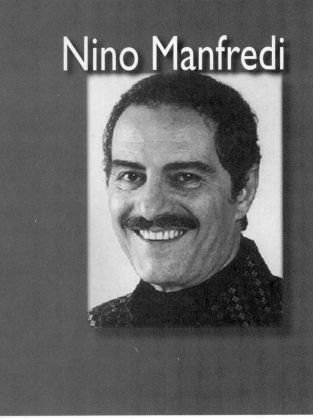

"Sex is very limited in a Catholic marriage."

San Francisco

It's impossible not to laugh when Nino Manfredi talks about problems with his Catholic background and his life-long struggle to escape death. He tells his dire stories with such a volcanic eruption of words that the interpreter can't keep up with him.

And he has such a bewitching mixture of sincerity, self-mockery, gusto, and fun that a translation seems almost superfluous.

Although Manfredi, sixty-two, has been making Italians laugh for nearly forty years, his comic genius won international recognition in 1974 when he gave a brilliantly Chaplinesque performance as an eager—but bewildered—Italian immigrant worker in Switzerland in *Bread and Chocolate*.

Manfredi is a droll picture of puzzlement in his latest film, *Nudo di Donna* (*Portrait of a Woman, Nude*), which he directed, co-wrote, and stars in as a middle-aged husband pursuing a mysterious stranger who resembles his wife.

Nudo is HIS story, Manfredi declared emphatically. Yes. His. AND that of other middle-aged Italian men, he added.

"When I was about fifty, I felt death closer and closer to me. The gates were coming too close together and I couldn't free myself. This had an influence on my sexuality. I lost interest in a sexual relationship with my wife, although I loved her very dearly."

He tried to explain, manfully: "Sex is very limited in a Catholic marriage. My wife is a very extraordinary person, but because of our background, there was not much fantasy between us.

"My marriage was in a state of crisis. Even though I thought I could never meet a better person than my wife, I wanted to find a reason to leave her. I almost left her. I went to doctors and psychoanalysts. I went through a terrible depression. Terrible. Terrible, but my wife helped me."

It wasn't clear how fantasy crept into their lives, but no matter. At any rate, Manfredi was able to make good use of his torment and introspection in *Nudo*, and—ironically—his wife was also to do so.

She had given up a career in fashion to raise their three children, but in this film she designed the extravagant costumes for the two women (played by one actresss, Eleonora Gorgi) and the fabulous Venice carnival sets.

"Venice is a very strange city to me," Manfredi said. "It has always been said that it is really one of the outer circles of Dante's hell. All that beauty and all that decay. I always think of death when I'm there. You realize you are mortal."

It was a good "theater" for his story, Manfredi said. His protagonist, Sandro, goes on a search for the model of a nude portrait he is convinced is his wife. When he finds a flirtatious prostitute, he is confused about whether she is his bookseller wife in disguise or another person.

Although it is deliberately vague in the film, Manfredi says that they are two different women. "Sandro is just fantasizing that it is his wife because of his problems. Whichever woman he finds in front of him, it is important that she be able to be both wife and mother to him.

"I feel it is important that a woman be both whore and saint for the man she loves. When the carnival is over, Sandro takes off his mask and he will accept the woman he keeps dividing in two and find an equilibrium with his wife."

Although he was in San Francisco to promote *Nudo*, he spoke with much more affection of Ettore Scola's *Ugly, Dirty and Bad*, a film made in 1975. In it, he plays Giacinto, a cunning, one-eyed pensioner living in the slums with his huge family.

"I loved that film like I would love a difficult child. It was a very difficult character to portray because he shoots his son. I had to act like an animal. I had to communicate the deep human reason of why he became that way."

For the first time, Manfredi went about constructing a character the way he would prepare for a part in the theater.

"When I read Scola's script, Giacinto reminded me of MacHeath in Brecht's *The Threepenny Opera* and of the buffoon in *Twelfth Night*. Brecht knows how to describe poor people with extraordinary strength," Manfredi said.

"Brecht's assassins have a certain kind of humanity. It's full of poetry like in a court of miracles. Every morning, the thieves try to figure out what character to put on to wangle money from people.

"In spite of this, they never make anything different out of their lives. Joining together the humor of MacHeath and the buffoon, I gave birth to this character of Giacinto."

For Manfredi, his difficult childhood memories are very real. His father was a peasant who became a shoe repairman as he kept moving his small family closer and closer to Rome in order to give his two sons the opportunity for an education.

"We had no water," Manfredi recalled. "No electricity. It was a very good reason for not having more children. I was so sick, that every two years, I was supposed to die.

"When I was sixteen, I almost died from diphtheria but my grandmother—who was a midwife—saved me. I had already been given last rites."

It was supposed to be a great honor to die young, Manfredi said with a grimace, "but I didn't want to go to that beautiful place."

Instead, he was sent to a sanitorium for three years. As soon as he was released, he was called up for military service by the German army then occupying Italy. Then he was put into a military hospital, from which he escaped.

He was finally captured as a deserter, but sympathetic young German soldiers, who had been university students, let him escape on Christmas Eve.

"That's why I'm still here today," Manfredi said. "I still feel death on my back, but I've stolen sixty-two years from all that. Death helped me to become a good actor because fear and torment made me very involved with my own feelings. Until today, when I cough, I still think I could die any moment."

He's absolutely serious, but the total effect of his words is miraculously comic. Manfredi had achieved a similar effect when he created a satirical weekly TV comedy in which he played a naïve man from the provinces whose innocent palaver unmasked the pretentions of Italian politicians.

Originally, after getting a law degree, he went into theater because the best filmmakers were into neo-realism and not interested in developing actors.

When film producers wanted to continue using his TV personality, he was so angered by their harping on the qualities of his voice that, in 1962, he wrote, directed, and starred in a voiceless role, *The Adventures of a Soldier*, a half-hour episode in the compilation film *Difficult Love*.

His first feature, *Between Miracles* (1971), which he directed, co-wrote, and starred in as a man summing up his life before undergoing an operation, won the Cannes Festival's prize for Best First Film.

He did not start out directing *Nudo di Donna*, but took over during filming from Alberto Lattuada when that director appeared on the verge of a nervous breakdown.

"I'd rather not direct myself," he insisted, "because I'm a perfectionist. I love to act. When I'm acting and directing, nobody is there to judge whether the scene was good. It's better to have someone else with that responsibility."

Manfredi may feel that way because he thinks he still hasn't solved all his problems. The crisis, he says, "is still on, but I learned how to cope with my problems. I console myself with the thought that I have many feelings that are important to me. I'm not a superficial man."

Billy Wilder saw those complexities in his personality, Manfredi recalled. Wilder invited Manfredi to be in a film with Jack Lemmon, but said he would have to learn English.

Manfredi replied that he would love to work with Lemmon, but felt that he couldn't express himself in English.

"So Billy told me this important phrase: 'It would be enough to take a close-up of your face to understand your world. I can see your tragedy in your eyes. You do well to take it with irony.'"

September 2, 1984
San Francisco Chronicle

Francis Girod

"A Don Juan type — homosexual and heterosexual."

Sarasota, Florida

The philosophical murderer who loved Arletty in *The Children of Paradise* is finally getting his own feature film treatment. *Paradise* director Marcel Carné and his scriptwriter, Jacques Prévert, wanted to follow their 1945 film with a sequel devoted to Pierre-François Lacenaire, the nineteenth-century real-life scoundrel and bisexual rake who fascinated the French when he played out his last days in prison like a flamboyant gentleman.

It took nearly fifty years before director Francis Girod realized Carné's dream. His film, *L'Élégant Criminel* (originally entitled *Lacenaire*), starred Daniel Auteuil in the leading role. *Variety* called the film a "masterwork . . . stylistically audacious and savagely witty."

Interviewed at the 1990 Sarasota French Film Festival, Girod said he had wanted to make the film ever since he read Lacenaire's frank and incisive memoirs twenty years ago. It wasn't until he met Auteuil that he felt he had exactly the right actor for the part of a complex man who combined a number of unique characteristics.

Delighted to meet his fate on the guillotine, Lacenaire was dubbed "one of the first black humorists of France" in *The Anthology of Black Humor*, a collected compiled by the surrealist André Breton. During Lacenaire's trial, the urbane Girod observed, "He could talk in the same language as the judge. And years before Freud, he explained in his memoirs all his behavior as an adult by his childhood. His language is very beautiful," Girod said, "as he analyzes his own case. He was a sort of Jekyll-Hyde. He was capable of the worst things, and was able to judge himself with humor and without any self-indulgence."

The film opens with Lacenaire in his final days, waiting for a stream of visitors in his luxurious cell. He is sardonically resigned to having a "master of phrenology" measure his head for the marks of a born criminal; boastful that novelist Prosper Merimee has asked to see him; and touched by the visit of an Austro-Hungarian princess who loves him. He is eager to present his memoirs to Allard, the police chief who brought him to justice, and Arago, a famous author interested in his manuscript.

Flashbacks reveal Lacenaire's misery as the unloved son in a conservative family, his rebellion against hypocrisies in his Jesuit school, and the wound he felt when his father predicted he would end up on the guillotine. After killing a gambler who cheated him at cards, he embarks on a life of petty crime, living high on the hog all the while. He is scornful of proprieties, but capable of tenderly caring for an orphaned girl who becomes his ward. He finally is brought to trial for the murder of a crooked pawnbroker and the pawnbroker's mother.

Girod based the script—co-written with the late novelist Georges Conchon—on Lacenaire's memoirs and books written about him by Allard and Arago.

"Everything that was put into Lacenaire's lips are sentences from his memoirs. I couldn't separate him from his taste in showing off," Girod noted. "In the memoirs, he speaks very clearly about his relationship with women. Because of censorship, his relationship with men is an underlying theme, but he's very clever at making you understand what he wants to say.

"He used his power of seduction toward homosexuals to make them his accomplices, but it's difficult to know if he had pleasure in that kind of sexual relationship. I think he felt no physical pleasure at all. The *idea* of pleasure was more important to him than pleasure itself. He is unable to have lasting relationships; he's a Don Juan type, homosexual and heterosexual."

Auteuil got right "into the skin" of Lacenaire, Girod said. "The actor illuminates every twist and turn of this intelligent criminal's mind. It's a very important part for him because it really shows his talents." Auteuil's skill previously made a great impression in the role of the crafty, dim-witted Ugolin in Claude Berri's *Jean de Florette* and *Manon of the Spring*.

Girod, who directed Gérard Depardieu in several films, felt that Auteuil was better than Depardieu in *Jean de Florette*. "At first, Auteuil was unknown. Now he's the challenger. They are the two best actors in France today. Gérard creates as he's interpreting, without thinking. It's instinctive. While playing, he has an acute critical sense about his own work.

"Auteuil does a tremendous work of reflection. He reads a lot about the person. He memorizes the part—then he forgets completely. But under his work he has this incredible base. He can handle subtleties and summon up his original freshness and instinct although he did all the work before.

"Gérard is now in a state of grace where he enjoys everything and everything can be accomplished," Girod added. "I think the best thing that's happened to Depardieu is the arrival of Auteuil. It's good to have two actors like that who can stimulate each other."

L'Élégant Criminel is the best Girod has done in an up-and-down career. After a fling at journalism and a few youthful years as a producer of non-mainstream films, he attracted considerable attention with *Le Trio Infernal*, the first film he directed when he was twenty-eight. Starring Romy Schneider and Michel Piccoli, it was a hit at the 1974 Cannes Film Festival.

Nothing matched that success until *Le Bon Plaiser* (*Our Will and Pleasure*) created a sensation in Paris in1986. The black comedy is based on a novel by Françoise Giroud, Minister of Culture under Valery Giscard d'Estaing, who also wrote the script, a penetrating view of political expediency at the top.

Girod's current concern is the cultural battle ahead involving the deteriorating quality of films. "In ten years," Girod said, "we will celebrate the centennial of cinema, but I hope it won't be the death of cinema. If we want film to be a live art we have to be ambitious for it. We need to raise the level of cinema, not to go down the way TV is doing. It's demagogic when we play down to the audience with the worst films by pandering to the lowest common denominator. I think the big opportunity and responsibility for European cinema is to challenge audiences. European cinema shouldn't concentrate on science-fiction or special effects, trying to copy American films. An audience is smart when it's encouraged to be smart."

October 18, 1992
San Francisco Chronicle

13

Balkan Bombshell

Ademir Kenovich

ADEMIR KENOVICH AND DANA ROTBERG. PHOTO BY JUDY STONE.

"We worked like Charlie Chaplin, with humor and tragedy."

San Francisco

By the time the siege of Sarajevo ended in 1995, 15,000 people were killed and 73,000 lost their limbs or were otherwise wounded. Nevertheless, Ademir Kenovich and friends had filmed 400 hours, documenting days and nights of "outrageous behavior." But, Kenovich said, "we worked like Charlie Chaplin, with humor and tragedy." Still something else remained to be done: a dramatic memorial to the courage of the Bosnian people. Despite horrendous logistical problems, when the war finally ended, Kenovich had finished the first step in directing *The Perfect Circle*, a superb film about three survivors: a lonely poet and two orphaned boys, one a deaf-mute who can't hear explosions and snipers.

"What is it like when you don't hear?" Kenovich asked during a visit to San Francisco while the siege was still going on in 1993. "We had the feeling that everybody in Sarajevo was shouting as much as possible to other people about what was happening and nobody heard. We were like mute people; we couldn't transmit to the world."

When the Serbs began shelling Sarajevo in 1992, it was a beautiful, multi-cultural city —"a kind of artificial paradise in which most of the people were not religious— whatever that means," Kenovich said. He was living in the hills near a lovely orchard. For a couple of days, he didn't understand what was happening, although there had been indications before the siege that an intense nationalism was developing in Yugoslavia. Everybody felt uneasy that something was roiling beneath the surface. Then Serbs began raining mortar shells from the hills. Kenovich's mother died when a shell hit the family home and Kenovich had to leave the hillside and stayed down in town throughout the siege. "We had no army strength, no media strength and no outside support. We didn't have anything that [Slobodan] Milosevic, the Serbian leader [later indicted for war crimes] had. At a certain point in time, everybody in Sarajevo despised everybody else in the world."

In order to show the horrors of the siege to those outside, Kenovich overcame "nightmarish" problems to bring rough videos of the war to the San Francisco Film Festival. "When I got there, it was like landing on Jupiter. Although I used to travel abroad before, this time I felt like I was leaving prison or a concentration camp where they were shooting. It was unbelievable to be in such a beautiful place with such a friendly ambiance with so many people who wanted to share the experience. At the same time, I was in complete shock. It was not easy to switch on and off. My family was still in Bosnia and I was worried. There was the horror of knowing they were killing people there and nobody was doing anything for us."

Six months after living in the "unbelievable" siege atmosphere, Kenovich thought it was important to make a dramatic film about it. Before the war, he had already directed two feature productions after studying cinema at Dennison University in Ohio. He and a colleague started to write the script for *The Perfect Circle* in October 1992 and began casting. "We looked at more than 4,500 kids from all possible nationalities. They loved the idea of being in a film. Even though it was dangerous to walk in the streets and they were cold, they liked anything that was a change. Some were from two different villages in the mountains where their houses had been burned, so they were refugees. For some kids, it was like a new beginning. Others thought if a film was being shot it would look like peace."

The idea that one boy in the film would be a deaf mute was a metaphor for the failure of the world to hear what was happening in Sarajevo. "I hate to say metaphor," Kenovich mentioned, "but the boys took it for granted. For them, it was absolutely natural that the younger boy was having problems with his hearing because a mortar landed close to his house. A lot of people were used to shock: some members of their family had been killed."

A couple of months after the peace agreement was signed in Dayton in 1995 ending the siege, Kenovich's crew began filming, although there was still some shooting. "They killed someone in a street car, not 100 meters from where we were working. For me, it was absolutely horrible to think that someone might be wounded by a mortar shell."

The production was helped considerably by Kenovich's new wife, Dana Rotberg, a Mexican director, who had seen his siege videos at the San Francisco festival. She said, "If you need anything, you can call me." He invited her to come to Sarajevo and then withdrew the invitation because it was too dangerous. She went anyway and wound up in the apartment Kenovich shared with four men who had lost their homes. There was no water and no electricity, but the men were very kind and supportive. When she wondered what she could do to be helpful, she thought of organizing a film festival because there had been no films in that city for years. She rounded up 170 videotapes of films from all over the world, eventually breaking her back carrying them onto a plane, and a crew of kids were kept busy making translations. "It was an amazing experience," she once said. "You could see snipers shooting and people lining up to see films." The festival lasted for three weeks, and 20,000 people had their first diversion in years.

Preliminary work on *The Perfect Circle*, trying to raise money and get equipment, was impossibly difficult with Kenovich commuting to Paris and communicating by phone with Rotberg, who had returned to Mexico to work on her next film. Although she was pregnant, she went back to Sarajevo. "I have no words to say what a significant part she played in getting the film made," Kenovich declared. When *The Perfect Circle* eventually premiered to great acclaim at the 1997 Cannes festival, "People saw this absolutely inexplicable situation and they finally understood what people went through and realized what had happened."

As for Rotberg, undaunted by her first experience of war, she learned a lesson in why making a film is "more than an ego trip. What I found out in Sarajevo changed my concept of why we make films. When I saw how these people really broke their bones and put their lives in danger in order just to prepare a little story, I re-evaluated why we are making images now. It comes from a real need to establish a dialogue between your reality and your people. It's not like a private artistic masturbation."

1998
Unpublished

Goran Paskaljevic

"In the Balkan mentality the people are very obsessive."

Thessaloniki, Greece

In 1998, Goran Paskaljevic was shooting a film in Belgrade that would throw a tragi-comic light on the "Balkan madness," but now that production, *The Powder Keg*, is seen as a grim prophecy of the current Yugoslav explosion.

Two years earlier, the director had joined the huge street demonstrations against the Serbian regime of Slobodan Milosovic, protests that went on for three months before they collapsed in futility amid the jockeying for power among opposition leaders.

"After that, I saw the biggest depression in my country," Paskaljevic said at the 1999 Thessaloniki Film Festival, where he was chairman of the jury. "It's a real depression when you don't know how you're going to survive tomorrow and what is going to happen in the future. I wanted to make a film about this tense atmosphere, so I put a couple of stories together which happen on one symbolic night when there is no exit. It was all shot at night because I think night has fallen on my country, which is in a kind of endless tunnel, without the slightest glimmer of light to suggest a possible way out."

Loosely based on a play by Dejan Dukovski, a Macedonian who co-wrote the script with Paskaljevic, the film juxtaposes the frenetic movements of a host of characters—a reckless car driver, an angry automobile owner, a crippled ex-boxer, a cabaret artist, a scary youth who terrorizes people on a hijacked bus, an irrepressible emigre hoping for reconciliation with his old sweetheart, a Bosnian Serb refugee family, a boxer who intimidates a desperate young woman in their train compartment—all ordinary people driven to extreme acts of violence. "In the Balkan mentality," Paskaljevic explained, "the people are very obsessive. When they hate, they hate; they love and hate at the same time."

Paskaljevic has lived in Paris with his French wife since 1994, but traveled frequently to Belgrade to visit his mother and two sons by his first marriage. In Paris, *The Powder Keg* opened on March 24, 1999, the day NATO began bombing Serbia. "I said then that the bombing campaign is an awful mistake because it will have the opposite effect. It will make Milosovic stronger and the Serbian people will become anti-Occidental and especially anti-American because it's clear that Madeleine Albright pushed it very much. Even the American generals and Clinton were not so sure," Paskaljevic told me. "These bombs are also killing any possible democracy in Serbia because it is definitely no time for opposition. Serbians are united now against aggression. There's a lot of hypocrisy in this very dirty and cowardly war and a lot of propaganda on both sides. The American generals say this war will have zero American victims. They don't want to risk the flyers' lives, but these pilots are flying very high, so they are less precise and make mistakes, killing innocent people like sixty Albanian refugees on the border. NATO says it's not a war against the Serbian people, but they are not just destroying military targets. We know who Milosovec is, but the West has to drop its vanity and stop the bombing before it becomes a real war. "

Ironically, Paskaljevic used to say, half in jest and half seriously, that his earlier film *Tango Argentino* was "the first Serbian war film." In fact, it was the gentle, humorous story of a ten-year-old boy's helpful friendship with a number of elderly, hopeless people, shot in 1991-92 during the chaotic breakup of Yugoslavia into separate countries: Croatia, Slovenia, Bosnia.

"I was so depressed by all this nationalism that I left. I decided to go somewhere, anywhere," he recalled. Greece was the closest alternative and he felt a certain kinship with the country because his paternal grandfather was a Greek named Paskalis and his father was born in Thessaloniki.

The family had moved to Serbia during the first World War and their name was changed to the more Serbian-sounding Paskaljevic. Goran was born in Belgrade in 1947. "I came from the very upper class in Serbia, if you can say that. My father was a journalist and novelist; my mother was a university history professor. They were leftists who opposed Tito's Communist regime. My maternal great-great-grandfather wrote the constitution when Serbia became independent in 1882. When the Communists came to power, they destroyed that upper class. They took everything from my family. If you were from my background, you were nothing. When I was very young, I was very ashamed of it because if you were not from the working class, you were not in a good position. I never mentioned I'm from that family because it's very famous and my name is different. Now I'm very proud of it."

As a youngster, he wanted to be a poet and at sixteen, a book of his poetry was published, but then he fell in love with film, particularly the simplicity and honesty in the work of Vittorio de Sica. Later, he attended FAMU, the famous film school in Prague where one of his favorite teachers was Milan Kundera, who, he is not embarrassed to say, "is an absolutely adorable man!"

Once, in lieu of an exam, Kundera asked Paskaljevic what he liked to read. "Dostoyevsky!" "Wonderful," Kundera responded, "let's talk about Dostoyevsky." They discussed the novelist for half an hour and Paskaljevic got an A for the "exam."

Now Paskaljevic gets high marks for being "devoid of dogma or preachiness." Pierre-Henri Deleau, former artistic director of the Cannes Festival's Directors' Fortnight, made that assessment on the occasion of a French retrospective of Paskaljevic's nine films in 1997. "Paskaljevic," he wrote, "first and foremost seeks to understand the human heart and the contradictions of his protagonists, plunged as they are into situations beyond their control (war, exile, poverty, social struggle) and without, a priori, criticizing or exonerating them. This warm-hearted humanism, with its mistrust of systems, be they political or religious, is rooted in an innate belief: that of the mystery of one person's quest for another's love . . . "

Paskaljevic is also a risk-taker. "Without risks," Paskaljevic says, "you can't do something special, something better." *The Powder Keg* was a risk. First of all, it wasn't easy to get financing in Serbia. He got an "insignificant" amount of money from Belgrade, some help from Greece and Euroimage, and "very good support" from his French producer, Antoine de Clermont-Tonnerre.

It was also a risk to shoot in Belgrade's strange atmosphere. "We had lived under an embargo for four years. It was supposed to hit the regime, but it hit the ordinary people so they became really poor under the power of the Mafia, which started to take over the black-market economy. The middle-class disappeared. I wasn't personally affected because I worked abroad. But you cannot be happy if just you survive and your family and friends are in trouble. I saw rudeness in Belgrade every day because people are living under tension and criminality is very high. Sometimes it's a crime just for nothing—because of depression—so we all become little powder kegs ready to explode.

"Ten years ago, in the first year of Milosovec's regime, we thought maybe he'd be the guy who would open Serbia to democracy. We didn't know what was going on. The Serbs in former Yugoslavia were somehow under pressure of others. If I say that, someone will call me a Serbian nationalist, but it's true."

When *The Powder Keg* was due to open in Belgrade, Paskaljevic couldn't use state-owned theaters. He couldn't get publicity because the town asked him to put up an enormous amount of money. "I took a risk again. I said, 'If the film is good, it will have good word-of-mouth,' and that happened. It opened in three independent cinemas in Belgrade and a record number of 220,000 saw it; and 300,000 more in the rest of Serbia and Montenegro. It beat all the records, and there were standing ovations."

Although the production had good reviews in Belgrade, *Politika*, the state paper, attacked him for his interviews. "They objected because I am openly against the regime. They try to make the atmosphere in Serbia that the guilt is from the Americans, the Germans, the Pope, but we have to face it and ask ourselves, 'Are we guilty also?' This question is repeated and repeated in my film."

The fifty-two-year-old director said that all of his generation is responsible for the events in his country. "I think that sometimes silence shows a lack of responsibility. You have to react to all non-democratic acts. We're responsible that we were pulled into nationalism, which is the worst thing that can happen to the nation."

April 29, 1999
The San Francisco Examiner

Danis Tanovic

That bomb "is a metaphor for any country."

Toronto

Black humor seemed to be the only way for Danis Tanovic to express the anger still haunting him about the wartime massacres he filmed in Bosnia and to show his contempt for the hypocritical "neutrality" of the United Nations that equated the aggressor and the victim.

"I had to be smart to make a film about my country that people are going to want to see," Tanovic said about his first feature, *No Man's Land*, which won the Best Screenplay award at the 2001 Cannes festival and became Bosnia's Oscar nomination for Best Foreign Film. *No Man's Land* has been receiving rave notices around the world as an extraordinary anti-war statement. It features a Bosnian and a Serb trapped in a trench with a wounded soldier lying on a spring-loaded bomb that would blast everyone to kingdom come if he moves. Waiting for an expert to defuse it while the U.N. command dithers is as absurd as waiting for Godot.

A native of Sarajevo, the capital of Bosnia, Tanovic enjoyed a typically carefree adolescence in the city, which was renowned for the harmonious co-existence of Croat Catholics, Eastern Orthodox Serbs, Jews, and Muslim Slavs. That tolerance was shattered in the spring of 1992 when the Serbian military forces of Yugoslav president Slobodan Milosevic fired the shots that began the four-year Bosnian war. Tanovic was twenty-two then, in his third year of film school. He spent the next two years on the front lines with a camera because he felt that a camera could be as important as a gun.

Interviewed at the 2001 Toronto International Film Festival, Tanovic insisted that the point of *No Man's Land* is to raise a voice against war and not to accuse those who did wrong. He also emphasized that the war in Bosnia was imposed by Serbia. "It was a tough job to take such a complex theme and make it simple and watchable. So I had to use humor to present certain things," Tanovic said. He doesn't know what gave him the idea for the film, cryptically saying only, "I lived through it." As for the bomb under the man, Tanovic's tightly coiled tension momentarily dissolves into a laugh: "That's my twisted mind."

But he's serious about that bomb. "For me, it's a metaphor for my country. Even the world today. We're lying on a mine. We all pretend that everything's fine, but if you look around, you only see a few places with democracy. The rest of the world is in misery, in war, in hunger—things which people shouldn't live in. So I just needed to say something. It's an absurdity that we're killing each other. What bothers me is that people think it's always happening somewhere else, in some uncivilized countries. People just forget history. Until the eleventh of September, people thought it couldn't happen to them. Everybody made war on everybody and still does and what's worse [if we don't change], it will continue."

The ongoing struggle to get people to understand what's happening makes Tanovic, a tall, husky, handsome thirty-two, feel like Sisyphus, forever condemned to roll a huge stone up a hill only to have it roll down again. "Every morning you wake up and the burden is there, so you push it. You leave it and it's there again. It's like Don Quixote-ism. You have to show repeatedly the mistakes of the human race so we can have a better place. If you don't do it, what are you living for?"

Although he is occasionally irritated by uninformed interviewers, he realizes how difficult it is for someone who has never experienced war or a concentration camp to empathize with those who have. "I don't think people would be ready to see what I was filming if I would present them the way they were happening: children being mutilated by mines or blown to pieces or women being raped. I made lots of documentaries that nobody wants to see. They show at some festivals, but you don't see them on any major channel at eight o'clock in the evening."

What also bothers him is lopsided reporting. For instance, "One day it was like hell in Sarajevo, 3,000 grenades exploded. On all the news shows, they only reported that ONE grenade landed on a U.N. barracks. And there were THOUSANDS of grenades. Is that news? It's ridiculous!"

Tanovic didn't say whether he absorbed any feelings about news coverage in his home. His father was a journalist and editor; his mother a professor of music. Although he wanted to be a filmmaker since he was a youngster, he first studied piano at a music school and later composed some of the music for *No Man's Land*. When a film and theater college opened in Sarajevo, Tanovic was one of 400 applicants for four places. Nobody passed the first tough exams. When he was told he lacked knowledge about theater, he spent the next few months studying drama and was accepted. "I think they thought I wanted to be a director so badly that I'd be one whether they accepted me or not. I was lucky."

Today he lives with his wife, a human resources worker, and their one-year-old daughter in Paris because there are more job opportunities there. It was France's Noe Productions, impressed with Tanovic's script, that got the ball rolling for the international production team that backed the film. However, Tanovic returns frequently to Bosnia where he is dismayed by the post-war conditions. "There is fifty-percent unemployment, and people are starving. A lot of the politicians are infantile or criminals doing things they shouldn't do. Nothing worked when a few tried to do something. We can't have a normal civil society until the economy functions." But, he likes to say, "I'm optimistic. It can get worse!" He enjoys the ironic touch: "Still, it's the best moment of human history. It's better than the Inquisition times!"

When he was filming every day on the front lines, he felt that the work helped him "to stay more like normal. I was sometimes doing things that when I think about them now, I think I was completely crazy, but in that moment I didn't care. A lot of people were working for money and I was filming for the sake of filming. I thought I could sell the images to TV for good money, but I was just giving them away. I thought if I made money out of my images, I would die because they were my friends being killed. I thought if I made money on their backs, I would not live. It's stupid, but you keep to something in this kind of situation. I didn't survive thanks to that but I survived thanks to whatever it is—luck. "

Although Milosovic has finally been imprisoned for war crimes, Tanovic is furious about two who have survived: the Serb leader Radovan Karadzic and Serbian army General Ratko Mladic. They have been charged with genocide and other crimes by the U.N. War Crimes Tribunal for the siege of Sarajevo and the massacre of some 7,000-8,000 Muslim men and boys and the torture of women and children in the U.N.'s so-called "safe haven" of Srebrenica in June 1995.

Tanovic doesn't think a comparison can be made between the Srebrenica massacre and the events of September 11, but he recalls that "we were all afraid of how America was going to react. Your president today is not my favorite, but I'm quite happy with how things are turning out. How it finishes is what counts most, but you have to get bin Laden. If you don't, the whole world is going to be in a very dangerous situation because any other maniac is going to think he can do the same thing. And Mladic and Karadzic should be brought to justice too."

It hasn't happened yet, Tanovic believes, "because nobody cares. If America wanted to, those two men would have been arrested a long time ago. After all, Bosnia is a small country and where they're hiding is smaller still. How would you feel if you didn't have an air force like you have and you didn't have the marines and army that you have and the 11th of September happened and it was Bosnia who could get bin Laden and didn't want to. How would you feel about that? Then you know how I feel when America doesn't want to get Karadzic and Mladic and all the others. Not doing anything is NOT neutrality. It's letting those people go."

October 2001
The San Francisco Examiner

14
Another Way of Life

Aktan Abdykalykov

"Windows to another world."

Thessaloniki, Greece

What can a boy think when he learns why he is called "Beshkempir?" The word means "five old women" in an ancient tradition of adoption carried on in Kyrgyzstan, a Central Asian nation, formerly a Soviet Republic. In the opening scene of *Beshkempir: The Adopted Son*, five wrinkled grannies, sitting on a colorful patchwork quilt, bless yet another baby boy with that name, setting the stage for a traumatic revelation in his adolescence.

Beshkempir was not the name given to Aktan Abdykalykov, the film's director, but there is more than a little similarity between him and the fictional protagonist of this remarkable debut feature, a realistic, subtly erotic, coming-of-age tale and the first independent film to come from Kyrgyzstan.

Born in 1957, Abdykalykov was thirteen when he learned that his mother and father were not his biological parents. "Why did it happen to me?" he recalls asking himself, a question that continued to haunt him. But he buried his emotions for years, until they emerged, artistically transformed, in the Beshkempir character's hurt confusion when his friends taunt him for being a foundling.

Whatever feelings of rejection may have lingered in Abdykalykov, they were not in evidence when two American journalists ecountered him by chance along a sidewalk one rainy night at the Thessaloniki Film Festival. Hearing one of them speak Russian, the director grinned, his face alight with friendliness.

Later, he explained in Russian that it was customary in his country for parents of a large family to offer a baby boy to an infertile couple. (Baby girls are considered un-reliable.) In a time-honored ritual, five old women pass around the infant and name him Beshkempir. Abdykalykov's birth mother was a geography teacher who already had nine children and so she gave away her eight-month-old son to her brother. Ab-dykalykov's biological and adoptive fathers were chairmen of the collective farms in their respective villages.

Like the Beshkempir character, the director had a carefree childhood with no bound-aries between him and his pals. He studied the required Russian language in school and roughhoused with other boys in the dusty primitive village of Kuntu, where he still lives. Everyone told him he was fated to be an artist, and he would "wish on a fall-ing star," he said, that it would become true.

His life changed in 1974, when he was drafted into the Soviet Army at seventeen. When it was time for him to fill out his induction papers, his adoptive parents were forced to show him his birth certificate, and that's when he finally learned the truth. Only then did he meet his biological mother, but he has had little contact with her since.

The army sent him to East Germany, where for a year he was confined to a huge base doing routine chores and drawing posters with slogans like "Glory to the Soviet Army." He laughs at the memory. "At seventeen," he remarked, "I was virtually un-conscious."

Still eager to become an artist, he entered a four-year program at the Frunze art school in the Kyrgyz capital now known as Bishkek. In his fourth year, he met his future wife, Aichurok, who was studying medicine and is now a practicing nurse. They have three children: two daughters—Mirgul, nineteen, and Nurzat, twelve—and seven-teen-year-old Mirlan, who is the star of his father's film. The children did not known that their father had been adopted until they read about it in a newspaper. "Why did you give that interview?" Mirlan asked, afraid it would hurt the feelings of his father's adoptive mother.

As a youngster, Abdykalykov enjoyed the Russian and Indian movies shown at the little theater in his village. (In one scene in *Beshkempir*, villagers watch in wonder as a movie, showing a gaudy Indian song-and-dance number, is projected onto an outdoor screen.) His favorite films were dubbed versions of *Spartacus* and *Tarzan*. He thought of films as "windows to another world," he said, but he didn't dream of becoming a director until he began working as a set designer at the Frunze studio.

Subsidized by the Soviet Union, the studio had a long tradition of filmmaking, turning out about four productions a year, including Larissa Shepitko's *Heat* and Andrei Konchalovsky's *First Teacher*. As Abdykaykov observed other directors, he was convinced he could do a better job. Three times he traveled to Moscow and applied for classes in direction at the prestigious VGIK film school. Three times he was rejected.

"Even though I was a man," he recalled, "I felt like a kid each time I was turned down. There were student quotas for all the Soviet republics, but those accepted were the children of influential parents. I turned those negative experiences into something positive and beneficial. I think they gave me a creative personality."

In 1990, he made a seventeen-minute film, *Dog Season, Black and White*, a parable of good and evil about a dog's fate. He followed that, in 1993, with a short feature, *The Swing*, a semi-autobiographical tale about the discovery of the world by an eleven-year-old boy who is infatuated with an older girl. It won the Locarno International Film Festival's Gold Leopard prize for short films and brought him to the attention of Noe, the French firm that had produced Milcho Manchevski's prize-winning *Before the Rain* and Idrissa Ouedraogo's *Africa, My Africa*.

Beshkempir: The Adopted Son, produced for $500,000 by Noe and Kyrgyzfilm, was made in the village of Bar-Bulak, 100 miles from the capital, using nonprofessional actors and mostly black-and-white film stock. Interludes of color represent the director's memories.

The film, he said, is constructed like a Kyrgyz patchwork cover: "Each piece of fabric represents the memory of someone who has died. When people die, the Kyrgyz custom is to distribute pieces of patchwork to those who were close to them. The patchwork represents their memory and their lineage. My film attempts to weave the woof and warp of the collective memory of the Kyrgyz people."

January 1999
The New York Times

Zacharias Kunuk

PHOTO BY JUDY STONE.

Putting a face on "Invisible" people.

Toronto

Atanarjuat (The Fast Runner) is an ancient Inuit legend, but Zacharias Kunuk, the director who brought that oral tale to worldwide attention in the first Inuit film, is now becoming a legend in his own time. Winner of the 2001 Cannes Festival's Camera d'Or for best first feature, *Atanarjuat* was hailed as a masterpiece.

Kunuk's father, who still hunts seals and carabou in the far north, wanted Zach to follow him in that tradition, but somewhere along the line the kid became mesmerized by John Wayne and American Cowboy-and-Indian movies. Later, seeing Philip Kaufman's *White Dawn*, set in the Arctic with some Inuit actors, made him want to do his own version of the life he knows. He still goes out hunting whenever he gets the chance, but now he's more likely to be casting about for the next screen project.

At the 2001 Toronto International Film Festival, Kunuk, forty-four, talked about his early days in Igloolik, a small island in the north Baffin region of the Canadian Arctic. He looks severe but he showed the same glints of humor that sparkle through this story of love, jealousy, murder, revenge, and a naked flight over the spring sea ice. And there is muted pride in his voice as he told how and why the people of Igloolik resisted the government's instillation of television, although it eventually led to the production of this first feature film.

Kunuk, the fourth eldest in a family of twelve, always wanted to express what he had learned about Inuit tradition, whether it was by listening to his father's stories of the day's hunt or watching his father cut moss into bricks for a house he built on Baffin island. Then when he was nine, a new government decree put him on a boat to Igloolik to be taught English. "It was very hard to learn English," he said with an accent that still echoed that difficulty. "I had to learn how to write my name from the blackboard. And we had books like *See Sally Run*. There were no books for children that related to the Inuit experience, but they're starting to have them now. I was interested in art and began carving. If I was lucky and sold my carving, we had twenty-five cents to buy a ticket for the movies. Math was one of my favorite subjects, but I was terrible in spelling."

In 1975 and again in 1979 the community voted against bringing in TV because there were no Canadian Broadcasting Corporation programs in their Inuktitut language. But Kunuk couldn't wait for the introduction of television. By 1981, he was a famous carver and sold three sculptures in Montreal in order to buy a Betamax video camera and begin experimenting with his own work. Finally in 1982, an Inuit Broadcasting Corporation was formed with Paul Apak Angilirq, one of the first Inuit producers. He hired Kunuk who worked there for eight years on all aspects of production, including a ground-breaking, thirteen-part, half-hour series on Inuit life, and was finally promoted to station manager.

Although Kunuk started winning awards for best programs and best series, "I never got patted on the back," he said with a trace of bitterness. "I never got recognition or help, so I just quit."

In 1990, Kunuk became president and co-founder with Apak of Igloolik Isuma Productions, Canada's first Inuit independent production company. They were joined by founding shareholders Pauloosie Qulitalik (who acts in *The Fast Runner*) and Norman Cohn, the only non-Inuit, who was director of photography. It was Apak who began work on *The Fast Runner* by interviewing and recording eight elders telling their own versions of the oral legend as it had been passed on to them. Then he led Isuma's team of five writers to combine these into a dramatic Inuktitut screenplay with an English version that became the basis for the subtitles. Sadly, Apak died of cancer before the production was finished.

438

It took six months to shoot the $1.3-million film with performers who had experience acting on the TV shows. When it was completed, Kunuk said, "We showed it for three nights in the largest auditiorium, a gym that held 500 people, and some came for all the screenings. The first time I was so afraid they wouldn't like it, but at the end everybody was clapping and shaking our hands. Then I knew we did our job."

That response was just as rewarding to Cohn, who shot the spectacularly beautiful production in video (which was later transferred to film). A native New Yorker who has lived in Igloolik for a large part of the last ten years, he calls himself an "itinerant video artist." He was living near New Haven, Connecticut. and successfully doing "very visual narrative work about people who were normally invisible" when a friend suggested that he come to Prince Edward Island in Canada and help him build a house. Later, meeting Kunuk and Apak, and seeing their videos, he began to work with them, regarding it as another challenge to help put a face on a people who have been largely invisible to the rest of the world.

If he expresses qualities rooted in a Jewish humanistic tradition, he said he doesn't know "how that articulates or informs my work." He emphatically has no "interest or respect for organized religion of any kind because I think all the world's worst practices have been carried out in the name of fanatical philosophies, almost all of which are extremely exclusive and have been used to justify doing the most terrible things to other people on earth."

He says simply that he believes his work "is in the service of putting more—rather than less—justice into the Canadian political system, into the world of the historical relationship between a whole universe of exploited and manipulated peoples who have had a very raw deal. So you can say I work for the underdog. Maybe that's a Jewish quality. It's certainly not a universal Jewish quality. Our film warns against extreme chauvinism. It articulates as clearly as possible the price of embracing vengeance. The logical conclusion of vengeance is that we're all gonna die. Maybe people who see that message in an Inuit context don't think it applies to them, but I think one of the ways our film is having an extraordinary impact is that a significant percentage of every audience thinks that the message of our film, which is so blatantly articulated by the old lady at the end, DOES apply to everybody. She banishes the troublemakers who had been hell-bent on vengeance."

September 2001
The San Francisco Examiner

Patrice Chereau

"Most films dealing with homosexuality are too positive, too romantic, too sentimental."

San Francisco

Patrice Chereau, one of Europe's most controversial and innovative stage and opera directors, is very comfortable with his homosexuality, but he believes that most films dealing with that subject are "too positive, too romantic, too sentimental."

Before he began writing *L'Homme Blessé* (*The Wounded Man*), the story of a teenaged boy who falls in love with an older man, a thief, Chereau wondered if it was even possible to make an honest film about homosexuals.

He never expected the anger the film provoked among Parisian homosexuals. "Some homosexuals who saw the film in Paris said, 'It's so negative, so hard and shows so many difficulties. Stop it! We're happy to be homosexuals,'" Chereau recalled at the

439

Mill Valley Film Festival, where the production had its U.S. premiere in 1984. "I answered, 'I'm happy too, but that's not the problem.'"

Chereau, a charming, relaxed, and humorous man of forty—best known for his controversial 1976 Bayreuth production of Wagner's *Ring of the Niebelungen*—spoke about *L'Homme Blessé*, his first major feature, with unusual candor.

Most films about homosexuals, Chereau said, "never tell the truth and never present the real reactions and never show the real relationships between men." The only exceptions, he feels, are Fassbinder's *Fox and His Friends* and Genet's short autobiographical, *Un Chant d'Amour*, about the fantasies of imprisoned men.

"Sometimes it's so stupid what people say in films about homosexuals: 'Beautiful love between two beautiful men, how it's beautiful to be homosexual.' It's so stupid," he repeated, hitting his hand against his forehead in irritation. "It's like in Soviet films on communism: 'Our reality is so beautiful.' It's propaganda. When homosexuals say, 'It's *better* to be homosexual,' I don't support this attitude."

Chereau was surprised to discover that the treatment of homosexuality on film still makes people fearful. "I thought I would have a larger audience for this film. The best audiences in France are the women. They don't feel threatened. The men and the homosexuals do. Although French homosexuals are more open now, the real problems of daily life and passion are still there. We can be more open, but . . . "

There was a long silence as Chereau struggled to explain his feelings. "I know what I mean but I don't know if it's right. I don't know why I don't like homosexuals. It is a very personal question. I'm not answering quickly because I'm asking myself if I can give a good answer. Probably I'm a *real* homosexual because I always fall in love with people who are *real* men. I think it's difficult to be a homosexual because they sometimes go outside the real world. I think the solution is *not* to make groups of homosexuals or to meet only homosexuals in life. It would be terrible not to meet women or other men. Nightclubs with only homosexuals—I hate that."

Although *L'Homme Blessé* is set in a provincial city, Chereau shot at the Gare du Nord, a Parisian railroad station that is a homosexual hangout. One scene there implies a brutal sado-masochistic episode.

"I thought, when you do a film about this subject, you have to show everything. The station is like that. *Exactement la verité*. People said, 'It's too bad. It's too hard. It's ugly,' and they are the same ones who go to the Gare du Nord and do the same things. They don't want you to show the reality. Sometimes people say to me, 'It's so terrible. The young man is so unhappy,' and I say, 'It's exactly the contrary. He's much more happy than if he had stayed with his family. What he's experiencing is exactly what he wants.'"

Chereau said that he and his script writer, Herve Guibert, also a homosexual, discovered that the only way they could tell this story was if nothing overtly sexual happened between Henri, the boy, and Jean, the older man. "It was a strange discovery. It's impossible to show a fully realized love and, for this reason, it's a film about frustration. Jean never gives himself and it's always a disaster to fall in love with someone who never really gets involved. Jean loves the younger man, but he feels the need to dirty him too in a way."

Originally, Chereau wanted to adapt Genet's *Diary of a Thief* for the screen. "After a few months, I discovered it was impossible. We can take influences of Genet but not the book. We take just the point of departure—a young man falling in love with someone older, and the man is always disappearing. With good books like Genet's *Querelle*, it's impossible to do good films."

When Fassbinder was shooting *Querelle*, Chereau spent the last three days on the set. "I have great admiration for Fassbinder," Chereau said. "He made terrific things, but not this one. For me, it was crazy to be there because he works so fast. Fassbinder's discussion with his mother in *Germany in Autumn* was the most intelligent thing I ever heard on terrorism, but we had a strange relationship. He was a good friend of a singer at Bayreuth. The singer was terrible. A real fascist, full of admiration for Hitler and Speer. He wore a ring with a swastika on it and always forced me to look at it. When Fassbinder came to see the *Ring* cycle, I was very angry against the singer and told him. Fassbinder was very cold to me."

Chereau said he didn't have to have lived during the Nazi period to have opinions on the history of the time. "Many people in France collaborated with Hitler. Not all. But only a small part of the population was fighting against the Germans. In a sense, we were with the Germans. My grandfather was very near to the Germans. My brother and I didn't learn English in school in 1950; we learned German because my grandfather was a Germanophile. I never knew what the situation was during the war with my father, who was an artist. I know that when he was young, he was extremely right-wing."

In his late teens, Chereau began his work in the theater, first as a set designer. He says his major influences have been Brecht, Luchino Visconti, and Roger Planchon. (He and Planchon are co-directors of the prestigious Theatre National Populaire.) Chereau has directed more than forty plays in Paris, including two "very beautiful" twelfth-century Chinese plays: *The Man Who Stole Women* and *Snow in the Midst of Winter*.

Although Chereau calls *L'Homme Blessé* his first film, he has actually directed two others: *The Flesh of the Orchid*—based on a James Hadley Chase book, starring Simone Signoret and Charlotte Rampling—and *Judith Therpauvre*, featuring Signoret. But he is very critical of both works. He took on the offer to act in Andrzej Wajda's *Danton* just to remind himself of "practical things and how bad a French crew is on the set."

He thought it was difficult for Wajda, a Pole, to attempt to direct in France. "In Paris, he was an international product of the producers, Gaumont—without soul. It's not a very good film. We don't learn anything in it and I'm terrible in it. I wanted to be close to Gerard Depardieu and observe him. Although he's not very good in the film, as an actor he's fantastic. He can do everything, but the director has to be direct. In *Danton* he did some fantastic things, but it was like a game. He throws something and the director must throw it back, but Wajda says, 'It's okay, it's very good.'"

Every time Chereau plans a film he screens John Huston's movies. "Before *L'Homme Blessé*, I made a screening of *Fat City*. It was fantastic. *Wise Blood* was fantastic. Huston seems to be in the right relationship to reality. Sometimes it's so perfect and so simple. He doesn't pretend to be a *creator*. He *is* a filmmaker."

Now Chereau would like to make a film on the German occupation of France. Although he's continuing with his theater work, he's not too interested in doing more opera. "It's dead. You just make works from the eighteenth and nineteenth centuries. The kind of pleasure you have in making opera is the same you would derive from making dead things live again. I think it's impossible to make an opera on film. It's almost stupid. I think it's more important for me to make a good film.

"I want to make a film about the intellectuals like Celine who collaborated with the Germans. It will be based on the story of an actor who appeared in several Renoir films and then ran away to Argentina in 1945 when the war ended. He's dead now. It will be set in this beautiful eighteenth-century castle at Sigmaringen where Petain and other collaborators stayed in the last days of the war. I think we French have never to forget that we were the only population in Europe to have had the most collaboration with the Germans."

May 1981
San Francisco Chronicle

Alexander Payne

A human link among the losers.

San Francisco

There's a mysterious, indefinable human link among the losers in Alexander Payne's remarkable four films: the paint-sniffing, pregnancy-prone drifter in *Citizen Ruth*, the driven high-school cutie who goes for broke to win in *Election*, the cynical Midwestern widower in *About Schmidt*, and now in *Sideways*, the frustrated, divorced writer and his unlikely pal, an unsuccessful actor, determined to get laid before settling into marriage.

It's not easy to get a handle on the Omaha-bred writer/director's uncanny ability to draw out their unpredictable complexities, while slyly unmasking pretension and hypocrisy in a way that's almost unknown in today's Hollywood.

Whatever that magic touch is, *The New York Times* noted, "The emergence of Mr. Payne into the front ranks of American filmmakers isn't just cause for celebration, it's a reason for hope."

In *Sideways*, Payne leaves Nebraska for the grape-growing vistas of California, but what attracted him to Rex Pickett's novel was typical. "I was impressed by the humanity of the characters, the banality of the situation, the melancholy of the story, the comedic set pieces, and the wine. The characters are so human and so sad. Each is at a delicate, painful time in their lives." Perhaps what is most extraordinary is the delicate and painful way Payne turns a conversation on the appeal of wine between Miles, the sad-sack writer, and Maya, a divorced waitress, into a moment that is more erotic than many overtly sexual scenes in mainstream movies.

What is immediately appealing about Payne, forty-three, is his rare gentlemanly quality—and his boyish enthusiasm when he says, "I'm just so happy, so grateful to have a career." He introduces himself quickly as "a Greek-American from Omaha, educated by Jesuits. Both grandfathers and my father were restaurant owners, which, as you know, is what Greeks do in this country," Payne broke away from that tradition by getting a B.A. in history and Spanish literature from Stanford University and an M.F.A. in filmmaking from UCLA.

Despite all the wine talk in *Sideways*, Payne does not consider himself a connoisseur, assessing the merits of pinot versus merlot, but he does allow that he likes the formidable retsina, which he says is written into his Greek DNA. During four years visiting a girlfriend in Italy, he learned "quite a bit" about Italian cooking, but would like to attend cooking school to improve his way with pasta, gnocci, minestrone, et al. Now, he "largely" does the cooking at the Los Angeles home he shares with the Canadian/ Korean actress Sandra Oh, his wife of two years. In *Sideways*, she plays the biker who wields a mean helmet at her duplicitous boyfriend, the actor, when she hauls off and cries, "But you said you loved me!"

Returning to the subject of his education, Payne went to a Jesuit high school by accident, after a tornado destroyed his public school. "My high school experience was very different from the sprawling co-ed public school that you see in *Election*. I'm very grateful to the Jesuits because I was educated with rigor and discipline. It wasn't a school about bringing everyone up to average. It was about helping and encouraging you to excel. Excellence is often not good enough."

His parents emphasized the importance of education too, but they also gave him an education in movies. Omaha was not an alien location for offbeat and foreign films. By the age of fourteen, he had seen *Chinatown*, *The Garden of the Finzi-Continis*, and *The Night Porter*. His favorite directors became Kurosawa, Buñuel, Sergio Leone, Anthony Mann, and "currently I adore Zhang Yimou, a master." And he thinks that the Iranians have been making the best films consistently in the last few years. They excel in the human films he prefers to fantasy.

"On a trivial note, I ended up being the editor of the high-school yearbook, and it taught me about seeing a long project through over a year, which is like making a film, having the patience to have a large idea of what it can be and to manage the day-by-day details." He thought of being a journalist, and excitedly refers to a *New York Times* article on blogging. "Blogging on the one hand and satire on the other—like Jon Stewart's—have moved in to fill the gap left by the mainstream press.

"I think it's important for filmmakers now to be thinking about the difficult times in which we're living. There's a lot going on politically and culturally that's bad. It's pretty strange that we have a culture that becomes complicit with the lies of the government. I think it's interesting culturally that digital technology essentially makes viewers complicit with the lies of digital technology in film. We've come to accept images which lie and we're complicit in it. I think a larger number of films now should be more real in terms of real issues and real emotion. We need to bring films back to reality. Not all films, but a larger number of films which may wish to function as a mirror to our society. "

Despite his criticism of digital technology, Payne is excited about its prospect for the future. "Just as a few hundred years ago, only monks knew how to read and write, so now with filmmaking. The means of production are so readily accessible that anyone can make a film. We may not be alive to see that seven-year-old girl from Pittsburgh who picks up her daddy's camera and starts shooting images and goes to her computer and puts them together in a way that is suddenly brand new. It's gotta happen. If Mozart could begin playing at age five, it's gotta happen in other artistic media as well."

2004

The Oakland Tribune

Postscript: So how does he feel after an avalanche of prizes for *Sideways* and the one he liked best: chosen by the Directors Guild as Best Director? "I never anticipated the success the film would eventually have, and I feel as if I've awakened from a dream—or a nightmare. When *Election* was nominated for an Oscar five years ago, my dad said, 'Don't let it go to your head.' I said, 'I'd like it to go to *other* people's heads.' Producers and studios latch on to these awards, but I'm still the same."

Don McKellar

PHOTO BY JUDY STONE.

"*Personally, I don't think the world is going to end.*"

San Francisco

When Don McKellar was a kid—before he became Canada's triple-threat talent—he had recurrent nightmares about the end of the world. He would wake up, sick and feverish, and run out into Toronto's streets and tell everyone the Big Bang was coming.

"I remember my parents sitting on my bed and looking at me as if I were insane. They tried to get me to talk myself out of it," he recalled when he was in San Francisco to promote—of all things!—*Last Night*. The film that he wrote, directed, and stars in just happens to be a comedy (of sorts) about the last six hours in the life of several Toronto residents.

Those early nightmares must have burrowed deep in McKellar's subconscious because the producers at Rhombus Media asked him to do a film about the coming of the millennium. McKellar had already worked with Rhombus on two films he wrote, with Francois Girard, *Thirty Two Short Films about Glenn Gould* and *The Red Violin*, and had bit parts in both productions. This time, the producers wanted him to make his debut as a feature director.

McKellar decided to do a takeoff on the end of the twentieth century. With his usual quirky, anti-Hollywood humor and deadpan panning of his fellow Canadians, he focused on the way a few folks choose to spend their last night on earth. Patrick (McKellar) wants to be left alone, but he reluctantly attends his mom's Christmas dinner (though it's not the season to be jolly.) Craig (Callum Keith Rennie) wants to have sex of every ethnic kind, including with his old French teacher (Geneviève Bujold). Utility company executive Duncan (David Cronenberg) efficiently reminds every household that the gas will be with them until the very end. Canadian/Korean Sandra (Sandra Oh) wants desperately to get home to her husband, but finds a tiny bit of solace with Patrick.

Asked if he takes *Last Night* seriously, McKellar gulped. "Oh, my God. My strategy is *shit* . . . that is, I'm skeptical. I'm resistant to emotional manipulation, and I'm resistant to aggressive manipulation—like in every movie I see on an airplane. My strategy is to trick people into a genuine reaction of some kind, responding to a genuine moment with irony or humor. The film starts ironically and maybe half-way through, people think, 'Oh, my God, he's actually going to end the world.'

"I feel I put a lot of myself into the movie, and I take myself seriously to some degree. Not totally, but sometimes I surprise myself with my own seriousness. My film is not a prophecy. Personally, I don't think the world is going to end. I don't take it that seriously—I think that's what allows this thing to resonate because if I really thought the world was going to end, I would have made a more depressing film."

McKellar said he simply wanted to show the reactions of ordinary people generally overlooked in Hollywood apocalyptic blockbusters. When the production had its world premiere in the 1998 Directors' Fortnight section at the Cannes Film Festival, critics dubbed it the "anti-Armageddon" entry. It also won the Prix de la Jeunesse, the young filmmaker prize once awarded to Martin Scorsese and Spike Lee. In Canada, it won the Best Canadian First Feature at the Toronto International Film Festival and received twelve nominations for the 1998 Genie awards, including best picture, best director, and best screenplay.

Growing up in Canada, McKellar, thirty-five, said, "The idea of being a filmmaker was pretty inconceivable. David Cronenberg was the only [Canadian] director I knew at the time who built a career, but his films were so idiosyncratic. I didn't want to be Cronenberg. I loved his films, but I never thought 'that's me.' He's so calm, so articulate, and has such a great sense of humor. His early film *Shivers* is stunning to me now. He summed up a certain ugly side of Canada. He's like the godfather of English Canadian films."

Cronenberg was on the 1989 jury that gave the Best Canadian Film award to *Road-killer*, Bruce McDonald's offbeat road movie, written by McKellar, who stars as a shy serial killer. The next year, McKellar co-wrote McDonald's *Highway 61* and played the lead role of a small-town barber who is persuaded by an attractive stranger to drive a drug-filled corpse from Thunder Bay to New Orleans. With growing confidence, McKellar wrote and directed a short film, *Blue*, in which Cronenberg plays the lead—a carpet-factory worker who is a porno addict. After completing *Last Night*, McKellar played an "anti-existential Russian double agent" in Cronenberg's *eXistenZ*, a "virtual reality espionage game." "It allowed me to have an elusive accent," McKellar said with a grin.

As a teenager in a "happy, upper-middle-class family," McKellar's most perverse act of rebellion came through music. His father, a lawyer who founded several theater companies, and his mother, who taught in a hospital for crippled children, were eager for him to be exposed to theater. Since his parents and his peers alike were fans of pop music, McKellar would blast from his turntable twelve-tone pieces by Arnold Schoenberg and Gyorgy Ligeti. And Lukas Foss's *Baroque Variations*, which end with really difficult percussive sounds that might alarm anyone. "I would watch for their reactions," he said, "and would use that to prove my own tortured-artist proclivities." He also enjoyed "free jazz" and "the more atonal work" of Ornette Coleman and the latter Miles Davis.

While indulging that side of his personality, McKellar managed to get into trouble as the high-school clown and smart-aleck. He and his friends started a theater company and he began acting. The theater remained his primary preoccupation at the University of Toronto until he dropped out in his fourth year, landing a gig acting in a critically acclaimed TV "anti-sitcom" called *Twitch City*, which he called an intellectual comedy about a gang of Generation X slackers. More recently, he took on musical comedy: he helped write the book and will also act in *The Drowsy Chaperone*.

What McKellar didn't realize when he began his film career was that cinema would be a great way to see the world. In preparing *The Red Violin*, he got to visit all the places where the violin in the story popped up through history: Shanghai, Vienna, Oxford, and Cremona, Italy. As he prepared to set off on a world tour with *Last Night*, he was grateful that his stop in Israel would not take place in Jerusalem at the end of December. With a shudder, he said, "I wouldn't want to be there when all those end-of-the-world nuts show up."

November 18, 1999
The San Franciso Examiner

Patrice Leconte

PHOTO BY JUDY STONE.

Life's quixotic turns.

Paris

From the moment one enters Patrice Leconte's breezy sixth-floor office on Boulevard Montparnasse and sees hundreds of the director's hand-painted pebbles scattered on the floor, something special seems in the air. There's already a magical play of humor on the filmmaker's face, so it came as no surprise later to hear him say that he finds someone without humor "terrifying, a Martian."

Leconte has an elfin-like appearance, but there is nothing funny or comic about that look, nor about his films, which resonate with a warm, subtle appreciation of life's quixotic turns. These qualities are nowhere more evident than in his last two productions, *Intimate Strangers* and *Man on the Train*, its predecessor.

In *Intimate Strangers*, a troubled woman (Sandrine Bonnaire) enters a door to what she thinks is a psychiatrist's office, but it turns out to be that of a tax attorney (Fabrice Luchini). Before the mistake is discovered, she continues to tell all about the sexual problems in her marriage to the fascinated, introspective accountant, who is in no rush

450

to correct the mistaken identity. In *Man on the Train*, two aging characters—a retired teacher (Jean Rochefort) and a bank-robber (Johnny Hallyday)—also keep talking to each other after the teacher offers the stranded robber hospitality in his home and they discover a wistful regard for the other's lifestyle.

"My biggest fear," Leconte confesses in his newly learned English, "is to bore people. If I'm bored, the audience is bored. If I am entertained, the audience is entertained, and I'm happy. I work seriously, but I never take myself seriously. I've always tried to be lighthearted, but it's very difficult to stay lighthearted because film costs so much money and you have to think about the public's reactions and sometimes it's very difficult to deal with it."

Although he doesn't see a common thread in the last two productions or in *Monsieur Hire*, *Ridicule*, *The Widow of St. Pierre*, and *The Hairdresser's Husband*, he says his films always start with daily existence, daily living. "But then I try to change it subtly, to make it maybe more strange, to make it different, to make it less quotidian, less banal. What I try to do is to open the audience's eyes to the world as I perceive it. My inspiration is always reality. And I've often invented stories that take place in a world apart."

The psychiatrist's office in *Intimate Strangers* is totally invented. "I don't know the world of psychiatry," he says, laughing off the interviewer's question. "My auto-analysis is to make movies. It's better because it's less expensive." Sandrine—whom he adores—also has never been to an analyst, but "Fabrice has gone for twenty years and talked about it all the time. Mainly to see that things were in the right place on the set. He never talked about why he went because you don't know exactly why yourself."

The key to his own dreams might be found on the pebbles he paints while he's musing at bedtime—he himself carefully dusts them by day, but he's not about to tell all to inquisitive interviewers. The son of two physicians, he grew up in the provincial city of Toures and has been married for an "unbelievable" thirty-three years, despite "storms and hurricanes," to the same wife. She is still an "intimate stranger," he says, "because if a woman doesn't have mystery for me, what's the fun of continuing to live with her?"

He did admit to being nervous when he showed the film at a private screening before it opened. A psychiatrist in the audience told Leconte he was very happy with the movie. He said, "'You don't know anything about psychology, but you understood everything!'"

The story developed from a twenty-page proposal from Jerome Tonnerre, a well-known scriptwriter, about a woman entering a wrong door. "He told me, 'Read it, Patrice, and if you like we can invent the rest together, and it's a good way to follow our imagination to see if it's a comedy—just to open a wrong door. It's maybe vaudeville or it could be a very dark movie. Who knows? Or it could be a sentimental thriller mocking analysis.'"

If *Intimate Strangers* needs definition, Leconte now defines it as a "sentimental thriller because it contains mystery, uncertainty, fear, doubt, and suspense like any thriller—yet all of these are built around emotions more than actions. I never dared to call it a love story at first because it is more perverted, more atypical than what you would expect from that. But I enjoy defying expectations."

He thought it was very funny that when shooting began and Bonnaire had to talk about the sexual problems in her character's life, she had just been married for one week to her second husband, a successful French scriptwriter. Earlier, she had been married to William Hurt, with whom she had a daughter, now fourteen. "She is so happy with her new husband," Leconte said, "that although she's speaking about problems in the movie, you can see a perfect light in her eyes. And with Sandrine when I operate the camera myself, there's a huge emotion. When she smiles, I love her!!! When you see the light on her, she's so photogenic. You never see her work—it's so simple, so natural."

They had worked together before in *Monsieur Hire*, in which Bonnaire was the object of a peeping Tom. Although it was Leconte's ninth film, it was his first international success. He is rhapsodic about Bonnaire: "She's an extraordinary human being, and she has a sensibility and talent that I've rarely seen elsewhere. She also has a quality that is worth its weight in gold because she knows how to laugh!"

Intimate Strangers is a hit in France, but it was no laughing matter when he ran into problems with *Man on a Train* because it co-starred Johnny Hallyday in a serious role. Although Hallyday is famous as a rock star, audiences were reluctant to see him play a part that was contrary to his image. Actually, Leconte himself once had doubts about people moving outside their milieu until an encounter in Los Angeles when *Ridicule* had an Oscar nomination.

"Someone came to me and said, 'I know a person who loved *Ridicule* and would love to shake your hand.' I said, 'Do I know him?' and he said, 'Maybe, you'll see.' And it was Mick Jagger! And it really surprised me, but actually, maybe I'm the idiot because of course people move outside their milieu, but it's always surprising when someone likes your work. And that isn't false modesty."

So he wasn't totally surprised several years ago. When Hallyday was presenting a special tribute to Jean-Luc Godard at a Cesar ceremony, he met Leconte backstage after the program and said, "One day I would like to be filmed by you."

After Leconte cast the two men, they both had stage fright. "Johnny felt that maybe he wasn't up to the part, and Rochefort asked himself, 'Can I act with a rock star?' But I was very lucky because I was able to shoot the film in chronological order. If you watch the film closely at the beginning, you notice that maybe they're not exactly on the same wavelength, but then as the film continues, there's a harmony that comes into play."

452

Nevertheless, Parisians resisted going to the film, but those who did see it changed their minds about Hallyday in a serious role.

And if Hallyday defeated expectations, Leconte will more than confound expectations when his "very personal" wordless film *Dogora* opens in France. He shot most of it himself in Cambodia, and he hopes that the final production—with only pictures, music, and noise—will have an appeal that is "humanist, but also militant." Two years ago, during a holiday visit to his brother who works in Cambodia, he felt extremes of emotion he never knew before when he observed desperately poor men, women, and children, some with amputated limbs, going about their lives with incredible joyousness. He felt that after so many years at war, they at last knew peace and hope. He watched the children scrambling in the garbage dumps at night and filmed them singing in an invented language to the music of Etienne Perruchon's oratorio "Dogora." To capture this experience, Leconte was inspired by *Koyaanisqatsi*, the wordless, musically unrelenting 1983 movie by the American director Godfrey Reggio, who used a Hopi word for the title, meaning "life out of balance." In contrast, Leconte later learned, *Dogora* is actually a Polish word meaning "towards the light," and that seemed apropos indeed for the childen's lively struggle for existence.

August 17, 2004
Toronto Globe and Mail

ERIC VALLI AND THILEN LHONDUP (*HIMALAYA*).

Humanity, quiet, dignity, tolerance.

Toronto

Eric Valli, who has the soul of a nomad, left his work as a cabinet maker in Dijon, France, in 1974 for a five-week climb in the Himalaya—and returned to live in Nepal for twenty-five years. Falling in love with the "incredible" people he came to know, their "humanity, quiet dignity, and tolerance," he had long dreamed of making a film about their hazardous journeys across the dangerous snow peaks to exchange salt from the high plateaus of northern Tibet for grain in the temperate southern lowlands of Nepal. He went on those five-week treks with the salt caravans fifteen times, taking photographs for *National Geographic* and writing books about the virtually unknown Dolpo, the northwestern region of Nepal, long off-limits to foreigners. Those particular Nepalese people retain their Tibetan cultural traditions.

Finally, after four years, Valli finished his first feature film, the $7-million *Himalaya (Abode of Snow)*. The Nepalese-French co-production was one of the five Oscar nominees for Best Foreign Film in 1999. Valli's friend, Thilen Lhondup, inspired by Kurosawa's *Seven Samurai*, had suggested making a film about the Dolpopas before their traditions disappeared; Lhondup played the leading role of an old chieftain.

"My big problem was not to make a pretty film," the tall, rangy Valli said in his rapid, French-accented English at the 1999 Toronto International Film Festival. He and his producer, Jacques Perrin, did not want to do an "exotic" film about the Dolpo region so memorably explored in Peter Mathiessen's *The Snow Leopard*. "We wanted to go deeper than their incredible faces and their beautiful costumes. It had to be a human thing, which was to show their courage, their great dignity, and universal things like the conflict between generations and power struggles. Each time my writing stayed too much on the surface, Jacques would say, 'It's not right if we don't get to the core of these people. We have to keep digging and digging.' And the film kept being delayed and delayed, and we were losing money, with the budget being blown up by four or five million. It was like total madness, but he was right."

They settled on a storyline about a conflict between an old chieftain, Tinle (Lhondup), who has just lost his eldest son and blames Karma, the leader of the young Dolpopas for his death. Tinle forbids Karma to lead the annual yak caravan and insists that, old as he is, he will be in charge until his grandson and future chief grows up. However, Karma decides to challenge Tinle by setting out with the young villagers before the date decreed by ancient ritual. He asks the beautiful grieving widow and her son to join him, but she stays loyal to Tinle.

Many times, even before the cameras rolled, Valli would ask the Dolpopas, long-time friends who were not professional actors, "'What would you do in this situation?' If they said they would not say something the way it was in the script, I went with their words. They were my teachers. I was their student. Everything is totally authentic except for the plastic yak that falls off the side of the mountain."

In the Tibetan culture, when an important character dies, friends write a biography of the person, a historical record that is stored in monasteries, Valli explained. "The Dolpopas thought this film was like writing a biography of their culture with a camera. They're very proud of their way of life, but it is being transformed because the outside world is coming in. They thought it was important to do this film before their culture melts like the snow under the sun."

There is a certain irony for Valli in the fact that the film is very successful in countries as dissimilar as France and Japan because audiences identify with the Dolpopas' heartaches and humor and struggles. "For me," he says, "this is a story of similarities." But when Valli started his nomadic adventures as a teenager, it was the differences among people that excited him.

When he was sixteen at a summer camp, he heard about a boy who was going to Yemen and Egypt, and he thought that sounded like more fun than camp. He told his parents he wanted to travel instead of being a camper. His father, an artist who had given him some eye-opening books by great navigators, Jack London and Joseph Conrad, "flipped out" at the boy's request, but finally agreed. After working at a local mustard factory to earn travel money, Valli, a lover of trees who was also a skilled craftsman, took off to see the famous Cedars of Lebanon and then went to Syria. That trip only whetted his appetite to observe "the many different ways there were to live." Afghanistan was next and there he began his career as a photographer of largely unknown places.

"My life as an adult," he said, "is very much realizing the dream I had as a kid. It may seem naïve, but at forty-seven, I still climb trees and go to these weird places. Sometimes I flip out and say to myself, 'At your age, you should be more responsible.'"

Valli's nomadic existence agreed with his first wife, Diane Summers, an Australian writer who collaborated with him on four books, including the stunning salt-caravan book *Les Voyageurs du Sel*. On two treks between Nepal and Tibet in 1992, they took along their two daughters, then four and one. That French publication was also illustrated by their friend, the artist Lama Tenzing Norbu (who inspired the *Himalaya* character of Norbu, Tinle's second son who leaves his monastery to help his father).

In September 2000, Valli collaborated with his second wife, Debra Kellner, a Canadian, on a *National Geographic* article about the unique Rana Tharu women's community in southern Nepal. It will be the basis for a future film.

Two of Valli's short films, made for the National Geographic television channel, *The Shadow Hunters*, about men who harvest birds' nests on the west coast of Thailand, was nominated for an Oscar eight years ago, and *The Honey Hunters* of Nepal brought him to the attention of Jean-Jacques Annaud. The French director was planning to make *Seven Years in Tibet* in the Argentinian Andes and he needed a second unit director to shoot in the Himalaya.

"That's when I learned what it was to be a feature filmmaker," Valli said. "Jean-Jacques told me two things. 'Now your job is different. Before you were an image-catcher. Now you make the image.' We worked on the storyboards together with incredible precision. Once in Paris I apologized for asking him some questions. He looked at me in a funny way and asked, 'Why do you feel so bad? The work of a director is to answer questions and find solutions.' So I have to say Jean-Jacques taught me this kind of perseverance and incredible determination."

One of his next projects will be produced again by Jacques Perrin, who will also act in it. Happily for the nomad Valli it will be shot in America, Africa, and Asia. "I can only say it deals with Vietnam and is about the absurdity of war."

March 26, 1999
Toronto Globe and Mail

Satyajit Ray

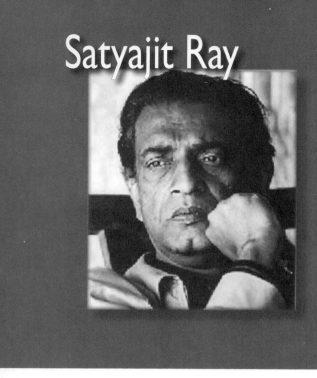

"My first love is music."

Berkeley

Satyajit Ray looked every inch—at 6' 4 1/2"—a man to match his giant reputation as director of the *Apu* trilogy, graphic artist, composer, and novelist when he was honored with the University of California's highest commendation for contributions to the arts in 1975.

An awesome figure with a leonine head that might have been the model for an ancient Roman bronze, he turned out to be unpretentious, direct, and relaxed with a general air of good humor when he reminisced about the San Francisco Film Festival award he received in 1956 for his debut film, *Pather Panchali*. The story about a poor Bengali boy named Apu had earlier won the 1956 Cannes festival prize for the "best human document," but it was only a paper award, less imposing than San Francisco's handsome wooden plaque with a gold-plate engraving of the Golden Gate Bridge.

"It was the first time a film meant primarily for an Indian audience was recognized outside the country," Ray said.

Encouraged by the world attention, Ray made his second film, *Aparjito*, continuing Apu's adventures as a young man. "It was a flop in India. It has not done well anywhere," Ray noted, "but when it was included in the *Apu* trilogy, it picked up. I've found that if something doesn't do very well in Calcutta, it doesn't do well in New York."

Commenting on his film *The Golden Fortress*, Ray said that it was a totally new departure for him. "Don't look for symbolism in it," he warned laughingly. It is about the adventures of a fourteen-year-old assistant to a young detective, two characters in a series of novels he originally wrote for *Sandesh*, the Ray family magazine for children.

"I used to get letters from young people and phone calls—because I'm in the phone book—asking, 'Why not make a film for us?'"

In addition to the adventure series, Ray has written four or five science-fiction novels and two collections of short stories.

The Golden Fortress was shot in picturesque Rajasthan, near the Pakistan border, the only desert in India. "It is most remarkable because all the inhabitants—extremely poor people—are musicians. They play instruments unknown in the rest of India—with the possible exception of the flute that snake-charmers use.

"My first love is music," Ray said. He had used three famous musicians to improvise scores for his first six films: Ravi Shankar, Ali Akbar Khan, and Ustad Vilayat Khan. Later, Ray thought he should start composing himself.

"I don't play any instrument, although I have a piano for my compositions. I started with Western classical music, but of course I was surrounded by Indian music. When I was eight or nine, I began reading about Beethoven in the *Book of Knowledge*, admiring his face and temperament, but I didn't hear any music by Beethoven until I was thirteen or fourteen. A relative had a record with one movement of a Beethoven violin concerto. Then whenever I earned a little money, I would buy a movement. It would take three months to complete a symphony or concerto. In college, I got into the habit of listening to Western music and studying it with a miniature score.

"But now I use less and less music, particularly with a contemporary story. I prefer a drier approach. I use the soundtrack to make it as rich and expressive as possible. It's never elaborate."

Since *Golden Fortress*, he has finished *Middle Man*, a black comedy dealing with joblessness in contemporary Calcutta and featuring another father-son relationship of the kind that so fascinates Ray. His own father, a writer, died when he was three.

He is now working on *The Chess Players*, the first film he will make in any language other than Bengali. Based on a famous Hindi short story, it takes place in Utter Pradesh and deals with the annexation by the British of one of the last Indian states.

"It was a period of decadence when the nabobs reigned. The King of Oudh was a great musician, but a bad ruler. The story is about two chessplaying friends so involved in saving the chess kings, they can't be concerned by the fact that their own king is being captured."

Coming from a country that, until two months ago, had an embargo on foreign films, he was eager to see Antonioni's *The Passenger*, Polanski's *Chinatown*, Welles' *F for Fake*, and Coppola's *The Conversation*.

Ray maintained his traditional skepticism about the validity and honesty of explicitly sexual scenes in films. He was dumbfounded to learn that Berkeley students had seen several rough cut versions of *One Flew Over the Cuckoo's Nest*.

"I never," he said with dismay, "let ANYBODY see my rough cut!"

October 15, 1975
San Francisco Chronicle

Ivan Fila

Challenges in a rootless Existence.

Mill Valley, California

Filmmaker Ivan Fila, a Czech citizen, has walked across many borders only to find the most satisfactory challenges in a rootless existence. The boundary he has trouble with is the one between fact and fiction.

Everyone asks if the bizarre romance in *Lea*, his prize-winning first feature film, is a true story. The haunting tale tells of a Slovak girl who writes letters and poetry to her dead mother and is sold into marriage, by her foster parents, to a grizzled German veteran of the French Foreign Legion.

When Fila looked into the eyes of friends and producers, he saw their need to believe it was a true story. "I felt that I had to nod 'yes' if for no other reason than not to disappoint them," he said in a interview at the Mill Valley Film Festival. "I told them, 'I know the girl and have the poems at home.' However, I became so confident that I myself began to believe it was true."

459

He said he "played the game" until *Lea* won a warm reception during the 1996 Venice Film Festival. "Then nobody cared if it was true or not." Nevertheless, two months later, Hanna Schygulla, who has a supporting role in the film, asked why he didn't talk about the girl. "I said, 'Hanna, I told you several times it was a lie.' She answered, 'But I want to believe it's true.'"

In a formal statement, Fila wrote, "To many people I have swindled during this time, I beg their forgiveness. The fact is that in certain instances cinema induces us to lie. Perhaps this is necessary in order to contemplate the truth."

The idea for *Lea* came to Fila when he was in a funk after failing to get funding for an earlier script. A story flashed into his mind about a young Slovak woman who dies following complications from a masssive stroke. He imagined that after Lea's death her poems and letters were found in an underground shelter scattered around an urn containing the ashes of her mother, who died when she was seven. Fila originally wrote his fantasy as a newspaper story, but soon turned it into his first successful feature script.

Fila found Lenka Vlasakova, the Czech actress who plays Lea, when he saw her in a student production of a play based on Dostoyevsky's *The Idiot*. "She was very strange. I felt immediately that she was the one I was looking for, and I contacted her right after the performance. I told her it wasn't a true story."

Christian Redl, a well-known German stage actor who plays Lea's hard-bitten husband, Herbert, was not at all like the character Fila had envisioned. At the suggestion of a friend, Fila met Redl in Hamburg. "I was a little bit shocked because he was completely the opposite of the character in my head." He knew Redl was right for the part after viewing his work on two videos. "I followed my feelings. I'm not a rational writer or director."

When Fila was a teenager, he wanted to be a psychologist. "I was very introverted. I liked to observe people and see what is in their souls. Until today I watch people all the time. Being a psychologist is very close to being a film director because a director has to know characters very well and work in a very psychoanalytic way with the actors." Nevertheless, he views psychoanalysis with something close to contempt.

In the film, he has Herbert angrily reject a doctor's suggestion that Lea, who has strange nervous collapses, needs psychiatric treatment. "The man is strong enough not to need a psychiatrist and he's able to understand Lea without the help of a doctor."

Fila realized that his initial response to Redl reflected the way he sees German men. "They have a lot of harsh, violent, arrogant voices. They act as if they know they are the best, but behind this, there is something that makes them very weak. They are not so strong as they pretend to be. After twenty years in the Foreign Legion, Herbert doesn't know how to express his love for Lea. This may be for me a mirror for Germany."

Fila, who is in his early forties, says his mother, a physician, and his father, an engineer, didn't talk about the war. What he remembers is the Russian invasion in 1968. He was walking to the National Theatre with his mother when they saw tanks coming over the bridge.

He grew up opposed to the Communist system and refused to cast an obligatory vote in the 1976 election when he was nineteen. He wanted to attend film school, but was told that unless he changed his opposition to the regime, there was no way he'd be admitted to a university and he would have to go into the army. To escape that fate, he joined a tour group going to Yugoslavia and, the day before it was scheduled to return, he walked across the border to Italy.

Another border-crossing landed him in Germany, where he studied scriptwriting, photography, and film direction. His next stop was New York, where he spent seven years and took 1,500 photographs of Harlem for a book that never got published. Eventually, he turned to film and made fifteen documentaries for German and Czech television, including *A Bohemian Fairy Tale* about Czech president Vaclav Havel. A self-described nomad, Fila headed to Romania to begin shooting his next project, *King of Thieves*, which he describes as a "modern Oliver Twist story." It deals with children in borderline peril at the hands of ruthless adults and was written after Fila did extensive research into organized crime networks in Italy and Germany in the 1990s.

Despite the fact that *Lea* was co-produced by a German company and won sixteen awards, including the German Ophuls prize, the honors went unreported in Germany and the film had trouble finding a distributor. "Eighty percent of the German critics said it was a masterpiece, but not commercial enough," Fila said.

In Czechoslovakia, the critical reception was cool, said Fila, because he is considered an emigrant. But Czech audiences loved it and the film ran for more than six months. "The public," he grinned, "is more important for me than the critics."

1997

Toronto Globe and Mail

Leonard Wolf

Dracula–energy without grace and love without consequence

San Francisco

Leonard Wolf, the San Francisco State College professor who is a Chaucer scholar, author of the only known Yiddish poem on Oedipus, and calls himself "the Rashi"* of *Dracula* and *Frankenstein*, is going Hollywood. So to speak.

Wolf has just completed a script for the first film that will actually be *true* to Bram Stoker's original 1897 novel, even though at least forty movies have been made with the dread name of Dracula and 200, more or less, about similar blood-suckers.

Meta-Philm, a new company, took a four-page spread in *Variety* to announce "Bram Stoker's Original *Dracula*." Negotiations are underway to find a director for the $8-million production.

The call to Tinseltown was an inevitable fate for Dr. Wolf, author of *The Annotated Dracula* and his latest, *The Annotated Frankenstein*, both of which contain a plethora of fascinating footnotes** published side by side with facsimilies of the original versions of those classic horror stories.

It is significant—although perhaps "too simple a formulation," Wolf notes—"that in the early nineteenth century, there was *Frankenstein* that symbolized women's fear of men, and at the end of the nineteenth century, with *Dracula*, a book that symbolizes male fear of women."

The Dracula revival—with two plays on and off-Broadway and a third due—got the Significant Trend treatment last month with four pages in *Newsweek*.

"I am pleased to see that *Newsweek* and others have finally noticed that Dracula reflects the American state of mind in a unique fashion. Dracula is America's favorite monster. I don't think any other culture in the world would feed its kids Count Chocula breakfast food," Wolf said. "And if you look closely, you'll find a little cross on a circle-shaped wafer. I find that to be an unconscious parody of The Host."

Horror for Wolf is a newsperson wiseacre trying to make a joke about the objects of his impeccably scholarly affection. Or the coincidence of his birth in 1923 in the wild Carpathian mountains that spawned Count Dracula himself.

In creating his now-legendary monster, Stoker, an Irish writer who became manager of Sir Henry Irving's Lyceum theater, added a touch of peasant folklore to the historic figure of Vlad Dracula or Vlad Tepes, the Impaler, terror of the fifteenth century. Old Vlad conducted his own St. Bartholomew's Day Massacre in which, Wolf says, "some 30,000 persons were probably killed . . . There were nails in people's heads, maiming of limbs, blinding, strangulation, burning, the cutting of noses and ears, and of sexual organs in the case of women, scalping and skinning, exposure to the elements or to the wild animals, and boiling alive."

So far as it is known, Dracula stopped short at actually sucking blood, but local peasants certainly believed in the *nosferatu*, or vampires, who did. Their remedy for the most obstinate cases was to "cut off the head and replace it in the coffin with the mouth filled with garlic."

Leaving aside such gourmet*** considerations, Wolf went on to explicate how this most sanguinary symbol has come to "reflect America's most persistent anxieties and confusions." He ticked them off methodically:

1. "Fear of death. Dracula lives forever, as long as he drinks blood."

    (1) "Old age. This is a culture that doesn't want to be older than forty."

        (Without flinching, Wolf says he is fifty-four.)

    (2) "The fixation on violence and/or the repression of it.

"The next hardest part to say—and perhaps the truest," Wolf continued without hint of an impediment. "I think Dracula's mode of loving is instantly recognizable—sadly—as a solution to the sexual perplexities we find ourselves confronted with in an 'age of sexual liberation.'

"The image of Dracula is an image in which you get power without responsibility, energy without grace, and love without consequence. I mean by that only that there are no babies.

"I'll put it brutally—the usual embarrassments of sexuality are evaded in the vampire gesture. The men's failures need not be confronted, and the woman doesn't have to fake orgasms. She can just lie still. Sexuality, which is a complex interchange between men and women, is, as we see it on screen or on stage, reduced to a charming, if deadly, simplicity."

It's all there in a standard scene in the post-1956 *Dracula***** movies, Wolf noted, such as the Count Yorga rip-offs. "The young female victim waits for the Count to come to her, lying back on bed in a see-through gown, with the attitude of a woman waiting for her demon lover."

Dracula has been treated as sub-literature, but Wolf thinks it's a great book because it symbolizes "the unsettled state of the post-industrial revolutionary psyche; it symbolizes a lot of human despair and yearning of a special sort."

He hopes they can get that quality across in the new film by "skillful explicitness and implication.

"I've argued that the story of Dracula has one line, that Dracula is the anti-Christ. He is the satanic version of Christ, and the other characters, the good guys, are young knights combating evil. I hope we can create that on screen, making it clear that Dr. Van Heising and his band of young men are dedicated to the destruction of satanic power."

An unexpected mystery in most of the movies, Wolf said, is why Dracula goes to London. "The novel points to it. Whitby and Exeter are where two young women live, and I've developed his relationship to these young women before he ever leaves Transylvania."

Since Bela Lugosi, America's favorite Dracula (1931), is long since dead, what actor would Wolf like to see as the Count?

"There are problems. Dracula has been around 400 years and is still a sensualist. Think of the energy that requires! That's part of the attraction: his determination to cling to life in defiance of the rules that say 'you may not . . . '"

At any rate, in the novel and the film, Dracula has to get progressively younger, which wouldn't be easy, even for the likes of Richard Burton or Richard Boone, "who has the face of a man who's been to the wars.

"The kind of Dracula I would like to see is intelligent, brilliant, and turned-on, one with great wit. That power, that energy is a very important part of him. Dracula promises eternal life under the wrong sponsorship—you have to murder your fellow man. With Christ, you have to love each other. Meanwhile, it's exciting to see a guy who refuses to die and is still turned on by the world."

Although he was a fan of *Dracula*, the book, from the time he was a boy, Wolf said he had to grow older before he could appreciate the more "brooding terror" of *Frankenstein*.

The Boris Karloff movie, made in 1931,***** "authoritatively established an American myth that movingly grasps at the English myth created by Mary Shelley. In both cases, they've understood that ugliness and loneliness are universal fears that can only be assuaged by responsible love. I think that's the heart of the *Frankenstein* matter."

The Wolf footnotes tell it all: How Mary Shelley was only eighteen when she wrote her masterpiece and certainly had birth and death on her mind. Her own mother, the brilliant Mary Wollstonecraft Godwin, had died days after her birth. Mary Shelley's first child had been born dead, and she was pregnant with a third while completing *Frankenstein*. She must have been in some state when Lord Byron suggested they tell ghost stories one rainy night in 1816 in Geneva.

She was busy taking care of her four-month-old son, Percy Bysshe Shelley still had a wife and two children in England, Mary's half-sister Claire was making sheep's eyes at Percy *and* was pregnant with Lord Byron's child. Television wouldn't countenance this.

Although about forty movies have been made on the Frankenstein theme, Wolf thinks it's time for another, more authentic, one.

"There is no creature with pegs in his neck. In the '31 movie, Boris Karloff doesn't know how to talk, but in the novel, the creature speaks like a professor of English lit. He accomplishes this by reading only five books, including Milton's *Paradise Lost*, Goethe's *Sorrows of Werther*, Volney's *Ruins of Empire*, LaFontaine's *Fables*, and *Plutarch's Lives*.

"He is eight feet high and *ghastly* to look at, but full of sensibility and innocent desire to love and be loved, and a human desire for sexual experience that is anguishing. I never refer to him as a monster anymore. My heart is overwhelmed by his plight. He is a creature whose creator blew it. Victor Frankenstein made a mistake and didn't have the courage to take on the responsibility of love."

December 31, 1977
San Francisco Chronicle

Stone's Footnotes:

*Rashi (1040-1105): Jewish scholar, b. France–author of important commentaries on the Talmud and the Pentateuch. Real name was Rabbi Solomon bar Isaac.

**Enough to provide at least a dozen gripping contemporary (1) movies such as "A Prematurely Liberated Woman: Why Mary Wollstonecraft Failed to Obtain a Menage à Trois and Tried to End It All" or "Behind Lyceum Doors: What Did Bram Stoker REALLY See in Sir Henry Irving?"

(1) See Footnote above: Imagine the mesmerizing images that could be dreamed up by

Luis Buñuel or Dusan (*Sweet Movie*) Makavejev in which Wolf's footnotes about de Sade's *Justine*, Lord Byron's affairs (foreign, incestuous and boyish), Dr. Erasmus Darwin's (1731-1802) favorite prescription: "Opium. Wine. Food. Joy" would embroider the struggle of that eighteen-year-old unwed mother, Mary Shelley, to give birth to Frankenstein. With a flash forward to Victor Frankenstein's great-great-great grandson messing around with DNA at Harvard.

***Wolf supplies a nineteenth-century recipe for Chicken Paprikash in *Dracula* and went as far as the Orkney Islands to get an authentic Scottish oak cake recipe for *Frankenstein*.

****The infamous Dr. Cross-Ebbing-away suggests that the whole Dracula mythology is an absurd fuss over what is merely a primitive Transylvanian trick anticipating future Yankee refinements in *Deep Throat*.

*****There is no statistical correlation available about the effect of two movie monsters in the same year, 1931, upon 6.05 million unemployed Americans.

Gus Van Sant

PHOTO BY JUDY STONE.

"I'm probably an outsider in the gay community."

Karlovy Vary, Czech Republic

Gus Van Sant has been thinking that the much-celebrated 100 years of cinema have been as industry-dominated as the car and believes it's time for a change.

"The automobile continues to drive on, you know, and film, likewise, is about as tiresome as an automobile," he said over coffee at the 2003 Karlovy Vary Film Festival, which was showing *Elephant*, shortly after it won the Cannes Festival's top Palme d'Or prize and best director award. There is nothing tiresome about *Elephant* unless it tires people who prefer spoon-fed answers to such problems as to why two adolescent boys would massacre their fellow high-school students. Van Sant offers no clues in his fictional recreation of a Columbine-like murderous frenzy.

"Maybe in our culture we're not used to people running amuck," Van Sant noted, in a pleasurable discourse about the word amuck, pointing out that it is derived from the Malaysian word amok. In Van Sant's definition, it's "When you get a knife and run through the marketplace stabbing everybody you see. We don't have a term for running amuck, so we can't fit it nicely into a category. We think it's a world-ending event that somehow disrupted our perfect universe. I think in another culture, they'd go, 'Oh, he ran amuck. Okay.' It's like it was something that fit into their idea of how culture can be. I don't think we tolerate certain things, although within our culture we have this need for conformity. "

Van Sant has a problem with the way drama is dealt with in film. He calls it "industrial cinema." The films are vehicles for stars and their performances. It's not really about the cinema. It's a product of theater and someone trying to pretend it's theater and not really becoming itself. The language that we learned through D.W. Griffith and filmmakers of earlier times, when you learn it, you find that it's this fantastic sort of creation, the idea of close-up being an innovation until, like, when you come around to it and you can escape the thought of that innovation and its charm, even though it's just like this purely mechanical language, it has a strong effect on the types of things that we actually film and display."

The Portland-based director doesn't have much hope for a change in filmmaking. "In the same way, I don't really feel that cars are going to be replaced. It's a very leaden and cement-like process like, yes, we'll try and take care of the environment when we get around to it or work on transportation when we get around to it and then, artistically or culturally, we'll try to develop cinema when we get around to it, when we've stopped making money at the box office. It just gets worse and worse, so that even great cinema around the world is still influenced by pretty traditional methods of storytelling."

He recently drifted far afield from tradition, gaining inspiration from two totally unorthodox filmmakers: Bela Tarr, the Hungarian whose strong imagery in long shots inspired Van Sant's time loops, the repetition of a scene from a different angle, and Abbas Kiarostami, the Iranian who "invites" the audience to provide their own interpretation to his films.

The influence of both men is felt in *Elephant*. The title is taken from British director Alan Clarke's 1988 BBC-TV production about pointless killings in Northern Ireland. Clarke saw the elephant in the living room as a taboo that people could not acknowledge. Van Sant thought of the old story about five blind men who touch different parts of an elephant, but no one gets the big picture. "You can't get to the answer, because there isn't one," Van Sant said, just as there's no satisfactory answer to the causes of those high-school murders.

Van Sant himself took a turn at Hollywood tradition with audience-pleasers like *To Die For* (1995), starring Nicole Kidman in a chillingly funny satire on America's obsession with fame; *Good Will Hunting* (1997), and *Finding Forrester* (2000). But early on, he displayed his unconventional interests in a short based on *The Discipline of D.E.*, a story by his literary hero, William Burroughs, and his 1981 featurette *Alice in Hollywood*, about a girl who ends up working in porno movies instead of where she thinks she's going. *Alice* was never shown in the U.S. and rarely appears in his filmographies. His next three films explored the likes of hustlers, thieving junkies, and wild outsiders: *Mala Noche* (1985), *My Own Private Idaho* (1991), and *Drugstore Cowboy* (1993).

Still boyish-looking at fifty-one, with a quiet, well-mannered air, Van Sant said he guesses that he's drawn to people on the wild side "because they're very different from me." He recently told another interviewer that he was afraid of "becoming too reclusive."

Wild, self-destructive people certainly didn't come into view in the middle-class world Van Sant knew when he was growing up. His father had became president of a large clothing company in Darien, Connecticut, after years as a salesman traveling all over the country, including Kentucky—where Gus was born in 1952. Both his Episcopalian parents encouraged his artistic aspirations when he began painting at the age of thirteen or fourteen, and later his father helped to finance the early films he made in the seventies.

"I never really had any outward rebellion," he said, "not the type of rebellion that can tear families apart. I think I was iconoclastic, but not rebellious. I think that whatever it was that I was looking at, I wanted to change it. You know, whatever was the normal thing, I wanted to make it different."

Van Sant started experimenting at the Rhode Island School of Design, painting on film, playing in short-lived bands, as well as engaging in the "weird" mixed media efforts students were enjoying. Mostly he was inspired by the New York underground filmmakers. After graduation he took off for Hollywood to learn how to shoot a conventional film and later had a minor job in a New York ad agency to earn money for his own independent movies.

He was in his early thirities when he finally realized that he was gay and when he chose to make *Mala Noche*, a doomed gay love story about a Portland liquor store clerk who develops a crush on a poor Mexican kid. "I think that choice was informed probably by my sexuality," he said. "I think there were a lot of things that worked with, like, what subjects I was choosing and where I was going. *Mala Noche* was written by Walt Curtis, who is not somebody you feel is speaking for the gay community. I think he's an outsider in the gay community. I think I'm probably an outsider in the gay community, in that I'm not a gay politician. When I think about stories and making my films, I'm not doing them in a political way. It's mostly an apolitical kind of choice."

When he made *My Own Private Idaho*, starring River Phoenix, it was the start of a close friendship with the young star and the bohemian Phoenix family. River's death in 1993 at age twenty-three from a drug overdose devastated the filmmaker who later

470

expressed his sorrow in his idiosyncratic, sexually explicit 1997 novel *Pink*. It featured a middle-aged director and several friends who resembled River and the late rock star Kurt Cobain, who would later emerge as a tragic suicidal character in Van Sant's enigmatic *Last Days* (2005).

Asked about the controversial shower kissing scene between the two high-school killers in *Elephant*, Van Sant replied that he certainly didn't intend to say that they were gay and that they had a relationship which might have been the reason for their killing spree. "It was the one point of contention in making the film. Everybody said, 'That's going to be, you know, attacked.'" He said the scene was like many other little things that happen on their last day, but none of them were meant to indicate a reason for the rampage.

How would he expect an audience to react to the film? He said he always worries about whether he would choose the right words. After searching for the right response, he pointed out that each person in the audience is different. "I couldn't say I want the audience to conform to my ideas of what I want. Hold on. Yeah, it depends on the audience. I want the film to include each different person so it's not so much me explaining something to them as it is them experiencing the film together. I'd hope that they are inspired to think about the things they see on the screen and to think about high school—you know, ordinary high-school life and extraordinary high school life or the antithesis of high school life."

And that about sums up the matter.

2003
Unpublished

15
Journeys

Memories of Cairo

FAYSAL ABDULLAH. PHOTO BY JUDY STONE.

After Afghanistan was bombed, international filmmakers have flashbacks to horrors in their own lands.

Cairo

September 11 in New York was already becoming a distant event, but when I stepped into a San Francisco taxi on October 7, 2001, and learned that the U.S. had bombed Afghanistan, I had second thoughts about proceeding on my way to the Cairo International Film Festival.

However, once there, I was curious to learn the reactions of visiting directors from countries all over the world. In a distinctly unscientific round of conversations here, they all said their thoughts had turned to events in their own lifetimes: The bombing

473

of a German town in World War II, American support of military dictatorships in Latin America, a frightening fundamentalist demonstration in Algeria, battles between the Tutsi and Hutus in Rwanda, the Greeks who saved Jews from the Nazis, an Iraqi dissident's contempt for Saddam Hussein, sympathy for the plight of Palestinians.

The Moroccan filmmaker Hassan Ben Jelloun was right there on the sidelines when he saw the 9/11 attack on the twin towers of the World Trade Center. The director of *Judgment of a Woman*, he was in New York for an Arab film festival, which was almost immediately cancelled. When he observed the towers engulfed by fire and people rushing into the street, he thought, "Oh, my God! It's terrible!" Then he saw a shot of bin Laden on TV and thought, "This is an Islamic strike. I'm Muslim and Arabic, but I was very afraid and closed my eyes. I thought of the time I was caught in a fundamentalist demonstration in Constantine, Algeria, in '92 and felt a terrible fear." In Morocco, he said, the fundamentalists are controlled. "I don't think people in Morocco are for bin Laden."

Still, despite difficult moments in New York, he felt lucky to have observed a "very important moment in history. I think the world has changed. I think that U.S. support for Israel is the cause of what happened, but I'm not sure. Everybody is happy that Bush spoke up for a Palestinian state. I think he wanted to do it before September 11."

Hussein Fahmi, the handsome Egyptian movie star who is the amiable president of the festival, had his own taste of political demonstrations when he participated in anti-Vietnam war activities while studying film at the University of California in Los Angeles 1965-71. "This is a different situation. Now we're at war with terrorism. We in Egypt have suffered from terrorism early in the game. In 1994, there was an attempt to assassinate Naguib Mahfouz because he wrote a novel that didn't appeal to the fundamentalists. And there was the assassination in 1992 of Farag Foda, a great writer who wrote against fundamentalism and terrorism and against using religion to get power. And there was an attempt on Mubarak's life in the nineties.

"I have always been against the Taliban," Fahmi said. "I have never understood their kind of Islam with the oppression of women's rights in Afghanistan. It's not part of Islam at all." Referring to the bombing of Afghanistan, he added, "I don't feel sorry for the Taliban as I have felt sorry for the victims of September 11. The essence of the problem is the Israeli/Palestinian conflict. Palestinian land has been under occupation since 1948. People who are resisting with stones are being suppressed by Israelis with American weapons. The U.S. calls them terrorists and we call them freedom fighters. I think the solution is for the Israelis to withdraw with a peace treaty like the one with Egypt and have the two nations living side by side. You're feeding terrorists the more you continue the occupation. A state of Palestine is the only solution."

Costas Ferris, the jovial Greek director of *Rebetiko*, the Greek form of urban blues, music banned by the Metaxas dictatorship (1936-1941), was in Tel Aviv on September 11 at the home of Micha Lewinson, director of the Jerusalem Festival. Lewinson was planning a theatrical version of *Rebetiko*, based on the life of a Greek singer, for the Haifa Municipal Theater March 10 and then expects to take the production to London. Ferris immediately said, "It's more important now than before to stage *Rebetiko* with a half-Jewish, half-Arab cast in a way to preach peace among people."

Two weeks after September 11, Ferris said that everybody in Greece was afraid to say anything against the official view, but the popular, outspoken director opened up a far-more-ranging discussion when he went on TV to declare, "No healthy human being can say he's happy to see thousands of innocent people dead, but that cannot make me forget Hiroshima and Nagasaki. Or the bombing and embargo of medical supplies to Iraq. I consider it a crime of war. Even in a battle if you find a wounded enemy you have the duty to bring him to a hospital. And we must not forget the fights between the Greeks and the Turks. Remembering is the most powerful education tool for bringing people together."

Ferris, who calls himself a "non-violent anarchist"—and can quote with ease from Plato, Buckminster Fuller, or Madonna—has seen a lot of history in his time. Born in Egypt when his father and two brothers were serving in the British army under General Montgomery, he later saw the Nasser revolution and the nationalization of the Suez Canal. In Greece, arrested by the military dictatorship, he escaped through the efforts of French friends, crediting director Barbet Schroeder for saving his life, and spent from 1967 to 1973 in exile in Paris.

Referring to President Bush's comments about "civilized people," Ferris asked rhetorically, "Did he mean Western civilization? Doesn't he know about the great thinkers of Arabia in the eighth, ninth, and tenth centuries? Doesn't he know about the hurt feelings of the Arab world, which suffered through centuries from Western domination? And is Israel an Eastern or Western civilization? It's both at the same time. During the war, thousands of Greeks took Jews into their homes and saved them from the Nazis. As Madonna said [after September 11]—and she's not a philosopher—violence leads to violence. As long as the god of Western civilization is money we won't have peace."

Helma Sanders-Brahms, a festival juror who directed *Germany Pale Mother*, recalled her childhood under bombardment in Emden, a steel and coal town, close to the Dutch frontier. "In my eyes, bombing doesn't solve anything. It mostly kills the innocent. I feel deeply for the women and children who have to suffer. Later, living in Berlin was like living in the eye of a hurricane with Russian soldiers on one side and Americans on the other. We were sure if there was a war it would take place in Germany. After the Berlin Wall came down, so many hopes seemed to be fulfilled, the hope that the world would be united. After fifty years there was finally peace, but now the world seems again to be divided into two different kinds of thinking, two different lifestyles."

Argentine director Hector Molina said he felt very sorry for the people who died in the twin towers, but he could not forget the American support of military dictatorships in Argentina, Chile, and Uruguay and their subsequent abuses.

In his film, *Illusion of Movement*, there is a flashback to 1978, during Argentina's military dictatorship when 30,000 people—including intellectuals and pregnant women who gave birth—went missing or were killed. The babies were put up for adoption.

Molina's drama touchingly explores the prickly relationship between a father who becomes acquainted for the first time with his perceptive seven-year-old son, the child of a "disappeared" woman who was later found by his grandmother.

Molina also referred to inconsistences in American policy, which supported bin Laden when he was fighting the Russians. In comparison, he brought up the case of former Argentine president Leopoldo Galtieri. Trained at West Point, Galtieri was considered the most pro-American military man in Argentina, but when he declared war on Margaret Thatcher, invading the British Falklands in 1982, he was called a madman.

Hilde Duyck, the Belgian art director of *Pauline and Paulette*, the festival's choice for Best Film, discussed her experiences for five months in 1991-92 in Rwanda, where she witnessed tension and fear between the Hutus and Tutsis and their hatred of the foreign teachers. She had gone to the former Belgian colony because she "wanted to see more of the world."

While she worked on a campaign against AIDS in Rwanda's only official art school, she had the thankless job of trying to bring the Hutus and Tutsis together to work on one project.

She said the fundamentalists responsible for the terror in New York and Washington didn't know what they were doing: "They had their brains manipulated like the people in Rwanda. It's not only a question of manipulation but of the money bin Laden is giving to them. It's money manipulation."

Faysal Abdullah, educated as a solicitor in Iraq, has been away from his native land for twenty-three years. He is now a film critic in London.

He said, "When Saddam Hussein came to power, it was an insult to my intelligence—as if someone spit in my face. I was not interested in politics, but they labeled me in opposition, as simple as that. The consequence of being in opposition in Iraq means you are playing with death."

He talked with grim but still-charming humor about events that led to his departure from Iraq. "I changed countries more than I changed my shoes, to quote Brecht. I still have this accent and consider it salt to keep my otherness. Once in Miami, a Jewish women looked at my documents, which noted that I was a stateless person.

"'I'm envious,' she said. 'Why?' I asked. She answered, 'Being in a certain country is like being in prison. If you're stateless, you've got a free soul. You are a liberated person.'"

He obviously relished telling the story. "I'm Muslim," he said, "but I'm compatible to new ideas, to new ways of thinking. I know America from the perspective of Franklin and Jefferson. And I totally, totally, totally condemn that atrocity on September 11. I don't have any sympathy for those people. The response to that destruction should be well-calculated and should have an objective.

"Eleven years after liberating Kuwait from the Iraqi invasion, nothing has happened to the person who did that atrocity, despite the fact that Saddam was being labeled as a Hitler, as a most-hated person, as somebody you cannot do business with—but now he is still in power. And the Americans who labeled Saddam are doing business with him. Iraq is a major supplier of oil until now.

"I'm afraid after eleven years, the bastard is still there and innocent people have already paid the price. That's why I'm hesitant about the bombardment of Afghanistan. They'll impose an embargo with so many restrictions, and we'll have a human disaster rather than a political disaster.

"Unfortunately, the American government was highly involved in promoting Hussein in the first place and helping the Mujahedin against Russia. I hope they will not repeat the same mistake. America has the most democratic system in the world and should be aware of its image and its actions. They should dig deep to understand the reasons for those fundamentalists (whom I hate), who celebrate the death of other people."

He added, "But those people are being driven by despair to admire monsters like bin Laden and Hussein."

October 26, 2001
Los Angeles Times

* * * * *

Postscript: In November 2004, Faysal Abdullah returned to Iraq for the first time in twenty-three years. He felt "drunk with longing and loving, making my days into daydreams," he wrote in an article for *Al Hayat.* "I also got myself ready for moments of terror. Tough moments whose details are hard to hold came back to me. Bleak moments and definite death were meant for others and me in 1979."

After the dizzyness and shock of his first days, he wrote: "I did not find one person during my stay there who wanted to return to the past or long for the days of Saddam, contrary to the ludicrous remarks of some Arabic satellite channels." He found that a middle class was beginning to emerge, houses were being reconstructed, and "that the new life, regardless of its vulnerability, brought a type of hope . . . people were beginning to flock to the clinics of dentists and opticians to fix their teeth and eyes to see a world they had longed to see."

Baghdad, he wrote, "awaits for the one who will rescue her from its past's heavy heritage and its somewhat convoluted present. For the curse of the Baath is gone forever. Here we are promising a promised void of fear, promised cutting the long tongue of exile. I have a homeland I am no longer ashamed of and I am not ashamed to stand under its flag. For the exiled one is the only one who does not have a flag. And on the notes of these promises, I recall part of a poem by Sa'adi Yousef: 'At times I ask, does forgetting bring mercy—or does it bring damnation?'"

* * * * *

After the January 30, 2005 election, Faysal sent me an e-mail from his home in London: "I think the election has sent a clear, shocking message to the world and in particular to the Arab world, that the Iraqi have defied all obstacles and gone to the ballot boxes. I spent most of Sunday watching Arab satellite televisions, the present-ers and commentators could not believe or digest what is happening on the ground. Most of the talks were real rubbish, but the good thing was that the majority of the Iraqi people made up their mind and said in clear voice NO to terrorism and NO to occupation in a civilized way."

* * * * *

After February 22, 2006's destruction of the Al Askariya Golden Mosque in Samarra and subsequent rioting, Faysal sent me the following comments excerpted from his forthcoming book: "The impasse that the occupation brought on itself has led to dangers and can backfire on everybody, as what happened at the Al Askariya Golden Dome, with grave consequences. Fear and awe are spreading daily. The dismantle-ment of the state apparatuses by Paul Bremer in what was an already fragmented country—ruled by fear during the dictatorship—has led to the revival of sectarian, ethnic and tribal tendencies on the one hand. On the other, the vacuum of a viable state for the last three years has tossed aside the middle class, educated civil servants, academics and high calibre people. Not one of the new decision makers in the Green Zone is originally from Baghdad. As a result, fringe elements had a chance to leap in. I believe the Iraqi future is hostage for an indefinite period between an odious sectarianism and a power sharing quota system. Iraq has nothing left today except for the fruit of the land and a fatalistic silence, waiting for a local Godot."

Encounter in Montenegro

He saw an American and he detested what he saw.

In 1959, when the rickety old Yugoslav bus broke down along the precipitous passes of the Montenegrin mountains, I was relieved. I needed a calm and quiet moment. My back ached from the tension of mental back-seat driving as the bus twisted and turned on the hairpin curves, over roads almost completely washed out after a night of torrential rains. But I was so awed and exhilarated by the overpowering sight of the wildly formidable black mountains, as well as by the vitality and variety of my fellow passengers, that I was glad I had decided to take the bus.

Actually, I had no choice. I had planned to fly from Skopje, the Turkish-looking capital of Macedonia, poorest of the Yugoslav states, to Dubrovnik, the seaside city known as the "pearl of the Adriatic." There I still hoped to receive word that Madame Josip Broz, wife of President Tito, would grant me an interview. However, heavy rains had closed down the Dubrovnik airport. What would have been a two-hour flight was a two-day bus trip through the mountains. I groaned, but consoled myself with the thought that I would at least see Montenegro, the land that inspired Alfred, Lord Tennyson, to write:

> "O smallest among peoples: rough rock-throne
> Of freedom! Warriors beating back the swarm
> Of Turkish Islam for five hundred years.
> Great Tzernagora! Never since thine own
> Black ridges drew the cloud and brake the storm
> Has breathed a race of mightier mountaineers."

At twilight, the bus broke down after having been on the road since 4:00 A.M. The air was clear and cool, the sunset colors had softened the harsh outlines of the mountain peaks. Weary of trying to carry on conversations with the aid of a Serbo-

Croatian dictionary, I approached one of the two other foreigners on the bus. He was impressive, a tall, bearded African who was traveling with a young German girl. They had stayed close to each other during the rest stops and it was obvious that the Yugoslavs were also curious about their relationship. At the moment, he stood there alone, looking over the mountains.

"Hello," I said, "you are British, aren't you? I'm tired of trying to make myself understood in Serbo-Croatian." I showed him the dictionary and laughed, thinking of my poor efforts, as well as my attempt to speak high-school French to a Macedonian girl who obviously knew as little French as I did.

He looked down at me and spoke coldly. Yes, he was a student at Cambridge, on holiday. "And you are American." There was not even a trace of a question in his voice, and his hostility was unmistakeable.

It was the first time in my life that I had ever encountered such pointed hostility from a stranger.

I realized, and with the realization came a terrible rush of hurt, that he did not see me at all. He saw an American, and he detested what he saw.

Later it struck me that his reaction to me was the same as my attitude toward his German girlfriend. I told her about our conversation the next day when I spoke to her for the first time. "You know, " I said, "his hostility to me because I'm American is like the hostility I have been feeling toward you because you are German and I know how ridiculous my feeling is. After all, you are only twenty and had nothing to do with Hitler."

"Oh," she looked blank and, in impeccable English, asked politely, "did anyone in your family suffer in Germany?"

"No," I answered, "but then does anyone in your friend's family suffer in the United States?" I asked her, "What do people your age think about Hitler?" She replied, "We try not to think about this foolishness."

The similarity of our attitudes did not occur to me at the time, but I was determined to pursue my conversation with the young man.

"What country are you from?" I asked.

"Ghana," he replied shortly.

"Oh," I said, thinking that I had found the way to get through to him. "I once heard your Prime Minister Nkrumah speak when he was a student at Lincoln University in Pennsylvania and I was a college freshman in Philadelphia. He was very impressive even then."

He looked at me with an almost imperceptible raise of eyebrows. The chill was still on. He made a noncommittal remark, and I plunged ahead.

"Why do you react that way? Don't you like Nkrumah or approve of what he has done for your country?"

"No," he declared. "I am not an admirer of Mr. Nkrumah. He has adopted all the demagogic methods of your country."

Then I began to feel angry. "Demagogic methods!" I exclaimed, raising my voice and suddenly noticing that we were surrounded by Yugoslavs observing us intently, wondering just what was the argument between the tall, dignified African and the short American.

"How can you say that?" I demanded. "When Nkrumah has statues of himself erected all over the country, when he plasters his picture on all the coins and postage stamps, when your women wear dresses decorated with his picture. That certainly isn't American. I don't know what it is, but it isn't American."

I calmed down and added that I didn't think the business of Nkrumah's pictures was so all-important anyway; that I thought Nkrumah had done a great deal to unite the country. Perhaps it was necessary for him to establish this image of himself in order to break the power of tribal chieftains. I wasn't certain that these observations were accurate, but I was reflecting the opinion of a respected Negro reporter I work with who had studied the country.

He listened impassively and commented that Tom Mboya of Kenya was his idea of a real African leader. The British and whites generally were diplomatic double-talkers, sly and untrustworthy, he said. And Mboya knew how to beat them at their own game.

By now my anger had subsided and I listened with interest. I had heard Mboya speak at a Free Africa meeting in Carnegie Hall a few months earlier in the spring of 1959. As a Jew in America, I had rarely been made conscious of my minority status, but that night, I was conscious of being one of the white minority in the world.

There were comparatively few white people in the hall, and the Africans seemed very regal and impressive in their brilliant red, green, gold and purple robes and turbans. Mboya arose, cocky, handsome, articulate, flamboyant, intelligent. There was no demagoguery in his manner, but his opening gambit drew passion. He asked the audience to rise and shout the Swahili word for freedom—"Uhuru!" I stood up too, but I was unable to join in the ear-shattering sound that filled Carnegie Hall. For the first time, I had a moment of understanding for the white governing minority of Africa and for our own Southerners: both governed by terror. And pity. Because I know they are afraid that their own treatment and their own racial hatreds may one day be turned on them with equal lack of understanding.

I thought of this while my companion talked on about Mboya. I told him that there was one other African leader I was particularly curious about, one who seemed like such a tragic figure, Jomo Kenyatta, who had been sentenced to prison as the leader of the Mau-Mau in Kenya.

There was a flicker of surprise in his eyes as he listened to me. I was beginning to drive a wedge into his stereotype of an American, and that is what I was anxious to do.

I no longer wanted him to see me as a person and not his stereotype of an American. I wanted him to see that I was an American, free to think in my own way, conscious of his continent's problems, although perhaps not knowledgeable enough, and I wanted to break through the ice of his reserve with me, his contempt for my country.

"Are you surprised that I think of Kenyatta as a tragic man? I'll tell you why. A few months before I came here, a magazine in America called *Holiday* had a special issue on Africa. It is a large, mass-circulation magazine, not a little left-wing or liberal weekly. And there was an article by Peter Abrahams, whose work you probably know. He's a very fine writer from Johannesburg. Well, he wrote about a visit he had with Kenyatta. I had not known that Kenyatta had studied and worked in England, developed a fine reputation as an anthropologist, and had been married to an Englishwoman before returning to Kenya."

Abrahams had drawn a picture of a brilliant and cultured man, now isolated and bitter among the tribes he had chosen to help lead to freedom. A lover of books who now lived in a room without books. Abrahams showed him not as the leader of the blood-thirsty Mau-Mau, but as the personification of "the terrible tragedy of Africa and the terrible secret war that rages in it. He was the victim of both tribalism and of Westernism gone sick."

As I talked, I sensed that this student from Ghana was finally beginning to relax, to listen. And with the relaxation of tension, he felt free to argue with me. When I deplored the violence of the Mau-Mau, he said that more blood would be shed before Africa finally became free; that violence was necessary because the colonial powers would not give up their power peaceably.

In that fantastic setting, he spoke passionately about the necessity of violence. You could almost hear its echo from those black mountains we were crossing, mountains that had seen so much of violence; mountains renowned for their violent men, their fighters who fought each other and who fought and held off the Turks and the Venetians and the Austrians; mountains that were the birthplace of the rebel partisan Milovan Djilas, who fought the Fascists and then fought the new Yugoslav ruling class. But later I saw that the student's passion for violence was verbal only. When a fistfight broke out the next day in the overloaded bus about seats, all the passengers joined in with a loud chorus of insults and my friend recoiled. "Did you ever see anything like that?" he asked in a shocked voice. "The way they fought!"

So he said that Africa would not be free without more violence, but he also said that American Negroes would never achieve equal rights until Africa was a free continent. I disagreed, but acknowledged that there was a germ of truth in what he said. I reminded him that black men once helped to sell other black men into slavery and that all problems would not be solved when Africa was free; there would still be black men willing to take advantage of their brothers, just as all men do.

When I told him of the progress that has been made in the United States to eliminate segregation, he looked at me with amusement, but now it was friendly amusement. Even so, it made me uncomfortable, and I, who am so quick to criticize at home, came to the defense of America, even the South. Then he asked me critically about American foreign policy, McCarthyism and John Foster Dulles. In my heart, I understood the questions he was raising, but I could not agree and I could not answer. I thought of all the people and places I love and that make up America for me and I wanted to describe this America to him and I knew I would not succeed, but I tried anyway. I tried to explain our complexities and our contradictions. I told him that, despite our failings and weaknesses, we have all the potentialities and legal processes for improvement, more than any other country in the world. I told him that most Americans are not bigots, they are not "militarists," they do not want another war.

He listened attentively, as did the baffled Yugoslavs near us. Then, politely, he asked: "What do all those good Americans do about all they believe in?"

I felt shame and frustration when I finally replied, "Not enough, I guess."

He was almost gentle when he said, "When you do not act against a policy you disapprove of, you give it your support."

I was glad when the bus driver announced that we would be on our way. It was dark now, and a full moon lit up the perilous and beautiful mountains.

I looked at the stars and thought of our strange discourse in this alien place. I wondered if the pain I felt was what others call patriotism. And then I cried with homesickness for my America.

1959
Unpublished

Index